Him/
Her/
Self

HIM/ HER/ SELF

Gender
Identities in
Modern America

THIRD EDITION

Peter G. Filene

with a foreword by Elaine Tyler May

THE JOHNS HOPKINS UNIVERSITY PRESS
Baltimore & London

© 1974, 1975, 1986, 1998 by Peter G. Filene
All rights reserved. First edition 1974
Third edition 1998
Printed in the United States of America on acid-free paper
9 8 7 6 5 4 3 2 1

The Johns Hopkins University Press
2715 North Charles Street
Baltimore, Maryland 21218-4363
www.press.jhu.edu

First edition published as *Him/Her/Self: Sex Roles in Modern America* in 1975
by Harcourt Brace Jovanovich; second edition 1986, The Johns Hopkins
University Press.

Library of Congress Cataloging-in-Publication Data will be found
at the end of this book.
A catalog record for this book is available from the British Library.

ISBN 0-8018-5920-4
ISBN 0-8018-5921-2 (pbk.)

To Benjamin and Becky
again and always
And now also
to Rachel, Eliza, and Dan

Contents

Foreword

When *Him/Her/Self* first appeared, women's history was in its infancy. Gender as a category of analysis was barely a glow on the scholarly horizon, and the idea that manhood was a topic of historical investigation was practically unimagined. In that early dawn of feminist scholarship, Peter Filene's pioneering work was a godsend. It was essential reading for both undergraduate and graduate students eager to understand the workings of gender in history and desperate for models of scholarship that broke the mold of "traditional" historical writing. Peter Filene's pathbreaking study did both.

In 1974, women's history was just beginning to assert itself as a new field of inquiry within the discipline, sparked by the re-emergence of a mass movement for women's rights. Feminist historians like Peter Filene challenged the traditional approaches to historical scholarship in terms of both content and method: they turned the primary focus of their attention to women, and they insisted that gender was an important category of historical analysis. The publication of *Him/Her/Self* came at a time when much of the work in the field of women's history tilted toward one of two paradigms: women were either heroes or victims.

Both of these scholarly impulses had merit and value. There were, of course, female heroes who had been overlooked by historians. Most of the historical writing up to that time focused overwhelmingly on great men and their exploits on the battlefield or in the realms of power and government or on their important canonical writings.

Feminist scholars had to restore women to their rightful place in the historical record, where they had been rendered silent and invisible. At the same time, they faced the equally important task of exposing, explaining, and understanding the various attitudes, power relationships, and institutional realities that oppressed women in society. Women were often victims of forces beyond their control. Since they were excluded from government and from voting until well into the twentieth century, they were often forced to abide by laws and policies, enacted by men, that curtailed their activities and possibilities. As important as these historical excavations were, they did not tell the whole story. The full history of women went far beyond heroes and victims. It called for a consideration of women as historical actors themselves, agents in the process of change—often even collaborators in the creation of the shared beliefs and ideologies that constrained them.

Him/Her/Self was among a handful of early works in the field that mapped out the terrain in a way that moved the discussion beyond victims and heroines and toward an understanding of the dynamics of gender, both in everyday life and in political institutions. Remarkably, writing in the early 1970s, when there was very little scholarship of this sort upon which to build, Filene anticipated findings in the field that would emerge over the next twenty-five years. The contours of gender that he described at that time remain as foundations upon which other, more particularized studies continue to build. Although the body of scholarship that has developed in the field since 1974 is deep and wide, *Him/Her/Self* remains a model of analysis and insight into the subtle workings of gender in American history.

The original edition of the book also put forward a self-evident truth: It is impossible to understand the history of women without also examining men, just as it is impossible to understand men and their history without including women. This fundamental historical insight provided the basis for Filene's fresh and perceptive account of what were then known as "sex roles." Although sociologists had investigated the subject for many years, historians had not followed suit. Many theorists considered "sex roles" to be biological imperatives, determined and unchanging as a result of the physical differences between women and men. Others, especially anthropologists, saw them as creations of culture, rooted in long-standing attitudes and beliefs. But most scholars had not considered the possibility that "sex roles" have a history. Filene took the word "role" to suggest that people adopt behaviors that are in some sense scripted in the drama of history, acting in ways that are expected of them as women or men at a particular time. As society changes, so do the expected roles. He developed this historical approach when very few other scholars had even considered it.

In the early 1970s, graduate programs in history were bulging with students whose scholarly passions were fired by the social movements of the sixties. The new historical scholarship that emerged at that time focused on ordinary people, those outside the realms of power and influence. Social historians turned away from the traditional concerns about wars and leaders in order to write histories of African Americans, workers, Latinos, immigrants, and women. Thanks largely to what was then called the "new" social history, we now have flourishing research in areas of gay and lesbian history, Native American history, and the histories of men, families, and sexuality.

Him/Her/Self emerged from this flourishing of social history and quickly became a standard in the field. In many ways, the book was ahead of its time, even in an era when so many boundaries within the field were being broken. It was an interdisciplinary project at a time when everyone was talking about interdisciplinary work but few were actually doing it. Filene drew upon the insights of psychologists, the findings of demographers and sociologists, and the works of artists and novelists to weave together a complex story of the evolution of gender ideology in America. Without relying on any cumbersome theoretical references, he built the book on a subtle and sophisticated understanding of the workings of hegemonic culture and the power of shared ideological beliefs. Predating the many studies in recent years that have leaned heavily on such theorists as Gramsci and Foucault, Filene explained in clear and accessible prose the ways in which ordinary Americans helped to create and then tacitly gave their consent to the gender codes and expectations that governed so much of their lives.

Filene's focus on the white middle class displayed his understanding of the power of that group to shape mainstream culture, and to marginalize those who did not conform to its codes of behavior. Sensitive to the issues of race and class, he examined the ways in which men and women from inside as well as outside the white middle class resisted its precepts and ultimately forced changes in mainstream American life. He is aware of power relationships but avoids any simplistic account that renders ordinary people as passive victims of the forces emanating from Wall Street, Madison Avenue, Hollywood, or the centers of political power.

While locating the lives of women within the larger story of American life, Filene also revises the story of political history by bringing gender to bear. Few scholars, then or since, have so effectively used gender as a category of analysis to expand our understanding of American politics. His sophisticated rendering of the career of Theodore Roosevelt demonstrates how powerfully ideas about manhood—particularly manhood that seemed to be threatened at the turn of the century—influenced Roosevelt's life and actions as president. The extraordinary chapter on World War I, while recognizing the importance of developments in Europe and attacks on American vessels, nevertheless casts the American entry into that conflict in new light. Filene's brilliant analysis of the ways in which fears about American manhood affected the war on the home front as well as the battlefield remains a model for a fully integrated political history. At a time when historians often chastise each other for compartmentalizing the study of history, or claim that social history has ignored politics, Filene's approach remains a model for emulation.

The book also addresses some of the most important theoretical questions that have vexed scholars of gender for decades. Feminists continue to debate the question of "difference": Are women the same as men, or are they fundamentally different? The question has huge implications for women's rights advocates as well as policy makers, and Filene traces the roots of that controversy back more than a century. His discussion of the ways in which various movements for women's rights have addressed that question, mobilized around it, and ultimately divided over it provide a clear and concise synthesis of the best scholarship to date.

Similarly, the book uncovers the basic tensions between public and private life, especially for women, by looking closely at the workings of both. Each time Filene addresses the question of women moving more fully into the public arena, through employment, politics, or voluntary work, he examines the implications for family life and the ways in which those challenges were confronted at the time. He makes it clear that from the beginning, the advances women made in the public arena were hindered by a much slower pace of change in the domestic realm. Although men have increasingly accepted a more active role in housework and child care, and many have demanded time away from work to have a more enriching and fulfilling life at home, women continue to carry the lion's share of domestic responsibility. To this day, women struggle mightily to combine employment with the responsibilities of primary care of the home and children. Filene is also careful to point out that women have not always felt trapped by those domestic responsibilities, but often considered them to be valuable and rewarding and were not so eager to give them up.

Filene first explored these themes with what were then considered radically new sources and methods. The book was among the first historical studies to draw heavily on popular culture as a means for understanding mainstream ideology. Examples from novels, magazines, and films provide vivid expressions of widely shared concerns and beliefs.

The 1986 edition of Him/Her/Self reflected and incorporated much of the writing in the field of women's history up to that time. This third edition is a more ambitious undertaking both in scope and conceptualization. Perhaps the most dramatic alteration is the shift from an emphasis on "sex roles" to that of "gender identities," a term that incorporates a more complex set of considerations. Moving beyond behavior and attitudes, "gender identity" includes one's own sense of self. It connotes a process of developing oneself in interaction with others and in reference to culturally defined expectations and social institutions. The development of identity is a dynamic process that takes place over time, in the context of an individual's life located within the larger forces of history.

This new edition also brings the book up to the present, with new sections on gay and lesbian history and on the men's movement. These themes were covered in Filene's original 1974 edition. He was one of the first to claim that men had a history grounded in their gendered experience, as did women. He was also among the first to include discussions of gays and lesbians in historical writing. Many have followed since then, and this revised edition synthesizes much of that writing and adds some new elements. Filene's astute analysis of the men's movement, which he divides into five separate movements, offers a framework for understanding the ways in which men have responded to feminism and the changes in gender expectations that have so fundamentally altered American life in this century.

Since the first publication of this book, scholarship on men and masculinity, sexuality, popular culture, and gender ideology has flourished. Some have extended the analysis in new directions by adding the dimensions of race, ethnicity, and religion to the category of gender. These studies have expanded our understanding of the complexity of American society. We now have an expanding field of scholarship that investigates the many ways in which gender functions in various racial, ethnic, and religious communities. Filene refers to this recent scholarship but keeps his focus on the white middle class. Some readers may wish for a more inclusive approach, and those who do should consult the many books now available on specific minority groups.

Him/Her/Self does not pretend to be an all-inclusive survey. It maintains its original focus on the group that still holds power in most social, cultural, political, and economic institutions in American life. Although minorities have challenged that authority, which is now much more widely shared, the persistence of hierarchies of race and class requires that we continue to acknowledge and investigate the hegemony of the white middle class.

Remarkably, Him/Her/Self needed very little in the way of revision to bring it up-to-date. The staying power of the original edition is what marks this book as a classic. By insisting that women can only be understood in relation to men, by casting the light of gender analysis on such issues as politics and war, by seeking to understand the ways in which middle-class hegemony is reinforced as well as challenged, Filene's study continues to set a standard for scholars to follow. It combines complex analyses of large historical developments with vivid accounts of the real lives of ordinary women and men. It is written in a clear, elegant, and lively prose, making it accessible to students and nonspecialists without sacrificing theoretical sophistication. It examines the ways in which gender operates not only in the lives of women but also in the lives of men, and in the realms of power as well as in the domains of private life. For these reasons and many more contained in the pages that follow, the insights offered in Him/Her/Self are as fresh and compelling today as they were in the first edition, published nearly a quarter of a century ago.

ELAINE TYLER MAY

Preface to the Third Edition

Revisiting an old friend after a decade-long separation is risky, because one can't be sure whether the reunion will produce awkward silences or easy familiarity. Revising *Him/Her/Self* turned out to be both: more difficult than I had expected and more gratifying. During the twelve years since the second edition, much has changed not only in the lives and attitudes of American women and men but also in the ways that historians think about gender. As a result, I found that revision called for more than simply attaching new pages at the end, bringing the story up-to-date. I also needed to change and expand earlier sections (updating the past). And at a more general level, I wanted to modify the conceptual framework (rethink my earlier thinking).

The first change a reader will notice is the new subtitle: instead of "sex roles," I have substituted "gender identities." In keeping with recent scholarship, I thereby make clear that this book is about differences created not by biology (sex), but by society and culture (gender). Moreover, it deals not only with the various social roles played by men and women (spouse, parent, employee, and so forth) but, more broadly, with the ways men and women have defined themselves. Many scholars, especially feminist ones, have criticized the concept of "sex role." For one thing, they argue, it fails to describe historical change, because it is basically static, assigning men and women to fixed binary categories and thereby missing the dynamic interplay between social practice and social structure. As a result, they say, sex-role theory distorts power relations by presuming that actors passively perform their roles rather than shaping or resisting them. "Gender . . . is a process rather than thing," says R. W. Connell. "If we could use the word 'gender' as a verb (I gender, you gender, she genders . . .) it would be better for our understanding."[1]

Contrary to this critique, I believe that *Him/Her/Self* pays attention to the dynamic, often defiant ways in which middle-class Americans have enacted gender roles during the past century. Indeed, unlike most gender studies, it maintains a bifocal perspective, tracing the actions and reactions between *both* sexes. Nevertheless, I have realized the desirability of widening the book's conceptual scope beyond roles to identity. Although individuals achieve their sense of self from the multiple social roles they play (mother, Methodist, and saleswoman), at a more transcendent level, they shape their individuality (identity, personhood) by adding personal motives and initiatives. In other words—and here I'm borrowing John Hewitt's lucid formulation—we have identities and we also make them, by bringing our own histories (biographies) to the situations.[2]

In keeping with this focus on gender identities, I have added a large amount of material about gay men and lesbians to this edition. For they exemplify particularly clearly how an individual's sense of self does not necessarily conform to conventional gender categories. Conversely, the category of "homosexual" turns out to be a cultural product, invented in the late nineteenth century and given various medical, moral, and political meanings thereafter. I have paid particular attention to three eras of gay and lesbian history: the turn of the century, World War II and its aftermath, and developments since 1970. As an illuminating subtopic, I also discuss romantic (but not sexual) friendships between men in the nineteenth century.

Since the time that I was working on the second edition, "feminism" has fallen into popular disrepute, but the demands for women's rights continue to be felt in every sector of American society: the law, the work world, the family, and sports, to name only the obvious ones. Accordingly, I have carried this story forward into the 1990s with the latest data, opinion polls, and studies.

The male half of the gender story, meanwhile, has become even more fascinating and complex than it was in 1985. Where I had written about two men's movements, now I have written about five. Granted, to call each of them a social movement is an overstatement. Nevertheless, the commotion among men certainly signals that a remarkable number of them—gay and straight, liberal and conservative, feminist and anti—have been re-examining the meaning of masculinity.

While adding this new material, I also subtracted. Many references to data or events of the 1980s, for example, have been replaced by more current ones, and the corresponding footnotes have gone with them. Likewise, in the process of adding new titles to the essay on sources, I have deleted those that no longer seem useful.

I want to thank Bob Brugger of Johns Hopkins University Press for encouraging me to undertake this new edition and for waiting so patiently until I finished it. Erica Rothman provided enormous help by her critiques of the manuscript as well as our many conversations about gender and relationships. I am grateful to Elaine Tyler May for writing a foreword to this new edition. Having admired her contributions to gender history, I feel honored that she has enhanced my words with hers. Finally, I thank once again all those readers and fellow teachers whose loyal appreciation of *Him/Her/Self* has justified bringing out this new edition. No author could ask for a better audience.

Preface to the First Edition

In 1967 I began doing research on the equality of American women after they got the vote in 1920. Seven years later, I have written a book on the sex roles of middle-class American women and men from the late nineteenth century to the present. Between my intention and my outcome intervened a series of new perspectives. Each of them altered my course; all of them together account for the form that I have finally given this book. To describe them is to explain what I have written and why.

The theme of "equality" became the first casualty of my rethinking. As I read about women in the 1920s, I recognized that this concept was too limited to contain the scope of my interests. For I was asking not only about the objective ways (such as legal rights, education, employment) in which women were or were not equal to men, and not only about people's ideas on these matters, but also about their feelings. This three-dimensional question overflowed the concept of equality and led me to replace it with "sex role": the kinds of behavior and attitudes (the script) that are expected of an individual as a member of his or her gender.[1]

So now I was studying changes in women's sex roles. This perspective helped me to formulate my evidence more effectively, especially because I could borrow from the numerous social psychologists who have worked on role theory and analysis. This perspective also dissolved my original starting point of 1920. The equal-suffrage amendment, I quickly discovered, made little difference in women's roles. The significant changes took place at the more basic level of culture. In order to understand them, I would have to go back beyond 1920, into the Victorian era. Early-twentieth-century women were the cultural daughters of the late nineteenth. The roles that they chose to perform inevitably responded, whether in harmony or defiance, to the ones they had been taught as children.

Thus I realized that the kind of history I was writing must fit the cultural life lines of the women I was writing about. To understand the evolutionary, and therefore gradual, development of their roles, I must extend my scope from the Victorian era to our own. Moreover, I must organize it according to "generations," or what sociologists more technically call "cohorts": groups of coevals whose attitudes are influenced by the same event within the same time interval.[2] Finally, I chose to focus on the middle class—white-collar and professional people, with above-average amounts of education—because, as David Riesman has observed, "it is the middle class, the mediating class, the educated class, whose opinions shift and which is therefore largely responsible for fluctuations in cultural and political tendencies."[3] The working class also has a history, of course, as social historians are increasingly discovering, but the "woman question" has been posed primarily by more privileged people.

So now I was studying the evolution of sex roles through several "generations" of middle-class women. These categories of analysis were helpful tools for digging into the past. But as my piles of index cards became paper mountains, I still felt that something was missing. One day I discovered it: I could not understand the roles of women without considering the roles of men. Sex role is, by definition, a product of interaction between male and female; the history of one sex is only one half of the whole. The question of sexual equality presupposes men with whom women are to be equal. More profoundly, a woman's question of "who am I?" involves expectations she has learned from men as well as expectations she has toward them. The idea of braiding the genders now seems obvious, almost inescapable, but given the multitudes of books on women and the few on men, it still needs to be demonstrated.

This last perspective completed my research design. It gave the vital momentum, the "plot," to my book. Now I was ready to find answers for three questions: How have middle-class men and women defined themselves during the eighty-five years from the late Victorian era to the present? Why have these definitions changed? What psychological and intellectual dilemmas have people undergone, and perhaps resolved, as they tried to find satisfactory roles?

Answers to these questions entail innumerable themes—feminism, employment, child rearing, sexuality, among others—and crisscross the boundaries of political, economic, intellectual, demographic, and other kinds of history. I could easily have written a compendious survey. Instead, I have chosen to write a long essay, an argument about the function of sex roles in modern America and about the meaning of male as well as female liberation. Ultimately, I have tried to illuminate the interior experience of men and women amid rapidly changing circumstances.

In doing so, I have used the post-Freudian premises of psychologists such as Kenneth Keniston, Gordon Allport, and Robert W. White. Like them, I believe that a person thinks and behaves not only according to forces he or she absorbs during childhood, but also according to influences and options he/she encounters during adolescence and early adulthood. An individual is the product of biological drives, child rearing, socioeconomic class, and culture, but within that matrix of conditions he or she makes choices about what to do, what to believe, ultimately who to be. In this constant process of self-defining, moreover, I believe that people have diverse kinds of motivations. The need to satisfy basic drives, especially sexual drives, is one motivation, but only one. More important is the desire to attain what White calls "competence." An individual wants the sense of efficacy gained through mastering the environment in some way or other, ideally a way that fits his or her particular personality. The greater this sense of competence and the closer the fit, the more he/she feels a satisfying sense of authenticity, of being fully him/her/self.[4]

Modern American culture has generally expected a man to find primary competence in his work and a woman to find it in her family. I began this book believing that these expectations constrict the happiness and possibilities of individuals. I wrote it in order to learn how and why these roles have been prescribed and thereby to learn how men and women might go beyond "masculine" and "feminine" into roles that exclude as little as possible of their personalities. I complete the book with a chastened understanding of how difficult this ideal has been and still is. Yet I retain a belief in the (difficult) possibility of people living more fully as themselves.

Like all historians, then, I look at the past with a particular angle of vision—an angle shaped by certain values, which in turn are shaped by personal experience. A few autobiographical remarks seem appropriate, therefore. I was born in 1940, went to college during the "silent" fifties, and came of social-political age in the turbulent sixties. I belong to the "new generation" whom the Port Huron Statement announced in

1962, and I share its commitment to finding "a meaning in life that is personally authentic" and to building egalitarian "community" within American society.

I am also male. Through the years of research for this book and through countless conversations with friends in and near the Women's Liberation Movement, I have learned to understand the extent to which, as a man, I am necessarily an outsider to the experience of women. At the same time I also developed a determined conviction that men as well as women would benefit by liberation from conventional sex roles. This book is a part of my efforts to act on this conviction.

My first acknowledgments go to these friends, especially Kathy Meads, Sara Evans, Harry Boyte, Kathy Knox, Ron Aarons, and Joan Lipsitz. I am also indebted to those who read my manuscript and offered invaluable suggestions for improving it: William Chafe, Towny Ludington, Joan Lipsitz, and Anne Firor Scott, with special thanks to Kathy Meads and Peter Walker. The librarians at the Arthur and Elizabeth Schlesinger Library on the History of Women in America were exceptionally helpful and cordial. The University of North Carolina provided me with funds that expedited my research. And the Charles Warren Center for Studies in American History provided me with a fellowship as well as other kinds of support that allowed me to complete the book in an environment that was ideal for intellectual work.

I/
The
End of the
Victorian Era
(1890–1919)

Prologue/
As They Were

26th May, Thurs. evening, 1889

My very dear Charlie,

Need I say how much we miss you? It seems like many times ten days since the train carried you out of sight. No doubt every mother feels such pain when her boy leaves home, but that brings nonetheless small comfort.

Yet, I should muster cheerful words, I suppose, for the happiness you and Bob will share during your travels. What I remember of England from my own brief visit, now so many years past, still glows within me. Oh do visit Westminster Cathedral, Charlie, and of course Wordsworth's Lake Country where "a host of golden daffodils are dancing in the breeze." Visit these places for me.

Our garden has prospered from the uninterrupted sunshine of the past week, jonquils and roses in profusion. Perhaps it was their aroma that awoke me this morning with a feeling of uncommon vigor. Directly after breakfast I set to work with Fanny airing all my summer dresses, exchanging the parlor drapes, and generally turning the house inside out. We even managed to push the divan beside the piano, where I had always wanted it, and it seems like a new sitting room altogether.

Yesterday Fanny finished the hem to Anna's dress. Her first party gown! When Aunt Emily (who made her usual call, now that her rheumatism has relented) and I fitted Anna this afternoon, she looked positively a princess. You would not have recognized then your "little sister." She will in time make some man proud.

If only she learns to govern her temper. We had, I fear, another "scene" when I sought to fit the corset. She grimaced and complained and shrieked against the laces, until finally hurling it across the room where it broke the globe of my lovely yellow lamp. It was, I tell you, a mortifying moment—with Aunt Emily open-mouthed and the cook peering curiously from the hall and both Anna and I in tears. I dread what your Father will say when he comes home.

As always, such scenes renew my languor. I lay down the rest of the day and did not make or receive any calls.

This letter grows longer than planned, my darling boy, and I confess I am weary. The clock strikes seven. I await your Father's arrival momentarily. Another late day for him at the office. He will be weary, too, but I shall keep this letter open for him to add a few words.

I hold you in my mind and heart with unbounded affection. I am of course desirous of receiving a letter from you as soon as your busy travels permit.

Remember your waistcoat that I put at the bottom of your trunk, for English weather can be exceedingly damp. Don't expose yourself, please, to the chance of taking cold. If you want of any clothing, do not hesitate to purchase it, as I wish you comfortable and also dressed befitting every social occasion. A handsome young gentleman as you are now ought to dress the part, particularly as it will gratify your ever loving

MOTHER

My dear Son:

You have entered upon a new experience of life to you—somewhat of an early trial of your capacity of taking care of yourself and recommending yourself. You have talents, you have character—you have a manly bearing. I trust, therefore, you will make good use of this wonderful opportunity. Walk about the cities and countryside, see sights, and try to exercise your faculties for learning whatever is of interest.

It is now late, and I must awake early for a full day at the office. I often wish that the business would thrive more of its own accord and less by one's "shoulder at the wheel." But in a fortnight's time we reopen the house at Nantasket, and I can visit your Mother and sister there for a Sunday's vacation.

You may be sure of the warm, unchanging affection and constant interest with which you are remembered at home.

Ever yr. affc. father

OLIVER ANDREWS

26th May, Thurs. past midnight

Another sleepless night, this journal again the faithful companion to my spirit. Everyone lies in the peaceful sleep that headache denies me. The house surrounds me like a grey cave. I would take another nerve pill, had not Dr. Ash so strenuously forbidden more than one.

I'm feeling vexed by Anna. Her mischief confounds me. Oh what have I done wrong, that she displays this wildness? I see some failure of me in her, but I know not what, and can only pray for improvement.

Why was I so short toward Oliver tonight? Weariness alone does not excuse it. Rather, contrariness & self-indulgence—I *must* discipline these parts. Dear God, I pray you, help me put them to rest. Why do I fail my duty? I dreamed myself again a skylark looking down upon this house & then flying out across an ocean of daffodils. Oliver has been so considerate of my melancholies—the most patient husband imaginable, but he cannot be patient forever. I must deserve his trust.

No one's nature is so irredeemably delinquent that it cannot be taken in hand by the will. I am determined to be more contented in the future. With God's help.[1]

1/
Women and the World

In 1900 W.E.B. Du Bois greeted the new century as one in which Americans must confront the problem of the color line. That proved to be largely a wishful prophecy. In the United States only certain men—white men—were created equal. But Americans could not so easily ignore the plight of another group. Women constituted 49 percent of the population, barely a numerical minority, and were deemed the "better half," apparently a moral majority. In terms of rights and power, however, they suffered obvious, overt discrimination. Only white men were created equal. Yet the circumstances of modern America were rapidly undercutting this sexual arrangement. New social and economic conditions and correspondingly new states of mind—especially among the middle class—were forcing Americans to deal with "the woman question."

It was a question of equal rights under the law, in education, and in employment. But it went beyond the right of a woman to act outside her domestic sphere. When feminists demanded the right to vote or attend college or earn a salary, they were asking not only to do as men did but also to be other than women were expected to be. It was a question of women's role, the social script that she performed in response to the expectations surrounding her and inside herself. And beyond that, it was a question of female identity. If feminists had their way, she would no longer be man's better half, but his equal. She would be a "new woman."[1]

Americans were not certain who this "new woman" would be or what consequences she would bring. Feminists themselves were uncertain. But, in any case, they perceived possibilities that were momentous, reverberating with unsettling force beyond women's rights—to sexual mores, to the family, and to the definitions of manhood.

ON THE EVE OF THE TWENTIETH century America was still Victorian. The crowds surging through the Columbian Exposition in Chicago in 1893 might have marveled at such wondrous innovations as the phonograph and outdoor electric lighting. Henry Adams, walking among those crowds, might have discerned a fatal historical phase in the din of the dynamo. A Rip Van Winkle awakening from a half-century sleep would have barely believed the Chicago metropolis of one million people, the hundred railroad trains roaring from coast to coast carrying Rockefeller's oil along tracks of Carnegie's steel. Technologically, financially, demographically, it was a modern nation. Yet Queen Victoria did not die until 1901, and the era named in her honor lived as long and longer. Subjectively—in their cultural values—middle-class Americans of the 1890s remained eminently Victorian. Like their ancestors two and three generations earlier, they believed in work, individualism, progress, religion, the home, and "character."

Nowhere were they more Victorian than in their view of middle-class women—or, more precisely, of ladies. When they spoke, in the 1890s, about the female role, they were using a vocabulary that had been repeated over so many decades that it had become effortless, sanctified, and cliché. As a Philadelphia newspaper put it at mid-century:

> Our ladies . . . soar to rule the hearts of their worshippers, and secure obedience by the scepter of affection. . . . Is not everything managed by female influence? . . . A woman is nobody. A wife is everything. A pretty girl is equal to ten thousand men, and a mother is, next to God, all powerful. . . . The ladies of Philadelphia, therefore, under the influence of the most serious "sober second thoughts," are resolved to maintain their rights as wives, belles, virgins, and mothers, and not as women.[2]

And not as women! A woman is nobody unless she be a lady. This was the role that Victorians assigned to the female sex; these were the boundaries of female rights. In the era when a queen ruled an empire upon which the sun never set, Americans expected women to reign at home. Assisted perhaps by servants, a middle-class American woman earned admiration by providing loyal support to her husband, rearing moral children, and superintending an orderly household. But she was more than a homemaker. Ideally she was the "angel of the house," using her natural—or, as some said, her divine—sensibilities to create a cultured atmosphere by playing the piano, working with church groups, and displaying at dinner parties a social grace that made a husband proud. She was homemaker as well as culture giver, but first and last she was loving and beloved wife. "Mutual joy," Madeleine Wallin wrote to her fiancé, was what she hoped for in their marriage. Like other aspects of middle-class life, however, marital pleasure was not expected to have the same meaning for men and women. According to the ministers, physicians, and other authorities who prescribed social ideals, a woman was less driven than a man by sexual passion, more given to restraint and delicacy, and a creature of love rather than lust. Purity came naturally to her, whereas a man constantly struggled to subdue his animal instincts.[3]

A "cult of the lady" held sway in Victorian America. Placed upon a pedestal of piety and purity, she governed the domestic half of the middle-class world while men did economic, political, and military battle beyond the doorstep. A pair of complementary hemispheres, hers and his: this arrangement lasted throughout the nineteenth century as an ideal, but it never corresponded to the daily reality of most women's lives.

To manage a household was in fact an exhausting job that dragged mercilessly on a woman's muscles from early morning to bedtime, Monday through Sunday. Nowhere more starkly than on the farms, where approximately half of American women lived. The typical farmer's wife worked a ten-hour day in the winter, a thirteen-hour day in the summer, carrying water to the house (as late as 1920, only one of three farm families had interior plumbing), heating it on the stove in order to cook meals or (in movable tubs) wash the laundry and bathe the children, making soap and brooms and clothing, scrubbing the floors, tending the poultry and the garden, milking the cows. Merely the preparation of food was a long, tedious business. Being even more prejudiced against new-fashioned canned goods than her small-town sisters, a farm woman spent hour after hour in the kitchen shelling peas, peeling potatoes, churning butter, making jelly, preserving fruit, and baking bread. For all this work she had little help: the older children, although they often hindered her more than they helped; a hired girl, perhaps, although only a small minority of farm families could afford one; and, except for a (nonelectric) sewing machine, few if any mechanical appliances. As diversion she could look forward to church services, perhaps a meeting of the Grange, an occasional chatty visit by a neighboring wife, a shopping trip to town, a seasonal fair.[4]

Urban housewives escaped this pastoral loneliness but not much else of the daily hardship. As late as 1925, for example, the majority of small-town homes in Delaware, New Jersey, Illinois, and other states still lacked stationary laundry tubs. In larger cities, middle-class women had more technological conveniences but little ease. They baked, preserved, pickled, canned. They laundered the voluminous clothing by hand or, in more prosperous households, by hand-driven washing machines, without effective detergent to ease the job. They cleaned the clutter of Victorian bric-a-brac, heavy draperies, and wall-to-wall carpeting without the benefit of vacuum cleaners.[5] By the end of an average week they probably had devoted more than forty hours to housework—and that figure does not include the additional twenty hours of caring for their children.[6]

Technological innovation in the late nineteenth century was beginning to relieve some of this burden. Refrigerators provided more leeway; hot-water extensions on stoves and water backs on ranges expedited cooking and laundering; sewing machines simplified the care of clothing; aluminum utensils were lighter and more sanitary than the iron, tin, or granite variety. But even as these "labor-saving devices" began to enter middle-class homes, a much more effective kind of assistance began to leave. Servants, those familiar inhabitants of the Victorian tableau, were becoming scarce. In 1892, a book titled *The Art of Entertaining* described the shortage of servants as " the great unsolved American Question." During the next twenty years it became still greater. Although the European immigration brought thousands of girls, they increasingly preferred the higher wages, shorter hours, and greater autonomy in factories, shops, or restaurants. Upper-class families still managed to maintain their force of two or more servants. But middle-class housewives found it harder and harder to hold or replace the one girl whom they, like their mothers, had learned to rely on. Writing to her sister from Tuscaloosa, Laura Phillips lamented: "You have no idea how much the difficulty in getting & keeping servants—cooks especially—has to do with the social life of this place." If it was difficult in the South, it was even worse elsewhere. Whereas the ratio of servants to families declined in the South by 40 percent between 1870 and 1920, it declined nationwide by 50 percent and in the North by 60 percent. By 1920 only one of every sixteen American families, on the average, employed a servant. The acquisition of a washing machine hardly made up for the loss of a Bridget to work it. Meanwhile, the minority of women who were fortunate enough to find a servant also found that she gave less devotion. In drawing rooms and clubs and in letters to the local newspaper, women complained bitterly about their lazy, impudent help.[7]

The lack of servants represented more than a matter of household management. It became "one of the burning questions of the day," as a writer remarked in 1901, because it was jeopardizing the Victorian model of middle-class domesticity. Without a servant, a woman would have to perform the dirtiest housework with her own hands; more generally, she would lose a symbol of upper-middle-class status. A woman could be a lady partly because she hired a Bridget.[8]

An anonymous contributor to the *New York Times* in 1906 described her plight in vivid tones. Newly wed to a man earning sixty dollars per week (five times as high as the average industrial worker's income), occupying a five-room apartment in a genteel uptown section of New York City, she was willing to pay as much as twenty dollars per month for an experienced live-in maid. But even at this rate, which was two to three times higher than wages in shoe factories or restaurants, she found no suitable applicants. All maids, she complained, wanted to live at home, "in some dirty tenement doubtless full of all sorts of vermin, which they would bring daily to my clean little home." Further, they wanted an eight-hour day, which was impossible because in the morning her husband ate breakfast at eight o'clock and in the evening she did not want to clear the dinner table and wash dishes "with no opportunity for converse with my husband."

But her concern went beyond the physical details of cooking and cleaning. She wanted a maid to open the door for evening callers and, if need be, to say that the master and mistress were not at home. "Bohemians who care nothing for the niceties and conventionalities of life may live after this fashion [of answering the doorbell in person, or choosing not to answer], but I contend that those of us who aspire to live after the manner of civilized society cannot."

Apparently, though, "Bohemians" were not the only deviants from a civilized style of life. "I hear certain women asking why I don't do the work myself despite my husband's prohibition. 'What have you to do the livelong day but keep your home?' they ask. I have this to do, to keep my husband."[9]

Here was the Victorian cultural standard in all its resonance, but rendered plaintive in the face of new economic realities. These realities cut two ways. The cost of living was rising faster than middle-class incomes, and the availability of servants was declining. By 1911 a writer in *Good Housekeeping* was telling women that the time had come to learn how to get along without a maid. However much the role of lady survived in the minds of middle-class women, in practice it was faltering. The newlywed just quoted, for example, concluded her article by saying she and her husband would move to an apartment hotel, that recent urban innovation, which provided commercial laundry service and a dining room on the lower floors. Circumstances had defeated her and countless others who shared her aspirations toward gentility. The apartment hotel was no place for a lady.[10]

Only a privileged segment of middle-class women could play the ladylike role with all its serenity and grace. Most commuted between kitchen and nursery and parlor and sewing room in an exhausting devotion to "making a home." Most worked as hard as their great-grandmothers had, before the era of industrialization. Where, then, was all the leisure that we believe came with technological and commercial development? Not in a mother's daily routine. If she enjoyed more leisure, it was to be found in changes in her life cycle.

Whereas in the mid-eighteenth century the median age at which a woman gave birth to her last child was thirty-eight or older, in 1900 it was less than thirty-three. Correspondingly, the median age of an eighteenth-century woman when her last child married was sixty, as compared to fifty-five in 1900. (Meanwhile, the median age at marriage remained almost unchanged.) Over the century she had "gained" five years. (See Fig. 1.) The gain derived partly from the fact that she bore fewer children. Between 1800 and 1900 the annual birth rate dropped 40 percent, and even more among the middle and upper classes. Whereas in 1790 the average size of a household (including resident kin) was 5.7, by 1900 it had shrunk to 4.6. Most urban families in the late nineteenth century had between two and five members, hardly fitting the Brueghel-like scene conjured up by our imaginations. Motherhood also ended earlier for the typical woman, because as obstetrical and pediatric care improved she needed to bear fewer children in order

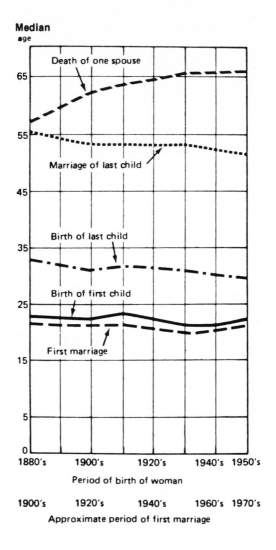

FIGURE 1. Median Age of Mothers at the Beginning of Selected Stages of the Family Life Cycle
Source: Paul C. Glick, "Updating the Life Cycle of the Family," *Journal of Marriage and the Family* 39 (February 1977): 7. Data are from U.S. Bureau of the Census Reports. Copyright 1977 by the National Council on Family Relations, 1910 West County Road B. Suite 147, St. Paul, Minnesota 55113. Reprinted by permission.

to have the same number survive. Infant mortality rates dropped sharply during the half century after the Civil War. Whereas in the 1870s at least 17 percent of the newborn died in infancy, by 1915 only one of every ten failed to survive.[11]

These changes significantly lightened the burden of motherhood. Women underwent the physical and emotional strain of pregnancy less often, and they typically were in their mid-thirties when the last child went to school. But that was not all of the "extra" life. The average twenty-year-old female of 1900 could expect to live until the age of sixty-four, four years older than her ancestor of a half century before. Thus, mothers could look forward to two decades of life after all the children had left home permanently.[12]

GIVEN THE IDEALS OF LADYHOOD—which seem narrow or even suffocating—and given the realities of homemaking—which seem heavy, even punishing—did middle-class Victorian women seethe with indignation? Before addressing this question, we must give second thought to the prejudices inside it. Late-twentieth-century Americans do not interpret experience in the same terms as people did a hundred years ago. Like tourists in a foreign country, we must try to understand the women of Victorian culture in their own terms rather than ours. It is easy to pity or attack their situation; it is harder and more instructive to comprehend how they dealt with it.

Although their lives were limited and arduous, most women responded not with indignation but with acceptance ranging from glad to grudging. At first we may be tempted to dismiss this acceptance as some kind of brainwashing. But that judgment again substitutes our standards for theirs. It also deprecates these women, implying that they were not intelligent enough to see what was good for them. In fact, there were considerable benefits in being a "true" Victorian woman: the privilege of being economically supported, the esteem of being a homemaker (in contrast to our "just a housewife"), and the nurture from husband's and children's love.

At least so a girl was brought up to believe. Consider the response of twenty-five-year-old Ellen Axson, for example, when her fiancé Woodrow Wilson asked about her plans for continuing art studies, reminding her that "of course there's that fact that marriage will take away almost all your chance for work." In her letter the next day, Ellen replied: "I think you do my love a great injustice"—not by asking her to give up her career ambitions, but by having thought he had to ask in the first place. She had no hesitation at all in wishing to "spend my life with [you]—and for [you]." Ten years and three daughters later, she had no second thoughts, only the same ones. "How I thank God for you, my darling—noble man, perfect husband that you are—my own true love, so absolutely *all* that a woman could desire the man to be to whom she gives her heart and life."[13]

Not all women were so fortunate as Mrs. Wilson, of course. Many felt gloomy or even resentful about their lot. Almira MacDonald, the wife of a Rochester, New York, attorney and the mother of three, filled her journal every second day with a patient refrain of "Baked today. Baked this morning. Baked as usual today." Once in a while, however, a dissonant note entered: "Baked. Am feeling miserable." Unlike their twentieth-century descendants, however, "miserable" housewives tended to turn their complaints back upon themselves. Charlotte Perkins Stetson, married less than a year and pregnant, lay for weeks in bed under the weight of illness and depression. But in her journal she criticized herself more than her circumstances.

> Jan. 30 [1885]: Bad night, lame all over.
>
> Feb. 2: I *must* be strong and not hinder him [her husband Walter]. . . . Feel so downcast that I take out my comforter, Walter's journal, and get new strength and courage thence, learning how good and brave he is.
>
> Feb. 4: Am very tired and lame at night which displeaseth and grieveth my Walter. I didn't *mean* to!

Fifteen years later, after leaving husband and child and then remarrying, Charlotte Perkins Gilman would write a book that defined housework as oppression. But not yet. She was still trying, like most women of her era, to be a "true wife."[14]

Their effort derived from religious conscience. Religion was not simply one among their beliefs but the framework of their lives. When in doubt (or pain or anger or grief), turn to God and regain virtue. They measured their lives by the yardstick of duty, not happiness, character instead of self-fulfillment.

Of course *ought* does not necessarily mean *is*. Try as they might, many dutiful Victorian housewives found themselves at odds with one or another part of their "appointed" role—the pain of unwanted pregnancies, perhaps, or the suffocation of their intellects by relentless baking and cleaning, or perhaps nothing they could specify except that, try as they might, they felt discontent. More precisely, they felt diseased. "I have such nervous attacks without any reason," Mary Helen Smith wrote to her husband from an ocean resort where she and her young daughter were vacationing. "I don't see what should cause them. One day I have a bowel complaint & the next day a headache & I haven't ambition enough even to go to the beach." Her body was expressing a rebellion that her mind could not or would not put into words. The modern label for her condition is psychosomatic illness; the nineteenth-century label was "nervousness." An epidemic of nervousness was sweeping middle-class women, producing insomnia, lethargy, bouts of weeping, vomiting, and panicky fears that had no apparent cause. In response, magazines like *Harper's Bazar* and *Ladies' Home Journal* published incessant articles prescribing self-help remedies such as exercise, nutrition, and firmer control of one's emotions.

A few women suffered to the point of breakdown or worse. Alice James, the sister of novelist Henry and psychologist William, spent most of the second half of her life in bed. The doctors found no physiological disease, but she did not get well. Finally, at age forty-four, she contracted breast cancer and died. In effect, Alice James had made a career of invalidism. Or one can say she performed a parody of the Victorian ideal of a refined, helpless lady. Either way, she was waging a tacit rebellion against the conventional expectations. "How sick one gets of being 'good,'" she wrote in her journal. "How much I should respect myself if I could burst out and make every one wretched for twenty-four hours; embody selfishness." But without saying so, she was doing exactly that—embodying selfishness—by lying in bed. She, or at least her body, had gone on strike. Always, however, it was a tacit rebellion, a passive aggression. The epidemic of middle-class female nervousness signaled a discontent that stayed hidden, usually from the women themselves. Illness was a symptom, not a solution.[15]

Indeed, when they took their illnesses to physicians, they found that the prescribed remedies reinforced the very situation that had made them diseased. For physicians treated female patients according to a model of health that embodied the Victorian stereotypes of gender. "Woman," Dr. Horatio Storer declared in typical fashion, "is what she is in health, in character, in her charms, alike of body, mind and soul because of her womb alone." Woman equals womb. Her anatomy defined her destiny as a creature of emotionalism, inwardness, and fragility, a dependent upon the power of men. Her procreative organs governed not only her traits, but her life's work. Given the nineteenth-century belief that a human body contained only a limited amount of energy, she should spend hers in motherhood and other domestic activities. Many physicians opposed education for girls after puberty set in, for example, because it diverted precious energy from ovary to brain. "Why spoil a good mother by making an ordinary grammarian?"

Avoid excessive mental activity, and also excessive sexual activity. According to Dr. William Acton's English study, *The Functions and Disorders of the Reproductive Organs* (1857), "The majority of women (happily for them) are not very much troubled with sexual feelings of any kind." And so Dr. Acton mentioned women only twice throughout his book. In the privacy of their bedrooms, countless women and men contradicted his claim. But in public, in prescriptions of what women ought to feel and do, the doctrine of weaker female sexuality prevailed until the turn of the century. Acton's book went through eight American editions, and was hailed by *Medical Record* as a "classic." In a typical marriage manual, a girl learned how to choose a eugenically sound mate, how to tend her health during pregnancy, and how to raise her children. But about sexuality she learned only that her husband ought to respect her milder needs. Specifically, manuals and physicians urged husbands to curtail their lust to weekly or even monthly intercourse.

And what if a woman fell ill in trying to perform her role, suffering "nervousness"? Working from their premises, physicians told her that she had abused her vital organs. According to *Woman's Complete Guide to Health* (1869), most female diseases "will be found, on due investigation, to be in reality, no disease at all, but merely the sympathetic reaction or the symptoms of one disease, namely a disease of the womb." The problem did not begin "out there" but "in here." So whatever remedy the doctors suggested (rest, exercise, hydrotherapy, surgery) was intended to return the patient to her "natural" place in the home. The cure was part of the disease. Doctors may have warned strenuously against the corset because it damaged lungs, liver, and uterus while compressing women to "feminine" proportions. But the medical definition of female health was as confining and often as injurious as the tightest corset.[16]

Fortunately, most Victorian women did not behave entirely according to the ideals held up for them. The experts may have said that "the better half" felt little or no sexual desire, but many females knew otherwise. "The physical effect of our close communion was unlike anything I ever experienced," Mabel Todd exclaimed in her journal the day after her husband returned home from a business trip "It was enjoyment, and yet it was very hard for me to feel the same kind of intensity as before—it was a thrilling sort of breathlessness—but at last it came—the beautiful climax of feeling I knew so well." Of course we cannot know for sure what took place in bedrooms a century ago, and so we cannot say whether Todd's sexuality was typical of her time and social class. Considerable evidence indicates, however, that she was not as uncommon as the Victorian prescriptions and our own stereotypes would have us believe. When Professor Clelia Mosher surveyed forty-five middle-class married women in 1892, for example, she was told that 33 percent reached orgasm "always" or "usually," while another 40 percent experienced it "sometimes" or "not always." Sexual intercourse "makes more normal people," wrote a thirty-five-year-old mother of four. "I consider this appetite as ranking with other natural appetites," a mother of three declared, "and like them to be indulged legitimately and temperately." The majority of Mosher's respondents agreed with the doctors and advice books in wanting less frequent intercourse, no more than every week or two. But we need not interpret their answers as proof of passionlessness. Victorian women had compelling objective reasons to prefer sexual temperance: namely, as a way of minimizing the risks of pregnancy, venereal disease, or the various gynecological afflictions that doctors usually could not cure. Passionlessness, like nervousness, was a social strategy as much as a socialized attitude.[17]

To combat the frustrations of their sphere, Victorian women also adopted a more positive remedy. Instead of turning away from their husbands or turning to physicians, they turned to one another. They visited (which was the form of calling one did in the pre-telephone era), perhaps for an hour on a set afternoon if they lived in a city, perhaps for a week or month if they lived in rural areas. They gathered, six or a dozen friends, in someone's parlor for tea or a session of quilting. They also formed more institutional settings for companionship—women's clubs. Taking advantage of the new leisure in their middle age, growing numbers of women in places as diverse as Watertown, Massachusetts, and Weeping Water, Nebraska, came together in weekly club meetings. By 1915 the General Federation of Women's Clubs, the national organization that coordinated this multitude, could boast a million members or more.[18]

They joined to escape the loneliness or the limits of their domestic sphere. But they wanted more than gossip and tea. Loyal to the Victorian model of womanhood, they earnestly devoted themselves to "culture." Hence the Shakespeare Club of Idaho Springs, Idaho, and the Homer Club of Butte, Montana, and the four standard General Federation groups, "The Bible as Literature," "Twelve Famous Novels," "English Poetry of the Nineteenth Century," and "Women in Education." These titles betray the clubs' conservative purposes and practices. Clubwomen were enacting the traditional role that they enacted at home by reading sonnets to their children or playing sonatas on the spinet. They were, it seems, merely moving their pedestals to a new location. But it did not work out exactly as intended.

They might have come to learn about Hamlet, but they discovered themselves. Although few if any clubwomen intended rebellion against their role, the very experience of organizing as women fostered unintended attitudes. Mrs. Mary E. Rumford, for example, recalled twenty years later "the revelation we clubwomen . . . were to each other" at the first meeting of the General Federation, in 1890. "As one and another appeared upon the platform to give her club report we nudged the neighbor next to us with surprised delight—'isn't she clever?' 'What wit!' 'How graceful!' 'What sound common sense!' To-day feminine ability does not surprise us. We expect it of clubwomen, but in that earlier day each one gave us a new and peculiar joy."[19]

Heightened self-esteem was the fundamental consequence of membership for most women. While cultivating the aesthetic sensibilities of a lady, they discovered their capacities for organization, public speaking, and intellectual analysis. Most would have been content to stop at this point. But a few carried the implications further, beyond the curtained club windows into the world outside. If the clubs could benefit their own members, they could also benefit others, by applying concerted female energy to the ills of society. So these women worked to build public playgrounds, improve street lighting and sewage systems, eradicate child labor, create tuberculosis clinics, expand public libraries, lobby in state legislatures for tenement reforms, and perform a myriad of other activities.[20]

The momentum of club experience took these leisured middle-class women directly into the male world, where, in unladylike fashion, they sought to reform the social injustices neglected or created by men. To this extent they had indeed departed from their traditional role. Yet their reforms stopped short at a significant point—equal suffrage. Not until 1914, after eleven states had granted the vote to women and when passage of the national amendment seemed inevitable, did the General Federation endorse suffrage. This reluctance measures the meaning of the clubwomen's activities. Although most members partly resembled the model of a "new woman," essentially they remained traditional women in a new locale. They did not question the concept of a feminine sphere, only its limits. A few leaders visualized the formation of female political power, but many more preferred political influence. Meanwhile, the rank and file was content with studying art and literature and music.

Ultimately, then, the members had left home but not woman's sphere; instead, they had stretched the boundaries of that sphere. In the process, they no longer matched the standard portrait of a lady, but remained nevertheless "true women," mothers of the society. Sallie Cotten, president of the North Carolina clubs, neatly defined the limits of female emancipation when she enthused, in a letter to her son, about the type of woman who was "freed from the bondage of an enforced extreme femininity—so-called refined womanhood—and seeing herself as God made her, man's comrade, helper, and stimulator." In short, the clubwomen descended gingerly from their domestic pedestal in order to fulfill more effectively the role as better half.[21]

WHETHER HAPPILY, DUTIFULLY, or resentfully, the large majority of middle-class women were performing their role as guardians of their appointed sphere. At the same time, however, social observers were increasingly obsessed with and alarmed by the "new woman" and the "woman question." If one believed their reports, some sort of gender upheaval was taking place. Who was this new woman, and what was the question?

According to some critics, she was the lady of leisure who spent her time and money decadently indulging herself. "Too many women are dangerously idle," muttered Edward Bok, the editor of *Ladies' Home Journal*. Without enough to occupy them at home they were going downtown to Wanamaker's or Macy's or one of the other new department stores. There they idled away the day with socializing, lunch, and, of course, shopping. Still worse, according to the critics, women were purchasing clothes that ill befit a lady. The "radical dress reform" at the turn of the century greatly upset the editors of *Harper's Bazar*. "What of woman's mission to be lovely?" they demanded. "A short-skirted woman on the street, except in a deluge of rain, is a blow to one's ideals." When the whim of fashion turned to long trailing skirts, puffed sleeves, feathered muffs and boas, and hats that hid the face, the critics remained unappeased. Women "have put their sex to shame . . . ," announced Margaret Deland, "by the wild vulgarity of their silly, and hideous, and selfish hats."[22]

Skirts and hats were a trivial debauch compared to the fact that some women were smoking—in public. Etiquette authorities of the 1890s issued clear warning that "the prospects for the future happiness . . . are small" for any young woman who smoked or even appeared in public with a man who smoked. But some females would not listen. Fifteen years later, things had gone so far that the New York City Board of Aldermen felt compelled to pass an ordinance forbidding women to smoke in hotels and restaurants. Various civic leaders applauded the move, denouncing cigarettes between female fingers as "a crime," an attempt to "corrupt our civilization," and, finally, "too disgusting for words." But prohibition had come too late. Some women were smoking—not only the "advanced" ones, but even some of the "most respectable"—at private dinner parties, in restaurants and hotel lobbies, on board ship.[23]

Here was "the new woman," her critics cried, and they denounced her as a traitor to her sex. "Is it to be wondered at," asked Anna Rogers in a widely read article, "that the indefinable charm, the sacredness and mystery of womanhood, are fast passing away from among us?"[24]

But the critics were wrong. Short skirts and smoking violated conventions of femininity, but they didn't raise questions about woman's role. Shopping carried more significant implications, no doubt. The thousands of women who daily crowded the new department stores in New York, Philadelphia, and other cities were participating in the trend away from production and toward consumption. By the 1920s, the economic function of housewives would center largely on what they bought (with their husbands' money) rather than on what they made.[25] Even as consumers, though, housewives remained housewives—not "new women" raising basic questions about their roles or rights.

WHERE, THEN, WAS A GENUINELY "new woman" to be found? Not in the home or the club or the department store, but in colleges and profes-

sions and "bachelor woman" apartments. And not in the older generation, but in the younger. The new woman was really the new girl and the
spinster—a minority of the female minority, but disproportionately
conspicuous.

The new girls created the largest commotion. With gusto they went
window shopping, attended theater matinees, played tennis or golf,
flirted, and danced. Household duties, sedentary "culture," chaper-
ones—these girls left them all behind as they romped into the public
air with their skirts revealing a full six inches of stockings. They had a
bravado that could not be ignored. Indeed, through Charles Dana Gibson's dexterous drawings they became one emblem of the era. "The
Gibson girl" was upstaging the lady.

Caroline Ticknor neatly epitomized the changing female scene in
1901 as she imagined an encounter between the new type and the old.
First we see the "steel-engraving lady," a figure of alabaster skin and
slender limbs, seated beneath samplers of curlicued biblical advice.
Enter the Gibson girl, whistling a melody from a comic opera, wearing
a short skirt, square-toed shoes, a vest and cravat, and a broad-
brimmed felt hat tipped at a jaunty angle. Even if she were to blush—
which is hardly her style—the blush would not penetrate through her
tanned cheeks. "We have done away with all the over-sensitiveness and
overwhelming modesty in which you are enveloped," she informs the
steel-engraving lady. "We have progressed in every way. When a man
approaches, we do not tremble and droop our eyelids, or gaze ador-
ingly while he lays down the law. We meet him on a ground of perfect
fellowship, and converse freely on every topic."

The lady catches her breath. "And does he like this method?" she
inquires. The girl shakes her head with impatience. "Whether he *likes* it
or not makes little difference," she replies. "*He* is no longer the one
whose pleasure is to be consulted. The question now is, not, 'What
does man like?' but 'What does woman prefer?'" The modern point of
view, she explains, begins outside the home and outside the notion of
being ornamental. Like others of her generation, she is economically
self-supporting. "This is a utilitarian age. We cannot set down to be admired; we must be 'up and doing'; we must leave 'footprints in the sand
of time.'"

Silently the lady rises and departs. Behind her, the girl pities this
"extinct type." Higher education, she thinks gratefully, has begun to free

her sex from the "chains of prejudice." But she has no time for contemplation. "I must be off, I'm due at the golf links at three-fifteen" to meet a man.[26]

This little vignette portrays quite accurately the themes dividing the female generations; but in reality the division often was far less verbal, far less polite, far more tumultuous. "Be sure to behave like a lady under all circumstances," Mrs. Mary Thomas wrote to her teenaged daughter, Minnie. "Do nothing that will attract the least notice." Like countless other parents of the later nineteenth century, however, she discovered—gradually and bewilderingly—that something was going wrong. Minnie Thomas insisted on jumping from roof tops too high for even the most daring boy, on dissecting mice, and then on going to college. Maud Nathan's mother discovered her daughter about to crawl along a plank propped between the third-story window sills of two neighboring apartment houses. Molly Dewson foreshadowed her political career when, during one November of her teenage years, she drafted and presented to her schoolteacher a petition for a holiday on Thanksgiving Friday. Rheta Childe Dorr's early years were punctuated by fits of screaming "Lil girls just as good as lil boys"; meanwhile, she regularly ran away from home. Young Margaret Sanger crawled across a towering railroad trestle near her rural New York State home, escaped death beneath a speeding locomotive only by hanging from the ties above the ravine, and then—trembling—forced herself to repeat the crossing. Something was stirring among the middle-class younger generation. "Mamma told me a few days ago," Mary Boit contritely confessed to her diary in 1891, "that she had given up trying to make a lady of me long ago."[27]

Many parents during the last third of the nineteenth century were sitting late at night and asking in worried tones: What is the matter with our Mary, our Minnie, our Maud? Why is she so reckless, so rebellious, so intent upon disgrace? They did not find easy answers, nor can we, even with a century of hindsight. A new female generation was coming of age—young women who resisted apprenticeship into ladylike decorum. That much is clear. But why did this new attitude take hold in this era, and why did it inhabit some girls and not others? Here the answers become more various.

Explanation begins at the most generalized level, with socioeconomic class. Most of these daughters were growing up in families that had acquired the style of, or at least pretensions to, considerable leisure. Their parents had made a kind of life in which they took pride. They had become substantial citizens, who earned respect for their economic achievement and civic service, and who wanted to pass on to their children the benefits.

As the widespread "nervousness" indicated, however, many middle-aged women were not quite finding fulfillment in their status. They would not or could not identify their discontent; indeed, denial was precisely why it found mute expression in nerves, chest, or bowels. If they could not hide the truth from their bodies, neither could they hide it from their daughters. Maternal teachings to "be a lady" were hardly very convincing when uttered from a sickbed. Without realizing why, the girls ran outside to jump off roof tops or play baseball or watch their fathers at work in the law office, bank, or store.

Even if their mothers were not diseased in the role of leisure-class women—and certainly many were not—daughters often had difficulty accepting the legacy. In fact, the greater the leisure, the greater the difficulty. After enjoying the privilege of higher education, for example, a young woman easily scorned the whist parties, the afternoon chitchat, the lavish dinners, the clubwomen's "appreciation" of Shakespeare or Liszt. Jane Addams quoted "a happy busy mother" who, while her daughter was performing her daily four hours of piano practice, looked up from her knitting and declared, "If I had had your opportunities when I was young, my dear, I should have been a very happy girl." In response, the girl gazed wistfully at her mother, not daring to speak what was in her heart: "I might believe I had unusual talent if I did not know what good music was; I might enjoy half an hour's practice a day if I were busy and happy the rest of the time. You do not know what life means when all the difficulties are removed! I am simply smothered and sickened with advantages. It is like eating a sweet dessert the first thing in the morning." In this scene Addams was describing herself. She was "filled with shame," she wrote to a friend in 1886; helplessly she was sinking into a "nervous depression."[28]

Earlier in the nineteenth century a girl would have found solace through religion, subjecting herself in prayer and diary to a confession that scoured her soul. But God had ceased to reply. Although the girls earnestly imitated their parents' habit of diary writing, they could not break through to confident affirmation. "If I could fix myself with my relation to God & the universe," Addams wrote plaintively to her friend, "& so be in perfect harmony with nature & deity . . ." But she could not.

Nor could Mary Boit. "On my [fourteenth] birthday," she promised her diary, "I am going to try to turn over a new leaf & be a better girl & try to please Mamma more to conquer my hasty ungovernable temper & be better in all ways. I am sadly afraid my resolutions will go to the wind but I must try to be a better girl. I have not said any prayers for a long time as I do not think they do me any good." And no one was there to help her; on the contrary, while she was vacationing with her siblings and a governess at the beach, and her parents stayed home in Boston, Mary was alone with her unmanageably fun-loving impulses. "I know dearest mother if you were here you would tell me to tell God my troubles & he would help me but I do not feel as though I could tell him." In fact, "I do not really feel as though I loved God. I am positively ashamed to write it down, but I really do not think I do."[29]

As these troubled passages suggest, the girls often were rebelling not in gladness but in anguish, almost despite themselves. Tormented by doubt and shame, they would have welcomed a more conventional identity if only there had been one that could have satisfactorily expressed their needs. But the conventions of femininity did not fit them. And so they must suffer rebukes—from their consciences and from their elders. The "new girl" became a favorite target of vilification in the public media. Men and women, especially the latter, railed at her hedonism, her conceit, her penchant for discussing risqué topics at the dinner table, her "positively hideous" tanned face and arms, her attempt to "convince the world that she is a man in a different body."

But the vilification was not pure. Mixed in with the abuse was a significantly different tone. Some of these same critics had to admit that they also found delight in this brash daughter of the day. There was something magnetic about a creature who had abandoned the swooning and tears, the fragility, the genteel deference of a lady. Reluctantly the critics confessed "a queer feeling of comradeship." They were saying more about themselves than about the younger generation. They saw the "new girl" enacting the choices that they had been denied or that they had denied themselves. "If I had had your opportunities when I was young, my dear. . . ." It was more than a queer feeling of comradeship; it was a tacit complicity. The "new girls" were rebels-with-consent. Their mothers opposed not with wholehearted disapproval, but with anxious envy; the rebukes served to conceal their guilt about this vicarious transgression of the ladylike role that they had chosen—long ago and irrevocably—for themselves. Via their daughters they were betraying their husbands and, in both senses of the word, betraying themselves.[30]

But sometimes the route toward emancipation did not run over even these halfhearted maternal objections. Sometimes quite the contrary. Living within the loneliness of rural New England and an unhappy marriage, Mrs. Blanchard turned to her only child, Phyllis, as an ally. She taught the girl to hate men, stay unmarried, and take up a career. Meanwhile, far to the south, in a genteel Tennessee home, Lorine Pruette was listening to her mother recall the agonies of giving birth to the girl. "Before I was six," Lorine wrote many years later, "I knew that men could do something terrible to women, and I flamed with the injustice of it. I ached with the longing to make it up to my mother and I braced myself against the dining room table to tell my father that I hated him, then fled in terror before his threatened vengeance." By the time she was a teenager, she understood that the world deprived women of what they wanted, that nature singled them out for the pain of childbirth, and that God watched indifferently "because he was a man." So she worked steadfastly toward a career in psychology and away from marriage.[31]

Sometimes the maternal encouragement was not bitter, but happy. "The story of my background is the story of my mother," Crystal Eastman declared, as she described the influences that had led her to a distinguished career as a social investigator and radical feminist. When her father suffered a nervous breakdown, her mother took up teaching and then the ministry, constantly dynamic and cheerful and intelligent, constantly an inspirational model to her daughter. The story of Virginia Gildersleeve, dean of Barnard College, had the same maternal heroine: "More than any other single person she influenced my life."[32]

Analyses of rebellious women have tended to ignore the mother's part. Whether through masculine prejudice or Freudian prejudice, the tendency has been to focus on the father, because, according to the usual theoretical assumptions, deviant women were envying his role, his power, or his penis.[33] Even a lifelong feminist like Doris Stevens accepted this interpretation. Addressing a conference of the National Woman's Party in 1946, she remarked: "Feminism, after all, is nothing more than the attitude of women toward the relations between them and their menfolk." "Some women I've known," she continued, "have become feminists because their fathers were tyrannical."[34]

But this formula collides with historical fact. Although many Victorian daughters fought for equal rights in outrage against a father's tyranny or, conversely, at his neglect of the family's welfare, just as many were following the route that their fathers had already begun. Growing up "under the influence of my father's genuinely libertarian nature," Elizabeth Stuyvesant received respect and intellectual stimulation that propelled her into college, social work, the suffrage movement, and—briefly—jail for her militant suffragist tactics. Michael Higgins was more picturesquely libertarian: an ex-Catholic atheist in a small town, a supporter of Henry George's single-tax doctrine, a socialist, an advocate of woman suffrage. "Leave the world better because you, my child, have dwelt in it," he liked to tell his daughter. Margaret Higgins Sanger would remember his maxim as "something to live up to" when she endured persecution, expatriation, and prison in her fight to legalize birth control.

And then there is the case of Harriet Taylor Upton. In her mid-twenties, Upton went to a speech by Susan B. Anthony, curious to see this notorious suffragist in person. Curiosity soon turned into indignation; surely men did not deserve to be blamed for all those wrongs. Agitatedly, Upton returned home to tell her father about the meeting, only to hear him say that he supported suffrage and was president of the Ohio Suffrage Association. At least, that is how she told the story a half-century later, after her own tireless career in the suffrage movement. As with O. Henry's jack-in-the-box endings, one is tempted to disbelieve. But there can be no doubt that her father remained "my inspiration throughout my years." As a child in his arms, Upton recalls, she had "a peculiar feeling which I never quite experienced with any other person." As an adult, after her mother's death, she invited him to live with her and her husband.[35]

A simple psychological derivation of feminism, whether from mothers or fathers, does not work. The same diversity holds true for those women on the opposite side of the fence, namely, the antisuffragists. Like Upton, Alice F. MacDougall confessed that "my father was my first and perhaps my only great love"—a classic patriarch who delighted her with carriage rides and intimidated her with stern moralism. But otherwise her life and personality contrasted sharply to the Ohio suffragist's. By the time that she was writing these words about her father, MacDougall had departed from an unhappy marriage and built a lucrative restaurant business. For suffrage she had no time or tolerance. Women should prove their worth, she claimed, by ascetic, unsentimental, individualistic competition in the marketplace, and she offered her own career as a parable. MacDougall published her autobiography in the 1920s, at the same time as a contemporary, Mildred Aldrich, was completing her own melancholy "Confessions of a Breadwinner." Both women had made careers; both opposed suffrage. Aldrich's father, however, was anything but a dominant force in her life. When he built a doll house for her, she inhabited it with three dolls—a war widow and two daughters. "She had to be a widow," Aldrich explained. "I could not bother with a man in the house, as I could not make his clothes. Besides he would have complicated the family life." Shortly afterward, her father left his family and would visit only on occasional weekends, conspicuously absent from Mildred's life, earning only brief and emotionless mention as he suffered two strokes and died on page 157 of her memoirs.[36]

"What is happening to our Minnie, our Mary, our Maud?" parents were asking in the prime of the Victorian era. Emancipation was happening. It was encouraged by the social and psychological climate: the spread of leisure, the want of traditional religious authority, the preachings of suffragists and other reformers. But only some daughters of the middle class responded, while others did not, and each for reasons of upbringing and temperament so various that no neat formula can contain them all. Father and mother and daughter interacted in a complex psychic triangle that resists any single theorem. A trend was increasingly apparent, however: more and more girls were refusing to become ladies.

THIS REFUSAL BECAME STILL MORE overt and decisive when daughters went to college. The decision to depart from home signified a departure from the role that their mothers played and that they themselves were expected to emulate. In college, many girls decisively grew into "new women."

Even a high-school education in 1890 was a rarity; only 4 percent of all seventeen-year-olds received high-school diplomas, of whom three-fifths were female. College education was not merely rare but, in the case of women, almost bizarre. In 1890 approximately one of every fifty women aged eighteen to twenty-one attended college; in that year, fewer than 3,000 received degrees (as compared to 13,000 men). Growing up in Baltimore, "Minnie" Thomas had seen only one college woman before going to Cornell in 1876. She remembered visiting this Vassar graduate with fearful curiosity and being relieved to find her tall, handsome, and dressed like other women. Molly Dewson, during her childhood in Quincy, Massachusetts, had never met an alumna before attending Wellesley in 1893. No wonder that most girls who wanted to go to college faced the resistance or ridicule of parents, relatives, and friends.[37]

But go they did, and in swelling numbers. Between 1890 and 1910 female enrollment almost tripled, and in the next decade more than doubled, a rate that greatly surpassed the increase of male college students. Hundreds of thousands of girls were attending college—still a tiny minority of their sex, but a growing minority. At the turn of the century, 35 percent of all undergraduates were women. As this trend continued, its personal meaning began to change. For pioneers like Florence Kelley, going to college in 1875 was "almost a sacramental experience." For those who followed her, especially the "coeds," it was considerably more mundane.[38]*

Approximately seven out of ten college women attended coeducational institutions in the Middle and Far West. By 1900, the days were long gone when they had to endure mockery from professors in the classrooms, nasty comments from townspeople on the streets, and curt rejections by landlords. What the University of Michigan regents had once termed a "very dangerous experiment" had become a familiar feature of the academic world. Women, those frail vessels, survived the physical rigors of campus life as well as men did. And they not only demonstrated equal intellectual capacity, but often won disproportionate numbers of Phi Beta Kappa awards. They had escaped the domestic apprenticeship for becoming a lady. But emancipation did not produce feminist transformation. Even as the coeds integrated the western universities, 70 percent of them segregated themselves in teacher-training and home-economics programs. They were making a pragmatic choice, considering the limited occupational opportunities available to them after graduation. But they also were preserving a large part of their traditional role. Even if they were training to teach other women's children and to manage other women's housekeeping, they were simply putting femininity on a vocational basis. That was a notable extension, but not more. And their entry into humanities courses—so thorough an entry that male students began to shy away

*For a statistical table on women in higher education from 1890 to 1990, see Appendix B.

from these "feminine" courses—reaffirmed their traditional responsibility for "culture."[39]

The coeds met men more often outside the classroom, at dinners, fraternity parties, football games, and other social events. In this nonacademic realm they deviated further from society's expectations of young womanhood. The visiting board of the University of Wisconsin, for example, in 1904 criticized those "seasons of festivity" when the twenty-five fraternities and sororities held so many dances so often throughout the week that they generated "an undesirable dissipation for all the students." Soon even the university's President Van Hise, a strong defender of coeducation, publicly conceded that "in the coeducational institution there is a tendency for the men to fix the standards not only for themselves but for the women." More and more women, he added, were coming to college not to develop intellectual leadership, but to attract men. The appointment of a dean of women ten years earlier had not sufficed for Wisconsin any better than for Ann Arbor, Chicago, or other seats of higher learning. In the early twentieth century, a giddy wave of funmaking (and lovemaking) swept across male and coeducational campuses, and many women were riding it in very unladylike fashion. As one sorority girl allegedly said to another, "You must talk frivolously to fraternity men—or you will ruin our reputation."[40]

The situation at women's colleges was significantly different. It may not have reached the level of Kelley's "sacramental experience," but neither did it reach giggling sorority heights. Vassar women awoke each morning to the seven o'clock bell and attended compulsory chapel services. At Wellesley, where one of the most select social organizations was the Shakespeare Club, the women frolicked in biweekly theatrical productions, treeplanting ceremonies, and glee club. On May Day seniors in academic gown and mortarboard rolled hoops across the carriage road in front of College Hall. At Smith the faculty refused to let the *Weekly* staff members go downtown to solicit advertisements from Northampton businessmen; that would be improper for young women. Finally the students promised to solicit by mail.[41]

If the women's colleges would not stoop to male social standards, they were determined to meet male intellect standards. Equality was their driving purpose from the beginning. Sophia Smith spoke for her academic descendants when she bequeathed the funds for a college "with the design to furnish my sex means and facilities for education

equal to those which are afforded now in our Colleges for young men."
Consequently the students at Smith, Vassar, Elmira, and the other
women's colleges contended with a curriculum as heavy in science,
classical and modern languages, history, and philosophy as their
Amherst or Harvard brothers confronted. Deviation went, if at all, in the
direction of greater stringency. Moreover, because skeptics stubbornly
asked, "Can they stand the strain of such an education?" the women's
colleges put special emphasis on hygiene, physiology, and physical education. No "nervousness," no swoons. The graduates of this education
were, as Vassar's president said, "sane, healthy, frank and wholesome
young women, free from morbidness." More than that, however, they
were the intellectual equals of men. With a decisiveness quite different
from coeducational institutions, these colleges rejected the role assigned to the Victorian female. Or, rather, they rejected some of that
role. Their graduates would be intellectually equipped to work in the
male world as equal partners with men. Equal, but not identical. Indeed, the alumnae—as cultured and chaste as the most orthodox Victorian could ask—would be socially and morally superior to men.[42]

It was a demanding education. It was also troublesome, because it
led students to the edge of an uncertain future. "What came after college? I didn't know," recalled Hilda W. Smith, class of 1908 at Bryn
Mawr. Nor did most of her classmates. They knew what the conventional "nice girl" of the middle class was expected to do: stay at home,
help mother entertain, be an apprentice angel in her parents' house
until a man asked her to be the angel in his. But after years of Milton
and invertebrate anatomy, college women regarded the female sphere
as a vacuum. The thought of returning home suffocated Jane Addams
and thousands like her. "We turn in our sleep and groan," Ruth Benedict wrote in her journal, "because we are parasites—we women—because we produce nothing, say nothing." Boredom and parasitism were
the meaning that higher education had taught these women to read
into the destiny of a "nice girl." They needed to put their capabilities to
some public consequence.[43]

So, whether immediately or after further education, they entered
careers. If that brought them under the suspicion or ridicule aimed at
"advanced women," so be it. "Of course I came in for a good deal of
staring," Ethel Puffer Howes reported to her mother after her first graduate class in Germany, "but I am accustomed to that." When the opposition came from one's parents, it was harder to bear. "My mother wept

and my father said solemnly: 'I would rather see you dead,'" but Agnes Meyer nevertheless took a reporter's job with the *New York Morning Sun*.[44]

College had rendered these women, in the phrase of the time, "unsexed." With their intellectual pretensions and their careers, they violated the conventional female identity. They also were "unsexed" for another reason: most had no husbands. In 1915 only 39 percent of all living alumnae from eight major women's colleges and Cornell were married. The rate was higher, of course, for older alumnae; but it never exceeded 57 percent. And among the younger groups it was considerably lower. Of Vassar, Smith, and Wellesley women between twenty-six and thirty-seven years old in 1903, only about one-fourth were married. Marriage was, for graduates of women's colleges, an exception. For the mass of American women in the early twentieth century, by contrast, it was the rule. Less than one-fifth of women between the ages of twenty-five and thirty-four were single; three out of four were married, and the rest widowed or divorced.[45]

The alumnae's spinsterhood occurred partly by default, partly by design. They almost had no choice but to postpone marriage for four years; then, after graduation, they found relatively few men willing or able to match their intellectual level. They had survived to become too fit. But some were more likely than others to marry. The graduates of coeducational institutions married at a significantly higher rate than their eastern-college sisters. Much of this difference reflects the coeds' good fortune of geography. In 1900, western regions contained more men than women (the excess ranging from 2 to 10 percent), while the eastern half of the nation contained only an equal balance or, in New England and the Old South, a female excess. This geographical contrast was intensified by an urban-rural contrast: between 1890 and 1900, while the nationwide excess of males remained higher than at any time since the eve of the Civil War and actually increased in rural districts, women in the cities suddenly outnumbered the men. By an arithmetic of the sexes, then, a Radcliffe or Randolph-Macon graduate had less chance than a Stanford alumna to find a husband.[46]

After the demographic argument is said and done, however, choice also enters the equation. Many college women remained single not only by force of circumstance, but also by intention. One of the things that higher education had taught them was that they should put their intellectual abilities to work in the world. To marry meant giving up this opportunity and, instead, going home to serve a husband's needs. Marriage seemed to them a surrender rather than a triumph. As a married Wellesley alumna remarked with obvious defensiveness, ten years after graduation: "'Happy domesticity' has been my lot, a state often looked upon with scorn in our ambitious college days." Likewise, when Harriet Burton surprised her friends with the news that, at age thirty-two, she was getting married, they were less than thrilled. "How could [you] desert the ranks of Bachelor women . . . ," one wrote, "when you have sworn that no man under the sun would ever get you to pay allegiance to him."[47]*

For a man, professional ambitions did not compete with domestic ones; he could become a physician or architect or banker and also have a wife and children. For a woman, the two alternatives were mutually exclusive. The job of child rearing, even with servants to help, made any full-time career impossible or at least heroically strenuous; as for a childless marriage, that contradicted the expectations of almost all prospective husbands. Home versus career—a drastic choice, an almost inexorable choice, and one that burdened women only. A society with different values would have offered less sacrificial alternatives. Victorian America did not. A woman had to choose, and a majority of alumnae chose a career.

Approximately 25 percent of them managed nevertheless to combine marriage (and even children, in the case of Harriet Burton and others) with employment. Many others worked because no man proposed marriage; in their cases, career was effect rather than cause of spinsterhood. But most entered professional life with the expectation of giving up a conventional home. They happily refused to bury their intellectual talent beneath housework. And, according to one extensive survey, although most of them in their middle age regretted not having married, nine out of ten remained happy. Here was truly the "new woman." They dismissed the half-pitying, half-contemptuous label of "old maid." Instead, they defined themselves, proudly, as "bachelor women." Although society prevented them from enjoying men's option of home with career, they would be equal at least to unmarried men.[48]

THESE PROFESSIONALS JOINED a rapidly growing female labor force.† Between 1880 and 1900 the number of employed adult women more than

---

*For a glimpse of Harriet Burton Laidlaw's marriage, see Chapter 2.
†For a statistical table on the female labor force from 1890 to 1990, see Appendix A.

doubled; between 1900 and 1910 it increased by another 50 percent, approximately twice the male rate. In the latter year, one of every five women above the age of fifteen was at work. Unlike college graduates, however, the typical employee worked because she had to. Necessity or misfortune drove her into the labor market. One-fourth of the female jobholders in 1910 were married, working because their husbands did not earn enough to sustain the family. Most of these wives stayed at home sewing dresses, taking in laundry, rolling cigars, maintaining boarders; the rest left early each morning to tend a textile machine, to clean and cook, to sell candy or clothing, or to perform some other of the jobs endured by the lower and lower middle classes. As necessity coerced these women to work, calamity coerced another 15 percent, those who had lost their husbands through death or divorce. The remaining three-fifths of the female labor force were unmarried, mostly in their twenties or younger.

For very few of these women was employment anything like a glorious adventure. The great majority labored long, menially, and patiently in domestic service (36 percent), manufacturing (24 percent), and agriculture (15 percent). Sales work in 1910 still employed relatively few (8 percent), while the growth of business and the invention of the typewriter had just begun to make the secretary a female stereotype (clerical service involved 4 percent of working women in 1900, 8 percent in 1910, 17 percent in 1920). Most worked because they had to, not because they wanted to. The job was just that, a job—an economic expedience rather than an intrinsic satisfaction or a new self-definition. As one cap maker remarked, "Work . . . spells no gateway to freedom." The young, single wage earner might enjoy the chance to be away from home and to spend her income on new dresses, but she was awaiting a husband to rescue her from the factory, the department store, or someone else's kitchen.[49]

Employment meant emancipation only for the minority of women who rejected the leisure that the working class dreamed of. They turned away from "parasitism" toward the public world and confronted the question of how to employ their talent. Seventy-five years earlier they could have entered occupations as diverse as shopkeeping, photography, and medicine. During the nineteenth century, however, more and more of these areas became exclusively male preserves. The trend toward professionalization (requiring specialized training and licensing) combined with the Victorian cult of the lady to restrict the opportunities for "nice girls." They became casualties of economic development.

What alternatives remained for "advanced women" in the late nineteenth century? Among white-collar female occupations, the most rapidly growing were clerical and sales. But working as a secretary or a saleswoman was beneath the education and also the dignity of upper-middle-class daughters. Owning or managing a business, as so many colonial women had done, was more respectable, but—in the corporate industrial era—rather unlikely. Alice F. MacDougall's *Autobiography of a Business Woman*, a female version of Horatio Alger's pluck-and-luck tales, told an untypical story. The commercial world of 1910 employed more than 150 clerks and saleswomen for every female insurance agent, realtor, bank official, proprietor, or manager.

If not business, what then? One of ten employed women found an answer in a professional career. In 1910 there were those 9,000 whom the Census Bureau classified as "religious, charity, and welfare workers," but the Florence Kelleys and Jane Addamses had not yet made social work a genuine profession. Agnes Meyer and 4,000 others were working as journalists or editors, but they constituted a small band of interlopers in the world of cigar-smoking, profanity-uttering newspapermen. Free-lance writing was a more familiar female activity, but in 1910 a mere 2,000 women had talent or luck enough to survive by their pens.

The most prestigious professions were law, the ministry, medicine, and teaching. But the first three were closed except to an unusually bold and determined woman. In 1880 there were exactly 75 female lawyers; thirty years later, despite the proliferation of women's colleges and the fervent woman's rights movement, there were only 1,341. Meanwhile, some states were forbidding women to practice law, while dozens of the leading law schools excluded them from learning it. Clergywomen in 1900 numbered fewer than 700. Medicine proved somewhat more accessible. The dauntless Dr. Elizabeth Blackwell had opened the way for more than 2,000 of her sex as early as 1880; by 1910, when one of every twenty physicians and osteopaths was a woman, that number had increased fivefold. But it was an arduous path, discouragingly so. Nursing and midwifery, those "feminine" areas, were easier alternatives because they posed no discrimination and required little formal training. "We don't mind the nurses," explained one male medical student at the University of Pennsylvania. "They are a sort of servants, you understand." For every woman doctor in 1910, consequently, there were six trained nurses and nine untrained ones or midwives.[50]

Of all the professions presumably open to the "new woman," in the end there was only one besides nursing that was readily accessible: teaching. In 1880 almost nine out of ten professional women were teachers; in 1910, after another generation of struggle for emancipation, two out of three still chose this course. Some made of it a brilliant intellectual highway. Ethel Puffer Howes went on from Smith College and two German universities to become the second woman to receive a Harvard Ph.D. certificate; thereafter she taught philosophy and psychology at several elite colleges, published numerous books and articles (while also doing suffrage work), married, and raised two children. Lucy Salmon, chairman of the history department at Vassar, won a national reputation for her research about domestic servants. M. Carey Thomas, equipped with a doctorate *summa cum laude* from Zurich University, became president of Bryn Mawr at the age of thirty-seven.

But these intellectual stars in no way represented their fellow teachers. Of the half million women educators in 1910, only 3,000 worked in colleges and universities. The masses were those overworked, underpaid creatures known as "schoolmarms." Most were young, and, partly because so many communities would not employ married women, all but a few were single. The large majority worked in one-room schoolhouses. Their imposition of grammar, multiplication tables, and French declensions, rhythmically interspersed by the slap of a birch stick on squirming hands or bottoms, hardly seems to warrant the description of intellectual activity. More important, teaching had a professional status only by the most generous interpretation. At the turn of the century, the majority of teachers possessed no more than six or eight years of elementary education. The National Education Association was just beginning to set entrance requirements, tenure rules, and other regulations that would professionalize public-school teaching.[51]

Employment emancipated women from dependence. It also accentuated the limits of emancipation. Although the proportion of employed women expanded from one-seventh to one-fifth between 1880 and 1910, the overwhelming majority of them held jobs only as a necessary economic evil, earning less than men and often less than a decent standard of living. If they thought of equality at all, they sought it in a better job rather than a woman's rights movement. Few even joined the National Women's Trade Union League. Most hoped for the freedom to stay home and raise a family as "true" or "womanly" women.[52]

For the upper-middle-class minority of employed women, work provided emancipation from that role. But these career women purchased independence by earning lower incomes than their male counterparts and, often, by staying unmarried. Furthermore, they had left "woman's sphere" for "woman's work," because most of them inhabited sexually segregated professions. This was particularly the case in the two fields employing three-quarters of female professionals: eight out of ten schoolteachers and nine out of ten nurses were women. The force of men's discrimination, along with women's inclination to follow the course of least resistance, produced a largely segregated economic world.[53]

IF HIGHER EDUCATION AND A CAREER brought emancipation, they brought a decidedly partial version and certainly nothing like genuine equality with men. Many "advanced women" were nonetheless content, but others felt all the more keenly the continuing discriminations against their sex. What value did even the most illustrious career have, after all, for a wife in Georgia and thirteen other states where her earnings belonged to her husband? Or for a wife in Pennsylvania and other states where she could not enter a business contract without her husband's approval? But the legal inequities touched much more personal matters than income and contracts. In thirty-seven states, at the turn of the century, a married woman had no right to her children; they were her husband's property (as were her furniture, jewelry, and other possessions), and he could dispose of them as he wished, Spinsters escaped this "civil death," but spinsterhood sidestepped, rather than dissolved, the injustice. And even that did not suffice when a New York City restaurant could legally refuse to serve a woman without a male escort. Of what value was a Ph.D. to a professor if she could not use her salary (which was lower than a male professor's) to dine alone in public? All women, married and unmarried alike, said Susan B. Anthony in 1875, must acquire "equal power in the making, shaping and controlling of the circumstance of life. That equality of rights and privileges is vested in the ballot, the symbol of power in a republic. Hence, our first and most urgent demand." In subsequent years, especially after 1900, a growing number of women agreed with her. First and most urgent of all, the vote. Only with political power, it seemed, could women achieve effective equality in the world.[54]

Support for equal suffrage came slowly, exhaustingly slowly. Fifty years after the first Woman's Rights Convention (1848), women could vote in only four states—Wyoming, Utah, Idaho, and Colorado—where they were too outnumbered to make a difference. A half century of dogged campaigning—most of the lifetime of suffragists such as Elizabeth Cady Stanton—had produced defeat after defeat. Indeed, opposition hardened in the 1890s, as prestigious civic leaders formed numerous Associations Opposed to Woman Suffrage in order to mobilize "antis." Men, of course, resisted surrendering their monopoly of politics, but women too were indifferent or even hostile. "'The women don't want the vote' is the 'stunner' that we friends of the cause have to meet at every hand," one suffragist confided to another in the 1890s. In 1902 Susan B. Anthony and Ida Harper confessed, as preface to their official history of woman suffrage, that most members of their sex did not want the vote. In 1908 the president of a women's college in Minnesota warned Maud Wood Park not to hold suffrage meetings in the community because "there is a prejudice in town against the very title of Woman Suffragist." Six days earlier, in New York City, a Wall Street audience bombarded suffrage speakers with water, apple cores, and hard rolls.[55]

How do we explain this hostility? The tempting answer is privilege and paranoia—a defense of male power and a hysterical fear of change. But this quick answer does not help us understand exactly what the antis were afraid of nor, still more puzzling, why so many women opposed their own enfranchisement. If we listen to what the antis said, we can hear beneath the furious, sensationalistic, often silly rhetoric a profound fear of social disorder.

The basic issue was not that suffragists were "unsexed" women, spinsters who were trying to compensate for "their barren hearts and lives." It was not that female voters would produce "freak legislation." It was not even that women would "soil their skirts" by getting "down on the level with men in corrupt politics." At stake was the moral role of woman and, beyond that, the integrity of the family. Equal suffrage signified to the antis—female as well as male—that a woman ought to put her self-interest above duty to her family; she should vote as an individual rather than as a wife and mother. And that, they said, was a

misguided way to look at gender roles. Morally speaking, no good
woman would want to be selfish. And practically speaking, she did not
have to be selfish because her husband would vote for her interests.
According to a Brooklyn antisuffrage group in 1894, for example, "the
household, not the individual is the unit of the State, and the vast majority of women are represented by household suffrage."

To suffragists, this seemed a false and dangerous presumption.
Given the fact that most females endured inadequate education, inferior wages, unwanted pregnancies, and undue amounts of housework,
how could one presume that husbands, fathers, and brothers were voting in the interests of "their" women? But antis worried about the contrary presumption. If one gave women the ballot to defend themselves,
then one was inviting a war between the sexes that would rip the family in half. Pointing to the higher divorce rate in western states, for example, Alice J. George warned that "WOMAN SUFFRAGE IS THE LAST STRAW
IN MANY A FAMILY." And without the family, American society would
crumble.[56]

Fundamentally, then, the antis were defending the spheres assigned to each gender. Some quoted the Bible, others quoted nature
and anatomy, but all agreed that the two sexes should not have equal
suffrage because the two sexes were not equal, but different and complementary—hemispheres of a social whole. In Lyman Abbott's terse
postulate: "Because their functions are different, all talk of equality or
non-equality is but idle words, without a meaning." Like the suffragists,
the antis wanted social improvement, but they believed it would occur
through men's exerting power in the political realm and women's exerting moral influence in home, church, and benevolent club.[57]

Year after year the antis reiterated their position, tenacious and
tireless. Year after year the suffragists responded with logic, anger,
mockery, or dignified silence. In 1896, women could vote in four states;
by 1910, in five. Stanton and Anthony died in their eighties, and still
the struggle went on.

But suddenly public opinion turned around. The hundreds of campaigns for state referendum and amendments, the thousands of articles and pamphlets, the millions of speeches had finally taken effect.
The movement "is actually fashionable now," Inez Haynes Irwin rejoiced to her friend Park in 1910. Suffrage was being discussed everywhere—in newspapers, among society people, in lectures, in political
campaigns. "Altogether, dear Maud Park, the movement which when we

got into it had about as much energy as a dying kitten, is now a big, virile, threatening, wonderful thing." The public had awakened. Anna Howard Shaw, campaigning from one midwestern city to another in 1913, described "magnificent" and "splendid" audiences. "Such crowds!" she exclaimed in St. Joseph, Missouri. "I have never addressed so many people in the same length of time in my life." From upstate New York another suffrage worker reported that "these country districts are apparently just thirsty to lap up the doctrine." One poultry farmer was stamping all her eggs with the slogan "Votes for Women." By this time, 20,000 suffragists, male and female, could march down New York City avenues with only scattered jeers from the bystanders. The National American Woman Suffrage Association (NAWSA) claimed 100,000 members; in New York State alone, the Suffrage party enrolled one million workers to win its amendment. In 1910 only five states allowed women to vote; during the next seven years came a deluge of ten others, from California to New York.[58]

The public grew more receptive because the suffragists' arguments grew softer. Until the end of the nineteenth century they had demanded the vote in the name of justice. In effect, they would amend the Declaration of Independence to read: "All *persons* are created equal." Making a case for natural rights of individuals, they also were demanding power. Once armed with the vote, women would use it to outlaw other legal discriminations, open up economic opportunities, and generally have an equal voice in public policy.

This argument from principle was clear-cut, but it also was too threatening for most Victorians of either sex to accept. Toward the turn of the century, therefore, suffragists began to clothe their demands in more attractive terms: on the basis of expedience rather than justice, and in terms of women as nurturers rather than individuals. Women should be enfranchised, they said, because the female ballot would bring morality, compassion, and peace into public affairs. "To extravagance they will oppose economy," promised Ida H. Harper; "radicalism they will temper with conservatism; to physical they will add moral courage; masculine brain they will supplement with feminine heart." Natural rights became mollifying righteousness. The argument pivoted now on influence rather than power. After 1900 most suffragists no longer raised a fist against masculine oppression, offering instead a feminine hand.

It was a tactful tactic, persuasively conservative in tone, politically successful. A rapidly growing number of influential men and women publicly endorsed suffrage as a moral benefit to society; state referendums won larger and larger support from male voters; and *Good Housekeeping* demonstrated with photograph and prose that suffrage leaders had beauty, charm, and domestic interests, like the truest of true women. But the new tactic revised much more than the suffragists' vocabulary and effectiveness; it also made a drastic change in their definition of female identity. When women finally won equal suffrage, they claimed it not as equals, but as "the better half." They accomplished political innovation on old-fashioned premises.

One might almost say that they were claiming "maternal suffrage." Such was the implication in the increasingly, and soon monotonously, repeated theme that women should be allowed to carry into the masculine realm their talents for keeping an orderly household and rearing virtuous children. On the one hand, the source of a woman's problems lay beyond her own doorstep: impure food, inadequate garbage collection, venereal disease, child labor, and other problems afflicting her family must be solved by public rather than private action. On the other hand, she could not depend on men to make the solutions. "In fact, and without any accusation of men's motives," Maud Wood Park told a large New Hampshire crowd, "we can say that much of our municipal and state and national housekeeping is a good deal like the housekeeping of a bachelor who is trying to run a house without the help of a woman." This domesticity motif eventually dominated suffragist propaganda, as in the following flyer distributed in 1917:

> A FOOLISH MOTHER loves her children only in the house. A WISE MOTHER loves her children wherever they go. AN EFFICIENT MOTHER follows her children out of the house, into the street, to the school, to the movie, the factory, and stands between the child and evil influences, low standards, bad sanitation, disease, and vice. THESE CONDITIONS ARE CONTROLLED BY VOTES. HOW MUCH DO YOU LOVE YOUR CHILDREN? Answer by joining the women who LOVE CHILDREN EVERYWHERE. JOIN THE NEW YORK WOMAN SUFFRAGE PARTY.[59]

This argument of expedience, deftly invoking the feminine virtues of the disenfranchised, conquered state after state. But victory came at a price. It was not merely, as several historians have remarked, that feminists had magnified the meaning of suffrage to the point where the ballot dwarfed all their other goals. This distortion injured feminism as a political movement, producing after the Nineteenth Amendment a vacuum of complacency and then disillusionment. But the real difficulty in the suffragists' position lay deeper than political strategy; it lay in their definition of womanhood. They claimed equal suffrage because women were morally superior to men. They asked for public power because of their experience as housekeepers and mothers. These tactics successfully co-opted the arguments that traditionalists had been using to keep women in their sphere. But the co-optation also backfired upon its authors. By exploiting the Victorian premises, the suffragists never fully abandoned them. While insisting that a woman was as intelligent, civic-minded, and self-reliant as a man, they also ascribed to her certain innately distinctive traits and functions. In the end, they made her the better half, a woman on a public pedestal, and to that extent still a Victorian creature.

Suffrage was a door from the domestic sphere into the world. Higher education and careers were two other doors. All opened toward more rights for women; none, toward equality of the sexes. When women finally made their way to the ballot box, they would be carrying with them a self-definition almost as traditional as the one that matrons were taking to club meetings. The women who went to college and into professions developed a more egalitarian identity for themselves, but they typically achieved equality with men by forfeiting marriage and motherhood. Effective equalization of the genders—that is, feminism—required more than opening the doors of the female sphere. Changes would have to be made among the family inside.

2/
Women and the Home

If equal suffrage came, the home would go—such was the prophecy by Cassandras of both sexes. This dire foreboding accounts for the polemics and hyperbole of the "antis." In their view, the question of the ballot went deeper than a struggle for political power: it touched society's basic institution, the family. The more the proverbial homemaker entered the public realm by acquiring the vote, higher education, and career, the more she must neglect the home. And without her support, would not the home degenerate and, along with it, the moral order of American society?

Apocalyptic questions of this sort did not trouble feminists as they proposed solutions to sexual injustice. Yet their answers contained questions asked or unasked. In pursuit of a career, for example, must a woman give up marriage or at least children? That was the price paid by most of the "advanced" women. But was equality worth that sacrifice? Or was there some way to avoid it, perhaps by redefining marriage? In any case, what did one mean by "being equal"? If a woman tried to be "as good as a man," she was deferring to male criteria; self-assertion paradoxically became degradation of her sex. Yet what were the alternatives to the traditional "feminine" role?

These were the questions besetting middle-class women who struggled for emancipation. They added up to the problem of defining a theory and practice of equality—the problem of feminism. As feminists encountered these questions, they entered an identity crisis far more acute and demanding than any man's, because they were formulating not merely their own individual selves, but the identity of their entire sex. It was more than a search for personal redefinition; it was a redefinition of the female class.

IN THE SPRING OF 1914 the United States Congress took time away from its deliberations on Panama Canal tolls and naval appropriations to pass a joint resolution. "Whereas the service rendered the United States by the American mother is the greatest source of the country's strength and inspiration," asserted the 500 male leaders of the nation, "and Whereas we honor ourselves and the mothers of America when we do any thing to give emphasis to the home as the fountain head of the State; and Whereas the American mother is doing so much for the home, for moral uplift, and religion, hence so much for good government and humanity," the Congress declared that henceforth the second Sunday of May would be celebrated as Mother's Day. The resolution received no debate and no dissent. But such swift unanimity did not mean that the bill was some lighthearted triviality. Although only a gesture, it was a serious one made by men with heavy hearts. They wanted to commemorate motherhood and the home as much as they wanted to assert American commerce and defense. And they believed that these sanctified domestic institutions were in no less peril than national honor.[1]

On this occasion the nation's political representatives were indeed representing their constituents. In countless speeches, articles, and conferences, Americans of the early twentieth century lamented "the breakdown of family life." The evidence for calamity seemed unmistakable. In the first place, divorces were increasing in a relentless trend, from the almost inconspicuous total of 7,000 in 1860, to 56,000 at the turn of the century, to 100,000 in 1914. While the annual marriage rate stayed constant across this half century, the divorce rate per thousand marriages quadrupled. As one character remarked in a Broadway play entitled *The New York Idea* (1906): "A man can't be sure he is married until he's divorced. It's a sort of marry-go-round to be sure. Monogamy is just as extinct as kneebreeches." But few commentators could achieve even this darkly humorous view. Divorce was too serious, too ominous, because it signified the disintegration not only of a family unit, but also of a moral commitment. In an era when many people still believed that a kiss signified engagement and a marriage was forever, divorce meant far more than social disruption and personal distress; it meant vice. Even a sociologist like Edward A. Ross, urging his readers to recognize that "accelerated divorce is produced by the modern social situation rather than by moral decay," ended on the moralistic note that it was "the symptom of a great evil."[2]

Most American marriages stayed intact, but they too were demonstrating an alarming pathology—namely, a drastic decline in the birthrate. Whereas 1,000 mothers in 1800 were tending 1,300 children under the age of five, in 1900 the same number of mothers had fewer than 700 children. At a time when child-rearing experts were advising women to produce *at least* four offspring, the majority of mothers—especially younger ones—stopped with four and, typically, three children. But these general statistics disguised an even more disquieting trend within the trend: the decline in childbearing was strongest among native white families, especially those in the middle class. According to experts' studies at the turn of the century, the birthrate among immigrant women was nearly twice that of American women. More pointedly, recent graduating classes from Harvard, Yale, Wellesley, Vassar, and other private colleges were not bearing enough children to maintain the population of "superior stock" in the next generation. As scores of eugenicists, sociologists, psychologists, and journalists embellished this arithmetic of infertility, public consternation spread. The American family was in crisis. Social scientists were persuasively documenting the situation, and then, in 1903, the president of the United States himself gave a name to it. With his talent for the pungent phrase, Theodore Roosevelt announced that Americans were committing "race suicide."[3]

If people read the divorce and birth rates as evidence that the home was tending toward collapse, how did they explain the peril? At first glance, their explanations seem to lash out randomly, but then one notices that all share the same theme: one way or another, they blamed women. According to the *New York Times*, for example, nine-tenths of New York mothers had undermined their household systems by buying ready-made food at delicatessens. Others blamed the wives' decisions to take jobs outside the home. Ida Tarbell, herself a famous journalist, rebuked those of her sex who perverted their feminine qualities by doing the business of men. Professor Ward Hutchinson told the American Academy of Medicine that the employed woman "commits a biologic crime against herself and against the community. . . . Any nation that works its women is damned and belongs at heart to the Huron-Iroquois confederacy." Still others focused specifically on the suffragists, warning that these agitators were working to replace the marital bond with weekend marriages, state phalansteries for children, and even polyandry. Most commonly, critics attributed the crisis of the family directly to female higher education. The causal link seemed indisputable, given the low rates of marriage and fertility among alumnae. As the eminent psychologist G. Stanley Hall explained to the 1903 conference of the National Education Association: "The first danger to woman is over-brainwork. It affects that part of her organism which is sacred to heredity. This danger is seen in the diminishing number of marriages. The postponement of marriage is very unfortunate in its influence upon civilization." To Margaret Bisland, it was more than unfortunate; it was reminiscent of the fate of the Roman Empire. Anxiously she implored women to turn away from "over-education and abnormal public activities" to motherhood.[4]

It was, then, an eclectic analysis. Less generously described, it was haphazard and hysterical. From it the American public could understand only two things clearly: first, that crisis was stalking the family, and second, that it derived from women. Why a crisis? Why not call it an evolution in family patterns, one of many new developments brought by socioeconomic modernization? For most Victorians, this impersonal perspective was impossible. They were moralists, who understood the world in terms of "good men" and "bad men." Confronted by graft, monopolies, labor strife, and slums, they blamed city bosses, robber barons, radicals, and immigrants. But ultimately they extended blame beyond the public sphere to the private sphere, to the home, where boys were supposed to be taught to become good men, and therefore to the mothers, who were supposed to teach them. "A race is worthless and contemptible," said Theodore Roosevelt, "if its men cease to be willing and able to work hard and, at need, to fight hard, and if its women cease to breed freely." He was echoing the truisms of three Victorian generations before him.[5] Social progress began at home, the warm greenhouse lovingly tended by a woman. When the last Victorian generation, born in the 1850s and 1860s, discovered rising divorce rates and declining birthrates, it saw the ethical order being undermined. And it blamed women, at least certain women.

The "devouring *ego* in the 'new woman,'" warned Anna Rogers in the *Atlantic Monthly,* has created "the latter-day cult of individualism; the worship of the brazen calf of Self." Instead of acknowledging that "marriage is her work in the world," she has tried to enter the masculine realm with ambitions for education, careers, and other public activity. "Apparently her whole energy is to-day bent upon dethroning herself." A woman who would leave the pedestal "has the germ of divorce in her veins at the outset." Mrs. Rogers gave ferocious articulation to the thoughts that hovered in the cultural atmosphere of 1907. According to one report, "no magazine article for a long time has been so widely exploited and discussed." The "new woman" was the enemy of marriage, the home, and therefore civilization. Indeed, outside her feminine sphere, how much of a woman was she? "That is the Woman Question in a sentence," said Lyman Abbott. "Does she wish to be a woman or a modified man?"[6]

His answer was obvious. Much less obvious was how the defenders of the traditional realms would keep women where they belonged. Rhetorical questions, alarmed arithmetic of divorce and childbirth rates, angry attacks on the suffrage movement—these were only verbal devices and, what is more, defensively negative. Legal barriers to women in higher education, the professions, and other masculine arenas were also negative and increasingly ineffective. Advocates of the traditional female role in the early twentieth century had to invent a better strategy if they were to drown out the siren call of the new women.

Mother's Day! That congressional genuflection to "the greatest source of the country's strength and inspiration" symbolized one part of the conservative strategy. During the 1890s, and particularly during the next two decades, a child-care movement developed throughout the United States. In the process, motherhood became not merely a biological fact or a pious social value, but a scientific accomplishment. That additional emphasis was new, and it reflected the troubled feelings about what was happening to the family. During most of the nineteenth century, the "cult of the lady" had told women to stay home and bear children, but it had not instructed them how to do it. Nature, grandmothers, and common sense seemed sufficient guides. The only exception, significantly, occurred in the pre-Civil War era, when the first spurt of feminist agitation erupted. During those years, *Mothers' Magazine*, *Mothers' Assistant*, and *Parents' Magazine* emerged to direct women on proper techniques for rearing children. Thereafter, mothers were left alone again until the 1880s, when a new wave of interest began. Natural motherhood was no longer good enough. Journals began publication, ranging from the pedantic (such as the *Pedagogical Seminary*) to the popular (such as the *Child Study Monthly*). Newspapers and women's magazines offered regular advice columns. Countless books discussed *The Management and Training of Children* or *Hints on Child-Training*. Most fa-

mous of all was L. Emmett Holt's *The Care and Feeding of Children*, published in 1894. During the next twenty years this "Catechism for the Use
of Mothers and Children's Nurses," as Holt subtitled it, went into millions of mothers' hands and through eight editions.

Meanwhile, women were forming and joining groups with such
names as the Society for the Study of Child Nature, the Mothers Discussion Club, or the Congress of Mothers. By 1912, when almost fifty
major child-care associations and countless smaller ones existed, the
Federation for Child Study was founded to coordinate their work. Parenthood had become a national concern—a problem that required no
less deliberate reform than did forest conservation or railroad rates.
Appropriately, the federal government was taking action, convening a
White House conference on child welfare in 1909, forming the Children's Bureau in 1912, and then, in 1914—the year of the first Mother's
Day—publishing *Infant Care*. That child-rearing manual quickly became
the best-selling federal publication.[7]

This sudden surge of interest in child care, amounting to a verita-
ble social movement, gave the role of mother a new importance. The
raising of children was no longer simply a duty or a joy, but a "scientific" vocation that required intelligence and training. It was "mothercraft." The nursery became comparable to the factory or law office. In all
likelihood, the redefinition did little to change the actual practices of
middle-class mothers; after all, people read and accept what they already believe, whether the topic be as remote as foreign policy or as intimate as raising children. Most mothers probably continued to treat
their children as they always had, although perhaps with more attention to diet and hygiene. And those wealthy enough to hire servants
continued to delegate much of the child care to these understudies.
(The well-educated wife of a Boston doctor, diligently keeping a daily
journal of child care, found it "annoying" that her one-year-old son
would cry for his mother to take him from Sadie's arms.)[8]

Nevertheless, the professionalization of motherhood had some intangible effects. Even as it exalted mother, it tended to make her anxious. When mothering was made deliberate and complex, a woman no
longer could rely on her "instinct" or on memories of what her own
mother had done. When little Priscilla was screaming in the middle of
the night, should one feed her, cuddle her, spank her, or let her scream?
It was important to make the right choice; after all, experts emphasized
the formative importance of a child's early experience. But what was

the right choice? Before 1910, experts urged mothers to serve as a moral and loving model; thereafter they urged discipline, sternness, even ridicule if necessary. A conscientious mother became confused and anxious. And if her children in later life were unruly or unhealthy or unhappy, she suffered guilt for having failed to perform "mothercraft" well enough. Caught in this dilemma, mothers perpetuated it by writing to advice givers like "Ruth Ashmore" of *Ladies' Home Journal* (at the rate of 10,000 letters per year).[9]

Thus the angel in the house was being professionalized. In retaliation against the "new woman," the gauzy Victorian model was refashioned along the more modern lines of science and expertise. Women could feel, however anxiously, a part of the nation's progress toward efficient productivity. And not only as mothers. Housework, too, was translated into professional terms. "There is no more drudgery in the work of the housewife," Lyman Abbott reminded his readers, "than there is in the work of the lawyer or the editor or the physician or the politician or any other profession which women are these days being urged to enter."[10]

This new approach to housework had begun tenuously, during the last quarter of the nineteenth century, with the establishment of cooking schools in a few large cities, with the recipes and marketing columns in women's magazines, and the home economics courses in some midwestern universities. Toward the turn of the century, prodded from one side by the decline of servants and from another side by the restlessness of housewives, these efforts coalesced into an evangelical movement. "Home economics" was the name, or, more often, "domestic science." Women's groups created courses and even entire schools to teach nutrition, cooking, efficient use of household appliances, budget making, and marketing. New journals like *Domestic Science Monthly* began publication. By 1917, one-fifth of public schools offered home economics courses, while 200 colleges and universities instructed 18,000 students in this new discipline. By then, the American Home Economics Association had been founded as a national agency to coordinate these proliferating activities. Finally, the U.S. Congress sanctioned the new doctrine by defining "homemaking" as a basic vocation for women and, in the Smith-Hughes Act (1917), including housekeeping education in its vocational appropriations to the Office of Education.

Domestic science served the traditionalists as a convenient weapon to keep woman "in her place." Housework is a "vocation," they said, for which a wife needs as careful a technical education as a physician, as much managerial ingenuity as a factory owner, as much pedagogical skill as a college professor, and as much artistry as a museum curator. But "antis" were not the only evangelists of home economics. William Hard, the liberal muckraker, sincerely praised domestic science as a means, not to drive women back into the home, but to bring them and the home into the mainstream of modernity. Lucy Salmon, an M.A. from the University of Michigan and head of Vassar's history department, was sure that systematic, businesslike management of the home would "command the respect as well as the sentimental consideration of men," making men and women "co-workers in all efforts to secure improvement." Soon even the women's colleges, still defiantly dedicated to intellectual equality with men, were succumbing to pressure from alumnae and students demanding home economics courses.[11]

When the president of Wellesley declared, in 1910, "I hope the time may soon come when we can have a department of domestic science," the revisionist view of wife and mother had come far indeed.[12] The antisuffragists were on the eve of losing their battle to exclude women from political citizenship, and antis in the areas of higher education and employment were steadily retreating. But defenders of the traditional home had discovered, it seemed, more positive and effective avenues for salvaging at least part of the feminine sphere. The child-care movement seemed to be reassuring women that motherhood was an important and satisfying vocation. And the domestic-science movement was doing the same for housework. The "new woman" now confronted a revised lady, the professional homemaker. It was hard to say whether domestic science meant artful entrapment on a neo-Victorian pedestal or genuine emancipation from the corset of angelic ladyhood. According to their prejudices, people had different views. But one thing was unmistakable: feminists—those who sought equality beyond sexual spheres or roles—would find their task more difficult than ever. In assailing political or economic or educational disqualifications, feminists could invoke the conventional American principle of fair play. But how, especially after the "professionalization" of housewives, could they criticize that hallowed institution, the home?

IN THE SUMMER OF 1914 Frances M. Björkman was campaigning in upstate New York on behalf of the equal-suffrage referendum. While boarding with the Gavit family, she wrote home to her husband in North

Carolina: "Watching [Mrs. Gavit] and her struggles with the problems of this establishment has confirmed me in my opinion of the institution of the family. As an enslaver, it takes *all* the prizes. Mrs. Gavit thinks likewise, believe me; altho she's a very fond and devoted mother."

Such indignant outbursts occurred often among suffragists. "So you think it better to be married and have companionship?" Anna Howard Shaw wrote to a long-time friend. "Well, I believe an ideal marriage is the best for both men and women. But any other kind—Heaven deliver us! Just think of the men along your street, beginning with old Dr. Whitney, Mr. Crawford, Mr. Wilson, Mr. Green, Mr. Robinson, and others. If a human being or a god could conceive of a worse hell than being the wife of any one of them I would like to know what it could be. In my long life of opportunities for observing, I have seen only six married people whose life would not have been perdition to me." By then in her fifties and in the prime of her career as suffragist and minister, Shaw was confident that marriage could never have made her "one half so happy or helpful as I am." Indeed, every night she thanked God for saving her "from the misery of marriage."

Some feminists had had to use prayer less complacently. When twenty-year-old Carey Thomas happened to fall in love, despite the fact that she had "declared against" such a distraction from her intellectual career, she wept in despair. "It was an awful trial," she said. "You see, I never came to anything before I could not, partially at least, manage." She finally exorcised the young man from her emotions, but only after a long depression punctuated by frantic moments of kneeling by the sofa as she "prayed against it." Even the daughter of the model egalitarian marriage between Lucy Stone and Henry Blackwell recited to her cousin how she had informed a suitor that "I had never had the misfortune to meet anybody I wished to marry; & hoped devoutly that I never should."

In public and in private, "advanced" women attacked the conventional family as a kind of slavery, more subtle though no less oppressive than the bondage of blacks. Of course, the chains were not iron, but economic or psychological. And they were put on by choice rather than by birth. But they were chains nevertheless. According to feminists, the typical wife sacrificed her creative talents, her legal rights, and her personality either to the tedious rounds of child care and housework or, if she belonged to the privileged class, to the "parasitism" of idle leisure. Whether in gingham or taffeta, marriage amounted to subjection—love and honor, perhaps, but mostly her obedience and his power. A half century after the Emancipation Proclamation, said the feminists, one-half of the American people remained unemancipated. For Shaw and Thomas and others, the best solution was to avoid marriage altogether. As a twenty-nine-year-old woman wrote to the *New York Times*, why should she give up her career, her comfortable income, her autonomy in choice of food, clothes, amusements, and friends, "for a risky experiment in matrimony with a man earning probably less than half as much as I?"[13]

Easily or arduously, they renounced marriage in the name of female rights and independence. They would be women of the world, not angels of the home. At first glance, this brave choice seems also a cold one; love and domestic comfort were sacrificed to self-assertion. For many feminists, it was indeed just that—a forced choice bringing as much private loneliness as public achievement. Others, however, did not give up domestic and emotional life, but found it, instead, with another woman. Their sense of sorority went beyond politics, beyond ideology, to sexuality. The exact extent can never be known, but Katherine B. Davis's survey in the 1920s of 2,200 college alumnae, ranging in age from twenty-two to sixty-eight, reported that one-third of the married ones and more than one-half of the unmarried had at some time entered intense emotional relationships with other women. For one-half of each group, the relationships involved physical contact such as mutual masturbation. If one divides the respondents into age groups, the incidence of homosexuality follows a gradual but steady line upward, reaching its peak among unmarried women born in the 1890s and among married women born after 1900. More than one-third entered homosexual relationships before college, and another third during college; 80 percent continued them after graduation, in most cases with only one other woman.

Because of her sampling techniques, Davis's study is not perfectly reliable; moreover, it disagrees with Kinsey's report, twenty-five years later, that no more than 10 percent of women born before 1920 had ever engaged in physical relationships with other women. The exact truth lies buried with the dead. The more important truth, however, is that our modern emphasis on a dichotomy between homosexual and heterosexual identity—and, indeed, our emphasis on sexuality in general—can easily cause us to misunderstand what was happening. Many professional women at the turn of the century enjoyed romantic friendships with each other, involving more or less physical affection. But amid the Victorian style of gushy "lovemaking" in words as well as touch, such expressiveness was not unusual. Homosexual and heterosexual feelings moved along a continuum instead of falling into mutually exclusive categories.

"I fell in love with Mrs. P. like a schoolgirl," twenty-seven-year-old Alice Stone Blackwell told her adopted cousin, Kitty, "& felt rather ashamed of it. . . . I had supposed I was past that." During the preceding years, Alice had sent numerous letters declaring, jokingly but ardently, her hopes of "marrying" Kitty. In one of them she wistfully recalled how they shared a bed during a Martha's Vineyard holiday. And in yet another, while a student at Boston University, she told of being surprised by the night watchman as she and a friend lay on a sofa in the darkened girls' parlor, "I in Leila's arms—for she has a chronic desire to hug me, & indulges it when there is no one around to see." Other women went beyond "crushes" to lifelong romantic relationships. Jeannette Marks was a student and Mary Woolley a professor of biblical history when they met at Wellesley College in 1895. During the next fifty-two years they stayed together, first at Wellesley, then at Mount Holyoke, where Marks taught and Woolley was president. Social settlement houses, like women's colleges, were female institutions that nurtured romantic friendships. "Let's love each other through thick and thin," Jane Addams implored Ellen Gates Starr as they founded Hull House. After Starr moved away, Addams achieved with Mary Rozet Smith a new "healing domesticity" that lasted forty years, until their deaths. "There is reason in the habit of married folks keeping together," Addams remarked. In the name of everything but law, couples like these were truly married. While Anna Howard Shaw was away campaigning for suffrage, for example, she wrote almost every day to Lucy Anthony about politics, clothes, health, dreams, and gossip, always with the warmth between two intimates.[14]

One-half of Katherine Davis's homosexual respondents described their feelings as wrong or abnormal, looking back upon themselves from the 1920s, and two of three no longer continued their relationships. A good many others, however, gratefully enjoyed "healing domesticity." Although the cultural conventions offered them either subjection to a husband or a career of ascetic independence, they found a third path. According to their example, a woman did not have to be "unsexed" if she chose paid employment. Or to put it in terms of psychological identity, she did not have to think of herself always as almost a man and therefore less than a man and less than herself.

A few women in America understood the possibilities of independence. A very few chose to act on this understanding. The great majority accepted marriage not only as a conventional option, but also as a desirable one. Recognizing this fact, most feminists tried to talk within that framework. Even if Alice Stone Blackwell would herself remain "devoutly" single, for example, she made clear in the *Woman's Journal* that feminism did not mean a general "revolt against matrimony," but, rather, a revolt against the unjust conditions put upon wives. She and others urged women to regard marriage as only one portion of their lives. Just as any man expected to continue his vocation and interests after getting married, so should a wife continue hers. No woman should settle for less.

Furthermore, if she found—as so many wives of the late nineteenth century were finding—that the marriage was not making her happy, then she should have the right to obtain a divorce. "Until death do us part" was a pious mask for female enslavement. Divorce, said Susan B. Anthony in 1905, "is just as much a refuge for women married to brutal men as Canada was once a refuge from brutal masters." Feminists regarded the rising divorce rate as a sign not of social disintegration, but of progress toward a society where marriage would provide women with love, respect, and individuality. They disagreed on how easily a couple should be able to get divorced. But they were unanimous in believing that without equal access to divorce a woman must yield helplessly not only to her husband's economic dictates, but also to his sexual delinquencies.[15]

In the tarnishing golden years of Victorian patriarchy, these ideas were scandalous. To demand suffrage or employment was bad enough; but to question marriage and family was to be "unsexed." Women who expressed these attitudes suffered ridicule or worse. Even wealth gave little protection. When Mrs. William K. Vanderbilt sued for divorce on the grounds of adultery, "society [she later recalled] was by turns stunned, horrified, and then savage in its opposition and criticism." After 1910, many middle-class Americans did at last begin to give grudging tolerance. National magazines, Broadway plays, and even some ministers began to concede that divorce might form a moral way out of an unhappy marriage. To this extent the feminists had found acceptance for a part of their program. But it was a part taken out of context, and it thereby lost the meaning of the feminist whole. In granting the legitimacy of divorce, these grudging advocates intended to reaffirm the family as an institution rather than to affirm the woman as an individual. In seeking to make marriage a voluntary union of love and respect, they assumed that she found fulfillment as wife—or, rather, *happy* wife. They were refurbishing the feminine sphere. This view was remote indeed from the views of someone like Elizabeth Cady Stanton, who exhorted the Senate Committee on Woman Suffrage to think of woman first as an individual—a Robinson Crusoe with her woman Friday on some island—second as a citizen, third as "woman . . . [possessing] her rights and duties . . . [to] individual happiness and development," and finally, in "the incidental relations of life," as mother, wife, sister, or daughter.[16]

STANTON AND HER FELLOW FEMINISTS offered a fundamentally unorthodox definition of woman's role in the family. Theirs was a new consciousness. They failed to convert the senators to it, but—more important—they also failed to reach the vast majority of their own sex. Although Stanton argued that a woman was first an individual and lastly a wife and mother, most American females reversed the order. "They are more conservative even than men," conceded Susan B. Anthony and Ida Husted Harper in 1902. Ten years later the picture seemed depressingly similar. "I am surprised beyond all things to find how many men are favorable," Harriet Taylor Upton informed a friend while campaigning for suffrage in Ohio. "Now if only stupid women would get awake and yell we might make it." But feminine silence remained smothering. As a fair young belle told one NAWSA organizer in Mississippi, "You know we women do not desire to be other than we are."[17]

Shaken by despair or fury, the feminists would see their fellow women as the enemy. But when these moods passed, they steadied their analytic sights again; if women were timid or complacent or silly, deaf to the trumpet of "equal rights," they were enacting the role that patriarchal society had taught them since birth. Do not blame the women but, rather, the men who had made them what they were—victims. Methodical conditioning by state, church, and school, generation after generation, had produced this creature of curls, coyness, docility, and fear. It was an effective process, remarkably so. There were, after all, the rewards of dependency for those who submitted; and for those who dissented there were ridicule, risk, and especially the "awful doubt" as to whether they were right, whether, perhaps, women were indeed inferior. Even brash young Carey Thomas was "terror-struck [in the 1870s] lest I, and every other woman with me, were doomed to live as pathological invalids in a universe merciless to woman as a sex." Thirty years later, after a Ph.D. degree and the Bryn Mawr presidency had given her the proof of herself, she knew better: "Now we know that it is not we, but the man who believes such things about us, who is himself pathological, blinded by neurotic mists of sex."[18]

This angle of vision led many feminists to a philosophy and a program that despised men, even hated them, as oppressors of "the better half." Defiantly, they waged warfare between the sexes. Women formed a class, a disfranchised class. Women must free themselves by themselves, because the liberation was from masculine oppression. "Why don't we trust the men?" Inez Milholland asked a group of suffragists. "We have and we don't like the results. Men have let things get into the present bad condition." Mankind, wrote Margaret Sanger, confined wives within his boundaries, "like a priest who watches and wards the young ideas to keep them forever within the enclosure of the Church— some Church 'virtue'; 'marriage'—'respectability' they are all alike." Even the ostensibly radical men in the Socialist party acted like men more than radicals, often openly contemptuous of female comrades, relegating them to making cakes for fund-raising, and virtually monopolizing party offices. As one Socialist woman complained in 1900, "To those of us who have had the courage and initiative to strike out for ourselves, the path is being covered with more thorns than roses." Like a mirror to misogyny, this sort of feminism blended anger at male power with condescension for male ineptitude. When Anna Howard Shaw traveled on her numerous speaking tours, she often was outraged at men's attempts to block her efforts ("I will not be muzzled or dictated to by any man"), but also commented sarcastically on their gullibility or sheer inefficiency. Either way, these feminists could feel equal, and sometimes even superior, to their opponents.[19]

Shaw kept her anti-male hostility private. As the president of NAWSA from 1904 to 1915, directing the campaign to win men's votes for equal-suffrage amendments, she took a diplomatic stance. Patient persuasion and organizing, state by state, fueled by speeches and pamphlets and meetings and more speeches—this was her strategy as well as NAWSA's. She transmuted her interior militancy into the tempered heat of oratory.

Other feminists, however, especially those in their twenties or thirties, were impatient. In 1900 four equal-suffrage states, in 1912 only eight—how long continue the politics of persuasion, how long try to reason with male oppressors? Their smoldering indignation wanted not only fiery words, but fiery deeds as well. Overtaken by "a kind of sinister despair," Inez Haynes Irwin imagined a pact among women who would—one at a time, throughout the country, on successive days—commit suicide, leaving "explanatory rebellious screeds" beside their corpses. But the English suffragettes were offering more feasible versions of militancy. After 1904, the Woman's Social and Political Union began to throw stones, break windows, pour jam or acid into mailboxes, bomb buildings, even attack members of government with whips or bare hands, and then, in prison, go on hunger strikes and suffer the horror of forced feeding through nostrils and mouth.

Young American feminists who visited England returned home with inspiration. First they took suffrage to the streets, holding outdoor rallies and parades with a noisy theatricality that contrasted vividly with NAWSA's usual style. Then, in 1913, twenty-eight-year-old Alice Paul—with the marks of English prison imprinted on her mind and body—formed a rival national organization, initially named the Congressional Union and soon the National Woman's Party. She promised to lead a fight for a national suffrage amendment, instead of NAWSA's state-by-state strategy, and to use whatever means necessary. Immediately thousands of younger feminists like Mary Beard, Crystal Eastman, and Harriot Stanton Blatch (daughter of Elizabeth Cady Stanton) flocked into Paul's new organization. Inez Haynes Irwin now found a program less apocalyptic than a suicide pact, but—in the view of moderate suffragists, not to speak of average Americans—no less abhorrent. Parades, hunger strikes, pickets at the White House gates seemed the work of anarchists. And the effort by the Woman's Party in 1914 and 1916 to unite all women in suffrage states as a "sex bloc" against the Democratic party seemed to NAWSA a dogmatic, self-defeating strategy. To hold all Democratic candidates responsible for Wilson's anti-suffrage views, said NAWSA, would only alienate the needed voters of both parties.

But Alice Paul never hesitated, never swerved. Thinking of nothing but the objective of political equality, spending no more than thirty cents a day for food, directing her party of women with an autocratic energy that left no space for sentimentality or humor, she fought for feminism. When the campaign for a sex bloc collapsed in what even she called "ignominious defeat," the party did pause in consternation. Perhaps, she and her lieutenants brooded, "our theory of the solidarity of women in helping each other to liberty is wholly fallacious." But the doubts of a moment were quickly put aside. The male enemy remained unmistakable; equality remained unachieved; there was work to be done. "We *never* must be on the *defensive*," Ethel Adamson exhorted one of her fellow party officials, "but always aggressively *attacking*—this time those women[-]hating and women-baiting men who show such violent 'sex antagonism' toward suffragists."[20]

But the war was not simply political or economic, with victories scored in objective terms of votes or laws or jobs; ultimately it took place on the field of culture, where subjective matters like personality and social values were at issue. Here the belligerent feminists learned that they could not draw the line between the sexes so easily. Instead, they struggled with troubling ambiguity. It began when they occasionally confessed to finding men more interesting than women. As Ethel Puffer Howes wrote home in the midst of graduate study abroad, "I have been accustomed so long to know clever men, & to have their minds to keep me going that I did miss it awfully in Weimar and here [in Berlin]." Of course, a feminist could explain this masculine intellectual "superiority" as just another aspect of the discrimination suffered by the female sex; most women were as boring as the housework that patriarchy had assigned to them. Because of the "double standard of experience," Inez Haynes Irwin explained to *Harper's Bazar* readers, "the dullest man who ever lived is more interesting than the most brilliant woman. What he knows he knows. What she knows she guesses." But where did this recognition take a woman? Toward "sex discontent," in Irwin's case, toward righteous anger, but also toward "the most shameful of all my discoveries"—namely, the desire to have been born a man.

She went on to write that she was glad to be a woman because she could join in "the rebellion of a whole sex, the reorganization of an entire world!" Nevertheless, the shame still seethed beneath the triumphant exclamation, creating an undertow of confusion. If Irwin despised women and envied men, did feminism mean, to militants like her, the transformation of women into men? Did they support the Woman's Party as the weapon by which the oppressed female class would assimilate itself into the oppressor class? Equality meant identicalness, then, and the egalitarianism derived from a kind of self-hatred. But to hate oneself as a woman is not the way to produce a secure sense of identity; on the contrary, it produces that most basic form of alienation, which is self-alienation. In the effort of the anti-male militants to unite women lurked a deprecation of their sex.[21]

Feminists who rejected the notion of a war between the sexes seemed, at first glance, to have escaped the self-deprecatory implications. "We represent the solidarity of a sex," Carrie Chapman Catt proclaimed. But whereas the militants went from this premise in one direction, Catt and the majority of feminists went in quite another. "We oppose a common enemy," she said, "whose name is not man, but conservatism." As president of NAWSA after 1915, she continued Shaw's diplomacy of deed and word toward men. And when the Nineteenth Amendment was ratified, she felt confirmed in her conviction that female solidarity should not become anti-male exclusiveness. Women and men could be equal but distinctive partners. One year after the suffrage victory, in fact, she was urging the leaders of the League of Women Voters, NAWSA's successor, to "do away with sex segregation" and invite men to become members. That was the best way, she believed, for women to win the political "race of progress."[22]

But the issue of partnership went far beyond political expediency; it involved the definition of woman's social role. Charlotte Perkins Gilman, for example, wanted to make clear that "I am not primarily 'a feminist,' but a humanist." Advocates of a woman's party, she said, imagine that women constitute a class with interests drastically opposed to men's. In fact, "women are folks, just folks, like the rest of us. Their whole claim to the ballot rests on their being human creatures, not on being females." Even in this "man-made world," as she titled one of her books, it is fallacious to attribute "a wholly evil influence to men and a wholly good one to women." One should not suppose the sexes polarized into a kind of class conflict, but, rather, should support "an alliance between the women and all the best and most truly progressive element among men." Together these two forces could go beyond not only the unnatural subjection of women, but also the unnatural division of society along sex lines. Steadfastly she argued that "*women* are not undeveloped men, but the feminine half of humanity is undeveloped human."[23]

Most advocates of woman's rights in the early twentieth century shared Gilman's "humanist feminism," looking forward to a society in which gender differences would be minimized. With this ecumenical perspective, they avoided slipping into a tacit exaltation of the masculinity that was oppressing women. They defined equality in human terms, not male terms. But if they escaped one kind of ambivalence, they nevertheless leaned sometimes toward its counterpart by exaggerating the effects of female emancipation. Driven by political necessity, the tacticians of the suffrage movement resorted to promises of a "social motherhood" that seemed perilously close to duplicating the traditional image of the "true woman," except that she would vote. Even Gilman, concerned with theories rather than campaigns, occasionally colored her ideals in feminine tones. When "andocracy" was overthrown, she promised, the world would no longer be a battlefield littered by disease, crime, and wars, but a garden, a school, a church, a home. Masculine capitalism threw away food while children went hungry, but women would replace selfish and unjust competition with beneficent, creative cooperation. "They are the born teachers," she declared, "by virtue of their motherhood, as well as in the human joy of it." Feminist fervor tempted her and others to glorify woman into humanity's better half.[24]

THUS EARLY-TWENTIETH-CENTURY feminism forked, one branch emphasizing militant tactics and vehement hostility toward men, the other seeking cooperation in tactics and objectives. To the one, equality meant emulation of the male role; to the other, it meant liberalization or even transcendence of roles; and for both, their egalitarianism contained a bedeviling ambivalence.

Despite these divergences, the feminists shared an extensive common ground of doctrine. Unanimously they cried that woman was subjugated, and unanimously they believed that one means of liberation was paid employment. Theirs was a doctrine of salvation by work. The suffrage campaigners did not simply preach the doctrine, but lived it during weeks and months, even years, of exhausting activity. The organizers out in the field endured especially vivid hardship. Rushing from one meeting to the next across dozens, sometimes hundreds, of miles, delayed by punctured tires or sluggish trains, giving speeches with perhaps only a sandwich and coffee for dinner, living among strangers for weeks at a stretch, weighted by headache or fever or grippe, these women doggedly carried their crusade to the unconverted. Less vivid, but no less tiring, was the endless politicking among themselves: the national conventions, the executive sessions, the managerial details of tours or publications, and all of it demanding a patience flexed like a mental muscle against the sense of futility.

After thirty years in the movement, the fantasy of a secluded house amid flowers and birds surged through Shaw's mind with almost irresistible force. Almost. And then she felt again Susan Anthony's "dear hand on my head" and heard her "precious voice" asking her never to give up. So "I shall not," Shaw wrote to a friend, "I am sentenced for life, and I shall work out my sentence cheerfully." Not only because of Anthony's saintly inspiration, however, but also because Shaw and her fellow feminists felt a real passion for work. They might enjoy vacations, but never leisure. Without work their lives would lose meaning, because work was (in Gilman's words) the highest joy and duty, an end in itself. As Shaw remarked at a suffrage meeting in 1908, "I think God's greatest blessing to the human race was when He sent man forth into the world to earn his bread by the sweat of his face."[25]

The gospel of work sustained these women through the long struggle for equal rights. But not many others could commit themselves so easily to that life sentence. Even when the suffrage victory seemed near, in 1916, Carrie Chapman Catt complained to another NAWSA executive: "It is a far more difficult task than I would have believed to find women who are willing to give up everything for the National Board." If suffrage provided a fulfilling vocation for leaders such as Catt and Shaw, it was for most feminists—especially those who had children—only an avocational activity that competed with their domestic responsibilities.

"It is impossible for me to go to Ann Arbor tomorrow," wrote Mrs. Clara B. Arthur, president of the Michigan Equal Suffrage Association, to Maud Wood Park. "My cook has gone home for a few days, and you can imagine what that means to me." Mary Beard sent similar apologies to her colleagues in the Woman's Party. "I wish I could be down [in New York City] more," she wrote from her Connecticut summer home, "but the work I do in the winter is only possible because of my summer change. I have to catch up with the children and many other things which I wholly neglec[t] when I am in town." The letter came a year after she had resigned from the party's national executive committee, pleading family obligations. Sometimes the choice went the other way, as when Mrs. Darrow of Bismarck, North Dakota, a mother of five, gave up the chance to accompany her husband on a world tour because she preferred to direct the state suffrage campaign. But for every Mrs. Darrow there were many Mrs. Arthurs and Mrs. Beards.[26]

Here lay one of the crucial problems that feminists had to solve. "Equal rights" should mean for a wife what they meant for her husband: the joys of parenthood along with the satisfaction of nondomestic activity. But, in very practical terms, how was that possible? She could use the birth-control knowledge available (though illegal) to most middle-class Americans and bear no children. Even among the full-time leaders of the suffrage movement, three-fourths were married, and one-third were mothers. If a woman had children, however, how could she continue her public involvement? While father was in his office and mother was stuffing envelopes at NAWSA headquarters or working in her own office, who would be nursing Jonathan through his pneumonia or sewing the button on Henrietta's dress or basting the roast?[27]

For more privileged feminists, servants were an answer (at least until the maid got sick or the cook took a vacation). But cooperative husbands were much more of an answer. Even with a part-time cleaning woman, Ethel Puffer Howes survived "a perfect delirium of finishing an important article on aesthetics" only because "Ben has helped me out somewhat—cooked everything one day." James Lees Laidlaw—a banker, husband of a prominent member of the New York Suffrage Party, and himself a member of the National Men's League for Woman Suffrage—was still more helpful. "I reached home again in time to give Louise her bath & we had a loving time," James wrote to his wife, Harriet, while she was away on suffrage business. "We had supper together & some reading & had time after teeth cleaning for a talk & cuddle in my lap." Passionately, almost reverently, devoted to his wife, he practiced a true partnership of parenthood. It was not always easy. "I am lonely and rather cross," he wrote after she had been attending NAWSA's national convention for several days. But he complained in an egalitarian spirit. "Now that it is all settled why don't you come home to your loving daughter & husband or are you really having a good time? You see I am cross ('The husband of a suffragette')."

Laidlaw's wry parenthesis spoke not only for himself, but also for other men who tried to play the role of partner. To be "the husband of a suffragette" tested a man's love and patience. It was a difficult role, partly because it was so unconventional, and therefore he needed considerable reassurance to sustain him along the way. As Ethel Dreier engaged in her whirling activity at the New York City Woman's Club and in the Brooklyn suffrage crusade, therefore, she was also solicitous of her husband's feelings. "Edward dear, I was so sorry to get home tonight and find you just gone. I hope you did not feel that I was neglectful; I was at the meeting at Mr. White's house & it was difficult to get away—When you get home, wake me if I'm asleep and let me tell you how much I love you."[28] Some feminists managed to continue their responsibilities at home and also in the public world. But they had privileges given to few other American women: wealth, servants, and cooperative husbands. For the vast majority of middle-class housewives, circumstances continued to shut out a career or even strenuous volunteer work. Until feminists devised a way by which an unprivileged mother could have time for nondomestic activity, their preaching of equality would remain utopian.

Charlotte Perkins Gilman recognized this fact and, more articulately than any other American of her era, developed a program to cope with it. A *radical* program. Like the blades of sharp shears, the two premises of her theory closed upon the roots of orthodoxy and sliced through them. In the first place, she insisted, society determines the home, rather than the other way around. If there was a "crisis" in the family as an institution, then the cause lay in the external conditions, and any reforms must deal with these. To this literally "socialist" premise she added a corollary derived from Marxist socialism: the conventional home had become an outdated institution. While the American economy in the nineteenth century had developed specialized industrial production, the home continued to use primitive individualistic techniques. The captains of industry had demonstrated the efficiency of mass production based on technology and specialized labor, she said, but each housewife still cooked and cleaned and sewed in her own house with her own hands like an unskilled preindustrial craftsman. As a result, Gilman argued in book after book and article after article, the home not only condemned women to a mindless and enervating monotony, but also blocked "the blessed currents of progress that lead and lift us all." The increase of social welfare and social efficiency—that was "human duty, first, last, and always," she proclaimed. Because the home prevented the performance of this duty, it must go the way of the wool carder and the spinning wheel.

In its place she proposed a domestic factory—but of a socialist rather than capitalist sort. A group of families would live in neighboring houses or apartments containing only bedrooms, living rooms, and bathrooms. Professional cooks would work in a central kitchen and serve meals to the families, either in their private rooms or in a common dining room. Professional launderers would wash the clothes. Professional housekeepers would clean the living quarters. And professional nurses would tend the children in a common nursery. Once this specialization of domestic functions went into effect, the home would become a modern productive unit, women could at last be freed to join men in developing their human capabilities, and social progress would gain its full momentum.[29]

Gilman's program was not unprecedented. As far back as 1869, forty families in Cambridge, Massachusetts, had established a Cooperative Housekeeping Association, operating a common storeroom, bakery, laundry, and kitchen, until practical difficulties put an end to the experiment. But even if they had managed to keep the meals hot between kitchen and table, these innovators would not have made much difference. Ideas must draw their vitality from a supportive context. In the prime of Victorian America, there was no such context.

By the time that Gilman first published her ideas, in Women and Economics (1898), however, the triadic trends of urbanization and industrialization (abetted by the decline of servants) and the woman's rights movement were forming a more favorable environment. The traditional home and the traditional woman no longer were unquestionable. They were dubious enough, indeed, that conservatives resorted to "domestic science" and "mothercraft" as buttresses for these two pillars of the Victorian value system. While conservatives found a large audience after 1900, Gilman also managed to attract attention among a much smaller group as she applied the same theme of professionalization to radical purposes. Magazines ranging from the anarchist Mother Earth to Good Housekeeping outlined the virtues of communal households and cooperative nurseries. In 1915 the New York Times published a lengthy interview with Henrietta Rodman, president of the Feminist Alliance, in which she ardently sketched plans for a 400-room "feminist apartment house" modeled exactly along the lines of Gilman's vision. By that time, Gilman was being ranked beside Mary Wollstonecraft, Olive Schreiner, and John Stuart Mill as one of the leading theoreticians of the Anglo-American woman's rights movement.[30]

After all was said, however, little was done. Five or six hundred day nurseries were functioning, mostly in urban centers, mostly providing custodial care rather than education. Apartment hotels proliferated in large cities. Commercial laundries became increasingly popular. But the middle-class household remained an individualistic unit of production and consumption, enclosing a nuclear family within its walls—"this castle keep of vanishing tradition," as Gilman bitterly described it. If the tradition was vanishing, however, the traditionalists were not. People continued to believe that a man's home was his castle—and a woman's too. They could not consider it merely another institution, alongside of corporations or governments, equally subject to socioeconomic evolution; for them it was *the* institution of society, sacred, beyond redefinition. Despite Gilman and her exponents, therefore, most housewives adopted "domestic science" and "mothercraft" without revising their female role. They strove to become better housekeepers and better mothers rather than fuller individuals. Even the suffragists, demanding equal rights and opportunities, did not challenge the home itself. Arguing that a housewife's services were as valuable as her husband's income, they demanded that she be given the vote and even a salary. But most stopped there. As one suffrage leader commented to Gilman, "After all, I think you will do our cause more good than harm, because what you ask is so much worse than what we ask that they will grant our demands in order to escape yours."[31]

The resistance derived partly from the fact that the vision of domestic efficiency also carried with it a certain aridity. Who was likely to be tempted, after all, by Ada May Krecken's promise that "bye and bye, we are all going to live in something which our current hotels picture more perfectly than anything else of the present"? Even a castle keep seemed preferable to a hotel.[32]

But the resistance was more basic, involving not only the form of a household, but also the emotional relationships that would occur within it. After child care and housekeeping were subtracted, what would be left in the meaning of "family life"? A truly loving marital relationship, Gilman responded. Once they had accomplished "the cleansing of love and marriage from this base admixture of pecuniary interest and creature comfort," she prophesied rhapsodically, ". . . men and women, eternally drawn together by the deepest force in nature, will be able at last to meet on a plane of pure and perfect love." This picture of ethereal, monogamous love seems attractive or at least inoffensive. In the early twentieth century, however, it aroused perplexity, suspicion, hostility. For even if it incorporated the orthodox sentiments of what an ideal marriage should be, it placed them upon the radical premise of emotional equality between husband and wife. He and she would relate to each other as persons, without presumptions of his dominance or her deference, without the security of prescribed roles. Such indeterminacy was disquieting—to the husband because he would lose sovereignty, to the wife because she would acquire the responsibility of self-assertion.

Only to feminists like Henrietta Rodman did the prospect seem exhilarating. She speculated that a woman might support her husband economically one year and he support her the next, that a father might take the baby for afternoon strolls, that women would dress simply and discard their coquettish, kittenish tricks while men would dress beautifully. But few people shared Rodman's enthusiasm for a domestic world without binary roles and identities. Even outright socialists were uncertain. Like Gilman, they condemned the capitalist system for making women into "machines for child bearing" and imposing brutal, wasteful competition on citizens of both sexes. But most socialist writers, male as well as female, endorsed cooperative nurseries and communal housekeeping as devices for easing women's domestic duties, rather than as ways of transforming the category of "woman's work" into parents' work.[33]

The Victorian imagination, in other words, could not extend to the concept of a genuinely egalitarian family, a marriage beyond gender roles. The loss of prescribed responsibilities threatened the power and security within the orthodox balance. Understandably, Victorians could not imagine how to live apart from the roles they had grown up into.

If at all, they could imagine only what they had been taught to overcome—irresponsibility and debauchery, everything that they had been taught to control fearfully within themselves. Without roles, not equality but anarchy. If marriage entailed love freely given, it could collapse into free love. Only a few eccentrics, such as those writing in Emma Goldman's *Mother Earth*, wished to shred the marriage contract so that "the heart and the heart alone will bind and loose." The vast majority of feminists, even the most radical ones, adamantly believed in monogamy. Gilman called it "the highest form of mating." In this respect most feminists were entirely orthodox loyalists of the reigning ethical order. They might consider "trial marriage," in which a couple reevaluated their decision after a period of childlessness. But to step outside the marital framework altogether was to move into a realm that they neither desired nor comprehended.

Quite the contrary, on the question of sexual relationships the feminist spokesmen at the turn of the century sounded like the most Victorian of Victorians: chastity for both men and women before marriage, monogamy for both husband and wife thereafter. Their egalitarianism of sexuality, in other words, was new only to the extent that it insisted on applying the old code of continence equally. And behind that demand stood the upright attitudes of true ladies. "I have never read any of Havelock Ellis' books . . .," Alice Stone Blackwell informed her cousin in 1912. "I am sorry if his books are disgusting; but they deal with a disgusting subject & perhaps under the circumstances they can't help being so." The same feeling filled Inez Haynes Irwin when, in her teenage years, she came across *And Satan Laughs*. It was "a vile novel relating the life of a fallen woman," she wrote in her diary, and after twenty minutes she stopped reading, "happy to say such books never attract me long. I am disgusted soon and put them aside." These female reformers looked forward, in Gilman's words, to "clear continent life for men and women," a "world with men less obsessed by sex," and "sex-union" restricted to its normal purpose of reproduction rather than sensuality.[34]

GILMAN'S PROGRAM OF COOPERATIVE housekeeping was ahead of its time, but her views of sex and marriage suddenly proved to be lagging. During the first decade of the twentieth century a new generation of women emerged, young women who brought with them a kind of vitality that propelled the suffrage movement to victory but also sent shock waves through the ideological structure of feminism. As Jane Addams remarked in 1915, "I confess I am some times taken aback at the modern young woman; at the things she talks about and at her free and easy ways."[35] Those two rebellious female figures of the 1890s, the Gibson girl and the career woman, were fusing into a new model of dissidence. Combining the sensual expressiveness of the one and the serious ambitiousness of the other, this "modern young woman" began to articulate a post-Victorian feminism.

The generational change appeared most clearly within the suffrage movement. When twenty-nine-year-old Maud Wood Park attended her first NAWSA meeting, in 1900, in the dreary basement of a Washington,

D.C., church, she felt conspicuous and alien among the throng of middle-aged or elderly women. But the scene changed rapidly. During the next decade a surge of young college graduates joined the suffrage ranks. The established leaders, most of them old enough to remember the Civil War or even the Seneca Falls convention, greeted these newcomers with mixed emotions. Grateful at first for the fresh and zealous energy, they soon became nervous, then angry, when the zeal became militance. Octogenarian Olympia Brown, mourning "those dear old reformers of the last generation," berated the youngest suffragists as "uneducated, half-baked women." The young replied with defiance. "Many of these women are of a past generation," wrote Winnifred Harper Cooley, "and, while once radical, are now conservative." They thought of victory only in terms of the vote, she explained, but younger women in the movement "consider the vote the merest tool, a means to an end—that end being a complete social revolution."[36]

It was the difference between suffragism and feminism. But it was more. Some suffragists, after all, had goals beyond the vote itself; they too had a feminist vision of women enjoying equality elsewhere than at the ballot box. But even though they wanted women to have men's economic and intellectual opportunities, they wanted men to accept the single moral standard of women. On the question of contraception, for example, the older feminists advocated abstinence rather than birth-control devices, because they feared that the condom or diaphragm invited men to continue indulging in promiscuity, which, in turn, meant exploiting women. "Your reform is too narrow to appeal to me," Carrie Chapman Catt wrote to birth-control leader Margaret Sanger, "and too sordid." Considering that "a million years of male control over the sustenance of women has made them sex slaves," Catt said that she would not support Sanger until "the advocacy of contraceptives is combined with as strong a propaganda for continence." To feminists who came of age in the 1870s and 1880s, equal rights required a containment of sexuality by both genders.

By contrast, the younger feminists claimed the right to enjoy sexuality as fully as men. "My body wants to be the mate of yours, more & more," twenty-seven-year-old Dorothy Kirchwey told her fiancé in 1915. "I have absolutely no dread of that phase of our married life." In fact, she added, "I resent the idea that it is a thing that will be easy for you & hard for me . . . as if somehow it were a thing I had to endure. . . . I want it just as much as you do." Having proclaimed women's right to be simply the other half rather than the better half, these young feminists stepped across the borders of Victorian morality into a region where definitions were open-ended. There a woman had the choice on matters much more personal than politics or education or employment: namely, her emotional relationships with men. That signified indeed, in Inez Milholland's words, "revolution of a new and bewildering kind."[37]

After 1905 or so, more and more young middle-class women were exercising that choice. Where the older generation struggled, as Carey Thomas did, to "manage" their emotions, the younger increasingly agreed with Margaret Sanger's exultant exclamation that "I'll give myself the benefits of its emotions, its moods, its sympathies." So they petted—80 percent of those born in the 1890s, according to Kinsey's report, and 90 percent of those born in the 1900s. And some of them engaged in premarital sex—probably fewer than 10 percent at the turn of the century, but definitely more than their older sisters and less than their younger ones. They had love affairs, happy or unhappy, but in any case claiming the same right as men to have them. And because they increasingly practiced birth control, they escaped that apprehension of pregnancy that had previously shadowed the act of love. If they wanted to get married, they did not believe that marriage was "the be-all and end-all of life." Many experimented with "trial marriage." Others, particularly in bohemian circles, insisted on equal rights with their husbands, including the right to extramarital relationships. The result, according to Hutchins Hapgood's recollection, was "a more conscious companionship, greater self-knowledge, and a broader understanding of the relations between the sexes."[38]

SOON AFTER THE TWENTIETH CENTURY began, spokesmen of the younger generation were pronouncing the end of the Victorian era. "Those who are young today," Walter Lippmann wrote in 1914, "are born into a world in which the foundations of the older order survive only as habits or by default." Patriarchy, caste, the sanctity of property, the dogma of sin, obedience to authority, the whole rock of ages, he declared, have been blasted away. Now "we inherit freedom, and have to use it."[39]

For those who were young women, however, it could not be so easily said and even less easily done. They inherited a considerable emancipation from their feminist elders, but in 1914 they still had much left to win. And even when completed, their emancipation would not add up to gender equality if taken on the terms that older feminists were bequeathing. For the leaders of feminism remained, in some important ways, loyal to that "older order" which Lippmann joyfully declared obsolete. They led back to the Victorian era as much as they led forward to the modern era. They rebelled against their cultural milieu, but did not totally forsake it.

When they talked about work, for example, they endorsed the puritan ethic as staunchly as the most conservative men did; their deviance lay in the fact that they wanted paid employment for women too. When they considered the family, they wanted to liberate woman from domesticity, but few were ready to adopt Gilman's program for radically transforming the household. When they discussed sexuality, only some of the younger feminists advocated woman's equal right to pleasure. Most feminists instead preached a single standard of puritanism. They were rebels because they demanded equal rights for both sexes, but distinctly Victorian rebels.

By blending their new ideas of equality with these old cultural values, the feminists got into intellectual predicaments. As they demanded suffrage in the name of social motherhood, they reaffirmed women as the better half. As they emphasized emancipation through employment, they deferred to masculine definitions. And their sexual puritanism denied an increasingly obvious and accepted aspect of women's nature.

Feminist doctrine produced intellectual dilemmas, but, more immediately, it produced emotional ones. When women tried to bring the theory to life—tried to practice it in their daily lives—they experienced frustration, confusion, existential pain. Perhaps Margaret Anderson could flee from her parents, take a train to Chicago, rush from the station to the uppermost balcony of Orchestra Hall, hear the first notes of a Bach air and weep for joy "as one only weeps a few times in one's life," and then exuberantly enter the literary bohemian world with never a doubt, never a backward glance. But other women wept in anguish.

During the four years of her first marriage, Charlotte Perkins Gilman hovered in an emotional depression which became so severe that for six months she could do nothing but lie on a couch and cry until the tears ran into her ears. "I went to bed crying, woke in the night crying, sat on the edge of the bed in the morning and cried." She finally left her husband, launched her remarkable career, and remarried. But it was emancipation without joy. Her prodigious productivity (including twenty-five books, several hundred articles and poems, and countless lectures) slumped again and again into illness, exhaustion, melancholy. Unable to maintain her daughter, she put the child into her ex-husband's custody and for years thereafter would cry whenever she saw a mother and daughter together. Her second marriage to George Houghton Gilman, who provided constant intellectual and emotional support, eventually gave her a share of contentment.

The emotional price of feminism was high. Margaret Sanger left not only her husband and children but her country as well, taking refuge in Europe for a year as she developed the birth-control movement. Eventually she won the prominence and influence that she craved. But the death of her young daughter permanently blighted her spirit with a grief thorned by guilt for having left her family. Sanger's second marriage, to a millionaire businessman, was an arrangement of expedience rather than love. Frances Björkman, a decade after her zestful campaign for suffrage and her acid attacks on "parasite women," got divorced and became a successful businesswoman, "but I have to admit rather ruefully that I am now practically nothing else."[40]

A feminist life exacted pain and courage; it could hardly have been any other way in a culture so hostile to female independence. Joyfully or ruefully, the feminists paid the price for their rebellion. But in the process they violated some part of themselves, the intensely personal desires or needs for love. They knew that, and accepted it. "After all," Molly Dewson wrote to another aging feminist in 1939, "us old maids have been repaid in our secret hearts for what we sacrificed to some principles and standards thro' which I suppose we sublimated the sex instinct!!"[41]

But others were not so sure, and their doubts measure the limitations of feminism in the early twentieth century. The story of Ruth Benedict is telling indeed. This prestigious anthropologist, the first woman to lead an American learned profession, would seem to have vindicated the feminist doctrines. But the anguish to her secret heart was unappeased, the sacrifices unrepaid; hers was feminism by default. As a young woman, in the 1910s, Benedict had been anything but a feminist. Hearing around her the criticisms of female parasites, she replied in her journal that "a woman has one supreme power—to love." At Vassar, she and her classmates had been taught to plan a useful career in social work or a laboratory or a school. But after a year of charity-organization work and another of teaching, she had learned that "all the time we did not yet know we were women," that "the one gift in our treasure is love—love—love." At first her longing had nowhere to go except into the pages of her journal: "this loneliness, this futility, this emptiness—I dare not face them." Then Stanley entered her life, asked her to marry him one August afternoon in 1913, "and so the whole world changed." For a year there were no journal entries, only happiness, the delight, the transforming love that "gives meaning to all of life."

"What need has a happy woman to 'justify her existence'?" Benedict wrote to herself at the end of 1914. But the question turned upon itself, like a snake devouring its tail. The journal resumed. Beneath her happiness the discontent was beginning invisibly to gnaw. She had a notion of writing biographies of "restless and highly enslaved women of past generations . . . from the standpoint of the 'new woman.'" Two years later, on Christmas Eve 1916, "Stanley and I talked. We hurt each other badly." She told him that she had decided to undertake a "business in life" rather than drift into the pitiful boredom and routine of the women around her. He doubted that it would hold her any more than social work or teaching had. But she remained firm. She wanted "success—success in writing," and for that she was "willing to pay high."

A few years later there was only an unpublished essay on Mary Wollstonecraft and a revived torment of questions. "Why must we go on hurting each other so cruelly?" And on the question of feminism, an answer that led only toward vagueness: the issue, she said, was not paid labor versus parasitism, but "initiative to go after the big things of life—not freedom *from* somewhat; initiative *for* somewhat." For her those big things centered in "the emotional part of woman's life—that part which makes her a woman—must be brought up out of the dark and allowed to put forth its best." But she had no children. And it was about "children—chiefly children" that she and Stanley argued most bitterly.

Finally, in 1919, an answer began to evolve from courses that she took with Elsie Clews Parsons and Alexander Goldenweiser. She would be an anthropologist. By 1922 she had completed her Ph.D. and begun her illustrious career. Meanwhile, she and Stanley were living together only on weekends, until in 1930 they were divorced. "Down the vain ways where love has died." This was the last line to one of her poems in 1925. Even amid her busy professional activities, she continued to write poems, though fewer and fewer. And she continued her journal. In 1934, the year when *Patterns of Culture* established her as an extraordinary anthropologist, she confessed to herself that "work even when I'm satisfied with it is never the child I love. . . . It's always busy work I do with my left hand, and part of me watches grudgingly the waste of a lifetime."[42]

The contrast between the brilliance of Benedict's professional life and its shadowed interior marks the limitations of feminism in the early twentieth century. Economic independence and public achievement provided many women with neither self-fulfillment nor even satisfactory sublimation, but merely second-best surrogates for love, marriage, and children. Unlike Gilman or Irwin or Sanger, their personalities did not throb with the irresistible need to assert themselves outside the domestic sphere. Thus Mildred Aldrich looked back upon twenty-five years of journalism and saw "nothing but hard work" interrupted by two nervous breakdowns. "The paper was my child," she recalled; but it provided economic sustenance more than emotional.[43] Perhaps not even motherhood could have satisfied Benedict's restless romanticism or Aldrich's dourness. But certainly the feminist doctrine of work did not.

For women who were driven by self-assertive motivations, a career furnished much greater compensation, and, as Dewson said, it "sublimated the sex instinct." Yet compensation is still compromise, a bargain with circumstance to get some but not the whole. And sublimation appeases desire by deflecting it—fulfillment by distraction. Either way, feminism did not win equality for women. Equality without marriage or without children was not equal; men did not have to pay for their public achievement by subtracting so heavily from their private wants. But feminists did, and their ideology thereby fell short of success.

During the first two decades of the century, the gap between theory and practice was slowly closing: More women were more able to find fulfillment, as men did, in both the domestic and the public sphere—a home in the world. But, until two conditions changed, the gap would never vanish altogether, and feminists would never entirely win equal rights. First of all, men would have to be genuine partners. Tolerance or even passive respect for women's independence was not enough. On the most practical level, a mother who wanted a career needed her husband's help in child care and housekeeping. Servants would minimize this need for the few middle-class families who could afford them; and a communal restructuring of the household, along the lines Gilman

proposed, would minimize it still further. But neither solution elimi-
nated parental obligations to change diapers at midnight, play with
children on Saturdays, and perform other familial functions. And neither dealt with the situation on the psychological level, where a cooperative husband was even more necessary. As recent sociological studies have indicated, a wife needs his affirmation in order to go beyond
her conventional domestic role into the risky and demanding realm of
a career. Moreover, the happiness of a coordinate marriage is most
highly correlated with the willingness of the husband to share family
responsibilities.[44] Familial commitment requires a man to reduce his
commitment to work. He cannot return home from the office at five
o'clock and expect his wife, returning from her own office, to have
shopped for groceries and prepared the dinner; nor can he write his
memos or attend meetings until midnight while she does the laundry
and puts the children to bed.

This fact leads to the second part of the formula for ultimate feminist success. If women were to win equality, they needed to revise the
primacy of work as a cultural value—not only among men, but also
among themselves. Unless the husbands of working wives or mothers
accepted greater responsibilities for the household and children, female "emancipation" would entail a doubled burden. But the converse
was also true. Unless their careers left time for their wifely and moth-
erly feelings, women would stifle a part of their personalities. Being
equal to men would mean being less than themselves. Frances Björkman was a businesswoman and "practically nothing else"; Anna
Howard Shaw was a suffragist crusading to liberate women from domestic enslavement and dreaming of a little house and garden.

The feminists' gospel of work was a necessary phase in the struggle
for equality of the sexes, but only a preliminary one. They sought,
above all, to expand the meaning of women's lives to include the public achievements through which men defined their worth. In so doing,
however, they failed to recognize that thoroughgoing equality entailed
changes not only in the female role. It entailed revision of the traditional home into a coordinate or perhaps communal arrangement,
which in turn would demand of men that they place more importance
on being husbands and fathers. The "new woman" needed a "new man."
Before female emancipation became female equality, male identity
must also change.

3/
Men and Manliness

The "woman question" was, in fact, also a question about men. For one thing, in a wholly female world there would have been nothing to ask—any more than in a wholly black world would there have been a Negro question. The pedestal had, after all, been built by male hands. To be a "womanly woman" was to play a role before a male audience.

Sexual interdependence also operated in a second way. The men were more than carpenters of the pedestal and then audience to its occupants. They played their own roles in the drama of the sexes—as sons, husbands, fathers, or simply men. No one was off stage. Any revisions of the female part, in response to the "woman question," would inevitably also change the male counterpart.

This interrelationship is obvious in the matter of suffrage. Not only did women depend upon male consent in order to obtain the franchise, but also the doubling of the voter population would supposedly unsettle the political order of things. In a similar though less direct way, the expanding education and employment of women seemed likely to transform the male monopoly of the public world.

But feminism aroused such furious debate less because of what men thought about women than because of what men were thinking about themselves. They dreaded a change in gender roles because at the turn of the century they were finding it acutely difficult to "be a man." The concept of manliness was suffering strain in all its dimensions—in work and success, in familial patriarchy, and in the area that Victorian Americans did not often discuss aloud, sexuality. Masculine identity was uncertain. Therefore, many men—and women too—felt threatened, rather than benefited, by proposed reforms. Feminism seemed the omen of "feminization" in proportion to people's anxiety about the meaning of manliness.

"BE A MAN—THAT IS the first and last rule of the greatest success in life."
Albert J. Beveridge's resounding imperative to youthful readers of the
Saturday Evening Post in 1905 echoed countless American parents addressing their sons. And few had any doubts about the definition of
manhood. Ideally, a man was self-reliant, strong, resolute, courageous,
honest—traits that people summed up simply as *character*. At home he
governed absolutely but justly, chivalrous toward his wife and firm toward his children, defending them against all adversity. He provided a
benevolent patriarchy. Outside the home, he worked to earn the income that would feed, clothe, and shelter his family in happy comfort.
As breadwinner he must struggle against his fellow men and natural
forces, but with enough determination he would succeed.[1] This is the
Victorian man who gazes down upon us from the museum walls or the
mantel—his mustache curling above a resolute mouth, a robust body
within his dark three-piece suit. He seems as solid and confident as the
mahogany chair upon which he sits.

But one must look into his eyes. Behind their sternness lies the
further meaning of "character." For a man achieved manliness only by
earnest, often desperate suppression of instincts. If he acted as chivalrous husband and beneficent father, he did so only by taming his aggressive urges. Throughout boyhood he had been taught to become
the master of himself. Thus a student promised his parents, "When I
get home I will be less selfish & quick-tempered." Without restraint, his
strength and worldly ambition could cause him to injure his family by
brutality or neglect. Without control, his sexual appetites would make
a beast of him, abusing the delicate spirit and body of a woman while
also abusing his own. Marriage and the family provided an institution
for civilizing his animal nature. In particular, the wife—the "better
half"—served as the agent of moderation, morality, and "culture." With
her help a man would master the destructive urges inside him.

Yet control must not go too far, must not tame his manhood away.
Indeed, nineteenth-century men commonly believed that they would
injure their health unless they satisfied, at least partly, their sexual
drive. Likewise, a true man did not succumb to grief or fear; such soft
emotions, a medical student explained, were "a proof of weakness of
spirit." It was a matter of finding a happy medium—and if it was happy,
it was certainly not easy. "I am assuming," wrote Beveridge, "that you
are man enough to be a man—not a mere machine of selfishness on
the one hand, or an anemic imitation of masculinity on the other

hand." As a man, then, one must be neither too strong nor too weak, steering carefully between these polar temptations, defending against the pull of one's natural urges.[2]

In the public world he fought a similar interior contest. To win the family bread and social respect, he must compete without unleashing his violent impulses, must depend upon himself without losing decent consideration for others, must achieve without subordinating spiritual values to materialism. In this realm, too, a man sought victory as much over the elements within himself as over the elements outside. He needed strength of character rather than sheer muscle and energy.

Such was, in general outlines, the middle-class model of manliness at the turn of the century. It asked much of men, though not necessarily more than they could give. And no doubt millions of Americans performed the role well. But not enough of them and not well enough to silence a growing clamor of criticism from women and from men themselves. Benevolent patriarchy at home imposed upon many wives a despotism by harshness or neglect or both. Heroic and honorable achievement outside the home, meanwhile, seemed to many men an increasingly elusive goal. Feminist agitation coincided with male doubts about the traditional manliness ideal, thereby creating not only a battle of the sexes, but also a psychic civil war among men.

ON THE EVE OF THE NEW CENTURY, Theodore Roosevelt reminded the members of a Chicago men's club what their proper role should be: "I wish to preach, not the doctrine of ignoble ease, but the doctrine of the strenuous life, the life of toil and effort, of labor and strife; to preach that highest form of success which comes, not to the man who desires mere easy peace, but to the man who does not shrink from danger, from hardship, or from bitter toil, and who out of these wins the splendid ultimate triumph."[3]

This was familiar rhetoric. Americans throughout the nineteenth century had talked about the strenuous life, although in different eras they had located it in differing environments. The frontier context had given way, during the Civil War, to the battlefield, which in turn had been succeeded by the athletic field, the arena of civic corruption, and again the wild-west frontier. By 1899, Roosevelt had in mind the jungles of Cuba and the Philippines, where Americans would prove their nation's manliness. Although his militarism probably exceeded that of most of his fellow men at the time, his general emphasis corresponded to theirs. Judging from biographies in popular magazines of the 1890s, a cult of Napoleon had seized the middle-class imagination. The conquering emperor recurred constantly as a model for individualistic success. And in physique the magazine heroes tended toward the super-Napoleonic. Articles described their subjects, typically, as "in every way a large man—large in build, in mind, in culture. He is nearly six feet high, and with a kind of stately bulk which turns the scales at something like 250 pounds," a man with "steel blue eyes," "jaws wired with steel," "shoulders of a Hercules," "tremendous even gigantic physical endurance."[4]

If the 1890s magazine hero was essentially Napoleonic, however, he was neither soldier nor statesman, but businessman. More of the living subjects in biographical articles came from the ranks of business than from any other occupation. In "the day of the financier," as the editor of *Munsey's* termed it, public reverence no longer belonged to the orator, jurist, poet, or sculptor, but to J. P. Morgan and the other men of Wall Street. The *Century Magazine* vividly condensed the whole matter of modern manliness when it explained that businessmen are "the men who fight the battles of life where they must now be fought, in the markets of the world, not in the fields or forests, and among whom real progress can be made only by manly and moral qualities." The article concluded: "He who lives a modern business life with unblemished honor throughout, has had quite as much of the reality of the struggle, if less of the romance, as had the soldier in earlier days."[5] Such was the definition of a strenuous life, a few months after Roosevelt stormed San Juan Hill. He expressed the men's desire for virile self-assertion, but apparently they preferred to find it in the economic rather than the military battlefield.

Yet the business world of the early twentieth century was to present frustration, tragic frustration. For as men looked to Carnegie or Morgan or Hill for incentive up the strenuous path toward manly success, more and more of them found that the economic heights were already occupied, that the approach routes were barricaded by monopolies, that detours led only into bureaucratic swamps. Individual opportunity for the man on the make seemed to be a myth—not simply a belief charged with social meaning, but a falsehood. The speaker at the University of Chicago convocation in 1907 could not offer the hearty advice that usually spilled over students' heads. Rather, he told them about "the crushing out of opportunities for young men through the growth of capitalistic combinations." A man, he admitted, must feel "considerable anxiety by reason of the disappearance of traditional landmarks." As such charges multiplied, business leaders vehemently issued denials. Opportunity was as great as ever, they said, for a qualified, ambitious youth; unfortunately, too many young men were lazy and incompetent. But the more that these spokesmen issued angry rebuttals, the more they confirmed that people were doubting the reality of economic opportunity. "Splendid ultimate triumph," to use Roosevelt's words, seemed increasingly unlikely.[6]

The implications for the traditional meaning of manliness went beyond simply the wane of opportunity. After all, even in the heyday of the Horatio Alger mythology, few Americans really expected to become millionaires. They believed in upward mobility of a more modest sort; and judging from the rise in real wages during the later nineteenth century, the average family did improve its lot. If that was the case, why such consternation about dwindling opportunity? Because people were considering not simply the amount of income, but also the ways in which they earned that income. The masculine dilemma also derived from the changing definition of work.

Until the late nineteenth century, a middle-class man had little difficulty doing "honest" and "manly" work. In the field, in the blacksmith shop or locomotive cab, in the law office, in the hardware store, he could achieve literally with his own two hands or with his own mental effort. But by 1900 the middle-class economy was becoming corporatized and bureaucratized.* The future lay not in fields and shops, but inside the walls of enormous corporations. And what could a man measure as his own achievement out of the million-dollar annual operations of U.S. Steel or Montgomery Ward? As a corporate employee, even at a lower executive level, he lost touch with the product of his work. He put his hands only on the typewriter, the account books, the documents—on the process that created, somewhere else, a corporate product. Moreover, the operations of a large firm aspired toward effi-

---

*The "new middle class" (salaried and unpropertied workers) grew eightfold from 1870 to 1910, or from 33 to 66% of the entire middle class; of the total male labor force in 1910, 20% was white collar: U.S. Bureau of the Census, *Historical Statistics of the United States: Colonial Times to 1957* (Washington, D.C., 1960), p. 74; Richard Hofstadter, *The Age of Reform: From Bryan to F.D.R.* (New York, Vintage ed., 1960), pp. 217–18.

ciency and specialization, in deference to "economy of scale." By contrast, Rooseveltian strenuousness and danger seemed pathetically incongruous.[7]

Given this increasing impersonality and efficiency, a middle-class man found it harder to acquire the psychological satisfaction he needed in defining himself as a breadwinner. And for all men, work was vitally important; for some, it was all-important. Russell Sage declared in 1903: "Work has been the chief, and, you might say, the only source of pleasure in my life." Without it a man was emasculated, bereft of identity. "Work, work whether you want to or not," the novelist David Graham Phillips decreed. He himself wrote standing up for uninterrupted periods of eight to ten hours. "It is better to wear out than to rust out," advised Joseph Henry Dubbs.

But the problem was not whether men *wanted* to work. It was whether they could find the meanings they were seeking—whether, one might say, the work wanted them. An extraordinary number of middle-class men, after all, neither wore out nor rusted out but broke down. Under the forced pace and sedentary activity of white-collar occupations, they succumbed to listlessness, insomnia, inexplicable paralysis of the right hand, or some other psychosomatic symptom. William James, Woodrow Wilson, and Frederick W. Taylor (ironically, the father of time-motion techniques to speed up production) are a few famous examples among innumerable lesser-known men who, like women, suffered from "nervousness." However hard their wills pushed, their bodies pulled harder, staging a passive rebellion against the demands of their gender role. In order to become a breadwinner again, they first had to go to bed (like a woman) or hike through the countryside (like a boy)—that is, take a vacation from manliness. When they returned to health and work, however, they renewed their dilemma. For they continued to understand work in traditional manly terms although these terms no longer fit reality.[8]

Indeed, traditional Victorian values had given way in yet another respect—not only "work," but "success" as well. Until the 1890s, almost all writers agreed that a true man measured his success by the yardstick of character. They applauded the proverbial rise from rags to riches not because Ragged Dick had gained wealth, but because he had possessed enough pluck and morality to deserve it. Roosevelt himself, like so many other self-appointed counselors to youth, made clear that success usually—but not necessarily—brought economic gain. Toward the end of the century, however, success was being equated with riches.[9] By itself this new attitude would not have posed extraordinary difficulty for the Victorian notion of manliness. Moralists were used to pitting higher impulses against lower, spiritual against carnal, good against goods. Yet the new view of success did not remain isolated. On the one hand, it joined the problem of waning opportunity, making men doubly distraught; they held jobs that gave them less fulfillment by traditional standards of character and also less by the newer standards of materialism. On the other hand, the economic definition of success produced a wave of antimaterialistic reaction that almost smashed to bits that aging, wobbly intellectual construct known as manliness.

According to the patriarchal partition of society, man governed the domestic realm jointly with woman, while he held exclusive dominion of the public realm. But power entails accountability. And at the turn of the century men were being accused of woeful misrule. The editor of *Harper's Magazine*, for example, deplored "the hideously egoistic and erroneous development of our commercial civilization . . . the brutal and entirely man-made conditions" of the world. Women also received some blame, for adding to "the tide of wild excess" by their extravagant hats and scandalous dresses and costly jewelry, by their parasitic idleness and social climbing. Ultimately, however, the blame for materialism fell upon men, because they had created the urban-industrial world and claimed credit for its achievements. As a woman wrote to the *Independent*, the American man "is losing his own soul. . . . He prostitutes his energy, vigor and courage to one sole end—materialistic success. Mammonalatry is the great American religion." Thus the basic premise of public patriarchy was called into question: not just the availability of manly work, not just the meaning of success, but men's capacity to create a worthwhile society. The critique of materialism quickly became an attack on male rulership.[10]

As the fruits of economic progress began to stink with ripeness, men faced a dilemma. How could they attack immorality without also attacking their own claim to govern? One way was self-reform, with a highly masculine emphasis; the second way was social reform, in which the gender implications became interestingly ambiguous.

When seeking virtue in the early nineteenth century, men had turned to church and God. Toward the end of the century, they looked to more secular locales, where they worked to improve body and soul together. For those who fell ill with "nervousness," there were the offices of the mind doctors, neurologists like George Beard and S. Weir Mitchell. For those who wanted to avoid falling ill, there were the gymnasiums of the Young Men's Christian Association. Muscular Christianity—that was the prescription offered by the YMCA and that was what half a million middle-class boys and men gladly took. Working out on the mats and bars or playing the newly invented game of basketball, they competed either against their own bodies or against other men, not for selfish victory, but for self-improvement. Luther H. Gulick, the man who led the YMCA to success in the 1890s, constantly declared that the purpose of all this perspiration was to develop altruism, cooperation, and self-control—spiritual ends through bodily means. Look to Jesus, Gulick advised, if you want an example of "magnificent manliness."

At the same time, men were looking outward, trying to promote virtue in the world around them. This reform impulse, which began during the 1870s, took its final form in the set of ideas known as progressivism. Industrial capitalism had gotten out of hand, the progressives said. It had spawned gigantic trusts that stifled competition and individual opportunity, while it had also bred poverty, slums, child labor, and other kinds of human misery. To remedy these evils, the progressives proposed laws and regulatory agencies that would replace individualistic materialism with social justice. Soon after the new century opened, these principles dominated the middle-class value system. By 1908 even a J. P. Morgan partner was proclaiming publicly that old-fashioned economic competition had given way to the spirit of cooperation. Classic individualism had dwindled both in economic fact and in social mythology. The favorite hero in the biographical articles of popular magazines during the years between 1904 and 1913 was no longer the businessman, but the reforming politician. Meanwhile, the path to success, as described in these articles, had also changed. A man typically still succeeded by his own effort, but instead of embodying Napoleonic values, he won the trust of other people and worked for social reform. He was a democratic, social individualist.[11]

Given these new attitudes, what happened to the old image of manliness? "As a matter of fact," the editor Edward Bok wrote in 1915, "the standing of a man in the world of men has entirely changed within the last few years, until today he is beginning to be judged not alone for the applications of his capacities to the making of money, but in proportion as he applies those abilities to the betterment of his fellow men."[12] The unchecked lust of robber barons had impaired the Victorian definition of public manhood. If the patriarchs were going to rescue their ideals of personal character and social order, they would have to turn in the direction pointed out by Hull House ladies. An irony had emerged. While decrying women who would become "masculinized" by entering the realm outside the kitchen and parlor, men were plagiarizing the women's social values. In so doing, they acknowledged both a modified definition of their own role and a larger female sphere; the public realm belonged, more than before, to both sexes. The "new woman" was called in to redress the imbalance of the old masculine world. In short, circumstances coerced the patriarchs toward progressivism. By 1912 even that preacher of the strenuous life, that advocate of womanhood as motherhood, that "Bull Moose" Theodore Roosevelt was deferring to Jane Addams's demands for a variety of feminist planks in his Progressive party platform.

But the strategy of gender accommodation contained perilous ambiguity. In reforming the excesses of capitalism, how much of "manliness" had survived? Classic individualism had given way to regulation and cooperation; the laissez-faire society had been replaced by growing numbers of government experts and agencies; yeoman farmers and entrepreneurs had yielded to bureaucratic, corporate industrialism. In such a world, what did it mean to "be a man"? A roughrider galloping down cement sidewalks? A strenuous life within the rules of the Interstate Commerce Commission? Significantly, the heroes of popular-magazine biographies after 1913 no longer were Napoleonic individualists or even social-justice individualists, but organization men in managerial occupations.[13]

Regulation, cooperation, and progressivism all saved "character" at the expense of "the strenuous life." Their accommodation to social realities threatened to produce not only a compromise with women but also a compromise of their gender identity. How was a man to be manly in the twentieth-century world?

AGAINST THIS BACKGROUND OF MANLINESS in crisis, we can understand what otherwise might seem a perplexing phenomenon: namely, the surge of anxiety about homosexuality. Until the last third of the century, many Victorian men enjoyed friendships that were intimate to an extent that we would find astonishing. Daniel Webster and James Bingham, for example, met at Dartmouth in 1800 and formed an attachment that continued into law school, careers, and their respective marriages. They greeted each other as "Lovely Boy" or "Dearly Beloved" in their early letters. Shortly after graduating from college, Webster lamented, "I knew not how closely our feelings were interwoven; had no idea how hard it would be to live apart." Four years later, having failed to find a wife, he proposed (only half-jokingly) moving in with Bingham. "Yes, James, I must come; we will yoke together again; your little bed is just wide enough; we will practise at the same bar, and be as friendly a pair of single fellows as ever cracked a nut."[14] In other friendships, affection became more physical. James Blake, an engineer in his twenties, told his diary about one of many evenings with Wyck Vanderhoef. "Our hearts were full of that true friendship which could not find utterance by words, we laid our heads upon each other's bosoms and wept, it may be unmanly to weep, but I care not, the spirit was touched."[15]

Today these words carry unmistakable homosexual implications, but that is our twentieth-century bias. To be sure, there were a minority of men, especially in larger cities, who preferred to have sex with other men, behavior that was deemed "unnatural" and illegal. On the other hand, many men embraced in bed without crossing that line and without shame.

Significantly, the word "homosexual" first came into use in America only during the 1880s. It was a symptom of middle-class men's increasing struggle to define what it meant to "be a man." In response to new socio-economic conditions (and also to the New Woman), men needed to draw a more definite boundary line around their gender identity. Romantic feelings between men became categorized with sexual behavior between men, and both were labeled by doctors and psychologists as signs of degeneracy. A man who felt or acted that way was an "invert," a woman in the body of a man. During the 1890s, the public began using more colorful synonyms—"sissy," "nance," "she-man," and most popular of all, "fairy."[16] Middle-class Victorians originally defined manliness in contrast to boyishness; now they were defining it in contrast to femininity. They tried to fortify their sense of self not only by building their bodies and celebrating Theodore Roosevelt. They also created a category of person—the homosexual, or fairy—to represent their fear of "the woman within."[17]

BY SUPPORTING PROGRESSIVE REFORMS, on the one hand, and stigmatizing homosexuality, on the other, middle-class men struggled to fortify what they could of traditional masculinity. Meanwhile, they had to cope with a growing crisis in men's domestic role. The patriarch was not at home—that was the most apparent failure. As a writer for Harper's Bazar complained in 1900, "The suburban husband and father is almost entirely a Sunday institution."[18] To be sure, the situation was hardly a new one. Observers since at least 1820 had remarked that men played a minor role in child-rearing because they were so rarely at home. Even if familiar, however, the default of fatherhood had grown greater in the late nineteenth century, along with the growing distance between residence and job. Industrialization was taking more and more jobs and therefore men out of their homes and into factories. The expansion of cities was extending the commuting time. And streetcars, instead of shortening that time, gave rise to suburbs that removed homes still farther away from jobs. The average work week in nonagricultural industries had declined by seven hours between 1890 and 1910, but that left approximately fifty hours—and probably more than fifty hours for white-collar workers.[19]

More important, changing attitudes toward the family made the absence of men not merely a situation, but an accusation. The minor contribution of fathers was interpreted as a masculine failure. For the home served less and less as the site of economic, educational, and religious activity; even entertainment was being diverted to movie houses, sports arenas, and the automobile. Parental love and guidance became the prime surviving functions of the modern home and acquired unprecedented intensity among middle-class values. Indeed, the term "family" was automatically restricted to adults who had children. The torrent of child-rearing manuals and child-study groups after 1900 signified the middle-class preoccupation with doing expertly, "scientifically," what previous generations had assumed to be a natural activity.[20] Meanwhile, social reformers were expanding their efforts to protect women and children from the evils of the urban-industrial order. It was, according to a fashionable slogan, "the century of the child."

Attention focused primarily on motherhood, but inescapably it implicated fathers as well. If the breadwinners were away from home most of the day, that was all the more reason for them to devote themselves to fatherhood when they returned. Many men tried, and a good many succeeded. Theodore Roosevelt romped in the barn with his children, joined in pillow fights, and played hide-and-seek. He did not let even the duties of the presidency distract him from the fun of parenthood.

Once he delayed a state dinner by pretending to be a bear in a rollick-ing game that forced him to change his shirt before going to the table. Edward Everett Hale warmly described his son Arthur as "the one of all my boys (save Rob)—whom I understand most thoroughly and who un-derstands me most thoroughly—and we have beautiful times together." After visiting with her fellow suffragist Abby Scott Baker, Ethel Adam-son admired Mr. Baker's concern for his son, Henry. "It was too sweet for anything to see his solicitude to know if [Henry] had his coat or if he wanted any money etc. . . . . I have great respect," Mrs. Adamson added, "for any woman who makes a really good father of any mere man."[21]

Many Victorian patriarchs may have tried to be "good" fathers, but many failed to be good enough. Bruce Catton recalled his father as "a warm-hearted man, but somehow . . . out of my reach," and this was the way most early-twentieth-century sons remembered their fathers. Con-sidering the odds, how could it have been otherwise? A man's work pulled him "out of reach" six days a week, and the manly code kept him at emotional arm's length when he came home. Whereas a mother was encouraged to enter the intimate give-and-take of emotions, a father was also expected to provide discipline, advice, and money—love at a slight remove. Even though middle-class men were becoming *more* in-volved and affectionate with their children, observers were not satis-fied. Men lived for business and money-making, they complained, and gave their families only the leftover time and emotion.[22]

The indictment also went further. The patriarch's delinquency was not only that he gave too much attention to his work and too little to his home, but also that all too often he did neither. All too often, crit-ics said, he went to the corner saloon or the downtown brothel. And when at last he did come home, he staggered with drunken gait and empty pockets, venting his guilt with a flurry of profanity or fists upon his weeping wife—or, worse, infecting her with the venereal disease that he had acquired at the whorehouse.

How common was this sordid story? According to the scanty and unreliable evidence, there was a considerable business in liquor and sex, particularly in big cities. Probably one of every fifty men was an al-coholic, while more than 10 percent of Americans were infected with venereal disease. Only a male minority, then, were drunkards or adul-terers. But even if the majority of American men were decent husbands and fathers, there were enough others that tens of thousands of des-perate wives went to court pleading for divorce. Among the kinds of woes they told, liquor and sexual abuse ranked higher than any except nonsupport and desertion. Other women—and men—chose a more basic challenge to the antisocial behavior of men: not individual divorce suits, but large-scale social reform. The "purity movement" was under way.[23]

DURING THE DECADES SURROUNDING the Civil War, women had launched the movement in a kind of dress rehearsal. They did so through the domestic novel, an enormously popular mode of fiction written by female authors for a predominately female public. Hundreds of thousands of middle-class women turned eagerly, gratefully, perhaps somewhat furtively to the latest book by Susan Warner, Mrs. E.D.E.N. Southworth, Augusta Evans, and a dozen other forgotten names. All these novels articulated the same basic message, which was that each woman can make herself and the world better. The typical heroine was a young woman driven by some misfortune to go out and earn money. In the end she triumphantly returned to home and marriage, but not exactly the same home and marriage she had left. By her influence her family relationships have been reformed from mercenary and exploitative ones into affectionate and supportive ones. Meanwhile, the male figures in those stories either shrank into pathetic ineptitude or, more often, exposed themselves as insensitive, arrogant, lustful, and violent. Even when the novelists excused these masculine vices, they also arranged for the men to suffer and submit. Thus the domestic bestsellers served as handbooks of female indignation, promoting in their saccharine and oblique fashion the idea of woman's rights within her sphere.[24]

But fiction is, after all, fictional. Even after a hundred novels were read by a hundred thousand women, the power structure inside the American home went on essentially unchanged. Susan Warner was no Harriet Beecher Stowe inciting a sexual civil war. To correct masculine vices, a more direct approach was necessary. And in the last third of the nineteenth century middle-class women (along with many male allies) provided that approach with the so-called "purity movement." The term suggests more cohesion than actually existed. Even after the formation of the American Purity Alliance, in 1895, the advocates of social purity operated through numerous essentially uncoordinated organizations in pursuit of diversified reforms. Specifically, they sought to regulate or abolish prostitution (which they called the "social evil"), eradicate venereal disease, promote sex education, regulate or forbid liquor, and censor publications.[25]

If "social purity" did not develop into a consolidated movement, it certainly expressed a consolidated state of mind. The outstanding example was the temperance crusade, in which the male Anti-Saloon League and the Women's Christian Temperance Union (WCTU) mobilized their middle-class forces against the lower-class men of the urban slums. In millions of books, pamphlets, speeches, and posters, the drys blamed alcohol for almost every human disease, for crime, for poverty, and for a myriad of other social ills. They lavished particularly dramatic emotion upon the wives left penniless by drunken husbands and the children born feeble-minded because of the drunken fathers' genetic taint. "The homes of America," proclaimed one WCTU resolution, ". . . have no enemy so relentless as the American saloon." (Indeed, the WCTU in the 1880s wanted the Prohibition party to be entitled the Prohibition Home Protection party.) It was lurid, uncompromising, largely unempirical propaganda—but it also was effective. At the end of the nineteenth century the drys had won prohibition laws in only five states; by 1913 more than half of the nation's counties and seven states were saloonless.[26]

The trend was not wholly of female doing. At a time when women had the vote in just a few states, they necessarily depended on male voters to put the dry laws on the books. Nevertheless, the temperance crusade contributed heavily to the pressure that men felt as they tried to "be a man." Whether the dry spokesmen were male or female, their object of attack was always a man.

> Women and Children First, 'tis the law of the sea,
> But why not make it the rule wherever a man may be?
> Let it become the law where roisterers quench their thirst,
> Emblazon it over the bar—"Women and Children First."[27]

This bit of Anti-Saloon League poetry identifies its villain not by class or religion or ethnic origin, but by sex. Inescapably, the battle against liquor seemed a battle against men—especially when a Carry Nation or a Frances Willard led the charge.

The temperance movement affected gender roles more tangibly through its influence upon women. By working in WCTU chapters, hundreds of thousands of women found, as one southern lady said, "the golden key that unlocked the prison door of pent-up possibilities." They found a mission beyond the home, according to another woman, becoming "in the hands of God a mighty agency for good."[28] But many men wondered, good for whom? Certainly not for those who enjoyed the fraternity of the saloons, the "poor man's club." On an average day in Chicago, Boston, and other big cities, half the population visited a saloon in search of conversation, a card game, an hour of newspaper-reading, or perhaps a song with friends, and of course a drink or two.[29] To middle-class men, the temperance crusade posed a different kind of threat. The liquor issue not only brought women out of the home, but also led many of them into the suffrage crusade, thereby endangering the masculine monopoly of politics. A large proportion of the early leaders of the National American Woman Suffrage Association entered civic work via the WCTU. For many years, in fact, the two movements shared personnel and profited from each other's political progress. Although after 1900 NAWSA and the WCTU went increasingly separate ways, in the public mind they remained paired. Most people believed that the women who wanted to drag men home from the saloons also wanted to enter the voting booths.[30]

But all of this furor ultimately held only superficial implications for gender identities. A man did not, after all, measure his manliness in votes or rum. The social-purity movement meant most when it reached beyond politics or thirst to the sensitive question of sexuality. For men as well as women, sexual passion was the heart of the matter. It throbbed incessantly and noisily, like a distracting savage drum, beneath the genteel discourse of middle-class Victorian Americans. When they spoke of it at all, they called it by decorous names—the social evil, the double standard, disgrace. But the vocabulary did not mute its meaning for their individual lives and for gender relations.

TO "BE A MAN" WAS AN EXQUISITELY difficult and ambiguous ideal. A nineteenth-century boy arrived at maturity through a rite of passage more prolonged and subtly tortuous than any primitive ceremony. On one side, he felt the adolescent stirrings of his body and heard that a healthy young man must "sow his wild oats." As Alice Stone Blackwell reported to her cousin in 1882, "E. O. Putnam's husband (who is a very good fellow) tells her that there is a very general belief among decent men who are not inclined particularly toward licentiousness that it is necessary for their health, & though they dont [sic] do it, they would if it were not for the fear of catching disease."[31]

On the other side, the adolescent boy heard strenuous demands for chastity. A good man, said the moralists, must resist carnal temptation. To violate sexual purity, both a woman's and his own, was sin. More than that, it was physical impairment. From intercourse could come venereal disease, and from "self-abuse" (masturbation) came consequences equally hideous. According to prestigious psychologists and physicians, masturbation could produce acne, loss of weight, scanty beard, deterioration of schoolwork, sluggishness of the heart, epilepsy, "optical cramps," and even insanity. As one expert crisply told college men, masturbation may lead "to complete loss of self-control and to mental and moral wreckage." Newspaper advertisements and traveling doctors urged boys to purchase remedies for impure thoughts before their only cure would be "use of the knife."[32]

The journey through this fierce cross fire was perilous, but most men reached manhood safely. "Thank Heaven, I am at least perfectly pure," Theodore Roosevelt exclaimed to his diary in 1878, when, at the age of twenty, he was speculating on a future wife. Two years later, by then engaged, he again "thanked Heaven" and rejoiced that he could tell his fiancée "everything I have ever done." He took pride in having fulfilled his father's advice, written shortly after he entered Harvard, to "take care of your morals first, your health next and finally your studies."[33]

During adulthood and marriage, however, the cross fire of advice continued just as fiercely. On one side, men still felt sexual drive and still heard that continence would injure their health. Women should be chaste, and, because they had mild sexual needs, they could be chaste. Male nature, however, contained too much libidinal energy to be always smothered successfully or safely. On the other side, men were told that a good man not only was chaste, but also, after getting married, should respect his wife's delicacy of body and mind by limiting intercourse to once a week. More frequent activity would be injurious "excess" not only for her, but for him as well, because of "the great drain of the nervous fluid, and the loss of semen," one drop of which equaled forty drops of blood.[34]

Purity and wild oats formed a contradictory masculine mythology. Many men were therefore confused, others chose a righteous and anxious pursuit of purity, and still others—having come to terms with their consciences—quietly practiced the double standard.[35] But no position was entirely comfortable, because no man escaped the ambivalent teachings of "manliness."

This sexual dilemma was not new. It had existed as long as America and the Christian preaching of chastity, but for two reasons it became unusually threatening in the later nineteenth century. Victorian prudery was one reason the dilemma intensified. Seventeenth-century Puritans, for example, had not been puritanical about sex. They punished adulterers and levied fines on the surprisingly large number of pregnant brides in a rather matter-of-fact manner (the flesh, both male and female, is weak), and they also endorsed sexual desire within marriage (human beings should enjoy all of God's creation, bodily and spiritual). Nineteenth-century Victorians redefined sexuality into something both more exalted and more base. They pushed it so rigorously into the realm of the private and unmentionable that they suffused it with divinity but also with shame. As a result, proper middle-class people could hardly help being confused about how to regard sexuality and, to make matters worse, could hardly avoid being ignorant about sexual facts. A few days before her wedding in 1895, twenty-four-year-old Edith Jones (later famous as novelist Edith Wharton) went to her mother to ask "what marriage was really like." With a look of icy disapproval, Lucretia replied: "I have never heard such a ridiculous question." But Edith was too fearful of her wedding night to be afraid of her mother. "Mamma—I want to know what will happen to me." After an awful silence, Lucretia finally said with some disgust: "You've seen enough pictures and statues in your life. Haven't you noticed that men are . . . made differently from women?" Edith offered a brief and bewildered "yes." "Then for heaven's sake," her mother concluded, "don't ask me any more silly questions. You can't be as stupid as you pretend." But Edith and countless other well-bred young men and women were that "stupid" because the bourgeois culture had made sure they would be.

Victorian prudery began in England as a frenzied reaction to the French Revolution of the 1790s, an attempt to preserve English social and political order by constraining the lower (and also the upper) classes within safe bounds of behavior. Evangelical religion soon added its sanction to the code of sexuality. A few decades later, this Victorian ethic crossed the Atlantic to the settled areas of the United States, where middle-class urban spokespersons acclaimed sexual propriety as the distinction between the "better" classes and those beneath them. By the mid-nineteenth century, the Victorian ethic prevailed as the social ideal (though not always the practice). Sexuality was to be disciplined not only by law, but also by shame, and then concealed beneath silence as heavy as corsets and topcoats. When men felt the temptation of lust, therefore, they could deal with and understand it only in the euphemisms of righteousness or the lurid exaggerations of pornography.[36]

But changes in the female attitudes formed even more of the reason for the growing male dilemma about sexuality. Until the late nineteenth century, men had dispensed with the sexual delinquency of their fellow males by turning the responsibility over to women, "the better half." They argued, in effect: we must rely on women, those tender angels of virtue, to cure the base appetites of men. It was largely a sly and hypocritical argument, no doubt, but it also filled the prevailing stereotypes of sex roles and to that extent was sincere. A society's myths may violate common sense or rationalize injustice, but they are not necessarily therefore deliberate, conspiratorial lies; people often accept rationalizations because they cannot understand the world without them.

One could hear all the resonances of the traditional Victorian transaction about sexuality and sex roles in the congressional debate in 1900 about Brigham Roberts. He was the newly elected congressman from Utah; he was also, by his own admission and in violation of federal law, a polygamist. During the months before Roberts arrived in Washington, women's groups organized a campaign urging the House to exclude the Mormon. They succeeded easily. "To the everlasting honor and glory of American manhood," declared an Indiana congressman, "be it said that at this time the voice of woman does not fall on deaf ears." He gladly joined the protest "on behalf of the American mother and her child, and the American father who will never consent to the enthronement and deification of human passion." Another congressman professed no fear that polygamy would spread in the nation. "Noble womanhood is too steadfastly enthroned in the affections, too securely embodied in the religious life of this country to fear any evil from that execrable system."[37]

With their lopsided vote to deny Roberts his seat, the congressmen endorsed virtue, honor, and the monogamous family. But beyond that, they reaffirmed the chivalrous belief that women formed society's bulwark against male lust. For the same reason, the male inhabitants of four western states had instituted woman suffrage before 1897, many years earlier than the rest of the nation: they wanted to encourage a civilizing feminine influence in the wild West.[38] With patriarchal conviction, Americans believed that a decent society needed women to protect it against "the enthronement and deification of human passion," by which they meant the male passions of mining-camp violence, vigilante justice, and polygamy.

By 1900, however, some women no longer accepted this deference with gratitude and without question. Susan B. Anthony, for example, issued a press statement amid the debate about Roberts. "While abhorring the principles of polygamy," the noted suffragist declared, "I think the wives and mothers of the country might better enter into crusade against the licentiousness existing all around us and polluting our manhood. . . . If women would require the same purity in men that men require in women, and if mothers would refuse to entertain in their homes or to give their virtuous daughters to men whom they know to have transgressed the moral code, society would soon undergo a purification—a revolution."[39]

Anthony violated the Victorian strategy on sexuality, not by rejecting the female role as purifier, but by taking it more seriously than most men intended or could comfortably tolerate. In the polygamy of Mormons they were fighting an evil that was essentially foreign and thus unambiguous. But Anthony denied them their smug virtuousness by pointing out that non-Mormon men practiced their own version of polygamy—adultery—with prostitutes rather than with multiple wives. Perhaps they did not "deify" their passion, but they practiced it, nonetheless. In effect, she would not let them displace their crime onto Mormons.

During the late nineteenth century more and more women were joining this indignant opposition to the double standard. They refused to let men off the moral hook. A social worker and journalist, for example, recalled the time when she first learned from her mother of the conventional attitude, "which condones the pollution of the majority of young men; of the degrading submission in the intimate relations of marriage expected of the average wife, and of the different judgments passed upon infidelity in husbands and in wives. I rose in revolt. If women must live pure lives, so also should men, I declared. Never would I marry a man whose life had been sullied by unchastity." Her mother replied, with the voice of an older generation: "But a wife cannot think of herself. She must keep her husband satisfied or he will go elsewhere." The daughter had quite another view: "Then she should leave him." Eventually she found a husband who fulfilled her specifications; so one gathers that many, and perhaps most, middle-class men did not practice the double standard. But there were enough others so that, by the twentieth century, a "purity revolt" was reaching a clamorous pitch. The climax came with the campaign against "white slavery," which shook cities and towns from Maine to California and, in the process, nearly destroyed men's already insecure sense of manhood.[40]

"ON THE OUTSKIRTS OF ONE of the western cities," reported the director of the National Vigilance Committee in 1911, "there is a cemetery where 451 nameless girls are buried. It needs not the stories that have been recorded, nor yet the unwritten tragedies that have come to our knowledge, to point the significance of such unmarked graves." These girls were the victims of white slavery. They had met their fate in various ways. Some had come to a city in search of success and had innocently accepted a man's offer of employment or lodging. Some had been dragged into carriages. Others, while sitting in a theater, had felt a needle prick in the neck and, after hours of drugged sleep, had awakened naked on a brothel bed. By whatever method, they found themselves inside the "terrible doors" of the red-light district, through which, according to the *Chicago Daily News*, "unprotected girls, by thousands every year, are lured to slavery and early death."[41]

At least, so the American public was supposed to believe during the decade after 1906. Beginning with a muckraking article in *McClure's Magazine*, a torrent of books, articles, plays, and movies dramatized the operations of an international syndicate that seized innocent girls and sent them into the hands of pimps and madams. Women's clubs, civic leagues, ministerial associations, and WCTU chapters united to lobby for bills closing the red-light districts. Reformers organized local and national committees to publicize the commerce in female bodies, while mayors in dozens of cities established vice commissions to investigate prostitution and find remedies. The report of the Chicago Vice Commission conveys the crusaders' fevered pitch.

As plagues, epidemics and contagious diseases old as the world have given way before the onslaught of medical science; as slavery in this country has been rooted out by the gradually growing conviction of an American conscience; so may the Social Evil be repressed proportionately as the

American people grow in righteousness and in the knowledge of this curse, which is more blasting than any plague or epidemic; more terrible than any black slavery that ever existed in this or any other country; more degenerating to the morals and ideals of the nation than all other agencies against decency combined.[42]

No one could say exactly how large the evil. The president of the Florence Crittenton Mission estimated that the white-slave traffic had devoured 350,000 women, with more than 20,000 "fresh victims" each year. A survey by the U.S. Department of Justice found approximately 100,000 prostitutes in city brothels, with perhaps the same number working on their own. Between 1910 and 1915, the courts put more than a thousand men in jail for having bought and sold women. But the statistics were mostly guesswork and ultimately less significant than the sudden horrified zeal with which middle-class Americans fed upon them. Something more than white slavery alone was distressing the reformers and their audience. After all, prostitution had been a familiar part of the American urban scene for a century, campaigns against it had been busy for thirty or forty years, and the number of prostitutes had peaked at least a decade before the white-slavery crusade began. Nor was white slavery a new issue; Europeans had been agitated about it since the 1880s.[43] If the problem was chronic, why did people suddenly become so alarmed after 1905?

The *New York World* offered a clue when it called the white-slave episode "a new witchcraft mania."[44] The belief that men with drugged needles were enslaving girls' bodies and destroying their virtue did indeed echo the belief in seventeenth-century Salem that Bridget Bishop, with her black magic and dolls, was buying girls' souls for the devil. Whereas Salem's courts imprisoned and hanged witches, federal courts convicted white slavers under the Mann Act.

Witch hunts break out when a community feels threatened and tries to strengthen its social boundaries—to define what is orthodox as opposed to what is deviant. Salem citizens discovered witchcraft because they needed to identify an enemy. In the devil and his agents they found a way of explaining their anxieties, reemphasizing traditional notions of virtue and evil, and thereby (they hoped) restoring order to their society.[45] During the controversy over Congressman Roberts, Americans performed a similar therapy, though in much milder form. Mormons served as the witches threatening to corrupt the monogamous family that Victorians considered so unstable. By unseating Roberts they hoped to reinforce their own sexual order and values. But the explosion of the white-slave mania, seven years later, signaled that they had failed. The Mormon witches were dead, but the devil was still busily at work. Just as Salem's Puritan ministers preached ferocious sermons to goad the public into action, so did the upper-middle-class civic leaders, warning of "this curse which is more blasting than any black slavery."

The rhetoric was so frenzied, the claims so exaggerated, the descriptions so lurid, that we must suspect something beyond white slavery and prostitution was alarming the reformers. Their sense of social order was threatened not simply by the "social evil" corrupting fallen women. Ultimately they felt threatened by the sensuality that was running rampant among their own sons and daughters. "Sex o'clock" had struck in America, a newspaper editor quipped in 1913. A "mania for dancing" had infected young people. In the face of "the present indecent tendencies" produced by the turkey trot, the bunny hug, and the grizzly bear, the *Ladies' Home Journal* desperately reminded parents and dancing teachers that the man's right hand belonged at the woman's waist, not in the middle of her back. But young boys and girls were joining together in even more dangerous recreations, such as ocean swimming and unchaperoned picnics or buggy rides. (Even the daughter of that most unconventional woman Lucy Stone still took for granted in 1883, when she was twenty-six years old, that she and her girl friend would travel through the West only with a matronly chaperon.) Beatrice Fairfax, writing a newspaper advice column, was shocked by inquiries from girls as to whether it was permissible to "soul kiss" on a first date.[46]

Sex had struck adults, too. There was "'the great unrest' of which we hear so much." People were seeking new forms of excitement, craving amorous adventure and even enacting it, watching licentious plays, talking at dinner parties with unprecedented frankness about sex. Some intellectuals were reading European writers like Havelock Ellis, Edward Carpenter, and Sigmund Freud, finding grounds for a new morality of "free love." An erotic revolution was occurring—at least, so it seemed to social critics. Whether it was as large in reality as in their minds is hard to measure. But the clear fact is that reformers—male and female, Socialist and Republican, old and not so old—were increasingly perturbed. Between the periods 1905–9 and 1910–14 the number of magazine articles about sexual morals doubled, almost 90 percent of them hostile to the new sensuality.[47]

The reformers translated this concern into a campaign for sex education among children, young adults, parents, and even factory workers. Via the usual local and national committees, consisting of the usual array of upper-middle-class civic leaders, they organized and publicized. Riding the white-slave mania, they had unprecedented success in spreading the gospel of what they called "sex hygiene." It was a revealing label. Some citizens prudishly opposed sex education as salacious. But the sex hygienists were promoting, in somewhat less prudish form, enough puritanism to delight the most conservative mind. They wanted to educate against sexuality. In the words of one advocate, they sought "sanitary and moral prophylaxis." Theirs was a form of prohibition as reactionary as the program of the WCTU. Brand Whitlock, a former Toledo mayor, made a telling point when he deplored "the present recrudescence of that puritanism which never had its mind on anything else" but the social evil. Sex hygiene, like social purity, was not the vanguard of modern liberation, but the rear guard of Victorians who sought desperately to discipline the unruly appetites in others and themselves.[48]

The campaigns against white slavery and for sex hygiene were attempts to define the boundaries of the traditional social order. In demanding a purity that Americans had never fully practiced, reformers were seeking to reinforce the sexual values that Americans had at least preached. Like Salem's Puritans, they were defending orthodoxy against a threatening modernity—in this case, defending a Victorian code of chastity, character, and community against the more tolerant ethic that seemed to be emerging in cities and among the young. By the second decade of the twentieth century this modernity had become so threatening that civil leaders and a large portion of the public sought solace in a witch hunt.

The bewitched were those innocent girls ensnared into prostitution. The witches were the white slavers. And the devil was male lust. There could be no prostitution, after all, without procurers, pimps, and "johns." "It is a man and not a woman problem which we face today," the Chicago Vice Commission proclaimed, "commercialized by man—supported by man—the supply of fresh victims furnished by men—men who have lost that fine instinct of chivalry and that splendid honor for womanhood." And not merely lower-class men. According to some social-purity spokesmen, more than half of all adult males in American cities had contracted venereal disease. The statistics were wildly exaggerated, but they made the propagandistic point: the blame for prostitution must extend across the whole spectrum of American manhood.[49]

A woman living in Ames, Iowa, posed the issue with particular forcefulness in a letter to Walter Rauschenbusch, a famous social-gospel minister. Rauschenbusch had published "A Prayer for Mothers" in the *American Magazine*, beseeching God to preserve women's purity for their holy task. But this particular woman, like Susan B. Anthony in her comment on the Mormon issue, was not at all grateful for such chivalrous deference. "I say—cut it out! If Walter wants to pray let him pray for the fathers," she wrote. "You just call to mind the thousands of young women sold into worse than African slavery in the south, by Rauschenbush [sic] sex for the satisfaction of the beastly lust of Rauschenbush [sic] sex, and let him pray to make young men chaste, if he can, short of castrating them. Cut it out! Too much preaching to women, and praying for women. Let men pray for their own sex."[50]

MANY MEN DID PRECISELY THAT, of course, and with Theodore Roosevelt "thanked Heaven" for having stifled temptation. But in the face of such emasculating zeal as the Iowa woman's, one must wonder why so many men joined the social-purity ranks.

A part of the answer, surely, is that they sincerely believed in promoting the moral ideals they had been taught as boys. A more skeptical psychological answer is that they felt a profound need to appease their consciences. Out of the perilous passage between purity and "wild oats," they carried with them a terrible burden of guilt. Even if they managed to stay "clean," they could hardly avoid a fleeting carnal impulse. Understandably, then, men supported the purity crusade as a form of contrition. And in the white slavers they could objectify, then destroy, their own evil fantasies.

But there was more to it than that. The Victorian elite were dismayed by what they regarded as social disorder and, in the purity crusade, sought to restore the old gender order: his sphere and especially hers. On the most subterranean psychic level, men were fighting against *female* sexuality. The profoundest threat to their sense of social and personal order lay in the specter that woman—not only the "vicious" or "fallen" woman but also the proverbial "angel in the house"—possessed her own sexual drive. The patriarchs needed bodiless women to sanctify the home as refuge from the male world and to purify their bestial impulses. But in the early twentieth century they found (or thought they found) disturbing evidence that women would not perform that role. The white-slave mania became so intense because anxious nineteenth-century Americans feared that the devil of sexuality had found willing playmates among the angels in the home.

Everywhere they looked, they saw alarming evidence that respectable middle-class women were interested in and enacting—and yes, enjoying—sexual passion. There were, first of all, the writings and doings of those bohemians, socialists, and anarchists. But closer than Greenwich Village and the lunatic fringe were the dancing, spooning, and soul-kissing of young people. And even closer, dangerously close, there were the women entering universities, professions, clubs, and reform movements, women of the breeding a middle-class man would normally consider marrying. But now that sex o'clock had struck, men stepped back with anger and disgust, denouncing the "new woman" for her licentiousness.

Why this hostile reaction? Why did men dread rather than welcome the appearance of a sexual partner? Some of the answer has to do with men's concern that passion would impair delicate female health, but more of the answer derives from their fear that female passion would deplete their own masculine strength. If the medical presumption of limited bodily energy applied to women, it applied no less to men. A husband depended on his wife to prevent him from reckless "spending" (the Victorian word for orgasm). According to physicians, one drop of semen equaled forty drops of blood. That kind of arithmetic gave a man pause. Too frequent intercourse would drain away his vital fluids and leave him weakened, impotent, unmanly. For both physiological as well as moral reasons, then, a man expected his wife to perform the role of bodiless angel. "You are my *good influence* to keep me pure in heart," a Minnesota architect wrote to his fiancée in 1887. "Your influence makes me more manly." In almost identical words, meanwhile, a young professor of zoology was telling his fiancée, "You are the very incarnation of purity to me . . . and you shall help to cleanse me."[51] The wife should be—must be—the better half. If she abdicated her part and became an equal sexual partner, then she would drag a man into sperm-depleting, manhood-killing orgy. In passion lurked the seeds of destruction.

Derangement of the patriarchal order at home would be followed by derangement of patriarchy outside. If the angel left the house, then the symbiosis between virtuous, affectionate home and amoral, competitive society would be broken. Feminists might promise that they would spread maternal morality over ballot box and market place and battlefield, but their opponents predicted the opposite. "I dread the effect of this woman's movement upon civilization," said Senator Joseph Bailey of Texas, "because I know what happened to the Roman republic when women attained their full rights." Earnestly he reminded the feminists of their social responsibilities. "We cannot pay women a higher tribute than to insist that their behavior shall be more circumspect than ours." A female "anti" said it more bluntly: "Equal suffrage is a repudiation of manhood."[52]

Middle-class men were feeling besieged at the turn of the century, and they were holding women to blame. This had not always been the case. In their grandfathers' time, the opposite of manliness had been childishness, a stage which all men outgrew. In their own time, the opposite of manliness was femininity.[53] The shift measured how much of their identity men had invested in the distinction between "spheres." They needed each gender to play distinctive roles. Female equality posed a threat because men had depended upon women not only to tend the home, but to mask the ambivalences inside manliness. The patriarchal culture was disintegrating because the "better half" seemed willing to be only equally good. When this development joined with their growing difficulty in satisfying the patriarchal ideals of work and success in the public sphere, middle-class men asked with even more confusion: "How was a man to be manly in the twentieth century?"

In Time of War

Before the First World War, men did not really have an answer to the dilemma of modern manliness. In their psychic crisis, they clutched at a variety of desperate sublimations. Owen Wister provided one when he wrote *The Virginian* (1902). As the first genuine "western novel," it not only went through fifteen printings within less than a year (to the surprise of its publisher) and through eight years of dramatization in theaters around the country, but it also launched a genre that has become a hallmark of twentieth-century popular literature. Wister symbolized the meaning of his novel when he dedicated it to Theodore Roosevelt. By rewinning the wild West in fiction, men could satisfy those virile fantasies for which postfrontier America had no geographical room. The cowboy was a man's man, violent but honorable, fighting evil with a phallic six-shooter, defending women without being domesticated by them. The Virginian eventually married the Vermont schoolmarm, but on his wedding day he rejected her pacifist pleas, killed the villain who had challenged him, and returned to her admiring embrace.

If one can infer from the phenomenal popularity of Zane Grey, Clarence Mulford, and a dozen other western novelists who followed in Wister's wake, middle-class readers found some special satisfaction in the cowboy prototype. In a less subtle but still more graphic form, they obtained similar gratification from Edgar Rice Burroughs, who published the first of his Tarzan books in 1912. Before he was through, Tarzan swung through the pages of 36 million copies and across innumerable movie screens. The same psychological need was reflected, perhaps, in the popularity of the Paul Bunyan legends after 1910.[1]

Men also played out their frustrations in less fantastic locales than the range or the jungle. The surging popularity of organized spectator sports during the late nineteenth century was largely a function of growing urban population, public transportation, and mass-circulation newspapers and magazines. But it also derived from the psychological situation of middle-class men. The football field was an exclusively male world where the players could legitimately act out aggressions and win measurable victories, while the spectators achieved the same satisfactions in vicarious form. When college football became outrageously brutal as well as corrupted by professionalism in the 1890s, Theodore Roosevelt and others objected, much as they objected to the predatory trusts. But by then baseball was becoming "the national pastime." This less violent sport demanded qualities closely resembling the Victorian manly code: honesty, physical fitness, courage, initiative, self-control, teamwork. Baseball did more for the fans, however, than give a moral lesson. According to one writer in 1913, it provided "momentary relief from the strain of an intolerable burden, . . . a harmless outlet for pent-up emotions."[2]

More directly satisfying than either fiction or sports, and symbolically more complex, was the Boy Scouts of America (BSA). This was not to be simply an outdoor recreational club. According to its founder, Ernest Thompson Seton, who had been a naturalist and an author of animal stories, the BSA was a movement to redeem boys from the rot of urban civilization. As Seton proclaimed in the first Scouts *Handbook* (1910), "Realizing that *manhood*, not *scholarship*, is the first aim of education, we have sought out those pursuits which develop the finest character, the finest physique, and which may be followed out of doors, which, in a word, *make for manhood*." Here was the chance for a boy to escape the passivity of urban middle-class life. Like the frontiersmen of yesteryear, he could contend with raw nature. (Significantly, the Boy Scouts absorbed an earlier organization named the Society of the Sons of Daniel Boone.) Unlike the frontiersmen, however, the Boy Scout would test himself in adult-supervised groups and via methodically scheduled tasks. It was to be a disciplined adventure. In keeping with the Victorian manly code that pitted self-assertion against self-control, the BSA wanted to free youthful energies and also to curb them. Out of this tricky combination, a boy was supposed to acquire strength, honesty, altruism, and a duty to God and country—in a word, "character," or in a romantic phrase, a code of chivalry. "American Knights in Buckskin," one Scout leader exclaimed in a burst of medieval wild-West manly imagery.[3]

Within four years more than 100,000 boys had enrolled, and within three more years almost twice that many followed on their heels. By 1920 almost one of every ten American boys had worn a Scout uniform. Leading them were more than 30,000 Scoutmasters, who were governed in turn by an administrative hierarchy which was crowned by a National Council consisting of such manly men as Admiral George Dewey, Major Leonard Wood, and—inevitably—Theodore Roosevelt. It was as if American middle-class males had been waiting for Seton's summons.

But institutional success was not the same as success in solving the frustrations of manliness. In fact, the irony is that the BSA reproduced much of the stifling bureaucracy and passivity that it wanted to overcome. Boys who came with visions of fighting fires and canoeing white-water streams all too often found themselves sitting through moralistic lectures in church basements and memorizing first-aid procedures. At the top, meanwhile, the romantic, woodcraft-oriented founders were losing power to younger executives who believed in bureaucratic efficiency and control—"the strenuous life" according to rules. As a result, turnover among Scouts as well as Scoutmasters stayed near 50 percent. The typical boy quit within less than two years, at the age of fourteen, still craving manly excitement and fulfillment.[4]

Men would need a more thoroughgoing solution—or at least a more thoroughgoing sublimation—in order to relieve the crisis of their sex role. By 1917 they thought that they had found it in war.

"YOU ARE GOING INTO A BIG THING: a big war: a big army: standing for a big idea," wrote "Dad" to "Tom" in a letter published as an editorial by the *Ladies' Home Journal*. "But don't forget that the biggest thing about a principle or a battle or an army is a man! And the biggest thing that a war can do is to bring out that man. That's really what you and the other chaps have gone over for: to demonstrate the right kind of manhood, for it is that which weighs in a fight and wins it."[5]

When Congress declared war on Germany in April 1917, the American public responded with almost ferocious zeal. The nation launched a campaign to destroy those Huns who had mutilated Belgian women and children and who sought to crush freedom under their iron heels. It was a venture in which, as President Wilson had so nobly declared and a million publicists repeated, the United States wanted nothing for itself except the rights and happiness of people around the world—a peace without victory. It was a crusade.

This disinterested idealism was sincere. But middle-class American men also wanted some satisfactions for themselves from the war. Basically they envisioned the battlefield as a proving ground where they could enact and repossess the manliness that modern American society had baffled. Beneath the tidal wave of war propaganda issued by the government's Committee on Public Information and its imitators, the theme of manliness protruded again and again during 1917–18. Nowhere was this more graphic than in the hundreds of enlistment posters, such as the one depicting a gleeful sailor riding a torpedo into the ocean like a cowboy.

Americans entered the Great War to achieve not simply political principles, but psychological reassurance as well. And not simply for the doughboys in actual battle, but also for the citizens on the home front. Indeed, the incessant propaganda that filled newspapers, magazines, auditoriums, and street corners focused primarily on those who were not in uniform. The trenches represented only one part of the war's meaning; the rest of it took place among civilians. As Americans translated the ideals of progressivism to the international sphere, they hoped thereby to restore within the United States their Victorian values of pure, strenuous manhood. That had been William James's objective as he offered his essay "The Moral Equivalent of War." But instead, there were rampant materialism, licentious sexuality, and stifled individual opportunity. Now men turned to real war for the virtues that they had failed to find in symbolic substitutes.

The most immediate and tangible consequence of belligerence was rationing. Led by Herbert Hoover's Food Administration, civic leaders and publicists from New York to Keokuk to Seattle implored families to eat meatless meals, to walk instead of driving automobiles, and to patch their pants instead of buying new ones. "Four-minute men" exhorted theater audiences and sidewalk crowds to serve the national cause by buying Liberty Bonds. The rich were urged to volunteer their energy in government jobs and Red Cross work, while giving up servants and limousines. Many people welcomed self-denial. Thrift would be "a fine experience for us," they announced. It would save the American soul from "the leprosy of materialism," end the mad "extravagance and luxury" that had contaminated civilization.[6] In short, according to these writers, the economic sacrifices would produce purification after an era of materialism.

The war was more than an economic emergency; for males over the age of seventeen, it became a matter of sacrificing job or education, an arm, a leg, perhaps life itself. But that was, for many commentators, precisely its value. Through the crucible of combat a boy would emerge a man. Even as improbable a boy as Neil Leighton, the hero of a *Saturday Evening Post* story entitled "The Feminine Touch." He was the son of an actor, who had died soon after Leighton's birth, and a Fifth Avenue milliner. As a teenager, he worked in his mother's establishment, developed a taste for opera and ballet, and was teased by girls for being a sissy. Finally, he enlisted to fight in France, in order to "show them the sort of man I am!" Ironically, however, he found himself stationed, not as a doughboy in the trenches, but as an assistant in a French doctor's office. In fact, he agreed to take a woman's role in a play being produced by the soldiers. So far so bad for Leighton. But suddenly the Germans invaded during a rehearsal. Disguised in his female costume, Leighton managed to shoot three enemy soldiers with a pistol concealed in a muff. He then proceeded to save the town by discovering the Germans' code for retreat (church bells to be rung three times). By the end of the story, he had won several medals and the love of a French girl, while enduring an arm wound with manly stoicism.[7]

Almost all young boys suffered the anxiety of being considered sissies, and reluctantly or not, they got into fist fights to prove their masculinity.[8] The world war provided a larger arena for the same proof. At least, this is how civilian observers liked to interpret it. To risk one's life for America signified more than patriotic idealism; it defined manly character. When the poet Joyce Kilmer died as he was reconnoitering on a battlefield, a mass-circulation magazine offered this eulogy: "Kilmer was young, only thirty-two, and the scholarly type of man. One did not think of him as a warrior. And yet from the time we entered the war he could think of but one thing—that he must, with his own hands, strike a blow at the Hun. He was a man!"[9]

Manliness included more than physical courage. It included those moral qualities that Victorians had in mind when they spoke of "character." Whoever would save his soul must be willing to lose his life. The Great War became a "crusade" because Americans proclaimed enormous moral consequences for those who went off to fight. Consider Kelsey, the protagonist of a *Saturday Evening Post* story published in 1917. Throughout his life this ship's fireman had wanted only to drink, fight, and earn as much money as he could. If anyone talked about defending freedom and democracy against Germany, he sneered at such

sentimentality. "Mr. Nietzsche would have approved of Kelsey," the author remarks. "To look out for number one was his gospel." When a German submarine torpedoed his ship during an Atlantic crossing, however, Kelsey went out of his way to save a woman and child whom he
had met previously. On the lifeboat during the icy night he gave them
his fur coat. Eventually they reached England, whereupon he donated
to the Red Cross a gold-filled purse that he had stolen from a dead passenger. In the end, Kelsey gruffly signed up to fight against the Huns
who were killing women, children, and freedom.[10]

He had proved himself "a true man," the Victorians would have
said, demonstrating not only strength, but honor as well. Like the heroes of countless wartime stories and essays and sermons, he had vindicated the ideal of manliness that the Beveridges, Roosevelts, Stim-
sons, and other patriarchs so earnestly espoused. For them the war
represented a crusade—more precisely, a chivalric crusade, an adult
version of what the Boy Scouts embodied in more artificial terms. And
as more and more Americans went into uniform and into battle, as the
casualties increased, these civilian commentators were convinced that
their hopes were coming true. "The slouching, dissipated, impudent
lout who seemed to typify young America has disappeared," a *Washington Post* editorialist announced in 1918. Service to the nation, he said,
had molded a youth who was serious, active, courageous, "with the
ideals of his country stamped upon his heart."[11] When such men returned home, they would not be content with desk jobs or more education, those unmanly options that prewar America had offered. No,
said the narrator in one novel of 1918, "there will be a new movement
toward the ever-vanishing frontier, a setting westward in the search for
wider ranges, for life in the open air."[12]

Such was the meaning of the Great War as defined by observers at
home, interpreting to the American public the bloody events across the
ocean. But how did the soldiers themselves understand their experience? Did they see themselves as chivalric knights riding tanks or
planes in the name of democracy and manhood? As one might expect,
no single generalization holds true for more than 2 million men of diverse backgrounds and temperaments. For some, war was simply another job, one that they took with the same dispassionate attitudes
that they had applied to their civilian jobs. Russell G. Pruden, for example, never once, throughout his wartime letters and diaries, betrayed any ideological interpretation or personal feeling beyond com-

passion and humor. Similarly, several doughboys recounted the ferocious battles of the Argonne without a trace of emotional flourish,
merely depicting themselves and their fellows as working stoically to
win or at least survive. For others, however, the experience of Woodrow
Wilson's war aroused very vivid feelings. "Darling dear this is the most
tiresome trip that I have ever taken or ever expect to take again," one
soldier wrote en route to France. "Sophia if I could only get back to you
and have some of your mothers [sic] regular meals you cannot realize
how I would eat." But beyond disgust at sugarless porridge and tainted
fish was the pain in his heart. "It seems as fate has dealt us an awful
blow, and some times dear, the old tears are bound to come to my
eyes, and if I wasn't a man I certainly would cry. If I look at your picture
once darling, I look at it thousands of times."[13]

While many never surmounted this sense of personal deprivation,
others certainly did. "War is not a pink tea," Arthur Guy Empey conceded in his best-seller, *"Over the Top,"* "but in a worthwhile cause like
ours, mud, rats, cooties, shells, wounds, or death itself are far out-
weighed by the deep sense of satisfaction felt by the man who does his
bit." It may have been cliché, but it was a sincere cliché. Some performed their "bit" modestly. "Mother you asked if I dreaded my trip
across," Sergeant Thomas Cole wrote home while with the American
Expeditionary Force (AEF), "and in ans. I shall say I did not. I feel about
this thing as every other true American feels and that is; It is an honour
to be here and to fight for such a country as we have." Some tended toward self-grandeur. A young army lieutenant declared in one letter:
"You know, I think soldiering makes real men." Alan Seeger, the ill-fated
poet, echoed this sentiment with his characteristically romantic flair.
"Be sure that I shall play the part well," he wrote to his mother from
France, "for I was never in better health nor felt my manhood more
keenly."[14]

However breezy or brassy the rhetoric, it expressed genuine emotions. After all, more than 25,000 American men—Empey and Seeger
among them—enlisted in the Canadian, British, and French forces before 1917.[15] Their zeal was authentic. Yet it alone does not explain the
propelling motives. Which needs in them were seeking the "deep sense
of satisfaction" that Empey mentioned? Again, any generalization is
presumptuous. But perhaps the example of John Dos Passos is suggestive, in exaggerated form, of what prompted other young combatants.

In August of 1916, months before the United States entered the

war, the twenty-year-old Dos Passos wrote to his friend Arthur Mc-
Comb, "I am dying to get to Belgium & exhaust surplus energy." Almost
a year later, still not having reached his destination, Dos Passos expressed the same frustrations, but now specifying their source.

> I think we are all of us a pretty milky lot, —don't you?— with our tea-
> table convictions and our radicalism that keeps so consistently within the
> bounds of decorum—Damn it, why couldn't one of us have refused to reg-
> ister [with the draft board] and gone to jail and made a general ass of him-
> self? I should have had more hope for Harvard. . . .
>
> And what are we fit for when they turn us out of Harvard? We're too in-
> telligent to be successful businessmen and we haven't the sand or the en-
> ergy to be anything else.
>
> Until Widener is blown up and A. Lawrence Lowell assassinated and
> the Business School destroyed and its site sowed into salt—no good will
> come out of Cambridge.
>
> It's fortunate I'm going to France as I'll be able to work off my incendi-
> ary ideas.

By enlisting in the ambulance corps, Dos Passos finally found release for those "incendiary" feelings that burned so impatiently within
him. Writing from a small village in Champagne after experiencing his
first air attack, he announced to McComb, "I've not been so happy for
months." But from what precisely did this happiness derive? From the
violence surrounding him. The war's havoc fed the fire of his aesthetic
romanticism. An entry in his notebook, dated August 1917, almost vi-
brates with passionate delight in the violence.

> But gosh I want to be able to express, later, all of this, all the tragedy and
> hideous excitement of it. I've seen so very little. I must experience more of
> it and more—the grey crooked fingers of the dead, the dark look of dirty
> mangled bodies, their groans and jottings in the ambulances, the vast
> tomtom of the guns, the ripping tear shells make when they explode, the
> song of shells outgoing like vast woodcocks—their contented whirr as
> they near their mark—the twang of fragments like a harp broken in the air
> and the rattle of stones and mud on your helmet. . . .
>
> In myself I find the nervous reaction to be curious hankering after dan-
> ger that takes hold of me. When one shell comes I want another, nearer,
> nearer, I constantly feel the need of the drunken excitement of a good

bombardment—I want to throw the dice at every turn with the old rois-
terer Death . . . and through it all I feel more alive than ever before—I have
never lived yet.[16]

Dos Passos had come closer than ever before to fulfilling his
thwarted energies—and did so in literary rendition of suffering. Between the real violence and his imagery, he found resolution of those
"incendiary ideas" that had driven him to France.

"I KNOW THESE MEN WILL RETURN finer, cleaner, straighter men," a Harvard
alumnus wrote from a French battlefront. In the light of Dos Passos's
attitudes, however, one wonders. Finer and cleaner? Perhaps only because purged of the furious energy that so many adolescents turned
against the enemy and, in suicidal heroism, against themselves. For
many, especially the fervent romantics like Dos Passos and Seeger, war
meant the ultimate test of manliness—at the edge of death. Nothing
short of that could satisfy them. "A night attack is a wonderful thing to
see . . . ," wrote Charles Nordhoff. "Into the maelstrom of sprouting
flames, hissing steel, shattering explosions, insignificant little creatures like you and me will presently run—offering, with sublime
courage, their tender bodies to be burned and mangled."[17]

For others, less compelled by the need for total self-definition, war
meant physical action and adventure sanctioned in the name of patriotism. And for some, it gave the opportunity to enact a more bluntly
physical violence than the aesthetic college men could admit. "I do not
mind saying," wrote the author of *Gunner Depew*, "that I was glad whenever I slipped my bayonet into a Turk, and more glad when I saw another one coming." And an infantryman wrote home about killing three
Germans: "Why I just couldn't kill them dead enough it seemed like.
Believe me it was some fun as well as exciting." Finally, there were those
whose feelings were much more prosaic. A private, after being wounded
at the Argonne and therefore withdrawn from action, remarked, "I was
happy to be hit again, because life in the trenches, plugging through
the mud and water up to the waist, sleeping in wet, damp dugouts is
unspeakable." This same private would receive the Croix de Guerre for
earlier bravery in an Argonne raiding party that had captured forty-one
German machine guns and fifty-seven prisoners.[18]

Whether any of these experiences produced "finer" and "cleaner"
men is dubious. Yet Americans insisted vehemently that the war puri-

fied the young men who took part. War produced not simply stronger, more courageous, more honorable men, but purer men. Indeed, many Americans made it an extension of the purity crusade that the Victorian reformers had been directing for half a century against vice. This was the last dimension of manliness, which Americans hoped to vindicate by means of the war.

And they thought that they had. According to one reporter in 1918, "Our fighting force today is not only the cleanest body of fighting men the world has ever seen, but the cleanest group of young men ever brought together outside a monastery." Others, particularly those working in the social-hygiene movement, made the same boast. Venereal disease among the armed forces, they claimed, had been virtually eradicated.[19] They credited two factors for this achievement. First of all, the American Social Hygiene Association had persuaded the secretary of war to create a Commission on Training Camp Activities that would suppress vice in military camp areas. With the cooperation of other government agencies as well as groups like the Young Men's Christian Association, the War Department undertook a $4 million campaign to keep prostitutes (and alcohol) away from the recruits, to abolish red-light districts near the camps, to require soldiers to obtain medical examination if they had sexual relations, and to disseminate information on venereal disease. "How much sweeter and cleaner would our home lives be," remarked one lieutenant, "if we were to live like these [army] boys do?"[20]

But prohibition was not the whole reason for this uniformed purity. No, the soldiers themselves rejected sexual temptation; they were clean in body and mind. Or so the American public was told. Even when they came into contact with the proverbially promiscuous French women, these American men remained true to their principles and to their sweethearts back home, doing no more than to stroll with the *mademoiselles*. And again the civilian writers argued that the war itself sublimated the male passions. The hero of Willa Cather's novel *One of Ours*, for example, enlisted after suffering the humiliation of marriage to a woman of stronger will than his own. Thereafter he never again turned to women for erotic satisfaction. Instead, he reasserted his masculinity by embracing battle and making love to war.[21]

That civilians, especially the social hygienists, proclaimed the purity of the chivalric doughboys is not surprising. After decades of service in moral-reform movements, they wanted and needed to believe that Wilson's war was, in all its dimensions, a crusade—a culmination to their tireless efforts and energies. More surprising is the fact that so many soldiers also insisted on this theme. A group of engineers and medical students at the University of Minnesota, for example, drafted a resolution as they enlisted in April 1917: "Aware of the temptations incident to camp life and the moral and social wreckage involved, we covenant together, as college men, to live the clean life and to seek to establish the American uniform as a symbol and guarantee of real manhood." During the next eighteen months, soldiers at the front wrote home with assurances that they had not succumbed to sexual temptation.[22]

What had happened to the notion and practice of "sowing wild oats"? Had the Great War abruptly destroyed an attitude that decades of earnest Victorian moralizing and purity movements had failed to destroy? Hardly. Whatever people believed or professed to believe, the American men who fought during the First World War were not essentially different from those in other wars. According to the reminiscences of a madam operating a New Orleans whorehouse, the war had not at all inspired men to find "true manhood," courageous and celibate. "Every man and boy wanted to have one last fling of screwing," she declared, "before the real war got him. Every farm boy wanted to have one big fuck in a real house before he went off and maybe was killed. . . . The idea of war and dying makes a man raunchy. . . . I dreamed one night the whole city was sinking into a lake of sperm." From a training camp in Plattsburgh, New York, meanwhile, one soldier estimated that most of his comrades were "unchaste" and that one-half had contracted venereal disease. More precisely, the surgeon general of the army reported a venereal disease rate of 114 per thousand enlisted men in 1917, rising a year later to 150 (as compared to 81 per thousand in 1898).[23]

The vast majority of these patients had contracted the disease in civilian life, before they enlisted. Conditions were better after the men came under army supervision. Not much better, though, and certainly far from the life of a monastery. Strenuous efforts by military officials in France—including prohibitive regulations, propaganda, and medical treatment—kept the loss of manpower among the AEF to a lower rate than in any previous war. Of approximately 2 million fighting men, an average of 18,000 were out of action each day because of venereal disease (as compared to an average of 606 men incapacitated during the

Second World War). Nevertheless, 18,000 daily cases constituted a medical problem serious enough that, in mid-1918, the army created a venereal disease detention camp in France. The men of the AEF may indeed have been "cleaner" than previous armies, but they were not monks, either in body or, more important, in mind. "Wandering through dark streets," one lieutenant wrote in his diary. "Ever-present women. So mysterious and seductive in darkness. . . . A fellow's got to hang on to himself here. Not many do." According to one officer's study, 71 percent of the Americans stationed in France engaged in sexual relations.[24]

Obviously the spokesmen of purity were deceived by their own hopes or propaganda. The Victorian crusade for chastity had not abruptly achieved victory in the war to end wars. Soldiers' bodies may have been less contaminated, but not their minds. Nor had the Victorian male dilemma of ambivalence regarding continence and wild oats been resolved; if anything, it had intensified as the gap between public allegations and actual behavior widened still further. The prewar dilemma of manliness persisted—but not entirely. Some of its features had changed because of the war. For one thing, men had at last found, it seemed, an opportunity for the strenuous life that the corporate economy and the vanishing frontier had been steadily stifling. To this extent they could win manliness, even if some of them in the process failed to transcend brutality and sexual vice. Second, the prevailing myth portrayed the warriors as chivalric knights (while the public at home forsook materialism in a patriotic campaign of thrift). Whatever the facts of how the soldiers were behaving, people did not know those facts or refused to believe them. Until the Armistice and even beyond, the American public believed that the crusade for worldwide democracy was also purifying their soldiers and themselves. And many of the doughboys, too, insisted romantically on this interpretation. In war Americans found, for the time being, peace of mind about their national morality, in large part because men were manly again.

AND THE WOMEN? THE IDENTITIES of the two sexes function interdependently, changes in one causing as well as being caused by changes in the other. As the definition of men underwent such drastic developments, what was happening meanwhile to their counterparts in the dialectic between the sexes?

The clearest answer is that middle-class women went through a confusing upheaval. As men relinquished normal activities for defense jobs and uniforms, some journalists proclaimed "a time of supreme honor for women."[25] But there was also dismaying evidence of female dishonor. Sixty YMCA lecturers might tour the nation with social-hygiene pamphlets and lectures urging women to "Do Your Bit to Keep Him Fit." Yet by September 1917 the Commission on Training Camp Activities had received so many complaints about young girls' promiscuous activities among recruits that it created a Committee on Protective Work for Girls. Reformers were encountering a bitter irony. While relying as usual on women to curb male lust, they discovered that some women—and not simply "fallen women"—were betraying this trust. Thus, besides contending with immoral men, the reformers had to contend with what they called the "girl problem." Because of the "lure of the uniform," committee investigators reported, girls "often lose their heads in a whirl of emotion." Whereas under ordinary circumstances they would not have dreamed of speaking to a man without an introduction, now girls "are picking up soldiers on the street, going to shows and ice cream parlors with them, and gradually becoming demoralized." Nor was the decadence confined to military areas. Courts in cities like New York, Cincinnati, and Chicago reported sharp increases in female juvenile delinquency rates during the period 1917–18. Zelda Sayre (later Fitzgerald) in Montgomery was not the only girl, then, to discover the excitement that arrived with an influx of young soldiers.[26]

The prewar tension between younger and older generations was coming into the open. The "fast" girls, who had shocked their mothers by dancing and flirting and spooning, now, amid wartime conditions, behaved even faster, while their more reticent friends began to join the fun.

But their rebellious conduct formed only a part of the "woman question"—although a portentous part, one that would dominate in the 1920s. During the war years the question still revolved around those familiar pegs—family, employment, and the vote, but most immediately the family. If war meant for men the chance to prove themselves in combat, it meant for women the necessity of letting their sons and husbands go. This situation inspired an endless, and endlessly mawkish, amount of wartime propaganda. The song "Keep the Home Fires Burning" was among the more subtle expressions. There were also posters such as "The Greatest Mother in the World," in which a madonnalike nurse cradles within her arms a wounded soldier and his stretcher. And then there were exhortations such as this one in a soldier's narrative: "While [the death of her son in war] would be a bitter blow, what more could a real mother ask than to be the mother of a real man?"[27]

Females could not remain simply heroines of the hearth, however. Even if people had wanted to use the war as a reactionary weapon for keeping woman at home "where she belongs," they could not have done so. For, as everyone conceded, too many men had left their regular jobs, too many new social needs had arisen. The emergency demanded that leisured women contribute their energies and skills in the world beyond their doorsteps. But not necessarily in "unfeminine" ways. Millions of volunteers performed their classic nurturant role as they made surgical dressings, fed national guardsmen on duty in the vicinity, knitted socks for the boys overseas, organized the planting of victory gardens, and replaced nurses in the hospitals.[28] These women upset not at all the traditional gender roles. Indeed, they tended to reinforce them, as a wartime story in the *Ladies' Home Journal* pointedly demonstrated. Mrs. Gerold, a widow, had reacted with grudging lack of patriotism when her two sons enlisted in the army. Soon afterward, discovering that her husband's fortune had been embezzled by his partner, she was forced to take a job—in a flag-making factory. At first the assembly-line work only depressed her further. But suddenly: "She saw it now. They were there all together—women with work to do and glad to do it . . . all together making their country's flags. Whatever happened, her boys were safe in their country's honor; and she, serving her country too, was with them."[29]

Reality also had less complacent endings. As approximately 1.5 million women joined the wartime labor force, men often reacted with dismay, sometimes outrage. Much of the conflict was purely economic; male workers feared that women were taking away their jobs. Thus, the Kansas City Carmen's Union threatened to strike if the streetcar company employed female conductors. A shrapnel company had to fire some of its 125 newly hired women workers because the union raised such a furious outcry. A prominent New York labor leader warned that employment of women—particularly at below-average wages—would "antagonize and demoralize male labor, and it may even result in open revolt."[30]

But the controversy throbbed with noneconomic emotions too. At stake was a threat not only to men's jobs, but to the moral standards of both sexes. When girls began shining shoes in Boston's Twentieth Century Shoe Parlor, for example, they were surrounded every day at lunch hour by a large, curious crowd. To our eyes, these female bootblacks— dressed in overalls with bunched ankles, high collars, long sleeves, and belted waists—seem quaint. To contemporaries, they seemed porno- graphic. As one woman reformer wrote, "To see these 'shine' girls . . . , clad in a costume that reveals every line of their feminine figure, com- ing in contact so intimately with men, is a sight that is repulsive and full of horror to any woman who has the best interest of other women at heart." A male unionist vehemently agreed. "No person worthy of be- ing called a 'man' would allow his sister or his daughter to shine his boots. And if you watch the face of the man over the bent back of the girl cleaning his shoes, you will find there all the marks of the degener- ate." They might have been describing masseuses rather than boot- blacks. Indeed, Mayor James Curley urged the Boston City Council to pass an ordinance forbidding such employment to women under the age of twenty-one.[31]

Such bluestocking reactions occurred throughout the nation, not only in Boston, as thousands of women appeared in "unfeminine" cos- tumes in hitherto "male" occupations. The century-old controversy about whether a woman should work became, during wartime, vividly tangible. In contrast to men's traditional identity, which seemed to be rejuvenated by the war, women's traditional identity seemed more jeopardized than ever. Certainly there were the angels of mercy, who rolled bandages and knitted socks. But there were also those who op- erated elevators, pounded blacksmith anvils, handled cash in bank tellers' cages, dispatched locomotives, manufactured torpedoes, and served in the numerous other capacities that, until 1917, had belonged exclusively to men. As the United States began its second year of war, women appeared in almost every corner of the labor market. However incongruous, there they were; and, however outrageous, there they had to be if the nation was to mobilize for victory. "This is the new woman movement," one female journalist proclaimed. "And you're in it. We all are."

Then the furor subsided. In fact, many observers went out of their way to praise the efficiency of women workers and to report employers' satisfaction. Even the *Ladies' Home Journal*, after decades of telling its readers to stay home and be ladies, published an article applauding the female employees of a traction cab company.[32] Most Americans thus accepted women as custodians of the male realm that the chivalrous warriors had left behind.

Two issues remained unsettled, however. First of all, economic inequity. According to a survey by the National Industrial Conference Board late in 1918, for example, almost 20 percent of industrial establishments paid lower wages to women than men. A similar survey in New York State found that 60 percent of female factory workers were earning less than fourteen dollars a week, approximately two dollars less than a subsistence level.[33] If women were custodians, they seemed distinctly second class. Furthermore, as peace seemed imminent and the doughboys began returning from the trenches, people began to ask, Should working women go home? Predictably, many men said yes. Veterans would have enough difficulty finding jobs, they said, without competing against women. Many women agreed, particularly since they wanted to enjoy the family life that the military emergency had disrupted or postponed.

But other women emphatically disagreed. The victory for worldwide democracy, they argued, should also mean equal economic opportunity for the other half of the American population. The official journal of the National American Woman Suffrage Association (NAWSA), for example, verged into uncharacteristically anti-male language when it complained about "the inability of men to think in terms of women" regarding postwar employment. "Men are not only human beings; they are men. And women are not only human beings; they are women. There is common ground on which they meet and there is particular ground where each sex stands alone."[34] Goaded by the issue of jobs for women, the NAWSA spokesmen seemed to foresee the prospect of sex war. Only time would tell the need for such an offensive. But the women activists were not merely waiting and hoping; they were forging the weapon that would, they believed, guarantee their rights in the labor market and elsewhere. While the troops fought in Europe, women finished the fight for suffrage at home.

"THIS WAR SHOULD BE A GOOD ARGUMENT for suffrage," Carrie Chapman Catt remarked, a few days after the archduke's assassination. It would prove, she said, that men are "as hysterical as women, only they show it in a different way. Women weep and men fight." The female vote, she concluded, would have prevented the war from erupting.[35]

It was a familiar argument, facile and sentimental and therefore convenient, repeated tirelessly by suffragists of militant as well as non-militant factions and of pacifist as well as nonpacifist persuasion. Give a political voice to women, and then at least those manly swords would be made into plowshares.[36] So the suffragists argued before 1917, exploiting the feminine stereotype that in other ways they resented, invoking peace because it seemed as unobjectionable as motherhood and mother's apple pie.

When the United States itself went to war, however, this tactic suddenly lost its convenience. The public mood turned bellicose; pacifists and even skeptics were being harassed, jailed, sometimes lynched. Amid such a context, the case for suffrage as a deterrent to war seemed at best untimely, at worst disloyal. Indeed, suffragists were asking in 1917, Must we subordinate our own crusade to Wilson's until the war ends? Yes, the leaders of NAWSA answered. Although many suffragists had ardently supported the peace movement, they had always put the vote at the top of their life's agenda. Even before Congress declared war, the NAWSA Executive Council proclaimed that suffragists would dedicate their services to the government. They would campaign for the vote "as a war measure," as a part of the larger campaign that Wilson had undertaken. (Symbolic of the new policy, Anna Howard Shaw agreed to serve, under the secretary of war, as director of the Woman's Committee of the Council of National Defense.)[37]

It was a political move, typical of the NAWSA approach ever since the turn of the century. But, in seeking to head off an antisuffrage attack under patriotic guise, it provoked angry splits among the suffragists themselves. Fourteen of NAWSA's Executive Council dissented, in private and in vain. A group within the New York State Woman Suffrage Party objected bitterly and also publicly, refusing to devote their energies to the war effort. They resigned "until such time as it shall again be a Woman Suffrage Party." Massachusetts suffrage leaders felt "many heart-burnings," one of them wrote to a friend, and as a consequence their work virtually halted. Similar consternation and schism troubled almost every NAWSA chapter. Meanwhile, the National Woman's Party —true to the militancy that had caused its secession five years before—announced that it would continue to fight single-mindedly for the vote. In fact, war or no war the Woman's Party maintained its pickets outside the White House, a decision that provoked numerous res-

ignations by those members who felt that such tactics were unprag-
matic or even unpatriotic.[38]

Events proved NAWSA's political wisdom. On the one hand, most
of its followers soon accepted the policy and donated strenuous war
service to the Red Cross, army relief, or similar efforts. As they earned
public admiration for their patriotic activities, they also earned it indirectly for the suffrage cause. In the light of their well-publicized work,
the accusations by antis that suffrage leaders advocated pacifism and
"pro-Germanism" seemed preposterous, if not hysterical. And meanwhile the drive for the vote continued its momentum, using whatever
energies the women could spare.[39]

On the other hand, the Woman's Party provoked such fierce public
hostility that it probably lost more than it gained for its ultimate objective. In June 1917, for example, two Woman's Party leaders stood
outside the White House as envoys from Kerensky's Russia arrived for
a conference with Wilson. They were holding a banner proclaiming:
"We, the women of America, tell you that America is not a democracy.
Twenty million American women are denied the right to vote. President
Wilson is the chief opponent of their national enfranchisement." An angry crowd milled around the pickets. "Why don't you take that banner
to Berlin?" one woman cried. "You are helping Germany," another
added. A man stepped in front of the crowd and shouted: "Won't the police pull that thing down?" "Can't you wait," a policeman responded,
notebook in hand, "until I finish copying this [banner]?" But the crowd
couldn't wait, and tore the banner to shreds. No arrests were made. Two
days later the police began arresting, not the assailants, but the pickets.[40]

To the proverbial man (and woman) on the street, the Woman's
Party was not a passionate advocate of equality, but an agent of sub-
version. True, the brutal jail treatment of arrested pickets (such as
forced feeding of hunger strikers) evoked temporary sympathy; to that
extent the public still considered the militants to be women. But this
sympathy did not displace the prevalent patriotic outrage. Consequently, the leaders of NAWSA objected to the picketing as "the greatest drawback to woman suffrage of any form of opposition that has ever
been employed. The anti-suffragists have never done anything which
has so blocked the progress of the suffrage movement in the last three
or four years." Even liberal spokesmen such as the *New Republic* editors
beseeched the Woman's Party to call off its pickets.[41]

The war diverted and divided the suffragists. But for some of them it created a more subtle anguish, because it threatened their personal sense of a woman's role as creator and nurturer of life. The prewar suffragist propaganda, in other words, was not entirely opportunistic. When it invoked motherhood and womanly instinct for peace, it expressed some authentic emotions. Ten days after Wilson's war message in 1917, a vice-president of the Ohio Woman Suffrage Association wrote to her friend and fellow suffragist in Massachusetts, Grace Johnson: "It makes me ill to think of the New York suffrage women carrying enlistment poster [sic] around, getting babies to go to war, boys not old enough to know their own minds." Mrs. Johnson replied with even greater pain: "I was told the other day that it was 'ignoble' for me to desire to save these boys, mine and others, from fighting, and injury and death. The habit of protecting them was formed too long ago to be dropped in a moment, or to seem 'ignoble' so soon. I feel as if all my anchors were swept away and as if the charts were all topsy turvy. . . . Every mother of straight, sound sons need [sic] sympathy."[42]

It was women such as these for whom Jeannette Rankin, the first congresswoman, had spoken during the roll-call vote on war. Allegedly with tears filling her eyes, she uttered an almost inaudible "Nay." The feminists who were rallying behind Wilson's crusade often seemed to go out of their way to deny that Rankin represented all American women, as if they were ashamed of her feminine tears—or uncertain about their own emotions as they "mobilized womanpower" in support of the men at the front. What did it mean to be a feminist in the midst of war? Did emancipation from the traditional female confinements also entail denial of "feminine" qualities, such as protectiveness toward sons and horror of bloodshed? Feminist patriots were confused. "At heart we are all pacifists," wrote the editor of the General Federation of Women's Clubs *Magazine* in mid-1917. As women, she continued, the club members would "love to talk it all over with the warmakers." But, alas, they would not understand; during war, words lost their force. "So we give our men gladly, unselfishly, patriotically, since the world chooses to settle its disputes in the old barbarous ways." The million club members would dedicate their organized energies to war work. Yet women were also proud, the editorial concluded, of the pacifist minority, who would not commit murder and who thereby would provide the leaven for a new and better civilization after the war ended.[43]

The editorial zigzagged in honest confusion, true to the ambivalence that beset its author and innumerable other American feminists. The war accentuated the uncertainties that had emerged ever since the woman's rights movement had begun demanding changes in gender definitions. Women should be equal to men—that had been the constant battle cry. But to what extent should "equal" mean "the same"? For some realms the feminists found an easy answer. Women should have the same power to vote, the same legal rights, the same employment opportunities at the same rate of pay (although with special protective legislation), and the same educational opportunities. For more subjective values, however, the answers were not so easy—particularly as the war seemed simultaneously to reinforce the traditional manliness and to open untraditional possibilities for women. Among these possibilities, it seemed, was the chance for female workers to prove that they were "as good as men." Or was it really, some wondered, as *bad* as men—as efficiently and passionately murderous as the war-makers? Likewise, what about the girls who were reciprocating the lust of the average soldier? Here was that old problem of the double standard, now more problematic than ever. While many girls seemed eager to adopt a single male standard of sexuality, many of their mothers—still loyal to a Victorian code of purity—forsook their role as the pacifist "better half" and worked in munitions factories. What, indeed, did equality mean?

BEFORE THE ARMISTICE, SUCH questions troubled only a few feminists, generally on a submerged level. Most of these women felt that they had worked out a satisfactory part to play in Wilson's crusade. They managed to support the war effort with less extravagant patriotism and more respect for pacifists than antifeminists demonstrated.[44] In addition, they felt confident that they were winning from the war not simply the Wilsonian hope of a world made safe for internationalism, but also the much more tangible victories of Prohibition and suffrage. The Eighteenth Amendment was ratified in 1919, the Nineteenth in 1920. Combined with the breakthroughs that women apparently had made in employment, these two legal achievements inspired feminists to foresee the coming of true equality at last. The woman's rights movement seemed to have completed the agenda that those bold ladies had declared at Seneca Falls seventy years before.

Feminists were not the only ones who discerned a transformation of sex roles. Journalist Isaac Marcosson told the 2 million readers of the

Ladies' Home Journal that women had demonstrated unmistakably that they were not the weaker half but an equally competent half, whom men would have to respect after the war as partners rather than submissive assistants. The *Saturday Evening Post* made the same point with greater force: "Only an especially Bourbon type of mind can repeat that woman's sphere is in the home and society will disintegrate unless she is confined there." Newspapers from Seattle to Baltimore to Memphis were confident that most women would and should hold on to the jobs that they had obtained in place of men. Perhaps the editors of the *Delineator* defined the prevalent attitude most succinctly. Men have always tried to keep women on the so-called feminine side of the fence, the editors noted, but "the fence has a very large hole in it, which daily becomes larger." However much some might deny or protest, the trend of events was clear. "Only Heaven can help the men now."[45]

II/
The
Modern Era
(1920–1998)

5/
New Generations

There were many kinds of American deaths during the First World War—not only 115,000 doughboys, not only the Wilsonian illusions of worldwide capitalist democracy, but also the Victorian concepts of manliness and womanliness. The men who returned home found themselves in a bewilderingly new culture. Amid the raucous beat of the Jazz Age, the flapper danced and drank and smoked, talked bluntly about sex and often did something about it, demanded the right to a home *and* a career. In short, she was saying that she was as good (or as bad) as any man.

The flapper brought with her a sudden shift of cultural generations. Older feminists regarded her as a traitor to their ideals of equality. Men responded with discomfort or dismay. They still understood their identity in old-fashioned manly terms—as patriarch of the breakfast table, as breadwinner in the market place, as roughrider on the range.

These notions were becoming daydreams, however. An increasingly liberated younger generation of middle-class women was overturning the Victorian code of "purity." An increasingly urbanized, bureaucratized society was rendering patriarchy into a masculine mystique. In the history of American gender roles, the 1920s marked the beginning of modernity. The old questions of equality were being asked in post-Victorian terms—especially in the case of women, less so in the case of men. From their answers—or, rather, their lack of answers—we can take lessons for ourselves, caught as we are in the turbulent middle age of gender modernity.

AT LAST IT WAS DONE! WOMEN had finally gotten the right to vote. And what next? "When we contemplate the social and political storms that are going to burst in cyclonic fury upon this country when all these pretty girls get to voting and mixing up in politics," the McMinnville, Tennessee, *Southern Standard* announced, "we rather rejoice that life is short and that we haven't many more years to tarry here." But it was precisely this prospect of "mixing up" that roused suffragists to ardent optimism. Women now had the chance, they declared, "to strike out a new political method, not dominated by party, in which social and moral values shall outweigh all others." Female voters would raise politics as well as socioeconomic conditions from masculine dregs of corruption, selfishness, and injustice. Of course it would not happen all at once, they added quickly. Nor would it come without a struggle. Women could not await progress, but must make it.[1]

Impelled by this vision, the suffrage leaders immediately began putting it to work, only to find themselves fighting one another, fighting confusion, and soon fighting an ominous despair. The conflict swirled primarily around the question "How?"—the question of strategy. But inescapably it entered the question "Who?"—the question of female self-definitions. For neither of these could the former suffragists find satisfactory answers.

Even before the Nineteenth Amendment was ratified, NAWSA was converting itself to the League of Women Voters. As Carrie Chapman Catt handed over the leadership to her old friend Maud Wood Park, she rallied league members for a "crusade" to make an intelligent electorate, to democratize the political parties, and to obtain legislation protecting women and children. "The only way" to reach these objectives, Catt said, "is to get them done on the inside of a political party." The men in power would try to lock the door, but "you must move right up to the center." It was the same lesson that Catt had always preached and practiced: organize, infiltrate the power structure, and meanwhile educate, educate, educate.

When they had been fighting for the vote, most suffragists outside the Woman's Party had readily followed this strategy. In the 1920s, however, they divided and debated. If women joined the established political system, leaders like Jane Addams argued, they would forsake the distinctive identity and interests that they had as a sex. Their social idealism would be absorbed by the broils of partisan politics. The League of Women Voters, this faction contended, should neither integrate men into its membership (contrary to a suggestion by Catt) nor integrate itself into the regular two-party system.[2]

How, then, were women to exert political force? For Alice Paul and her followers, the logical answer was a third party, a party of and for women, a party that would support female candidates and would fight for the interests of their constituency. "Only women," Paul insisted, "can really put our program before anything else."[3]

That was an answer, but not for the league. As usual, Paul's logic was too fierce for most former suffragists (including many of her own followers). They too chose a separatist rather than an assimilationist route, but they preferred forming a "bloc" instead of a party. They hoped to win women's rights without a sex war. Mrs. Gifford Pinchot, for example, endorsed the idea of appointing women in numbers equal to men within the Democratic and Republican committees, but she worried about stirring up "latent sex antagonism." Along with numerous other NAWSA veterans, she insisted that women politicians should be chosen for their talents rather than their gender, and that they should represent constituents male as well as female. Most liberals outside the league heartily agreed with this critique of a women's party. "Even the women voters are more than women in these days," the *Nation* observed. "They are citizens, they are workers, farmers, housekeepers, not only females and voters."[4]

Inside the issue of strategy, however, was the even more explosive issue of goals. Specifically, the ideological gunpowder lay packed in the eighteen words of the Equal Rights Amendment (ERA): "Men and women shall have equal rights throughout the United States and every place subject to its jurisdiction." Soon after the Nineteenth Amendment was ratified, the Woman's Party proposed this new amendment as the way to end, immediately, all remaining legal distinctions between men and women, especially in employment, property, and divorce. The ERA would serve as the direct road to sexual equality. But social-welfare reformers were not so sure. What about maximum-hour and minimum-wage laws for women, they asked? In the name of equal rights, they said, the Woman's Party would wipe out these hard-won legal protections and expose women once again to economic exploitation.

Protection disguises discrimination, replied the Woman's Party. To "protect" some women is to penalize all women. This paternalistic legislation classifies the whole female sex as weak and dependent, handicapping individuals in their competition with men. As a result of so-called "protective" legislation, women printers were fired because they

couldn't work at night, and women streetcar conductors were fired because the work was too hard. If a woman wants to work at night or for
twelve hours at a stretch, why shouldn't she?

Easy for upper-middle-class women to say, replied the protectionists. The privileged members of the Woman's Party can afford to advocate equal competition, but factory women and laundresses have fewer
resources and options. They lack the protection that male workers receive through unions, so they must depend on the protection of laws.
Moreover, some protectionists argued, it is a question not only of class,
but biology. Nature has made women and men different in terms of
physical stamina and childbearing, and no constitutional amendment
can make them the same. Identical treatment will only produce unequal results. "A fair field and no favor—equal rights for women, nothing more"—these, said Florence Kelley, were "the slogans of the insane."

ERA versus protective legislation. The Woman's Party versus the
League of Women Voters, the Women's Bureau, the Women's Trade
Union League, and the General Federation of Women's Clubs. By 1922
the lines were drawn, and until the 1960s they remained locked in bit-
terness. At issue was not simply political strategy, but fundamental definitions of women as a gender. Year after year for a half century, Alice
Paul's Woman's Party gave single-minded, wholehearted attention to
the ERA. Anything else (whether birth control, disarmament, or maternal health) seemed a distraction from the goal of sexual equality; anything less than identical legal rights meant a subtraction from the principle of equality. In taking this stance, the party was once again on the
fringe of women's politics. The vast majority of activists in the 1920s
(and indeed until the 1960s) opposed the ERA. Despite the logical
problems of advocating equal rights via unequal treatment—or to put
it more harshly, despite the risk of opposing sexism in the abstract
while using it to support certain laws—they made ready to win the rewards of suffrage.[5]

At first the future seemed bright. The leaders of the League of
Women Voters enthusiastically launched their new organization in a
program of legislative lobbying and civic education. On the one hand,
they joined with sister groups in the Women's Joint Congressional
Committee to lobby on Capitol Hill for the passage of numerous protective federal laws, most notably the Shepard-Towner Act on behalf
of maternal and infant health. At the same time, league chapters,

women's clubs, and other groups were lobbying successfully in state legislatures on behalf of wage-and-hour laws, jury service, property rights of married women, and other reforms. On the other hand, local and state leagues scheduled innumerable lectures and institutes and study groups and forums and radio shows to educate women about public issues.

The achievements were exhilarating when they came, but they were not sufficient to dispel the gloom that was beginning to seep among the women activists. By mid-decade, lobbying efforts were colliding against legislative indifference on federal as well as state levels. Even friendly congressmen were advising the female pressure groups to ease up because Congress was tired of spending on behalf of women and children. Frustrated and desperate, the groups began to quarrel with each other, Republican versus Democrat, League of Women Voters versus Federation of Women's Clubs, in what Catt privately called a "subterranean, secret, maligning, lying, and thoroughly dishonorable" enmity. This was mild feuding, however, compared to the warfare that erupted over the ERA. As the Woman's Party launched its adamant campaign and other women's agencies mounted their counter-campaign, personal friendships splintered, conferences turned into shouting matches, and angry denunciations ricocheted back and forth in the public press.[6] So much for hopes of a "women's bloc."

The political fortunes of the equal-rights movement were also dwindling in other ways. The number of female delegates to national party conventions dropped sharply between 1924 and 1928, and their already minuscule membership on convention committees was cut in half. In state legislatures, the sharp increase of women (quadrupling to 141 by 1925) seemed very promising, but it stopped throughout the rest of the decade. Of those few who held higher office as governors or congresswomen, the vast majority were inheritors of their deceased husbands' positions rather than champions of equal rights. "I am myself old fashioned enough to believe that the real ideal of women is in the home and in motherhood"—thus spoke Mrs. Nellie Taylor Ross, governor of Wyoming, the first woman governor in American history. "It is clear," confessed the *Woman Citizen*, "that the barriers in the way of women being elected to any political office are almost unsurmountable." What should be done? the editors asked aloud, and replied wistfully: it is "an extremely difficult question."[7]

Educate, educate, educate—that was the old suffragist answer. As their lobbying activities became stymied, the league leaders gave more and more attention to the training of women voters. By the end of the decade, in fact, President Belle Sherwin was telling her national convention that "the League has become a living organism of education." This strategic retreat, however, ran into consequences even more demoralizing than those of the political efforts. If lobbying failed, the women could at least blame men. But educational activities uncovered the disquieting evidence that women themselves cared little, if at all, about the opportunity for which three generations of suffragists had struggled. In the heyday of its campaign, NAWSA had had 2 million members; during the 1920s, the League of Women Voters held on to perhaps one-tenth that number, tripling its expenditures over the decade without expanding its membership beyond this static tenth. The Woman's Party, meanwhile, remained an even narrower cadre of fewer than 8,000. As president Sherwin soberly told her league followers in 1925, women not only remained ignorant of elementary political processes, but they also did not care to learn. "One would give up if one did not know that this is the way the world advances," Sherwin concluded.[8]

The forward motion was so slow, however, that only a most optimistic eye could see it. In 1920, in New York, "the better half" cast only one-third of the total vote. Three years later, in Chicago's mayoral election, they cast only one-fourth. Why did they stay home on Election Day? Because, a sample of nonvoting women told two political scientists, they were not interested in politics, because their husbands had failed to remind them, and especially because they did not believe that women should vote. Eleven percent specifically said that females should stay home and leave politics to men. Elsewhere in the nation the same apathy prevailed, sucking relentlessly at the activists' confidence.

It all was "rather disappointing, don't you think so," they confided to each other, seeking solace. Some quit politics altogether. The Federation of Women's Clubs took up a program of home economics, no longer campaigning for protective legislation, but for wider use of home appliances. The remainder continued their political work, full citizens at last, but chastened by what they had learned not only about the resistance by male politicians, but also about the passivity of their sister citizens. "If we could only change our opinion of ourselves," Anne Martin lamented after her two unsuccessful candidacies for the Nevada

Senate, "our shackles would drop off instantly."[9] The celebration of suffrage had become a wake.

IT WAS THE SAME STORY IN THE world of employment.* After the surge of female workers during the war, some feminists proclaimed that "breaking into the human race has been accomplished." But the future betrayed them. At the beginning of the decade, one-fourth of women were working; at the end of the decade, one-fourth of women were working. And most of these were servants, waitresses, factory hands, salespersons, and secretaries, who had entered employment not as emancipation from domesticity, not as the avenue toward a new self-definition, but as economic necessity. They worked because they had to. Economic coercion weighed with particular force upon those working women who were married. Most of them took jobs because their husbands earned not enough or nothing at all; one of every seven employed homemakers in 1930 was the sole wage earner for her family.[10]

The feminist gospel of salvation by work still applied primarily to that upper-middle-class minority of women who entered business and the professions. But here, too, the feminists found the evidence of failure. To be sure, there were those 100,000 female newcomers on the business scene, working in banks and real-estate offices and elsewhere—a ten-year rise of 50 percent, larger than in any other occupational category except domestic service and twice the rate of increase of the general female population. But they still huddled within the "feminine" ghettos of the employment world. The overwhelming majority of female professionals, in the 1920s as in the 1890s, were teachers or nurses; the overwhelming majority of businesswomen were typists, clerks, and salespersons. Even after the numbers of female authors, photographers, draftsmen, architects, certified public accountants, and realtors doubled, they constituted a mere 2 percent of all women in business and professions. The 11,000 women dentists and physicians, meanwhile, actually dwindled by more than 1,000.[11]

Outside of the familiar feminine havens, it remained a man's world, and most men wanted to keep it that way. Feminists had won the right to vote beside men, but not the right to work beside them. Law schools from Harvard to Mercer excluded females. More than one-third of all

---

*For a statistical table on the female labor force from 1890 to 1990, see Appendix A.

medical schools had never graduated a woman, and more than 90 percent of hospitals refused to admit female interns. At coeducational colleges, only 4 percent of the faculty were female; at twenty-nine men's colleges, there were exactly two women professors. Bank officials were pleased with the work of the female clerks whom they had hired during wartime labor shortages, but the *Commercial and Financial Chronicle* assured its readers that "no one has an idea that a woman will eventually become a banker." In every field and at every level, meanwhile, women earned less than men.[12]

The barricades of discrimination remained high against a woman who wanted to enter a career. If she was married, they were even more formidable. Wives, said one bank vice-president, were "too independent and hard to manage for business purposes." They had husbands to fall back on, he explained, and so they did not give wholehearted commitment to the job. Furthermore, employers argued, one must consider the effects on family life. "There can be no real homes," according to one business executive, "when women are away from them all day and every day, and return to them at night as dog-tired as their husbands." These prejudices operated even in the "feminine" occupation of teaching; 60 percent of the school boards flatly refused to hire a woman if she was married. Despite these obstacles, the proportion of married women in the labor force increased 60 percent in the twenties, triple the rate of increase of all female workers. Although many of these wives were entering domestic service jobs, even more were entering white-collar fields. But in 1930 they were still a small minority. Of all employed women, 29 percent were married; of professionals, less than 20 percent.[13]

By the late 1920s feminists were discouraged. Their sex was no closer to "breaking into the human race" than it had been ten or even twenty years earlier. The attitudes of men had not changed—that was discouraging enough. The attitudes of young women, on the other hand, seemed to have changed in the wrong direction, away from the doctrine of salvation by work—that was discouraging to the point of despair. When feminists looked at college campuses, where they had learned to emancipate themselves from the "womanly" role, they were appalled by what they saw. To be sure, more women were attending college than ever before, and women were earning a larger share of bachelor degrees than ever before. But the meaning of higher education seemed to have diminished from the days of intellectual pioneers like Carey Thomas. Instead of ascetic dedication to equality, the feminists found a spirit of fun. Even at women's colleges, students seemed concerned with enjoying themselves rather than proving themselves.

Their behavior after graduation dismayed feminists still more. In striking contrast to their predecessors, a majority of alumnae in the 1920s quickly married—in some colleges, a majority that reached 80 or 90 percent.[14] From the perspective of older alumnae, so many of whom had scorned marriage as a surrender of self-esteem, these young women had forsaken the feminist faith. Nor were the elders assured by the fact that most college graduates in the twenties took not only husbands, but jobs as well. For the young were going to work with motives that seemed unfeminist. One Vassar newlywed, for example, returned from her Bermuda honeymoon and settled into being a homemaker—for three days. "I simply couldn't stick it," she explained. "By 10 o'clock in the morning the apartment was all cleaned, and there I'd be, with nothing to do until [my husband] returned at night." So she became an assistant buyer at a department store, but she still asserted that "I certainly don't work because I think I ought to." No ringing principles inspired her or most of her employed classmates. According to Chase Going Woodhouse's survey in 1927, of almost eight hundred married alumnae in business or the professions, three of every five worked first of all for economic reasons. Only a handful—twenty-nine, to be exact—mentioned a career or idealistic principle as their motive, and even these few spoke in nonmilitant terms such as "all my friends worked" or "to justify the expenses of my training." In this context, the four women who sought to "maintain my individuality" seemed very eccentric. "The day of the old style feminist is passing," Woodhouse concluded.[15]

Suffragists had thought that with the Nineteenth Amendment they had marked a turning point in the history of American women, only to find that history had somehow turned upon them. They had become outdated. Feminism as a whole, it seemed, was outdated. "Emancipated" women of the 1920s did not preach the gospel of work; they did not join in angry indictments of "parasitism" or in glorious visions of self-discovery through a career. The ideology of orthodox feminism found few followers among the postwar young, the supposed successors to Adams and Catt and Paul. Feminist leaders had imagined themselves in the vanguard of female progress, but as early as 1923 they seemed to have been shunted onto a siding. Down the main track rode a new generation of women, younger women, who barely noticed their heroic elders or, if they did, scorned them as "either the old school of fighting feminists who wore flat heels and had very little feminine charm, or the current species who antagonize men with their constant clamor about . . . equal rights." The young had no use for parades, campaigns, ideologies.

A generational split had occurred, and it brought feminism to a halt. So said most people at the time; so say most historians. Understandably, feminist leaders were baffled and embittered by this trick of fate. They were only partly correct, however, in thinking that their principles had become obsolete, just as the obituaries by later historians have mistaken a part of the truth for the whole. Reports of the death of feminism were greatly exaggerated. Although women's political and economic progress stagnated in the twenties and the organized women's movement fell apart, the doctrine of equality did not die. It survived among the younger generation in a revised version, less ideological but no less resolute than prewar orthodox feminism.

Instead of asking, "Should I choose work or marriage?" the young were asking, "How can I combine them?" Carey Thomas and Charlotte Perkins Gilman and Ruth Benedict had writhed in the anguish of a forced choice. The "newest new woman" (as one *Ladies' Home Journal* writer called her) refused to be forced. "It dates our [prewar] marriage," a woman remarked in *Women's Home Companion* in 1925, "that there should have been discussion about my keeping on with my work. Today in our circle[,] which likes to consider itself progressive[,] it would be a foregone conclusion that I should."[16]

The "woman question" was still being asked, but more in private than in public. The focus had shifted to the intersection between home and career and to male-female relationships. There, more removed from the public eye, the traditional roles of women (and men) were being questioned in lively fashion. And the younger generation was doing most of the asking.

ON THE EVE OF THE TWENTIES the editors of the *Smith College Weekly* enunciated the doctrine of revised feminism: "We cannot believe that it is fixed in the nature of things that a woman must choose between a home and her work, when a man may have both. There must be a way out and it is the problem of our generation to find the way."[17] It was a hopeful theory, but no more than that. The women of "our generation" would have to demonstrate, amid the daily circumstances of their adult lives, whether and how it could be put into practice.

The circumstances seemed unpromising. Childless women in the 1920s typically spent between forty-three and fifty hours per week in the routine of cooking, cleaning, mending, and shopping, less if they lived in cities, but more on farms. When children appeared, the job increased. For mothers the average work week reached a total of fifty-six hours—that is, an eight-hour day, Monday through Sunday (but, among farm families, ten hours in winter, thirteen in summer). Even the labor-saving home appliances saved little labor, and a surprising number of families in the decade of radios and airplanes were still living in primitive conditions. One-quarter of the homes in Cleveland, for example, lacked running water and stationary laundry tubs; two-thirds in Indianapolis; and nine-tenths in Atlanta. Across the nation, one home of every six had no kitchen sink, one-fifth had no flush toilet, and three-quarters had no electric washing machine. Electric irons and sewing machines were becoming fairly common, but their contribution was counterbalanced by the disappearance of full-time servants. Of course, middle-class housewives tended toward the privileged end of all these averages; but even they did not escape much of the sweat and exhaustion embodied within these dry statistics. At home they were doing a job that was—compared to their husbands—more than full time.[18]

How, then, were they to combine paid employment with domestic responsibilities? The usual middle-class answer was to defer it until the children reached school age. "I don't do anything but the baby," Elsie Hill wrote to an old friend in 1925. "My baby is exquisite—fifteen weeks old—13 lbs. 6 oz. of the most enchanting squeals and murmurings as she lies in her crib alone in her room." The letter, filled with rapturous descriptions of nursing and other details, is not what one would have expected of Hill five years earlier, when she was a national organizer for the militant Woman's Party. But she had not forsaken feminism for diapers. She ended the letter to her comrade of picketing days with the salutation "blessing you for the work 'for all women,'" and by the 1930s she was working once again at Woman's Party headquarters. Hill's biography exemplifies the solution that many other women adopted in the postwar decade. By regarding motherhood as only a phase of their careers, they extended the female role far beyond Victorian definitions. As one feminist mother and career woman said, instead of being thrust into the state of wifehood they were choosing "wife-ing it" as one profession among others.

Many women, however, could not divide their lives so easily. Having learned in college or employment to think of themselves as persons with talent and purpose, they balked against the domestic rhythm. Dishes that were cleaned after lunch became dirty during supper, laundry that was washed on Monday had to be washed again on Friday—an endless cycle of mechanical tasks punctuated by the staccato demands of children. "So goes the morning. So go many many days. So go the years. Why," Margaret Dunaway lamented in her journal, "why do I long for Achievement?" Fearful that "my pent-up thoughts would wreak some sort of destruction," she wrote poetry—or tried to. "I sit down to my desk in the morning, rejoicing that I may write an hour, but the big boy needs a letter of admonition and encouragement. The little girl needs a bunny rabbit stitched to take to school for completion and the elder sister must have a good hot lunch as she eats no breakfast." But she would not relent. "I shall do it all"—housekeeping, mothering, social duties—"and still find a little corner of nearly every day just for my own." Seven years later, she published a volume of poetry.

Compelled less by creative needs than by a furious boredom, Edith Clark took a part-time job writing newspaper articles at home. But every fifteen minutes she had to stop typing in order to tend the tears of her young son, or advise the nursemaid about the laundry, or praise her daughter's kindergarten homework, or contend with a chatty neighbor. "I have become of necessity," Clark wrote, "a bovine creature who has foregone completely the joy of having nerves or temperament." Nevertheless, "I hang on like grim death to my newspaper job," craving even that bit of independent income and achievement which she could call her own.[19]

One might see these as success stories except that the success came with such painful penalties. Was emotional desperation or emotional numbness what a woman must undergo if she wanted to live in both "spheres"? According to many employed middle-class mothers, it was. "The self-supporting wife who wants to keep her job and wants to keep her home, must sacrifice even her sense of sacrificing. It is the price she pays."[20] But such stoicism only removed the dilemma of a Carey Thomas or a Ruth Benedict to another sacrificial level, now *with* husband and children. It did not dissolve the dilemma, and thus, for less strenuously heroic women, it did not offer a way out of domesticity. If the principle of equal female opportunity was to become practicable, a wife and mother also needed some sort of help outside of her own inner strength.

Servants would have been the most effective resource in earlier generations, and they still were for a privileged 5 percent of American families. When the *Woman Citizen* ran a series of "how-to" articles by the "home-plus-job woman," for example, every one of the contributors employed a maid or nurse. The vast majority of their audience lacked that kind of daily domestic help, but all of them possessed another: a husband.

What might he do for the home besides winning the bread? According to a survey of 650 career women across the country, three-quarters of their husbands were taking a share of household chores. A few went even further, like the YWCA secretary's husband who bathed and dressed their children each morning, took the son to kindergarten, and cared for them on Saturdays. Still fewer couples went further yet, beyond the husband's voluntary contributions and to the principle of equal division of responsibilities. In these fifty-fifty marriages, each spouse pursued career, each paid an equal share of the family budget or a share proportionate to their respective incomes, and each did one-half of the household jobs and child care. Such instances of equality were exceedingly rare, of course, and they had their own kinds of tensions. But that they were happening at all, and were being reported to the 2 million ladies/women who read their monthly *Journal* or *Companion*, suggests how earnestly the home-and-career problem was being confronted.[21]

These were still individual efforts, though, whether by a wife alone or with her husband's cooperation. In order to succeed even among this adventurous minority, not to speak of the conventional majority, they needed institutional kinds of support: day-care centers at the least, and perhaps community kitchens and professional house cleaners too. These had been the banners of Charlotte Perkins Gilman's lonely twenty-year crusade during the era of old feminism. At last, in the era of revised feminism, her day seemed to have come. Public discussion of Gilman-like proposals was widespread, in women's clubs and women's colleges, in family magazines and books for the general public. And not only talk, but action as well. From Syracuse, New York, to a remote county of New Mexico, municipal kitchens, community canneries, and similar ventures began to appear. Child-care facilities were also developing. The 3 nursery schools operating in 1920 had multiplied to 25 in 1924, and then to 262 by 1929, teaching 4,000 children in 121 different cities. As for the less formal day-care centers, these probably numbered in the thousands. Mothers, at least urban mothers, no longer had to raise their young children entirely at home.

Nor were they *expected* to do so. Although scientific child-rearing advice rained as heavily and didactically upon mothers as it had since the advent of Mother's Day and before, during the mid-twenties the burden of that advice shifted significantly. The problem was not too little mothering, the columnists asserted; it was too much. "Smother love" would make children overly dependent, emotionally immature. As remedies, the experts recommended a larger role for fathers, a diversification of interests by mothers outside the home, and even the use of nursery schools. Mothers may have remained confused and anxious about how to raise a good child, but increasingly they were also relieved that the responsibility need not be entirely their own.[22]

Circumstances, both institutional and attitudinal, seemed more and more favorable for eventually dissolving the feminist dilemma of home versus career. "There must be a way out," the student editors of the *Smith College Weekly* had insisted in 1919. Six years later, the Smith administration established the Institute for the Coordination of Women's Interests to pave that way. The institute director was Ethel Puffer Howes, a Smith alumna of the Victorian 1890s, who had gone on to a successful "double life" as philosopher, author, and mother of two children. What Howes had done for herself she now hoped the institute would do for others, namely, "integrate the women's normal family life with a genuine continuous intellectual interest." To reach that goal, she and her staff created a cooperative nursery school, communal kitchen, communal laundry, and other model institutions. This was not a grandiose version of home economics, Howes emphasized. To be sure, she was working on the assumption that homemaking would be part of every woman's life, that, indeed, it was *"a way of life."* Yet she wanted to prepare women for that function, not by "life-adjustment" courses, but by intensive intellectual study and a revolutionized structure of the home.

It was a difficult distinction, acknowledging women in their traditional domestic role, but simultaneously crediting them with more extensive capabilities. Only a small but ideologically crucial distance lay between the feminist program of "coordination" and the feminine notion of a woman's proper sphere. Vassar College, for example, set up a School of Euthenics in 1924 in order to "raise motherhood to a profession worthy of [woman's] finest talents and greatest intellectual gifts," but this starched rhetoric barely concealed the gauzy presumptions of producing "gracious and intelligent wives and mothers." Howes would find it hard to make people understand the difference between "domestic science" and "coordination." Intellectually, the old-style feminism was simpler in offering women a polar choice between private and public roles, but it was thereby also narrower. In the revised feminist version lay more ambiguity and also more promise.[23]

That was 1925. Six years later the Institute for the Coordination of Women's Interests had closed its doors, while home economics was flourishing—not only at state-supported colleges, but increasingly within the once fiercely intellectual women's colleges. It may be "a little out of keeping with our cultural atmosphere," Mount Holyoke students remarked, but they nevertheless wanted a course in "plain everyday cooking, taught from a scientific point of view." No man can eat Latin, a Smith student said tartly. Meanwhile, Wheaton opened a nursery school as a laboratory in child care, and Vassar's course in "food chemistry" was bluntly renamed "nutrition." Increasingly the male presidents of female colleges and the male editors of female magazines were congratulating women for having proved their intellectual equality with men; at last, they said, women could attend once again to their special interests as "the other half." To which the young women nodded in agreement. Fifty-five to 65 percent in 1930 told interviewers that they preferred marriage to a career. How about combining the two? A majority replied that they did not believe it possible. Coordination had become euthenics. The promise of the mid-twenties had recoiled to Victorian platitudes.[24]

It was not, as they say, merely an academic question. The curricular trend expressed the mood of middle-class women far away from campus life. "Personally, I'm rather tired of rights," the first woman member of the American Bar Association told her fellow attorneys. "I'd love to have a few privileges. In all, I would say that women have lost a great deal in the process of becoming emancipated." A female journalist found the same feeling among most career women in 1930. No one believed that latchkeys and economic independence opened the door to happiness, she reported. "The very word 'career' is suspect, and you are much more likely to hear a discussion of 'the job.'" After all, exclaimed an industrial researcher in her mid-thirties, what had feminist ardor won for her except the exhausting double burden of home and employment! As the decade turned, people were talking about a drift back to the home.[25]

WHAT HAD GONE WRONG? WHY HAD feminists failed to move forward? Gilman had a ready answer. In the fever of their emancipation, she said, "some classes of women" were rioting in "selfish and fruitless indulgence." Of course, one expects this behavior from a suddenly liberated class, she added, yet "it is sickening to see so many of the newly freed using that freedom in a mere imitation of masculine weaknesses and vices." Instead of taking "their opportunity, their power and their long-prevented sex duty—race improvement," she said bitterly, these women were following "the solemn philosophical sex-mania of Sigmund Freud." Looking around her in the postwar decade, Gilman deplored the "indecency" that women were promoting on the "masculine" assumption that "the purpose of sex is recreation."[26]

What had gone wrong? A large number of observers, some feminist and others nonfeminist, arrived along with Gilman at the same answer. It was, in a word—in *the* word of the day—"flappers." Those girls with bobbed hair and powdered noses, with fringed skirts just above the knees and hose rolled below, with a cigarette in one hand and a man in the other, those girls who checked their corsets in the coatroom before they danced to jazz, who later drove with men in fast cars and kissed or necked or petted with neither discretion nor apology, who were (in F. Scott Fitzgerald's phrase) "lovely and expensive and about nineteen." Almost before the last cannon shot had stopped echoing "over there," the flappers became—on this side of paradise—a prototype not only of the latest "new woman," but of a generation. "Whenever two or three elders were gathered together in the last year," a journalist wrote at the beginning of 1921, "there was somebody to whisper about the outrageous new customs of the outrageous new generation." Yes, the young women shouted back in capital letters, "WE ARE THE YOUNGER GENERATION." Novelists wrote about "flaming youth." Sociologists announced a "youth movement" and a generation "gulf." "The whole country," remarked one character in a best-selling novel of 1923, "has gone crazy over youth."[27]

A cultural generation does not live or die by the demographer's strict cycles; it occurs when enough people, then or later, perceive it or, more precisely, construe it. If opinion leaders declared and opinion followers agreed that there was a new generation born from the ashes of war, then there was. The birth was not quite that abrupt, of course. They were forgetting their consternation about "sex o'clock" having struck among youth long before the war. Fitzgerald's model flapper was nineteen years old in 1920, but she had learned her style from sisters five or ten years older, whose cigarettes and jazz and petting in American bohemia were arriving only now in Middletown. To people of the 1920s, however, history began with the war. As the lunatic fringe expanded toward the middle-class center, birth announcements of a "new generation" appeared.[28]

In choosing this label, spokesmen were articulating their sense of a cultural divide, the end of the Victorian era and the beginning of something else. In choosing to identify the generation with the flappers, they were giving an explanation as to who had created the divide. Women! Floyd Dell's novel *Moon-Calf* offered a potentially catchy epithet and character for a male partner to the flapper, but it never caught on. According to popular opinion, women alone were the agents of upheaval. If the movies, dramas, and novels were disgustingly salacious, the female audiences were responsible, because they tolerated or even applauded. If a Baptist minister was appalled by the spectacle of "two practically naked men, pounding and bruising each other and struggling in sweat and blood" at a prize fight, he was appalled primarily because women were cheering at ringside. If the flask and the speakeasy were the new emblems of an old sin, the drinking woman was especially stigmatized.

More alarming than any of these new facts of life was smoking— and this issue focused exclusively on women. "Time was, and well within current memory," the *New York Times* editorialized in 1925, when a cigarette's "illicit, faint perfume" appeared only in the shaded boudoir. "When the average sort of chap first saw a woman smoke he knew very well what he felt about her, even though he also knew that it wasn't true." During the 1920s women took their cigarettes out of the boudoirs into theater lobbies, movie houses, restaurants, art galleries, clubs, school and college lounges, railroad trains, and even the open street. Nothing stopped them—neither sermons nor editorials, city ordinances nor campus prohibitions, International Anti-Cigarette League resolutions nor school boards' dismissals. "I can't feel that a real genuine womanly girl would form the habit," asserted one dean of college women in 1922. But more and more girls did. Smoking "is the beginning of the end," said the superintendent of the National Reform Bureau, because "virtually all the male vices will be feminine vices, too." But with the end already under way, the moral upholders and uplifters found virtue in compromise. At Nantasket Beach, Massachusetts, one could read a sign of the times. In 1925 the town fathers authorized public smoking benches for women (the first in New England) with signs indicating: "Reserved for Ladies—(Smoking Permitted)."[29]

These matters were peripheral, though, to the center of the cultural storm, which was sexual conduct—or, more exactly, the sexual conduct of the female sex. When Warner Fabian wrote *Flaming Youth* (1923), his sensationalist best-seller about the immoralities and amoralities of the upper middle class, he dedicated the novel to "the woman of the period thus set forth. . . . To Her I dedicate this story of herself." If the youth of both sexes were aflame, the once better half had thrown the match. The problem that parents faced, according to Janet Richards's report in the *New York Times*, was how to save their sons from "the girl 'vamp.'" She personally knew of five boys who had gone to their mothers and said: "Mother, it is so hard for me to be decent and live up to the standards you have set me, and to always keep in mind the loveliness and purity of girls. How can I do it with this cheek dancing, and if I pull away they call me a prude. And when I take a girl home in the way that you have told me is the proper fashion she is not satisfied and thinks I am slow."[30]

Five boys and their girl friends hardly constitute a sample of American youth. But systematic studies by Terman, Kinsey, and other social scientists have confirmed Miss Richards's anecdote. The generation of women born between 1900 and 1909 did indeed take an abrupt fork in the history of sexual behavior as well as attitudes. The rate of premarital intercourse was twice as high among those born after 1900 as among those born before. One-half of the wives born during the first decade of the twentieth century, and two-thirds of those born during the next decade, had slept with at least one man before marriage. What is more, an increasing number of them (though less than a majority) had slept with men other than their future husbands. The virgin was on her way to becoming a Victorian period piece.

That alone permits us to announce a sexual revolution, but in some ways the truly revolutionary behavior of the 1920s took place not

at the barricade of virginity, but somewhere short of it, on the middle
ground of sexual play. Dating, for example. The pairing of a young man
and woman who are romantically interested in each other but who are
not necessarily or even likely to marry—this arrangement, so familiar
to us as to seem universal, was in fact an "invention" of the 1920s.
Whereas nineteenth-century young people socialized in groups and
paired off only when courting with an eye to marriage, 1920s youth
dated as couples, finding space away from parents and friends in order
to discover and enjoy each other.

Which brings us to the next aspect of the sexual revolution: petting. Whether it meant a kiss or a caress or something more, petting
held back from intercourse—safe but not sorry. This was certainly not a
postwar invention; just as youth of the 1920s petted, their parents had
spooned and, in fact, had done so at a rate almost as high as that
among the "flaming youth." The difference—the revolutionary difference—was not in behavior but attitudes. Whereas only the more unconventional Victorians had approved of erotic pleasure among unmarried people, the vast majority of middle-class youth in the Jazz
Age—especially on college campuses—had no qualms. "There are only
two kinds of co-eds," proclaimed the editor of Duke University's student
newspaper, "those who have been kissed and those who are sorry they
haven't been kissed." Attitudes toward premarital intercourse were
hardly so permissive, of course, but nonetheless strikingly affirmative.
By the 1930s, almost two-thirds of college women said they were willing to sleep with a man before marriage, and even more said they had
no objection to others' doing so. From the other side of the gender
line, a majority of college men said they would marry a woman who
was not a virgin. The double standard was far from dead, but in the
1920s it began to die.[31]

Female cigarette smoking jolted the Victorian value structure, but
female sexuality smashed it. For many of those who had come of age in
that other age, the 1920s was a time of dismay. These people included
a large number of older feminists, women of Gilman's generation, who
saw in the flappers a perverse betrayal of their egalitarian hopes. As
one mother wrote (anonymously), she had provided her daughter with
education, winter sports, symphony concerts, and European galleries,
only to discover that the girl had necked with a boy she did not really
love and had "'permitted liberties' that were dangerous to self-control,

that were vulgar." Just think, the mother exclaimed bitterly, "in the days of our innocency we all believed" that feminism's single standard would be women's, not men's.[32]

In her lament one hears an echo of maternal voices thirty and forty years earlier. "If I had had your opportunities when I was young, my dear," Mrs. Addams and countless other baffled women had said to feminist daughters who rebelled against ladyhood in the name of economic independence. In the 1920s another generation of daughters was rebelling against the Victorian sexual code built into that feminism. What Gilman or Addams called "idealism" the flappers scorned as "sentimentality" and "puritanism." When older feminists called for an end to the double standard on behalf of chastity, "this new woman only shrugs her shoulders and smiles a slow, penetrating secret smile." She too was demanding equality with men, but on men's terms: not only career *and* home, but sexual enjoyment before and during marriage.

"Are we as bad as we're painted?" asked an Ohio State University coed. "We are," she replied, and went on to say blithely why.

> We do all the things that our mothers, fathers, aunts and uncles do not sanction, and we do them knowingly. We are not young innocents—"we've got the dope" at our finger ends and we use it wisely for our own protection. . . .
>
> . . . The girl with sport in her blood . . . "gets by." She kisses the boys, she smokes with them, drinks with them, and why? because the feeling of comradeship is running rampant. . . . The girl does not stand aloof—she and the man meet on common ground, and yet can she not retain her moral integrity?[33]

Gilman and a shrill chorus of others, not all of them middle-aged, denounced the flapper generation. But a substantial number of Americans, after a momentary recoil, took a second look. Yes, they said, these modern young women "are often a little hard, aggressive and obvious, and lack that gentleness of bearing and softness of voice which are so pleasing to every one who prizes culture." Yes, their candor, their ironies, their slang and swagger, their nonchalant indulgences shock the traditional sensibilities. But what a refreshing change from the meek or petulant Victorian type, who lived within her dim upholstered sphere of migraine headaches! Moreover, what a relief from the shame

and hypocrisy bred by the sexual double standard! Like the old feminists themselves, their postsuffrage descendants showed "a certain
fearlessness and gallantry" as they pushed open the doors and windows of their lives and walked out into experience.

The difference was that the flappers seemed so sensual and lighthearted in their fearlessness. They did not carry a ponderous ideology
of female rights, female power, and political process. In their own way,
however, they were very serious indeed. With suffrage, education, and
employment established in principle and at least tentative practice, the
newest female vanguard was giving serious attention to private rights.
Intellectual and sexual gratification, an income to buy chiffon stockings
or a trip to Paris, a relationship of mutual respect and enjoyment with
a man—"a simple philosophy perhaps," as one woman remarked. "A little lacking in subtlety, in profundity, in poetry." But in "this distracted
age" their parents' grandiose ideals had broken apart. The young had
grown up to find all gods dead, all faiths in mankind shaken. "So for
lack of other vision, they believe in themselves." They were continuing
the woman movement in their individual lives, as personalized rather
than collective experience. Whereas feminists had once been intensely
sex conscious, their descendants of the 1920s were intensely self-con-
scious. Feminism survived, Elizabeth Breuer insisted, as an attitude
rather than a program or solution, an attitude that was looking beyond
feminism and sex differentiation toward "plain human maturity."[34]

In short, things had not gone wrong, but simply different. The defenders of the new generation saw hope where feminists like Gilman
saw betrayal. This divergence occurred because the two groups had
conflicting presumptions, first, about sexual morality and, second,
about effective strategies for attaining equality between the sexes. The
first disagreement, like any value conflict, could not be settled by logic
or evidence. In the end, it was settled by popular vote, as a growing
number of men and women in the twentieth century rejected the principle of chastity.[35] The second disagreement, however, was empirical
and therefore can be assessed by objective criteria. On the matter of
strategy, Gilman's analysis soon proved correct. By the end of the 1920s
it was becoming clear that women were not winning equality in their
private lives any more than in their public lives.

Their failure derived from several causes. For one thing, the institutions that they needed for escaping domesticity did not develop beyond a tentative stage. For all but a few women, the nurseries, cooper-

ative households, and other such programs served as models rather than effective realities. Without a public institutional setting, feminism had to be practiced privately and individually, inside the confining walls of the female sphere. That was difficult enough. But it became close to impossible because young women dismissed the ideological and collective forms of "the woman movement." Without a doctrine as a yardstick, a woman easily lost the general meaning amid the particular and personal. Discontent became "a problem that has no name," maladjustment rather than oppression. Without a sense that other women were also contending with similar problems and toward similar goals, a woman easily lost hope.

Thus the new generation, which had turned away from sex consciousness to self-consciousness—or, one might say, from feminism to humanism—was acting prematurely. The institutional and ideological contexts were not sufficiently established to permit this next phase in the evolution of gender identities. Given more time, perhaps, their success would have been greater. But there was no time; the Great Depression abruptly ended the luxury of innovation. Even without the Depression, however, the new feminists would have had difficulty. For if they needed more institutional and ideological support, they also needed more support from their male counterparts before they could succeed in transforming the roles of the sexes. Women were failing ultimately because men were failing them.

FOR HUNDREDS OF THOUSANDS of Americans during the 1920s, especially women, the story of Carol Kennicott was partly the story of themselves. Sinclair Lewis's best-selling novel *Main Street* served as a kind of parable of revised feminism. As Carol searched for self-fulfillment, the most apparent obstacles were her smugly old-fashioned small-town neighbors, who scrutinized and criticized her every impulse like a pack of yapping dogs. A low-cut dress, a highbrow play, a political conversation with men, a job—all were suspect or taboo. But her basic obstacle was at home with her husband, Will. "Kennicott had five hobbies: medicine, land-investment, Carol, motoring, and hunting. It is not certain in what order he preferred them." He loved her, loved her greatly and sometimes incredulously, but he could not imagine her as anything other than his better half, Mrs. Will Kennicott.

If she was to express her personality and capacities, she would have to tear up the role in which he had cast her, to find a way of becoming "no longer one-half of a marriage but the whole of a human be-ing." Finally she left him to live in Washington, D.C.: "I'm—I'm going! I have a right to my own life!" And he: "I have a right to my life—and you're it, you're my life!" And she: "You have a right to me if you can keep me. Can you?" Two years later she was back in Gopher Prairie, home with her husband, pregnant with their second child. She had found that her freedom was empty and that her adventure was martyr-dom. She wanted to be back among family and friends. On the last page of the novel, she is again talking frustratedly about making com-munity reforms, while he, only half-listening to her, mutters about storm windows. She was "not . . . utterly defeated," wrote Lewis, but Will had the last word in the book.

Here the parable ends—in ambiguity. The feminist rebel has won no more than a compromise victory, at best; at the worst, she has com-promised her principles. But, Lewis makes clear, she has chosen her own fate. If accommodation turns as sour as rebellion, *she* will be re-sponsible. That is the lesson of the novel, which Lewis pointedly subti-tled "The Story of Carol Kennicott."

But the author misread the meaning of his own book. The woman's role cannot be played entirely apart from the man's; they share a trans-actional drama. Carol left home because Will frustrated her sense of in-dividuality. She returned not only because she decided that she was giving up too much for independence, but also because Will's constant self-possession and love throughout their separation offered her the promise of something better. "It seemed to her that she was of some significance because she was commonplaceness, the ordinary life of the age, made articulate and protesting. It had not occurred to her that there was also a story of Will Kennicott, into which she entered only so much as he entered into hers."[36] *Main Street*, then, was a novel about Carol *and* Will; the half-truth of its subtitle disguised the fact that the success or failure of revised feminism depended on men as well as women.

Lewis did not understand the meaning of his own book, just as he misunderstood the meaning of his own experience. In the wounding re-alities of his two marriages he represented even more vividly than in his fiction the failure of men to revise their own role. In 1914, at the age of twenty-nine, still an unsuccessful writer and unstylish midwesterner, Lewis married Grace Hegger. She was cosmopolitan, arrogant, "smart," and he gladly subjected himself to the will of this woman he called lady, princess, "Silver Maid." Ten years later, having vaulted into literary celebrity, Lewis walked out on his princess. "You have of late become extraordinarily bullying," he wrote to her. "Complete independence" was what he demanded. "I must run my life." Two years later, after several brief affairs and bouts of heavy drinking, Lewis described himself in the mirror of one of his characters: "He wanted a woman with whom he could be childish and hurt and comforted." On July 2 he wrote to Grace asking her to meet him. On July 8 he met Dorothy Thompson, handsome, intellectually effervescent, and, at thirty-three years of age, a successful journalist. On July 9 he asked Dorothy to marry him, and proposed again every time they saw each other until finally she consented.

"Why else should I have married him, considering my own position when we met," she later recalled, "except because of that pull of his genius and my faith in his almost agonized protestations, at times, that he *needed* me?" But she had her own needs, which she confided to her diary. "One is willing to be swallowed up by a man," she wrote, "if in his brain and heart one is transmuted into something 'rich and strange,' something better than one could be of one's self." Such was "the longing of the real woman." Impelled by this kind of love for him, and then giving birth to a child, she found it increasingly difficult to sustain her own career. Work was also a need. "My brain has gone *phut*," she wrote to a friend in 1930, "but that's due to domesticity—which is unavoidable. Show me a woman married to an artist who can succeed in her marriage without making a full-time profession out of it. Oh Jesus God!" It was the kind of letter that Carol Kennicott might have written.

Lewis was giving his wife less attention, preoccupied by his writing, by the tumult of winning the Nobel Prize, and by his drinking. At one point she wrote to him in Italy, "Sometime I think you don't see me at all, but somebody you have made up, a piece of fiction." By the third year of marriage, she turned to her journalism for the satisfaction and security that she could not obtain from her husband. Soon she acquired enormous public prestige, enacting a postlude to *Main Street* that Lewis would never have written for Carol.

In 1937 he walked out on his second wife, proclaiming that her work had ruined their marriage and that she had robbed him of his creative powers. Dorothy pleaded earnestly and passionately with him. "I *know* that [work] saved our marriage for the past six years," she wrote to him. "It was, for me, the outlet, the escape, from something too intense to be born[e]. Too 'devouring.'" She understood his "obsession" about "being the husband of Dorothy Thompson, a tail to an ascending comet." But "darling, darling, darling, there's only one thing in which I am a really superior person. I have a really superior capacity for love. I love you. And that's the truth and that's the last word. Go away for six months, or six years, or three years. I shall sit at home, in *our* home, and be there when you come back to it." But he never came home, because he never could admit what she was saying about their relationship. "American women are like that," he would remark in later years. "Killers of talent."[37]

His view was, as Dorothy had said, a piece of fiction. In each of his marriages he had invented a role for his wife and then stalked off the marital stage, each time shouting that she had failed him when in fact it was his fantasy of her that had failed. In the first case, he left because he felt strong enough at last to do without a princess; in the second case, because he felt too weak to live with an equally successful writer. For a moment, his marriage with Dorothy had seemed to exemplify everything that the new feminists were seeking—joint careers and joint parenthood. But it collapsed because his sense of self could not bear the weight of equality. Instead, as in *Main Street*, he denied that their marriage was the story of Dorothy *and* Red. He focused only on her part, because he would not or could not acknowledge his own. "You have a right to me if you can keep me," Carol had said. But Sinclair Lewis lacked Will Kennicott's self-confidence. Like "the great Gatsby," he clutched desperately at the dreamed form of a woman he had loved and thereby lost the real woman. Like Gatsby he lived a fiction—a masculine fiction—which, in turn, destroyed the possibilities of creating a new, egalitarian relationship between the sexes.

"YOU CAN'T REPEAT THE PAST," Nick Carroway protested. "Can't repeat the past?" Gatsby exclaimed. "Why of course you can!" Most middle-class men of the 1920s were trying to retrieve a time gone by, because only in the frame of the Victorian past did they know who they were and how to act. It had been hard enough even then, in the waning years of Victorianism, to "be a man." After the Great War, the task became even more baffling and frenzied. Men had invested in the war such grand hopes of themselves, only to discover them battered into grand illusions. "No[,] I believe no more in the gospel of energy," Dos Passos wrote wearily to a friend in 1918. "One thing the last year has taught me has been to drop my old sentamentalizing[*sic*] over action." The battlefield had been not a proving ground for manly courage, but a site for the technological ferocity of military machinery. War had been an experience of impersonality, not heroism, from which men emerged in diminished form. In his novel *Three Soldiers* (1921), Dos Passos described the wounded soldiers as "discarded automatons, broken toys laid away in rows." That tone typified the war stories of the twenties: saddened and cynical, tales of poor little tragedies rather than glorious ideals, a *Farewell to Arms*. But most veterans did not want to say anything at all. As the doughboys returned home from the great crusade, they met civilians' excited questions with stolid silence. "We have come back hating war . . . , disgusted with the prattle about ideals," a Chicago volunteer wrote in his diary.[38]

It had been a war without heroism or heroes. "How many readers," one journalist asked in 1920, "can name a single American general who commanded any one of the huge separate armies into which our troops in France were divided?" Several years later, when almost 700 New Jersey schoolboys were polled as to who they would like to be if they were not themselves, General Pershing was the only military man on their list, and he earned a mere fourteen votes. By 1929, in a similar poll of Alabama boys, he had vanished entirely. If there was a hero in the Great War, he was that collection of bones memorialized as the Unknown Soldier.[39]

Most men needed some vindication beyond cynicism and anonymity; they needed a hero with whom to identify in order to clarify (or at least fabricate) their own identity. Not having found him on the battlefield, they looked to the gridiron and the diamond. Before the war there had been popular excitement about spectator sports, but nothing quite so intense as in the 1920s. It was the "Golden Age of sport"; athletics "has been seated on the American throne"; baseball was the national pastime, but football became "almost our national religion." In the huge new stadiums one found heroes: the Sultan of Swat, the Four Horsemen of Notre Dame, the Galloping Ghost. Here one found real men. "I've seen moral courage in football as often as physical," a *Collier's* journalist declared. "I've seen football make men out of condemned material." Football was more than a game; it was combat. Grantland Rice wrote proudly about the "real physical suffering" of quarterback Harry Stuhldreher, who played an entire game with a cracked ankle, and of Notre Dame's captain, Adam Walsh, who played against Army with two broken hands. This was, said Rice, "the stuff men are made of."

Many commentators drew the parallel to the suffering that men had just endured in other uniforms. According to the president of the University of Minnesota, "The same kind of red blood qualities are required on the football field that animated the men on the battlefields of France and Belgium." As one psychologist has speculated, sports did indeed seem to evoke a warlike willingness to die.

But disillusionment soon began to enter this arena of manliness too. Whereas military technology had devoured the heroic possibilities of war, commercialism began to contaminate the "sporting" quality of sports. The fixing of the 1919 World Series was an omen. By the mid-twenties, the extravagant organization and expenditures and publicity surrounding college football provoked sportswriters and coaches to complain. The game was turning into a big business, they said, a "Frankenstein"; the great god football was becoming Mammon. People began to propose that college football be abolished.[40]

"Say it ain't so, Joe!" a boy supposedly pleaded to Shoeless Joe Jackson after the World Series bribery scandal. The more relentlessly that modern civilization closed or corrupted the possibilities for "the strenuous life," the more anxiously men sought it. They could not let go of the manly mystique. But, in this era of dead gods and tarnished heroes, where were they to find it? In 1927, Charles Lindbergh gave them an answer when he flew alone across the Atlantic. Within days the public made the young, handsome pilot into a national hero, *the* national hero, a symbol of the dreams that Americans wished for themselves. The Lone Eagle, one newspaper proclaimed, "stands out in a grubby world as an inspiration." The Boy Scout *Handbook's* cover showed a Scout marching beside the phantom figures of Boone, Lincoln, Roosevelt, and Lindbergh. The western frontier lay buried beneath highways and railroad tracks, but Lindbergh's plane had opened a new frontier. His exploit, Joseph K. Hart said, gave comfort to "the homesickness of the human soul, immured in city canyons and routine tasks, for the freer world of youth, for the open spaces of the pioneer."

For a giddy moment, Americans talked as if they could not only repeat the past, but repeal the present too. Yet the celebration of Lindbergh could never be more than fantasy. When the ticker-tape parade ended, Hart also said, "we . . . go back to the contracted routines of our institutional ways because ninety-nine percent of us must be content to be shaped and moulded by the routine ways and forms of the world to the routine tasks of life."[41]

For a middle-class man, the task was his job—typically, eight hours a day, six days a week, fifty weeks a year; and, more and more typically, not in the open air of a farm or even inside the walls of his own establishment, but inside the walls of someone else's factory or office building among hundreds or even thousands of other employees. During the 1920s the proportion of white-collar workers among the male labor force increased from one-fifth to one-fourth. But most of them did not resemble that economic folk hero, that lone eagle of the industrial world, Henry Ford. Most neither invented nor produced, but sold or helped others to sell. During the decade there were more and more stock-market agents, insurance agents, advertising copywriters, and especially salesmen, while there were proportionately fewer and fewer managers, proprietors, lawyers, and doctors. The business of America was business, but for most workers it was someone else's business.

They worked because they had to and also because—as disciples of the puritan ethic—they believed they should, but it was a joyless faith. As social psychologists have repeatedly demonstrated, the more specialized and repetitive and prescribed the content of his work, the more likely a worker will be bored, fatigued, and discontented. Much of the rising productivity in the 1920s derived from the assembly line and time-and-motion routines introduced by Ford and Frederick Taylor. Their techniques produced more goods, but hardly happier men. Quite the contrary: men often worked passively or sullenly or sloppily, provoking their superiors to angry rebukes. According to a writer in the *Independent*, "No worker should ever get the notion that work is play, that he should do a thing only when he likes it, or that he should waste time analyzing his emotions at all. Feelings are the most faithless, cruel and unreasonable tyrants that a person can obey. . . . A man is not a man until he makes himself do with a smile whatever he hates most." It could have been General Pershing talking to a squadron or Knute Rockne to his team.[42]

Toward the top of the corporate hierarchy the mood was quite different. There men worked with zeal. "I'm first and last a salesman," announced the forty-year-old president of Austin, Nichols, and Company, the world's largest wholesale-grocery enterprise. "I get more joy out of selling than anything else. Business to me is like a game of sport." A Standard Oil executive put work ahead of love, learning, religion, and patriotism. The manager of a wood-pulp factory found in his job "the opportunity for self-expression, which is synonymous with joy in work."[43]

Even for successful men, however, work no longer meant what it had for their fathers. The hearty Victorian phrases about self-reliance and character building rang discordantly amid a new and louder vocabulary: "spending," "service," "putting it over," "efficiency." Now success was defined, without apology or dismay, as wealth. Even less Victorian was the increasing emphasis on the science of "human engineering," the manipulation of people rather than of things. Salesmanship became the economic theme song, and journal articles instructed the updated Horatio Algers in how to sell their products and how to sell themselves: "There's Not Much Use to Grind Unless You Advertise Your Grist," "How to Play Your Game, Whatever It Is," or "Questions That Will Help You Get a Line on Yourself." Bruce Barton took the theme to unforgettable heights when, in *The Man Nobody Knows* (1925), he described Jesus as the first Rotarian, "the great advertiser," a go-getter, who made his dozen disciples into the most successful sales organization of all time. The gospel of work thus turned into the devices of salesmanship. The stern Victorian injunctions of "character" yielded to the pliant smile and handshake of "personality." Sinclair Lewis's novel *Babbitt* gave a name to this new middle-class man, along with a viciously satiric portrait. But, as a versifier for *Nation's Business* indicated, Babbitt's colleagues were unrepentant.

> Bill Babbitt is a hustler,
>   A regular go-getter,
> And when he's caught the thing he sought
>   He goes for something better!
>
> So when he's wanting money
>   He does his best to make it,
> (He makes no bluff to hate the stuff
>   While being glad to take it).
>
> Is anything he gets worth while
>   To pay for his expended vim?
> Well, William wears a pleasant smile—
>   I guess it's all worth while to him![44]

The Victorian prototype of manly work, already struggling against obsolescence after 1890, lay buried under this jolly epitaph. He who had once been a frontiersman, then a soldier, and then a captain of industry, had become a go-getter. By means of this redefinition, the postwar spokesmen were accommodating to the circumstances of the white-collar world; they were making a peace with realities that their fathers had not made or, rather, had not allowed themselves to make. But it was an uncertain peace. After all, the Babbitts and the Bartons still talked in the old terms of individualism and self-reliance, betraying an ambivalent nostalgia for challenges more strenuous than they could find in their real-estate or advertising agencies. Indirectly, they were expressing what other men were saying as they cheered Red Grange and Lindbergh, namely, that something in their work role was not quite right.

Nobody openly said that. Except in these inadvertent ways, middle-class men did not express dissatisfaction. They would have been mystified if someone had asked them to join a male-liberation movement. They may have wanted more money or shorter hours, but they were not aware of wanting any fundamental change in their role as breadwinner. In retrospect, however, one can see stresses that they could not. Instead of making some thing, a man was making money. Instead of offering a needed product or service, he was using "personality" to "engineer" his customers into buying something they had not known they wanted. During this process, it was perilously easy to forget what was reality and what was showmanship—not only in his product, but also in himself. If even Jesus was a go-getting salesman, how could a merely mortal businessman hold on to a clear definition of himself? The objective standards of work and worth were blurring, thus presenting middle-class workers with an ambiguous sense of their own identity.[45]

They would have to find personal definition elsewhere. The favorite choice was "service clubs," which quintupled during the postwar decade. By 1930, 400,000 middle-class men were lunching, discussing, singing, and fraternizing on a first-name basis at the Rotary, Kiwanis, Lions, or a dozen smaller clubs. They went partly for social status, but also for the feeling of fellowship. As one man explained, "You can't sit down at a table with a man and talk things over without getting to understand him better." According to another, "I have gotten more out of it than I ever got out of the church. I have gotten closer to men in Rotary than anywhere else, except sometimes in their homes." But if some members found genuine friendship, others found an impersonal atmosphere of bombast and competitive "kidding." Ultimately, the clubs were a way station between a man's public world and his home.[46]

"HOME LIFE IS THE CENTER of everything; if that is gone, everything is gone." Speaking from the heart of the heart of the country, this Indiana businessman pronounced in 1924 what all Americans already knew. Men depended on the home as the cornerstone of social order, as the nursery of morality, and as the measure of their own achievement in the world. These were commonplaces.

Equally common were the shrill tocsins ringing the news that the home was gradually disintegrating, that it was rapidly disintegrating, that it had collapsed altogether. It was old news to those who remembered back to the early twentieth century. And the reason was also familiar: women were abdicating their domestic responsibilities. Like his father and grandfather, a man of the 1920s returned at the end of his day expecting "a citadel of protection, an asylum and a refuge, a feather-bed for aching limbs and an opiate for bruised self-esteem." More and more often, however, his wife handed him a spatula or a crying baby instead of his slippers. She would listen to his problems or soothe his weariness, but she also expected him to hear and soothe hers. "Marriage is now understood to be a form of human teamwork," as one woman said, "to which each must do his share." The stereotype of a man's home as his castle was competing, in the 1920s, with the modern image of the family as a partnership.[47]

Just as the "antis" had warned during the battle over suffrage, the doctrine of equality had invaded the home. But even their fevered imaginations did not guess how far it would infiltrate male-female relationships. "In these modern days," one woman explained in a letter to the *New York Times*, "it is not a question of moral obligation to 'support' a wife, or to be criticized if she earns her own living." More married women were asserting their right to take a job, more were demanding an equal division of household duties and family budgets, and a few even proposed wages for housewives. Patriarchy was becoming almost as outdated as the mustache. If a man nonetheless insisted on playing the patriarchal role, he discovered—according to a woman in *Ladies' Home Journal*—"that modern families won't put up with him any more." His wife, she said, may learn to type or sell insurance, while his son will take the first opportunity to leave home. The modern father had to earn, rather than presume, respect from his family.[48]

A few middle-class men took up the challenge, encouraging their wives to pursue careers, agreeing to fifty-fifty household arrangements, spending more time at home with their children, attending or even presiding over the meetings of parents' associations. They worked at their new role with the determination that their fellow men gave to their jobs. And some found that the "freedom from invidious sex distinctions" had liberated not only women, but themselves as well.[49]

They were the exceptions. American culture had imprinted patterns of identity more deeply than a generation of feminist arguments or a cohort of flappers could erase. Most men clung to economic supremacy, not only for the privileges it gave them, but also because they could not imagine another way to be. Without the familiar balance of spheres, they dizzily lost psychic equilibrium. When father "slipped from his pedestal," wrote one man, he catapulted into being "poor dad," ridiculed or tolerated as "a dear old thing." Economic equality, most men believed, merged the two sexes into dangerous confusion. Women were becoming masculine and men effeminate—so warned Will Durant even as he prepared to write the ten-volume *Story of Civilization* in partnership with his wife, Ariel. Lawyers, bankers, and editors mourned that marriage to "intellectual tomboys" was deadening husbands' ambitions, driving them to drink or desertion, and causing the high divorce rate. According to the typical short story in family magazines, marital ties were taut to the breaking point because of women's demands for "rights." Sociological surveys reported that in fact the vast majority of marriages were happy, but they also found that the middle-class husbands of wage earners were more discontent than husbands of entirely domestic wives.

As men suffered, so did "their" women. Because economic equality was more than most husbands could bear, they levied a terrible guilt upon their wives. Some women, like Dorothy Thompson, defended their careers as their source of strength and self-esteem. But others succumbed. "*I have deprived my husband of his birthright,*" wrote a publishing executive, as she assessed her years of motherhood and career. By earning more than he did, she had supplanted his "privilege of safeguarding his little family against the world. I have robbed him of the greatest incentive to success a man can have."[50]

Female economic equality threatened men; sexual equality confused them. They had grown up relying first on their mothers and then on their wives as models of purity, moral lighthouses to guide them in the struggle against their stormy sexual drives. When women cast off that role, men were set adrift. "There are white kisses and red kisses," the eighteen-year-old heroine of *Flaming Youth* explained "unconcernedly" to her lover. "You have no right to that kind of knowledge," he replied sternly. In the same novel, avuncular Dr. Osterhut murmured, "The modern flapper knows so formidably much!" Female sexuality carried over into marriage, if we can judge by the fact that orgasm was considerably more common for wives born after 1900 than for those born before. Women were expressing passion and expecting gratification, not only in the marital bed, but sometimes outside it. Even the unflappable Judge Ben Lindsey was stunned when a well-to-do woman in her mid-thirties explained how, after discovering her husband's adultery, she had convinced him to accept "collusion in adultery": *both* spouses could enjoy discreet affairs. "I had suspected this kind of thing was going on," Lindsey remarked, "but here was the evidence."[51]

The proverbial dark lady and fair maiden were fusing into the same woman. The prewar boy, who had been taught by moralists and marriage manuals to be considerate of his wife as a frail vessel, entered manhood only to find that she was demanding sexual satisfaction. Instead of telling him to control himself, the newest manuals told him to awaken her desire until they both reached simultaneous orgasm. Likewise, nineteenth-century advocates of birth control had favored abstinence as a way of protecting women against male lust; advocates in the 1920s favored diaphragms as a way of freeing women from the dread of pregnancy and letting them enjoy their full share of pleasure. Procreative duty had become recreational performance. Scarcity had become abundance.* For women, the change brought new pleasure; for men, it brought a mixed pleasure, the release from inhibition being accompanied by the challenge to be a good lover. The Victorian code of moderation had provided some men a shield for their sense of inadequacy, but that shield was being removed. Even for the more "virile" ones, the

---

*The parallel trend of the economic and sexual "ethic" is striking. Instead of respecting vigorous self-restraint by customers against inordinate "spending," the entrepreneur was supposed to exert his personality in order to make customers buy, and especially buy on the installment plan, with money they did not yet have. Similarly, in the sexual realm scarcity ("spending") was giving way to abundance ("coming"), with greater emphasis on manipulation by personality than on production by self-assertion. This parallel does not explain, but it does illuminate, the close fit between the sexual and other cultural roles. See Charles E. Rosenberg, "Sexuality, Class and Role in Nineteenth-Century America," *American Quarterly* 25 (Summer 1973): 151–152, and Peter T. Cominos, "Late-Victorian Sexual Respectability and the Social System," *International Review of Social History* 8 (1963): esp. 216.

new code was disturbing. Beatrice Hinkle, a psychiatrist, described men as bewildered creatures. Another psychiatrist, this one male, reported neuroses and nervous breakdowns. During Dr. G. V. Hamilton's interviews of 200 middle-class persons, mostly in their thirties, one-half of the husbands complained of sexual dissatisfaction.[52] The exact truth remains necessarily out of reach, hidden in the privacy of bedrooms and in the diversity of the millions of middle-class couples who slept there. The problem of sexuality, so incessantly bedeviling to the Victorians, had become a new sort of problem—that much one can say with assurance.

But there is more to say, although people in the 1920s left it largely unsaid. Obsessed with the prudish and prurient heritage of puritanism, they tended to see relationships in sexual terms. Love also deserved attention, however. When Ben Lindsey proposed "companionate marriage"—a legal marriage with birth control and with the right to divorce by mutual consent for a childless couple—he provoked a public outcry. "Jazz marriage," said the magazines; "nothing but free love," said the Reverend Billy Sunday; legalized promiscuity, animal-like mating, pornography. Few people, whether friend or foe, dealt with the "companionate" part of his proposal, but it was precisely that part—companionship, affection, love—in which men were most delinquent. They declared that home life was the center of everything, but all too often they behaved like inert tenants. "When he gets home at night," one wife complained, "he just settles down with the paper and his cigar and the radio and just rests." Nor was mere conversation enough. The authors of one marriage manual scolded men for presuming to satisfy their wives with a dinnertime narrative of what they had done during the day.

Marital partnership entailed the sharing not only of money, jobs, and sex, but also of those intangible qualities of affection and companionship. Yet men seemed oblivious to these aspects. Love and sexual desire are essentially the same, a male novelist asserted in an article praising the new woman. Among Hamilton's 200 subjects, thirteen women complained of too little affection in their marriages, but only one man. Dad cares about two things, wrote Kathleen Norris—his job and golf. No, said journalist Florence Guy Woolston, men care primarily about being cared for. They are "the sheltered sex," expecting their wives to feed them, sew buttons on their coats, and shield them from tiresome relatives, quarrelsome maids, and the noise of the street. "In daily processes," Woolston remarked, "they've been taught that the greater their helplessness, the more their masculinity."[53]

She offered a shrewd insight. The patriarch was also a child, blending dominance with dependence. In the days of unquestioned male sovereignty he had dispensed and received attention regally at the head of the family table. But in the new days of domestic democracy the mask of sovereignty was pulled off, exposing ineptitude both practical and emotional. Father became "poor dad." The tensions that had been growing within the masculine role during the Victorian era seemed finally, under female pressure, to have reached the breaking point.

And what then? "Ultimately the woman movement should result in the emancipation of men," Woolston said at the end of her article. Significantly, it was a remark by a woman. Almost no men were saying that, because they had no sense that emancipation meant anything but loss. In place of superiority, they could envision only inferiority. If they descended from the pedestal of domination, they would be "henpecked." After they had learned so arduously to grow out of boyish tears and fears into the manly role of tight-lipped strength, soft affection seemed dangerously vulnerable. Having struggled to master their lust, they had little to say or feel about love. That emotion had been delegated to women. Enclosed inside a casing of masculinity, they resembled Dos Passo's war-wounded "automatons."

An occasional man in the 1920s understood that "man's superiority, once it is brought into the light of day and examined, appears to be a liability rather than the asset it has been considered heretofore."[54] Given more time, perhaps, more men would have reached this perspective. But it would have had to be a long time. In their patriarchal position, men occupied themselves first of all with defending their privileges against feminist attack, rather than with constructing alternatives for themselves.

At the turn of the decade, most men were still hoping to repeat the past. In his notebook, Gatsby's creator expressed the dilemma of their role with a poignant clarity:

> When I like men I want to be like them—I want to lose the outer qualities that give me my individuality and be like them. I don't want the man; I want to absorb into myself all the qualities that make him attractive and leave him out of it. I cling to my own innards. When I like women I want to own them, to dominate them, to have them admire me.[55]

6

The Long Amnesia:
Depression, War, and Domesticity

THE DRAMATIC CONFLICT ABOUT gender equality ended abruptly in 1930. The emergencies of the Depression and Second World War wrote another script, in which middle-class Americans played other roles in other costumes: the patched clothing of poverty, blue collars instead of white, then military uniforms, and overalls instead of aprons. Questions of common survival, both personal and emotional, pushed the battle between the sexes off stage. And there it remained for thirty years, preserved in the memories of those who had enacted it, but postponed again and again, until even many of them forgot its meaning. To the younger actors, meanwhile, it seemed an outdated genre, a morality play that they ignored or never knew or did not understand. They were too busy learning other roles—or, rather, relearning roles older than feminism. In the Depression, men tried desperately to be breadwinners for their families; in the war, they were defenders of the nation. Women served in whatever ways they could as helpmates in these two struggles for survival. When victory came at last, both sexes gratefully went back to normalcy, gratefully resumed the deferred middle-class dream of family, security, and upward mobility. At last they could be mom, dad, and the kids again, hoping to live happily ever after . . . after war, after depression, long after feminism.

ONE YEAR AFTER LINDBERGH FLEW across the Atlantic, Amelia Earhart did the same, landing in Wales at the end of a strenuous flight. Like him, she came home to ticker-tape parades, medals, and ecstatic acclaim as a pioneer, a heroine, an embodiment of the American dream. But it was not the same at all. "How does it feel to be the first woman to fly the Atlantic?" a man asked as she climbed out of the plane. To which she replied merely, "Hello." "What's the matter?" he persisted. "Aren't you excited?" "Excited?" Earhart echoed. "No. It was a grand experience, but all I did was lie on my tummy and take pictures of the clouds . . . Bill did all the flying—had to. I was just baggage, like a sack of potatoes." She had been not a female Lone Eagle, but a passenger, crouched for twenty-two hours behind a male pilot and a male mechanic.

Four years later, she finally made a solo voyage across the Atlantic, inspiring one woman journalist to exclaim that "social historians of the future might do worse than to use her flight as a marker of the new battlefield of feminism—a battlefield, symbolically enough, . . . of the atmosphere." But that was 1932, the darkest year of the Depression. Few people were looking up toward bright horizons of any kind. Five years later, while flying over the Pacific, Earhart vanished into a fate of unsolved mystery.[1]

The trajectory of Earhart's career offers a sorry symbol of feminism during the 1930s. The principle of woman's rights was thrust into the back seat as Americans tried to cope with the worst economic catastrophe they had ever experienced. If people spoke of a battle, it was against poverty, not sexism. If they thought of a revolution, it was against the capitalist, not the male, ruling class. And even these doctrines stirred only the fringes of society. The great majority of Americans, bruised and bewildered by the Depression that had abruptly fallen upon them, shuffled stolidly on bread lines, knocked patiently on employers' doors, tramped somewhere and elsewhere and back again across the country, or simply stayed at home to wait. The problems of food and shelter were too overwhelmingly immediate for them to see solutions in any "ism." And certainly feminism seemed more irrelevant than communism, socialism, or fascism. If at all, they might have professed pragmatism, but even that came down to doing something, anything, to give people jobs again. So they waited, through three years of Hoover's promises and an unemployment rate that climbed above 20 percent, until finally they elected Roosevelt and waited for whatever he might mean by "a new deal" on behalf of "the forgotten man." As he slowly proceeded, after 1932, to put the capitalist system together again, the remnants of feminism vanished almost as completely as Amelia Earhart had.

"The forgotten man." The phrase itself betrays how Americans de-

fined priorities in the Depression. Bread first, social reform later—and
the breadwinner was presumed to be male. Married women workers,
proclaimed a Chicago civic group, "are holding jobs that rightfully belong to the God-intended providers of the household." Working wives
with adequately employed husbands "cannot be dignified by the name
of workers," agreed the (unmarried) president of the Massachusetts
Women's Political Club. "They are deserters from their post of duty, the
home," she continued. Congresswoman Florence Kahn agreed that
"woman's place is not out in the business world competing with men
who have families to support." The City Council of Akron, Ohio, agreed.
In a Gallup poll of 1937, 82 percent of Americans agreed.

Opinions also turned to action. Banks and factories dismissed
married women; the mayor of Northhampton, Massachusetts, fired
eight wives working in city hall; three of every four cities across the nation excluded married women from teaching positions; and eight legislatures adopted laws excluding them from state jobs. On the federal
level, meanwhile, congressional legislation ruled that two married persons could not both work for the government. Although a "person"
could be either male or female, in fact four-fifths of those fired were
wives. The National Federation of Business and Professional Women's
Clubs, the editors of *Ladies' Home Journal* and *Woman's Home Companion*,
the director of the United States Women's Bureau, even the First Lady,
Eleanor Roosevelt herself, all protested bitterly against this discrimination. In vain. Although Congress repealed its law in 1937, popular
feeling toward employment of wives remained rancorous. As Kathleen
Norris remarked, "There is a real war going on."[2]

In fascist Germany, where Hitler was ordering women back into the
kitchen and commanding them to breed children for the master race,
feminists saw a chilling example of how thoroughly that war could be
carried out. In their own country it never reached such proportions, but
the components were present. Panicked by economic disaster, both
men and women once again made woman a scapegoat. It was almost
an automatic reflex, propelled by economic self-interest and sexual
stereotype, against which rational argument cried like a small voice inside a mob. No matter that the female unemployment rate increased
during the 1930s as the male rate fell, so that by 1938 it was more than
50 percent higher than the men's. No matter that most of these unemployed women were from the most vulnerable parts of the population,
namely, the young, the old, and the unskilled or semiskilled.

Single women? Why they're just discards [a New York City social worker reported, seven months after the New Deal began]. I'll tell you how they live! Huddled together in small apartments, three or four of them living on the earnings of one, who may have a job. Half a dozen of them, sometimes, in one room. . . . Just managing to keep alive.

No matter that the majority of women—whether married or unmarried, whether working, seeking work, or on relief—had one or more dependents. No matter that, although one of three women workers had a husband, she was all too often the sole wage earner in her family. And, most to the point, no matter that in fact women almost never displaced men from jobs during the Depression; in 1940, 70 percent of men still were working in occupations that contained only 1 percent of females.[3]

All of this was true, and all of it influenced only those few who cared to know. "Your average businessman," one federal relief official lamented, "just won't believe there are any women who are absolutely self-supporting." People believed what they wanted to believe. The president of Carnegie Technical Institute warned that women "have usurped all, or nearly all, of the white collar jobs." Almost half of Gallup's respondents (including 42 percent of the women) said that no wife should work, whether or not her husband could support her. A woman's place was at home.[4]

In the face of these circumstances, it is surprising how well women held on to their share of the economy. True, at the end of eight years of depression their unemployment rate hung at a terrible 22 percent, *higher* than in 1931. (And if one counts those working part-time or in temporary jobs, the rate would have been higher yet.) On the other hand, there was also good news. Their proportion of the labor force increased during the decade. So did the percentage of working women who were married, from less than 30 to more than 35 percent. All in all, by 1940, almost three of every ten women were gainfully employed, an unprecedented percentage. What were they doing? Much the same as women a generation before. Most of them were still in factory, domestic, and clerical work. Those in professions and business remained a minority, in fact a slightly dwindled minority by the end of the 1930s. Although these career women suffered much less unemployment than their sisters farther down the occupational ladder, they thereby left less room for newcomers to their ranks.[5]

Women, then, performed a holding action. In this respect, they did not differ substantially from men, whose unemployment rate in 1940 had dropped no lower than the atrocious levels of 1931. Men, too, succeeded only in holding on. But for women the same story had quite a different meaning. They had a special stake in employment. Ever since the mid-nineteenth century, a growing minority of the female upper middle class had been struggling to establish an equal right to a career. Slowly and arduously this feminist campaign had been gaining ground, less in practice than in principle, but the principle was ultimately more important. Slowly, arduously—until the financial earthquake of 1929 broke up the entire terrain. As people groped for the necessities of life—food, clothing, shelter—they clung to truisms, including "woman belongs at home." In the statistics of the labor market women managed to hold their place, but in the realm of ideology and attitude they lost it. They defended themselves as individuals, but not as a class. The weakness in the revised feminism of the 1920s had proved fatal.

In this crisis, the leaders of what had once been the feminist movement provided little that could be called leadership. "We of the League [of Women Voters] are very much for the rights of women," said Dorothy Straus. "But . . . we are not feminists primarily; we are citizens." Whatever this perplexing statement might have meant, the activity of her organization was clear enough. During the 1930s the league concerned itself primarily with child-labor laws, with disarmament, and with blocking the Woman's Party campaign for the Equal Rights Amendment. The Woman's Party, meanwhile, had dwindled to a cluster of white-haired veterans, ardently loyal to orthodox feminism and—as one of them confessed to Alice Paul—doing "a little of this and that, but we are getting nowhere." Meetings of the Executive Council, she said, dwelled on party housekeeping. "Sometimes I think it would be better if we had no house to keep! There is much dead wood on the Council, including myself."

If there was any hope of political leadership for women, it lay not in the petrified forest of feminist organizations, but in the flurry around the White House. For the first time women were appointed to the cabinet, to a diplomatic post, and to the U.S. Circuit Court of Appeals. Women took high positions in the Works Progress Administration and the Democratic party. And Eleanor Roosevelt was not merely a first lady pouring tea in her husband's parlor, but was surveying social conditions across the country, defending the rights of minority groups, advising the president, and working skillfully in the inner councils of the Democratic party. At the political pinnacle, women had never done so well. But at lower levels there was backsliding: fewer female members of Congress between 1930 and 1940, fewer female state legislators. And, in any case, all of this female commotion and promotion in Washington gave little direct aid to feminism. Molly Dewson, Frances Perkins, and their colleagues worked primarily for reform, incidentally for woman's rights. Their New Deal was on behalf of the "forgotten person," not the forgotten woman. They accomplished an enormous amount of good for a stricken society, but not for a stricken feminism. In 1937, two-thirds of the Americans whom Gallup polled—including 60 percent of the women—said they would not vote for a qualified woman for president.[6]

The organized feminist movement went moribund soon after the First World War. Now its principles lay beneath the Crash, apparently dead, apparently unmourned even by female public leaders. "Today there is no time for feminism," said Mrs. Chase Going Woodhouse, director of the Institute for Women's Professional Relations, in 1940. "The problems [women] consider are not feministic, but economic."[7]

SHE USED MARGARINE INSTEAD of butter now, cooked noodles and eggs instead of meat, bought day-old bread. She saved leftovers, saved broken crockery, saved rags, saved everything that could possibly be reused. But some things could not be saved—the piano in the living room and the fur jacket had gone. She did not miss them much, nor the new hat she had bought in other spring seasons but not in this one. These were small hardships in such hard times. No, it was easier to patch her dress or reweave her husband's socks than to tell the children that they could not have roller skates, could not buy ice cream, must wear hand-me-down coats to school without shame. Who would have imagined that she would be cooking two hardboiled eggs at breakfast, one for each of Susan's coat pockets, to keep the child's hands warm on her way to school, where she would eat the eggs for lunch?

But even these things were easier than the feelings she saw in Eric's eyes and in the children's. *Things* she had learned to cope with, but not those feelings. When she had married him, he would come home from the office tired, but not too tired to smile, swinging his briefcase. Now the smile came rarely, and sometimes simply to curtain the fear as he mentioned that Taylor or Simpson or someone else had been fired. She had never known him to be afraid, and it stirred the fear in her. What would become of them? Many nights, now, she lay awake while fear coiled inside her like a question mark. And often she knew that, alongside her, he too was lying sleepless, but neither of them dared to talk aloud. In the morning, exhausted, they would shout at the children. Last week, when Johnny asked if Daddy was going to be on relief like Mr. Baxter, before she knew what she was doing she had slapped him. And then blundered out of the kitchen away from his incredulous tears, half-blinded by her own. Two years since the Wall Street Crash! One-eighteenth of her life! How much longer would . . . ?

He had gotten used to some aspects of it: sharpening the old safety-razor blades; wearing the same corduroy jacket through fall, winter, and spring; canceling the subscription to *Popular Mechanics* and reading it in the public library instead. Doris had learned to cut his hair evenly. He had tried to stop smoking and couldn't, but at least he rolled his own. "You're smoking too much, Eric," she told him again and again. But what else was there to do, sitting at home every afternoon, every evening? He had repaired all the storm windows and the back steps and (twice) Johnny's bicycle, all the things he had never found time to do when he was working.

Time. He finally realized what people meant when they talked about "killing time." He was taking naps after the morning job hunt. "Why don't you do something?" she said again and again. "Let's have the Formans over for bridge, like we used to." But they'd probably expect to have the usual coffee and cake, and Bruce would ask him politely whether he'd found work yet—or, worse, would be politely *not* asking.

Come to think of it, they hadn't been seeing anybody at all. Maybe that's why he'd been so moody lately. Yelling at Doris just because she said something about the curtains being torn. His ears seemed to have become sharper these days. He heard too much. It was like living with three other people in a life raft for eight months. Everybody was always bumping into someone else. The kids never used to be so noisy. "Why don't you *do* something?" she kept saying. He had tried helping her with the housework, but the macaroni had burned twice, and pinching those little clothespins onto the line made him feel—well, he felt clumsy or foolish or something. And why had Ernie Lewis been laughing like that in the next yard? So he napped most afternoons now.

What was it she had said last night? Something about Mrs. Burns selling Two-in-One shoe polish door to door, earning fifteen dollars a week. She wondered if . . . No! Not that! They might have to eat corned-beef hash for Thanksgiving again, but he'd never let his wife work.

It had to end sometime. President Roosevelt promised.[8]

IF A MAN COULD NOT SAY "I am an accountant" or a lawyer or a pharmacist, it became harder to say "I am a man." There was the businessman in Arizona, for example, worth $60,000 before the Crash plummeted him into bankruptcy and forced his son to drop out of college. "All this—it breaks you down," he confided quietly to a federal relief investigator in 1934. "We men who have been the backbone of commerce, who have ambitions and hopes, who have always taken care of our families—what is going to become of us? I've lost twelve and a half pounds this last month, just thinking . . . Why, I've sat across from Jesse Jones [head of the Reconstruction Finance Corporation] and talked contract with him, running up into many thousands of dollars! But I'd be afraid to face him now. You get so you feel so whipped."

When a man had a job, just as surely the job had him. In it he invested one-half of his waking hours, every day but Sunday; out of it he took the paycheck that provided his family with the means of survival. The job was like a bank containing their life savings, both economic and psychological. And when jobs failed and the savings vanished, men were left holding onto emptiness. "I am going crazy," they said, "with so much time on my hands and nothing to do."[9]

Some in fact went insane; some committed suicide; some deserted their families and joined the tramps who wandered—anonymous behind beard-stubbled faces—from town to town, campfire to campfire. Some stood on bread lines or job lines day after day, caught in the endless slow motion of a marathon dance contest. But most went nowhere. With nothing to do, they did nothing except stay home. Inside their proverbial castles, they were safe from the glance of anyone who had known them as they used to be. But they were also more exposed to the family's scrutiny. The older children, especially if they had jobs, tended to lose respect for their fathers. "How can you be glad to see your wife and children when you come home," a New Haven man asked aloud, "when you see debts all around you and that's almost all you can talk about? And every time you think of them you know they cry to heaven that you're a failure. The wife may not say so, but she knows it the same as you do."

As the pressures of poverty increased, however, many wives did say so. Why can't you get a job? Mrs. Cohen challenged her husband, an unemployed musician, in New Haven. Why did you quit high school instead of going to college and becoming a lawyer? Lawyers are still supporting their wives, she said. Why did you marry me anyhow? retorted Mr. Cohen. Why didn't you marry that cabinet-maker you were in love with?

When the covering of economic security disintegrated, old grievances came to the surface, as wounding as the broken springs in the living room sofa. Some husbands shouted and "bossed," demanding the respect that they were losing. Some husbands became plaintive, "but when I tell her I want more love, she just gets mad." The rate of sexual intercourse dwindled and, in a few cases, ceased altogether. Many husbands retreated into silence, sat alone in the kitchen or bedroom, slid into the numbness of psychological depression.[10]

But hunger eventually penetrated even the densest numbness. If he could not find work, then maybe she could. Most husbands resisted this exchange of roles as long as possible, dreading the morning when she would close the door behind her and leave him to make the beds, prepare the dinner, be a male housewife. And if her paycheck was a welcome prospect, it was nonetheless *hers*—a domestic dole. After they had made the choice, some husbands found they could not live with it. One man joked about doing household chores while his wife was working downtown at the library, and he made plans for getting a Ph.D., but finally he left home until he could meet her halfway. Another solaced his ego by extramarital affairs. But most managed to make an uneasy truce with circumstance.[11]

Was there any alternative, after all? There was, but it was no less dreaded: the relief rolls. "We'd lived on bread and water three weeks before I could make myself do it," an engineer said. When at last he did, he "simply had to murder my pride." Another middle-class man still could recall vividly, thirty years later, how he put his hand on the doorknob a half-dozen times before he entered the relief office. In the minds of most Americans, "the dole" was the public badge of defeat. As the economic crisis spread, however, first the unemployables, then the working class unemployed, and finally the white-collar workers surrendered pride to necessity. From 1933 to 1935, more than one of every five wage earners accepted federal relief at some time or other, and throughout the decade an even larger proportion took local relief.

It was a hard fate, but the New Dealers tried to make it easier by providing jobs rather than money. The projects of WPA, CPA, FERA, NYA, and other federal agencies offered people a way of saving their bodies without forfeiting too much self-respect. If it was relief, at least it was work relief. "And did they want to work?" an official asked rhetorically when the Civil Works Administration began in Iowa. "In Sioux City they actually had fist fights over shovels!" As they picked up their first federal paychecks, some men wept in happiness.[12]

They were breadwinners again, even if it was government bread. They could go home and meet their wives and children without apology. "It all turned out O.K., you see," said one man, "and I kept my collar white." The emotional network of the middle-class family—taut to the point of rupture under the strain of male unemployment—began to ease with renewed confidence. For decades, experts had been predicting "the collapse of the family" because of war, liquor, woman suffrage, or race suicide. But under an attack more devastating than any they had imagined, the family had survived.[13]

In fact, even when husbands remained jobless, familial relations usually did not deteriorate. According to one systematic survey in a northern industrial city in 1935 and 1936, fewer than one-third of the unemployed middle-class men lost status with their wives, and even fewer lost affection and respect from their young children. An eight-year study in New Haven reported that most families eventually worked out an accommodation to their plight, developing new trust and cooperation between husband and wife. Whether a family slid toward fragmentation or found its way toward cohesion depended on its emotional health before the crisis of unemployment. Couples who had previously enjoyed harmony and mutual respect preserved happy relationships. As one wife remarked, "Money isn't everything; when you get a husband who is as good to you as my husband is to me, you can certainly consider yourself lucky."[14]

Like a flood or a hurricane or a war, the Depression stripped away incidentals and brought people face to face with the basic questions of existence—food and shelter and a job, but also personal identity and relationships. In the end, most men survived with their sense of manliness intact. Even most of those without work for months or years managed to hold on to their self-respect and to the respect from their families. For those who joined government relief rolls, the taint of dependence and the taunt of "boondoggler" were more troubling. But it was only a temporary necessity, they reassured themselves, and it was shared by 20 million other Americans, and, after all, it was *work* relief. Meanwhile, the majority of men—those who had undergone neither unemployment nor relief—survived more fortunately than any. They had succeeded not only in escaping destitution, but in doing so by their own efforts. They were the ultimate heroes of the crisis. They were, according to the editor of Muncie's newspaper, the "forgotten man," who is "too proud to accept relief and yet he deserves it more than three-quarters of those who are getting it. . . . He and his kind are the original spirit that is America."[15]

AFTER THE CRASH, THE AMERICAN dream seemed to have turned to nightmare. But in its darkest moment, in 1933, the new president told Americans that they had nothing to fear but fear itself, and Walt Disney's little pigs were singing "Who's afraid of the big bad wolf?" Five years later, the dwarfs were whistling while they worked, and Prince Charming had come to break the curse on the kingdom. Snow White awoke, her dream come true, and lived happily ever after.

The nightmare decade became an age of hopeful heroism, but heroes had a new size and character. Though usually not dwarfs and miniature pigs in pants, they were Little Caesars or life-sized Rhett Butlers or prince-sized Kingfish. They no longer soared into space like lone eagles.

Of course, Tarzan still swung through his comic-strip jungle every morning, flanked now by Buck Rogers and by Terry and the Pirates. But popular fantasy also came down to earth and back to the real world, away from the deserts of the Sheik and the prairies of the Virginian to the city streets of Sam Spade and Dick Tracy. Men were still he-men, but "hard-boiled" now, urban cowboys.

And some were no bigger than the forgotten man himself: Dagwood Bumstead bumbling through his trap-door life of boss, salesmen, wife, and pets; the Joads trekking toward the grapefields of wrath; and Charlie Chaplin struggling against the gears of modern times and coming out at the other end with a smile. Franklin Roosevelt could not lead the strenuous life of his uncle Theodore because of the steel braces on his legs, but he was the people's leader nonetheless.

During the nightmare decade Americans dreamed themselves in life-sized terms, hard-boiled terms, as forgotten men building houses of brick against the wolf at the door. Yet in the end they turned out to be romantic dreamers, because they awoke expecting to live happily ever after as Mr. and Mrs. Prince Charming (not with 7 children, perhaps, but at least 2.5).[16]

It began as a dream deferred. During the three years following the Crash the marriage rate plummeted lower than in any years before or since. This sudden celibacy was particularly prevalent among persons aged sixteen to twenty-four. A young man dared not take responsibility for a wife when he could not support himself. Then, in 1934, the marriage rate began rising again, until by the end of the decade it exceeded any previous year on record. The birthrate, meanwhile, went in similar directions, but less angularly. It had been dropping steadily for decades, but in the early 1930s it dropped abruptly faster. Then began a slow ascent. In 1940, however, white women of child-bearing age were still having only slightly more babies than at the nadir of the Depression, considerably fewer than on the eve of the Crash. The nation emerged from hard times with nearly 3 million fewer children than would have been born at the 1929 rate.[17]

There was no baby boom to match the spouse boom, but a shrewd demographer in 1940 could have foreseen which way the future would turn. Not in what people said; most Americans, especially the younger ones, believed that the ideal number of children was two or three. Not in what they said, but in what they—especially the younger ones—did. Between 1925 and 1945, young women had a lower-than-usual birthrate of first children *except* during the five years between 1935 and 1939. The average marriage age, meanwhile, remained unchanged. In other words, during the later Depression more young people were marrying and more were having children sooner. This fertility was not for lack of contraception. The vast majority of Americans, in Plainville or Philadelphia, rich or poor, young or old, approved of birth control and practiced it. The fertility was by choice. As hard times became not so hard, younger couples were impatient to make up for the frustration of having deferred marriage and parenthood.

Take the example of the Chases, Ted and Ginger. They met on a blind date in 1935, when he was a nineteen-year-old college sophomore and she was sweet sixteen. At the time, Ted had made up his mind that he could not marry before owning $5,000 in cash, $5,000 in insurance, and a house. Five years later they were husband and wife, living on his $33.32 weekly earnings as a cub commercial engineer for General Electric. Less than a year after that she was pregnant. They had not exactly scheduled a baby so soon, but after all, said Ted cheerfully, "people ought to take chances." When interviewed by a *Ladies' Home Journal* reporter, both Chases were waiting with joy for little Theodore or perhaps Theodora.[18]

There were many Mr. and Mrs. Chases taking up where their parents or slightly older friends had left off in the wake of the Crash. The Depression caused no revolution in their roles except in the literal sense of "revolution"—a process of revolving. People at the end of the thirties returned to the gender definitions of an earlier time, not of the twenties but even earlier than that. The song of victory against the wolf had the tones of a fundamentalist revival meeting.

The gospel of work received particular emphasis. From President Roosevelt and ditchdiggers and men in between, one heard familiar refrains: work is virtue; work builds character; work builds the nation; "The right of a willing man to work and live by his labor is paramount. There is nothing else important." And what about a willing woman, especially a married one? Here some men wavered momentarily. But most of them finally came down alongside the 80 to 90 percent of their sex who declared that "women should not hold a job after marriage."[19] Was it 1909 or 1939? One could hardly hear the difference in the scoring for male voices.

Nor on the female side. Girls would work if they had to, but they decidedly preferred not to. In home-and-marriage classes at the Young Women's Christian Association in 1938, the fiancées were far more unhappy than their future mates about the prospect of becoming employed. If finances permitted, they hoped to settle into suburban housewifery. At a Stephens College symposium, the girls burst into applause when Mrs. Douglas Timmerman, wife of a Junior Chamber of Commerce executive, asserted: "No! Marriage and career don't mix. I tried it . . . and I'm glad to be back home." A majority of senior women at Pennsylvania State College were convinced that a woman who continued her career was being unfair to her husband and children. Vassar seniors preferred homemaking over a career even if they could have professional child care and only a part-time job.[20]

The flapper's hem had fallen far below the knee; the bobbed hair curled decorously to the shoulder. It was as if the twenties had never happened. The articles about fifty-fifty marriages, the defiant pronouncements about combining work and family, the experiments in cooperative nurseries—all the pieces of revised feminism lay forgotten beneath the rubble of the Crash. But the women who had been one-half of those marriages, who had held those jobs, who had supported those nurseries—*they* were still alive. Why didn't they serve as models for younger women? And the thousands of wives who entered the labor force when their husbands lost work—why didn't they persuade other women that one could manage both home and career?

These personifications of feminism remained, but they could not compete against the compelling circumstances of the thirties. First of all, the massive male unemployment rate. As millions of men lost jobs and millions of others feared doing so, they turned with ferocious defensive hostility against wives who sought employment. But the men were not alone. A large majority of women themselves joined the attack, indicating how the Depression had transformed the war between the sexes into another kind of war. The revised feminism of the 1920s had based its egalitarian arguments on the assumption that men would be working alongside emancipated women. With 25 percent of men unemployed, the feminist argument was left standing on one leg.

This situation almost precluded any changes in the traditional female role. Without cooperation and support from her helpmate, a wife usually cannot sustain, financially or emotionally, the burdens of a career. More and more middle-class husbands were helping in housework and childrearing. But egalitarian practice was not necessarily egalitarianism, a genuine redefinition of gender roles on his part *or* hers. Usually he was "helping" her to perform what he considered essentially female work.

Beyond male opposition, however, there was the problem of women's own ambivalence—the old ambivalence now rendered more acute by men's economic plight. The wife of an unemployed worker in New Haven said she wanted him to do his share of the housework, "but," she added, "I suppose I'd lose my respect for him if he did." Her ambivalence exemplified what most housewives were feeling. In a national poll by the *Ladies' Home Journal*, 60 percent of women objected to the word "obey" in the marriage ceremony, 75 percent believed that men and women should make important decisions together, and 80 percent thought an unemployed husband should keep house for a working wife. Yet 60 percent also confessed that they would lose respect for their husbands in a situation where the wife earned more than the man, and 90 percent declared that a woman should give up work if her husband preferred her to stay at home.[21]

Women were confused about who they were and what they wanted. They talked about marriage as "partnership" but didn't know what they meant by it. Through such confusion, even the shrillest feminist arguments could not be heard or understood. "Women are very badly treated in America," Pearl Buck told them in 1938. They "do not feel as happy in their lonely hearts as they wish they did." But the problem was that they did not really know what they wished. And if there was Pearl Buck trying to tell them the secrets of their hearts, there was Rose Wilder Lane to warn that her life as wife, mother, and successful writer "has been arid and sterile at the core." She advised girls: "Your business is to be a woman. Your career is to make a good marriage." One opinion leader contradicted another, and some contradicted themselves. Dorothy Thompson, for example, told *Ladies' Home Journal* housewives in 1940: "I should hate to see most women exteriorize their lives as I have done. I have an ever-increasing respect for those women who stick to their knitting." But Thompson herself was not knitting as she traveled to report the war in Europe.[22]

In these circumstances, it is hardly surprising that young women did not learn or did not accept the teachings of revised feminism. Accomplished public women offered as much discouragement as inspiration. At home, their own mothers provided messages even more mixed. And, meanwhile, they had to cope with a much more personal and tangible circumstance: the Depression had curtailed employment for women, but it had also enforced postponement of marriage and children. Revised feminism had told women that they should enjoy career and home. As hard times began to ease, young women attended to first things first. "We cannot believe," the editors of the *Smith College Weekly* had written in 1919, "that it is fixed in the nature of things that a woman must choose between a home and her work. . . . There must be a way out." In 1938 the *Weekly* announced, under the headline "Marriage for All," the second annual campus symposium on marriage. So many Smithies attended that the lectures had to be moved to a larger hall.[23] Young women had chosen a way—even if not "the way out." But first they had to go through a world war.

THE JAPANESE ATTACK ON Pearl Harbor in 1941 killed the Great Depression. Two years after the United States joined the war against the Axis powers, the unemployment rate of 14 percent was reduced to almost zero. Before victory was achieved in 1945, the frantic production of tanks, planes, ammunition, uniforms, and other war material pulled millions of people into factories and government service, while the armed forces employed 12 million others to wear those uniforms and drive those tanks. Real war proved to be, after all, the most effective war against poverty.

The lives of Americans were wrenched into new shapes. For men the disruption was obvious, as they put on military uniforms and risked their lives in Europe, Africa, and Asia. But the Second World War never developed the intense psychic meaning that the Great War had. Although it lasted three years longer and drafted six times as many young males, it did not become a crucible of masculinity. Most men served with patriotic loyalty but felt surprisingly little personal commitment. They accepted military duty as a national necessity rather than a private test of manhood. On the home front a similar spirit prevailed. No enlistment posters of young sailors riding torpedoes, no hysterical cries of "slacker," just a dogged determination to get the job done.

The war had a more disruptive impact on the lives of women. Almost 200,000 put on the uniforms of the Women's Army Auxiliary Corps and its naval counterpart, the Waves, many of them going overseas in non-combat roles. Female soldiers were a startling phenomenon for Americans, evoking ridicule or suspicion, but their zealous, efficient performance soon earned praise, from military superiors as well as from the civilian public.[24]

Military service also subverted conventional gender definitions in a quite unintended way by giving homosexuals the opportunity to meet more easily and in greater numbers. Before the war, the great majority of gay and lesbian Americans, except in large cities like New York, suffered furtive isolation and self-contempt. As the historian Allan Bérubé has explained, the draft "placed a whole generation of gay men and women in gender-segregated bases where they could find each other, form cliques, and discover the gay life in cities."[25] When Pat Bond walked to the barracks on her first day at Fort Oglethorpe, she heard a short-haired woman at one of the barracks windows exclaim: "Good God, Elizabeth, here comes another one," and Bond thought, "Well, at least they recognize that I am another one." In the music room of the service club at Camp Beale, Marty Klausner played "The Man I Love" on the piano, hoping to attract men's attention.[26]

Gay and lesbian GIs socialized even more successfully off-base. Long lines of servicemen waited to enter the Astor Bar in New York City and the Top of the Mark in San Francisco, while women in uniform congregated with factory women at the If Club and the Flamingo in Los Angeles.[27] One night a twenty-one-year-old naval officer from Seattle walked through the Biltmore bar in Los Angeles, where 75 percent of the men were in uniform. "I asked myself 'Can what I think is going on here *be* going on?' I stopped to find out and sure enough it was. I was in that bar every night."[28]

When they were shipped out to the South Pacific or Europe, the men were brought even closer together. Some army and navy outfits instituted a "buddy system," under which pairs of men were responsible for each other's safety. In the confines of a navy carrier and the stress of danger, buddy relationships often evolved into romantic ones; sometimes sexual, sometimes affectionate. While watching movies at night on the deck of an LST in the Pacific, men held hands, kissed, hugged—not all of them gay men.[29] In other words, the war reopened the continuum that Victorians had enjoyed before the barrier of "homosexuality" was raised. The war, one might say, proved to be a large-scale coming-out event.

"Well, this is the way it's going to be forever," a navy woman exulted in the midst of her first lesbian relationship with a fellow recruit.[30] But even during the war, gay people couldn't help being aware of their precarious status. "Cocksucker" was a favorite put-down among GIs. During basic training in Texas in 1944, an effeminate-acting soldier wrote that the other men "sized [me] up as a fairy" and made life "one miserable hell with their jibes and taunts and petty persecutions."[31] On a more official basis, hundreds of homosexuals were court-martialed and imprisoned for sodomy, while thousands of others were diagnosed by military psychiatrists as "sexual psychopaths" and discharged.[32] Once the war was over and life returned to "normalcy," would gay and lesbian Americans continue enjoying their new sense of personal and collective self-esteem, or would they have to go underground again?

The vast majority of women neither were lesbian nor entered military service. They kept the home fires burning, saved tin cans, tended victory gardens, and frugally spent the government rationing coupons. But millions of home fires ended up far from home, as husbands and boy friends went to work in distant defense plants and wives and girl friends followed them. Within less than four years more than 7 million women changed their county of residence, living in furnished rooms, trailers, hastily built government homes, or "doubled up" with relatives.

Under the impact of war manufacturing, towns became cities, cities became metropolises.[33]

For these women, the change was not merely in where they lived or how. One-third of the female migrants joined the labor force, working alongside the 4 million other women whom war put to work. Because of the sudden manpower crisis, women became a precious asset. Thus, a cosmetics salesgirl learned how to operate a 1,700-ton keel binder, a beautician took over as switchman for 600 Long Island Railroad trains, women cleaned out blast furnaces in Gary, and a group of Maryland grandmothers manned the police radio in Montgomery County. In Detroit, Buffalo, Kenosha, and Wichita, more women took manufacturing jobs than had been employed in all American industries before Pearl Harbor. The same dizzy rate of female employment was found among clerical occupations. By 1945 the total number of employed women had leaped 60 percent. War had accomplished in half a decade what feminist agitation had failed to do in half a century.

There she was, Rosie the Riveter, a heroine in overalls. But, even more significant, she was a middle-aged mother. In sharp contrast to the typical employed woman before the war, three-quarters of the new war workers were married, and one-third had children under the age of fourteen. They transformed the composition of the labor force. By 1945, for the first time in American history, almost a majority of all female workers were wives, most of them older than thirty-five. Like a miracle, revised feminism's hopes of combining home and career seemed to be coming true.[34]

But miracle turned out to be mirage. Although the war drastically changed the activities of women, attitudes proved to be less elastic— and sex roles are determined by what people believe and expect as much as by what they do. At first, it seemed that new behavior was creating new attitudes. Whereas 80 percent of Americans during the Depression had objected to wives' working, in 1942 only 13 percent retained their objections, while a substantial majority favored the employment of wives in war industries. The views of male employers also turned inside out. As wartime mobilization intensified, industries and businesses took down their longstanding barriers and hired women of all ages and marital status for all kinds of jobs. "Meet MRS. Casey Jones," a Pennsylvania Railroad advertisement beckoned, under a picture of a middle-aged woman in overalls and kerchief, shouldering a wrench and sledge hammer. "Casey's gone to war . . . , so Mrs. Jones is . . . out where 'man-size' jobs have to be done: in the round house, in the shops, in the yards."[35]

Beneath the new facade, though, older patterns persisted. Even in their man-sized jobs, women continued to earn less than men. Moreover, they were still treated as women rather than individuals. They were Casey Jones's wife, whom male workers resented or, at best, patronized for being "good as most men, I reckon." Rosie's pneumatic drill did not break up male stereotypes of the "fair sex." One chesty female at the Vultee Company was distracting so many workers that the management forbade women to wear tight sweaters. On a North American Aviation tool shed hung a sign: "No Profanity. Women Working Inside."[36]

Whether in the kitchen or in the tool shed, whether in sweaters or shirts, working women remained women. But there was more to it than that. An unprecedented number of them were mothers. If men were uneasy about accepting women into the masculine world of work, how would they cope with this flagrant violation of gender stereotype, the employed mother? For it was not enough simply to end discrimination against hiring a woman who happened to have children. Something had to be done about supervising those children, especially the young ones, while she was on the job. In 1943 approximately 2 million children needed some kind of care. The Kaiser company in Portland, Oregon, acknowledged the situation when it created an around-the-clock community school for employees' dependents between the ages of eighteen months and six years. The city of Vancouver organized special after-school programs for students whose parents were working beyond midafternoon. But few industrial or government agencies followed their examples. Community child care was too expensive, they explained; but the real reason was that it ran too contrary to prejudices about a mother's rightful place. Only after two years of war did the federal government appropriate funds to build and staff day-care centers, and the funds were sufficient for only one-tenth of the children who needed them. Photographs of youngsters chained to a mobile home and reports of nurseries filled with beds, two children per bed, offered the pathetic evidence for "a national scandal," "probably the most important crisis on the home front today." But the crisis was juvenile delinquency, the scandal was maternal neglect, and the usual lesson was that mothers should stay home where they belonged.[37]

It was not wholly a man-made story. Women, too, played their part in perpetuating the traditional transaction between the sexes. *Vogue* might announce that in "our new life" of wartime service "it is time to stop all the useless little gestures, to stop being the Little Woman and be Women." But what exactly did it mean to be a woman? Only one of every ten working mothers put her children in a public day-care center. No doubt many of the other nine would have done so if more centers had been available, but many made clear that they much preferred using friends or relatives or, if need be, giving up work rather than violating their image of responsible motherhood. What exactly did it mean to be a woman? "I manage to get into trouble once or twice a day," a blonde factory worker said, "just so the foreman can help me out. That makes him feel manly and superior—and friendly"—and also, one suspects, made her feel womanly.[38]

As the Second World War neared its end, female identity was being stretched in a painful tug of war between behavior and attitudes. Although 20 million working women were not in their proverbial place, most men and many women carried proverbial concepts of "the feminine woman" and "the good mother" to the aviation plant or office. Cultural stereotypes had laid roots far deeper than four years of innovation could loosen. But as social psychologists have demonstrated, changed behavior does cause changes in attitudes. If not four years, perhaps ten or twenty would make a difference. In 1945 that possibility seemed very real, because three-quarters of the working women said that they expected to keep on working after the war. Particularly eager were single women and those above the age of forty-five, but almost 69 percent of working wives also said they wanted to remain employed. "I love it," a shipyard welder declared. "I don't know what I would do if I had to go home tomorrow and just take care of the children and be a housewife. . . . I'd hate to do it. I love the noise and the welding and all the people in the yard." So said the women workers. And a variety of other Americans, from Senator Harry Truman to the *Saturday Evening Post*, agreed. "It's a country where work needs doing," a *Woman's Home Companion* writer announced, "and you're just the 'man' for the job."[39]

WHEN THE WAR FINALLY ENDED, female employment did keep rising. By the 1950s, more women were working than ever before, more wives and more mothers, more middle-aged and more middle class, and the large majority (two out of three native white women) in white-collar occupations.[40]

But their hearts and minds were occupied elsewhere. One overheard them in the hit songs of 1944 and 1945. "I Dream of You" and "I'll Buy That Dream" and "My Dreams Are Getting Better All the Time" and simply "Dream, Dream, Dream." After fifteen years of depression and war, "It's Been a Long, Long Time." But at last "I'll Be Walking with My Honey Soon, Soon, Soon," because "My Guy's Come Back." When V-J Day lifted the evil spell from the kingdom, people began to make their dreams come true. First they married. Marriage license bureaus did more business in 1946 than in any year of American history before or since. It was a marital fever which continued throughout the next ten years, expanding the married proportion of the population to unprecedented size, pushing the average age at marriage to an unprecedented low. The effects were most pronounced among urban white women in their twenties, especially those who were college graduates. By 1956, in fact, one of every four was married while still in college. The days when young Carey Thomas had "declared against" marriage seemed long, long ago. According to a poll in 1957, only 9 percent of Americans thought that an unmarried person could be happy.[41]

First they married; then they had children—more quickly than their parents and grandparents (for half the newlyweds, within less than sixteen months) and more numerously. The rate of first births soared to historic heights in the late 1940s, followed a few years later by a record rate of second, third, and even fourth births. In 1945 an incredible 31 percent of white women thought the ideal number of children was four, but a decade later the total had leaped to a more incredible 41 percent. "Ray and I are just crazy about new little babies," exclaimed one mother. "And I love being pregnant." Amid this fertility fever, college graduates were again the most affected. Members of the class of '44, for example, produced more children within ten years than the class of 1921 had borne within twenty-five. If there was any alarm about race suicide, it could have been only about overpopulation.[42]

Young couples raced down the church aisle toward what *Time* called that "lovely light around the little white cottage," which they promptly furnished not only with the children they had had to defer, but also with the material lifestyle they had had to do without. "More than anything on earth, I wanted a husband, home and children," a twenty-nine-year-old woman confessed in 1954. Finally she had her wish: Dick, with whom she enjoyed the blue-and-yellow provincial print on the wing-back lounge, the braided oval rug, the maple rocker and cobbler's bench, bookcases loaded with favorite books, sunshine splashing through the sheer curtains, "unquestionably the greatest happiness that I have ever known."[43]

One has to wonder how gay Americans would find a place amid this giddy scene of nuclear familism. Many gay veterans married and had children, either suppressing their sexual identity or quietly engaging in homosexual affairs. Others couldn't perform that charade. During the first six months after he left the army and returned home to Manhattan, Robert Fleischer's family tried to find dates for him. "They were getting me the most eligible Jewish girls in New York," he recalled. "Finally one day at my sister's home, the entire family practically was there for a summer weekend having barbecue in the back yard. I lined everybody up and I said, 'Listen. Enough! . . . I prefer men and I'm not going to accept any more blind dates with women. Leave me alone! Let me live my life!' And all it did was make my life much easier and much happier."[44] But in rural or small-town communities, coming out was a more daunting, even physically dangerous possibility. Innumerable lesbian and gay veterans from small towns realized they could not go home again. Instead, they migrated to big cities, especially San Francisco and New York, where they could live more freely among people like themselves.

By the late 1940s, however, their hopes of social acceptance or even tolerance were blighted by Cold War politics. Feeling threatened by the red tide of communism in Eastern Europe and Asia, American officials launched a witch-hunt at home, but the witches turned out to be not only alleged communists but also homosexuals. It was the same process of scapegoating that had taken place a half-century earlier against heterosexual men during the white-slave panic. In this case, though, the logic was more cumbersome. Homosexuals who worked for the government were deemed "security risks" because they were susceptible to blackmail by Soviet agents. But logic was simply a vehicle for Cold War paranoia and politics. As the Republican party national chairman in 1948 warned, "sexual perverts . . . have infiltrated our Government in recent years," and they were "perhaps as dangerous as the actual Communists." Two years later, a Senate committee agreed that even "one homosexual can pollute a Government office." Gay federal employees were being fired in growing numbers: five per month between 1947 and 1950; sixty a month between 1950 and 1953. Meanwhile, far beyond Washington, D.C., FBI agents gathered information about gay bars, the post office established a watch on subscribers to gay erotic materials, and local police arrested lesbians and gay men in bars, public restrooms, parks, and beaches. There were a hundred arrests per month in Philadelphia during the fifties. On a single night in 1956 in San Francisco, thirty-six lesbians were arrested at the Alamo Club. The story was much the same in Baltimore, Miami, Wichita, Dallas, Memphis, and Seattle. After a young boy in Sioux City was kidnapped and murdered, the county attorney invoked Iowa's sexual psychopath law and committed twenty-nine local homosexual men to mental institutions.[45]

In Cold War culture, there was room only for straight gender identity—straight and narrow. According to what the media portrayed and what most people said, middle-class America was inhabited by happily married actors and actresses, all playing out the same script—a national Kodak home movie. "We live by you and your ever helpful editors," Jane Hill wrote to *Ladies' Home Journal*.

> In late '49, we led both our college classes in infant productivity. We think we still hold the title. Candy, Terry and Debby—7, 5, and 4—and Brian, born last July—these are our kids plus a pet duck and one turtle.
>
> Of course we think we have the most wonderful daddy in all the world. Lately, he has been made captain of the Westminster [Maryland] National Guard Unit, and his duties have taken up much of his free time. His regular position is Plant Engineer at Congoleum-Nairn, Inc.
>
> I make all the kids' clothes, most of my own, and pajamas and neckties for Raymond, on my new sewing machine. [She also put up more than 500 jars of food a year.] Writing is not my forte, but it's been fun telling you this. . . . My devoted passion for the Ladies' Home Journal is, I believe, just a natural woman's love for something womanly.[46]

For many women, though, happiness did not come so easily. The terrific postwar inflation drove prices much higher than the average middle-class income could reach. Would that little white cottage be filled with infants and diapers and not much else? Most American families would not let their dream slump into anticlimax. They wanted to smile the way that Mrs. Grace Sullivan smiled at them from the glossy pages of *Life*, where she posed in her home amid a washing machine, toaster, sewing machine, vacuum cleaner, and $650 worth of clothes that she had purchased during the past six years with her salary as a schoolteacher.[47]

"I'll Buy That Dream," the song had said. If a husband alone could not afford it, his wife could also go to work—and by 1960, 10 million were doing just that (triple the number in the Depression year of 1940). Before the war almost all working wives had come from lower-class homes; by the late 1950s an equal proportion came from the upper middle class. Wives of white-collar husbands, in fact, were seeking jobs more frequently than those of factory workers. With that third child in school during the day, they could afford to work, at least on a part-time basis (less than a majority worked full time); given their desires for a television set or a second car, they could hardly afford *not* to.[48]

"Work is the highest joy and duty, an end in itself," Charlotte Perkins Gilman had proclaimed at the turn of the century. Thirty years later, Dorothy Thompson had declared: "It was, for me, the outlet, the escape, from something too intense to be born[e]." Their mid-twentieth-century descendants ignored both orthodox and revised feminism. Employment was for them neither outlet nor end. It was the means to raise their family's standard of living toward upper-middle-class abundance. (According to a national survey of white employed wives in their twenties and thirties, one-half were working "to buy something," only one-fifth to fill "a need for accomplishment.") It was a detour on the path toward domesticity. (One-fifth of the working wives planned to retire temporarily in order to have children, while another two-fifths planned to retire permanently.) Most of the newly employed, like most employed women of previous generations, did not take on careers, but merely jobs. The percentage of women in professional and managerial fields remained almost static between 1930 and 1960.

Work was a joy for some, but housework was a higher joy for most. "On the whole, who do you think has the more interesting time," Elmo Roper asked in 1946, "the woman who is holding a full-time job, or the woman who is running a home?" A large majority of housewives responded in favor of "running a home," but so did half of *all* women; only one-third believed that a job was more interesting. Ten years later, a pair of sociologists asked, more subtly: "What are some of the things you do which make you feel useful and important?" Seven of ten employed college-educated women mentioned their jobs, especially when they occupied professional or managerial positions. But when one focuses only on the married and younger women in this group, the pattern of attitudes changes markedly. Only 60 percent of the wives found self-esteem in their jobs, and still fewer of the women aged twenty-one to thirty-five (that is, the daughters of depression and war). One wonders, moreover, how many felt "useful" because their earnings contributed to the family budget.[49]

The large female influx into the labor market effectively closed the century-long question of whether a woman, particularly a mother, should work. Although the debate persisted, it was becoming almost as antiquated as the issue of whether a girl should attend college. The facts had outdistanced it. In both education and employment, middle-class women had decisively perforated the sphere to which their Victorian grandmothers had been assigned. And yet in terms of their attitudes they remained "true women."

In 1956, at a *Ladies' Home Journal* forum entitled "The Plight of the Young Mother," Mrs. Robert Eberhardt described her morning routine, when "I find myself almost running back and forth" between making the beds and making breakfast for her four young children and her store-manager husband. But she was hoping for two more children. The editors of *Life* commiserated with housewives in 1955, "the largest, hardest-working, least-paid occupational group in the country." But nine out of ten women said they liked housework. Some child-care experts talked about "the modern mother's dilemma" and urged her to put the children in day nurseries so that she could have some time for her own needs outside the home. But when Gloria Tweten's husband jokingly wished that they had enough money for a maid to ease her burdens as mother of three preschool children, she retorted: "Oh fine. Then what would I do all day?"[50]

Should we believe these housewives, or should we suspect that they have been subtly brainwashed or coerced? In 1963, Betty Friedan depicted suburban women as the victims of "the feminine mystique" perpetrated by women's magazines, psychiatrists, sociologists, and Madison Avenue. More recently, historian Elaine Tyler May developed a more complex and persuasive interpretation. Americans embraced traditional gender roles, May argued, not only to compensate for the deprivations during the Great Depression and war but also to appease the anxieties of the Cold War. In this era when the United States desperately sought "containment" of the Soviet menace abroad, government spokesmen and social science experts promoted the nuclear family as the bulwark of security—"a psychological fortress"—on the home front.[51] And middle-class women said the same, with only hints of ambivalence breaking through the surface of satisfaction. "[Marriage has given me] my place in life," one housewife declared. "I feel I am doing exactly as I am fitted—with an occasional spurt of independence growing less all the time. I am settling down to a way of things. I am happy or content more of the time than I am not."[52] If housewives had been given role models of "independent" women combining home and career, and if they had been given the pragmatic wherewithal (child-care centers, for example, and an adequate salary), they might have chosen otherwise. But in the fifties there were few models and limited wherewithal. So these highly educated, energetic women chose domesticity and they enjoyed it—at least they said they enjoyed it. "I'm much more free than when I was single and working," said a Texas mother of four. "A married woman has it made."[53]

It was the story of the early twentieth century all over again: female emancipation without feminist consciousness. But the plot had turned inside out, because the doctrine of work had succumbed to the doctrine of domesticity. Even though an unprecedented number of middle-class wives had jobs, they disdained "the career woman" and cast themselves contentedly in the role of homemaker. From a feminist perspective, then, it was a story discouragingly older than the turn of the century. It was "the cult of the lady" transposed to suburbia and translated into Freudian and functionalist terms.

Three factors rendered it significantly different, however (though no more feminist). For one thing, regardless of their motives, more and more wives and mothers were away from home every weekday and bringing back a paycheck. That quite un-Victorian experience had important repercussions on their marital relationships and, as events of the 1960s would demonstrate, on their children. Furthermore, middle-class women had acquired a very un-Victorian sense of sexuality. They were not frail vessels or ladies, but corporeal persons who claimed the right to (at least) half of the sexual satisfaction once monopolized by men. And that brings us to the third new factor: the other half of the once better half. Middle-class men after the war were decidedly unlike the Victorian patriarch. Because the male part of the sexual transaction was different, the female counterpart could not be the same. If Friedan had been looking at both sides of the story, she would have had to write about "the domestic mystique."

SHE DID NOT WRITE THAT HISTORY because most Americans still thought of men primarily as public creatures. Male history, they assumed, took place in the world away from home, especially in the world of work. After fifteen years of depression and war, middle-class men looked more than ever to their jobs as the mirror of their identity. The job was for them what the family was for their wives. And more than ever they measured themselves not only by what they did, but also by what they earned. They wanted to buy the new car, the new refrigerator, the new house, the new everything that hard times had denied them. It was acquisitiveness that motivated them—but it was more than that, or, rather, less. Basically they were wanting "the good life," by which they meant security. They wanted just enough money to protect themselves against some future calamity like the one they remembered from their past. Rather than climb the perilous heights of occupational mobility, they hoped to go just high enough to find a secure resting place.

But enough never seemed to be enough in the white-collar world. The more a man earned, the more he seemed to have to earn, not only because inflation reduced the purchasing power of his paycheck, but also because he and his family always somehow needed something more: a second car, to drive the children to tennis lessons; a vacation in Yosemite; a fourth baby, and then a house with a fourth bedroom. The good life could always be better. And it could be bought in monthly credit payments. The typical young suburban middle-class family of the affluent fifties—once the children of depression—spent instead of saved, preferring the "security" of a regular, predetermined outflow to the anxiety of making budgetary choices.

This private Keynesianism succeeded in raising the average middle-class income by almost one-third between 1950 and 1960. But it did not let a man rest. He had to keep working hard—and the more he earned, the harder he had to work. There were no plateaus in the white-collar world. Not in the middle levels. "What it boils down to is this," one executive said, "you promote the guy who takes his problem home with him." But not in the upper ranges, either. "Sometimes I get up from one wage bargaining session," a utility company president remarked, "go home, lie awake thinking until it gets light, and then go back to the bargaining table with maybe only an hour's sleep. I've got an ulcer that acts up on me in times like that." While the average clerical or sales worker gave thirty-eight hours per week to his job, one-third of professionals and two-thirds of the executives gave more than forty, usually fifty or sixty, hours. Partly for the money, mostly for love. "Do I work too hard?" a union executive asked rhetorically. "My doctor and my wife think so, but I don't." And a company president: "You live only one time and you might as well do something you like."[54]

So they worked hard, ulcerously hard sometimes, and most of them derived satisfaction, especially those at the top of the white-collar hierarchy, who enjoyed the process itself and who could take personal pride in what they accomplished at the end of that process—a new wage contract, a record profit margin, an improved design. For men farther down, satisfaction was more elusive and more ambiguous. In the large organizations that increasingly characterized the economy, they were middle management, both supervising and supervised, belonging to the company rather than its belonging to them. They were "not their own men." If they looked for tangible definitions of their achievement, they found them less often in the job than at home, among the possessions that their earnings had purchased. Were they therefore "alienated," as so many postwar intellectuals claimed on their behalf? No, that was largely a projection by outsiders. The white-collar workers themselves were primarily seeking security, not achievement, and in the middle circles of bureaucracy they felt more secure than at the top. They could pass the risks and the responsibilities to someone above them.

And yet neither money nor nonresponsibility immunized them against another source of anxiety. "How well do you fit into the group?" This was the question that up-to-date organizations were asking in their personality tests and interviews, their "problem-solving groups" and role-playing sessions, and their daily conversations. Because the question focused more on personality (who are you?) than on production (what is your skill?), employees had to measure themselves by fluid criteria. And precisely because the emphasis was on cooperativeness, on not rocking the boat, employees had to navigate according to signals muffled by bland euphemisms. One junior executive vividly described this new "social ethic" in practice.

> We are all working in a very large room; an administrative section is simply a number of desks which are adjacent. I am not near the point where I will have a glass cubicle with a group of subordinates outside. So I carefully, week by week, effect small changes, to get an extra stenographer, to shift a file here, another there, to separate my section from the next.

Everything is done in an atmosphere of extreme amiability. No one ever does anything to rock the boat, and everyone keeps smiling. Honest to God, my face was sore at the end of the first month, smiling at everyone.

In terms of sexual stereotypes, it was a feminine world. The openly aggressive individualism of a robber baron or a would-be baron was out of place and out of date. The successful worker had to use the soft arts of personnel relations. To get ahead, he had to get along.[55]

When he left the office at day's end, the Smiling Man put down his mask and tried to regain a sense of who he really was. Home beckoned as a refuge where he hoped to validate his worth, amid the love of his wife and children and amid the possessions that he had provided for them. Because the occupational setting furnished increasingly tricky mirrors for his identity, he looked more than ever to domestic mirrors.

But the social ethic followed him home from the office. "Togetherness"—that was what the ideal family was supposed to achieve. According to the fashionable prescriptions of the forties and fifties, husband and wife were supposed to be partners in the family enterprise, living with each other and with their children in happy democracy. Decisions were to be made jointly, disagreements were to be resolved by consensus, and household chores were to be distributed among everyone. As the title of an article in *Parents' Magazine* explained, "Families That Play Together Stay Together."[56]

Thus the postwar "feminine mystique" had a double edge. The emphasis on femininity was one-half of a larger trend toward domesticating not only women, but men too. Father's Day had begun merely as an afterthought—a commercial afterthought—to the moralistic proclamation of Mother's Day. Following the Second World War, however, it acquired a genuine meaning of its own. "Being a real father is not 'sissy' business," a male psychiatrist wrote in *Parents' Magazine* in 1947. "It is not an avocation, a hobby to be pursued in spare moments. It is an occupation. And for the father and his children, it is the most important occupation in the world and for the world." If that were to be the case, home would provide no refuge, no masculine retreat. It would be, instead, a smaller organization making its own sort of troubling demands. When the breadwinner came home from work, he should begin his homework, taking his spot on the home team.

In 1947 there were few fathers among the audience of *Parents' Magazine* to receive this message, but there were many mothers who would quote it to them. And soon that message became more and more wide-spread among the media of the middle class, more and more imperi-ous. "What Every Father Should Know." "Let Daddy Take Over." "Men Make Wonderful Mothers." Fathers might manage to ignore the pres-sures coming from child-rearing experts and even from their own wives, but they found it harder to resist their peers. By the early 1950s, un-precedented numbers of husbands and husbands-to-be were attending classes on marriage and family. In response to male interest, the Visit-ing Nurse Service of New York began holding classes for prospective fa-thers. Meetings of parent-teacher associations were no longer just fe-male events. At home, one-third of the proverbial autocrats of the breakfast table were scrambling eggs and washing dishes. At day's end, instead of subsiding into their favorite leather chairs and waiting for slippers and pipe, they were on their hands and knees playing blocks with the children or barbecuing the steak in the backyard. More young fathers, though by no means most, were giving Junior his 6:00 P.M. feeding and then changing his diaper. Although children still usually turned to their mothers for advice and comfort, fathers were providing far more affection and day-to-day guidance than they had gotten from their own fathers. *Life with Father* no longer played only on the Broadway stage. By 1954 *Life* magazine was announcing "the domestication of the American male."[57]

Dutifully the men practiced their part in the play of togetherness. But some wondered how far domestication could go before becoming emasculation. The patriarchal role was dead, but the opposite role of "poor dad" was very much alive. Each morning millions of Americans snickered at Dagwood Bumstead; each week they laughed at Danny Thomas, Ozzie Nelson, and Robert Young. Of course, it was all in fun. The fact that almost half the men in the daily comic strips were shorter than their wives did not mean that real men were shrinking. And yet—status was a matter of mind, not physique. You were only as important as you and others thought you were. And by the mid-1950s some of those others were beginning to have second thoughts. Psychiatrists tanked ominously about the ineffectual man, the passive man, the man whose masculine ego had been robbed. Child-rearing authorities were concerned that "the currently advertised ideal" was depriving fathers of their rightful needs at home. Writers in *Life* and *Parents' Magazine* en-couraged men to summon up "what reserves of masculinity are left in them" in order to exert firmer parental authority.

Amid this cross fire of advice, men no longer knew what to think. A father of five children jokingly pleaded for "the care and feeding of Spock-marked fathers," but—as in the case of J. D. Salinger's "Laughing Man"—one shuddered at what lay behind his merry facade.[58]

And that was not the whole of the masculine predicament. There were cross fires within cross fires. The good father must also be the good husband in the kitchen, in the living room, and in the bedroom. The happiest marriage was a partnership: so said the experts, in their manuals and magazine columns, and so said the wives themselves. According to Robert Blood's systematic interviews of Detroit housewives in 1955, one-half selected "companionship in doing things together with husband" as the most important aspect of marriage, far more important to them than love, understanding, economic well-being, or children. They wanted to share in his job by entertaining his colleagues and clients at dinner parties or by talking over his business problems. They wanted to have fun with him at the bowling alley or on family picnics.

They also wanted to enjoy sexual recreation with him. The typical middle-class woman of the postwar era still desired intercourse less frequently than her husband. But the doctrine of togetherness governed the bedroom as imperiously as it did the rest of the house. Even if wives expected intercourse less often, when they did have it they expected full satisfaction. Female sexuality—in the nineteenth century a perversion, in the early twentieth century a radical notion—had become an undisputed fact of marital life (and, for a minority, of premarital life as well). The good husband must not think only of his own desires. Indeed, according to the cult of mutual orgasm that pervaded the marriage manuals, he must develop his lover's skill toward a literal togetherness. It was a difficult demand, an anxiety-provoking demand. But most middle-class couples subjected themselves to it. At whatever cost, they wanted to be marital partners—or at least to *think* they were. Two sociologists made the interesting discovery that no matter how often each spouse really wanted to make love, he or she reported that the other desired the same frequency. In their earnest loyalty to the partnership principle, they distorted each other's actual desires in the direction of congruence.

"Togetherness" thus produced self-deception and, one would suspect, considerable frustration for the more amorous spouse, who usually was the man. But most married couples *said* they were happy with

the love they were receiving. Almost one-half of the Detroit wives de-
clared themselves "quite satisfied. I'm lucky the way |my husband's
love| is," and another third rated themselves "enthusiastic, it couldn't
be better." A few years later, the large majority of upper-middle-class
wives told George Gallup's pollsters that their husbands were even
more attentive and affectionate than they had expected. Seventy-six
percent were sexually satisfied. In general, one-half of all American
adults said they were "very happy" with their marriages, and another
one-fourth were "moderately happy"; only 5 percent complained of being "not very happy."[59]

So they said, in sincerity but also in considerable deception of the
pollsters or of themselves. For the smooth surface of these testimonials covered a fierce undertow. The truth also was that wives became
progressively less happy as the honeymoon gave way to pregnancy, and
then pregnancy to child-rearing. The longer they were married, the
greater their discontent. They focused their complaints especially on
the aspect of marriage that they ranked most important, namely, the
companionship with their husbands. "He works too hard," they said.
"He stays in the office too late. And when he comes home, he's too
tired or preoccupied to pay attention to me or the kids." Men—especially men on the way up—apparently were reneging on their half of the
contract of togetherness.

But that was only half of the truth. For many wives were making it
almost impossible for their husbands to do anything but renege. When
a sociologist asked 600 middle- and upper-middle-class women in the
Chicago area to say what they considered the husband's most important role, two-thirds replied "breadwinner." In other words, even if their
white-collar mates had decided to emphasize success at home rather
than success in their occupations, they would have appeased one kind
of wifely discontent, only to arouse another. Men failed either way.
Wives who had their own jobs depended less heavily on the male
breadwinner for status and gratification, but their employment threatened his sense of authority and self-esteem. Marital conflict occurred
either way.[60]

IN THE END, THEN, THE IDEAL of marital partnership was flawed. The two
partners were trying to write a new, egalitarian script for their relationship but continuing to cast each other and themselves in essentially
their old roles. More husbands took up household responsibilities than

their fathers or grandfathers had, while more wives held jobs than their mothers and grandmothers. Nevertheless, the men remained "bread-winners" and the women remained "housewives," each reaching coop-eratively toward the other while standing in their separate spheres. Whatever "togetherness" they achieved was subtracted from what each considered his or her "real" purposes. The more they subtracted, the more tension and discontent developed in their marriage.

The partnership suffered strain because each of the partners was undergoing strain. In the twilight of patriarchy, middle-class males had found it hard to be a man. In the days of domestic democracy, they found it no easier. At work and at home, they acted according to new scripts which threatened their sense of masculinity. In combination, the two scripts produced the double jeopardy of a double bind.

Their wives, meanwhile, had an apparently easier script. Although unprecedented numbers of them were employed, that activity took place off stage. Their on-stage role was happy housewife—well, almost happy. In retrospect, one sees that they had denied their intellectual and nondomestic capabilities. At the time they did not see it except in glimpses or, if they did, found no encouragement for this larger vision of self. Women were supposed to be happy housewives. So they dedicated themselves to the home and achieved through their husbands.

But almost everyone smiled, at least most of the time. Not just because the group or *Ladies' Home Journal* told them to get along, nor because Norman Vincent Peale convinced them of the power of positive thinking. They smiled because their dreams were growing around them, in an abundance of chrome and brick and mink. And they smiled especially because their children were growing up. Through these future inheritors of affluence and parental devotion, the heroes and heroines of domesticity expected to live happily ever after. Whatever their own difficulties and doubts, they depended on their children to vindicate their lives.[61]

In the 1960s, however, the plot took an ironic turn. They would be betrayed by their own children because they had betrayed so much of themselves.

7

The Children of Domesticity

After 1960 the era of tranquil domesticity dissolved into hurly-burly scenes of rebellion. The camera eye swung from the pine-paneled family room to the campuses and streets, where young people chanted the birth of a "new generation." Suddenly the established cultural institutions and values shook under the assault of youth. Racism, capitalism and imperialism, higher education and professionalism, marriage and parenthood and sexual mores—all came into radical question.

The New Left proposed answers; the "counterculture" proposed somewhat different answers; and then the Women's Liberation Movement proposed its own, thereby translating the upheaval of the sixties into yet another chapter in the history of feminism. Among the daughters of domesticity Susan B. Anthony and her sister crusaders finally found descendants. But the newest feminism did more than revive the old. With unprecedented ardor, it challenged the institutions of family and marriage and, ultimately, the roles played by men. By the 1970s many Americans were asking, with fresh confusion or exhilaration: "What does it mean to be a (male) (female) person?"

AT FIRST, THE CHILDREN SEEMED ready and eager to live up to the inheritance that their parents were offering. Middle-class adolescents in the 1950s behaved like younger replicas of the organization man and the happy housewife. The girls worried primarily about their popularity and physical attractiveness, gathering around themselves a small circle of female friends and waiting or hoping for a boy to invite them to the Friday night dance or, better yet, to "go steady." They were social creatures, skillful diplomats in the world of adolescent relations. With their parents, too, they worked out an easy balance of power. Although only half of the girls had a part in making the rules at home, almost all were pleased with their parents' jurisdiction. They were closely supervised, and liked being so; they were not encouraged to be independent, and did not want to be.

From this undefiant present they looked forward to an undefiant future. Most expected to have a job, usually in some feminine field like nursing or teaching or secretarial work, but that was only a way station until the right man came along. Marriage formed the horizon of their vision; beyond it, few could imagine clearly how their individual lives might develop. And who was Mister Right? According to a poll of twenty-year-old women in 1956, their ideal husband was personified by Perry Como, followed by an odd assortment of celebrities including Eisenhower and Tab Hunter (tied for fourth place) and Marlon Brando, James Dean, John F. Kennedy, Jerry Lewis, and Richard Nixon (all tied for sixth). But this was the whimsical lottery of daydream. In reality, most girls looked forward to a husband who would be successful in his career as well as helpful at home. Many hoped that the career would not be unduly demanding, however, so that he could contribute plenty of time to raising their children.

On the male side, meanwhile, the adolescent story had different contents, but essentially the same plot. Boys generally were more troublesome and troubled than their diplomatic sisters, relating abrasively with authorities and resenting the constraints that their parents placed on them. Whereas girls worried about social acceptance, boys worried about self-control. Their friends served them not as confidants, but as a "gang" of comrades protecting them against the outside world and also, they hoped, against their own deviant impulses.

Less socialized they were, but rebels they were not. Indeed, Edgar Friedenberg lamented in 1959 that the traditionally defiant adolescent was vanishing amid the insidious coercions of "permissiveness" at school and at home. Certainly the boys expressed sober enough fantasies, so sober and realistic that one hesitates to call them fantasies at all. In a nationwide set of interviews conducted in 1955, two of five male adolescents could think of no way in which they wanted to be different. The rest tended to focus their wishes on their future work role. Unlike the girls, they sought self-definition primarily in their occupations. But it was a very unrebellious definition. The large majority looked forward to a professional career, preferably one that was interesting, but also one that was "steady." One-third said that "be your own boss" was among their least important criteria.

These junior organization men did not talk about marriage and family. That was the stuff that female dreams were made of. But the spurt in the teenage marriage rate during the 1950s could not have been wholly the work of women. Beside every bride stood a (somewhat older) groom, often because he had made her pregnant, but more often because he too shared the domestic mystique. When Dee Dee Floyd married John, she was a seventeen-year-old clerk for a plate-glass company. Two years later they were building the good life in frantic fashion. Having gone into debt by buying an almost new Chevrolet Impala Super Sport and expecting their first baby, they had to live with in-laws and eat baked-bean dinners. But soon they hoped to afford the down payment on a house for the four children they intended. "John and I do so want to have our own house."[1]

For the majority of middle-class children, however, marriage had to wait a few years. College came first. Higher education, which had once been the privilege of a small elite, during the 1950s became the increasingly usual expectation of the middle class. In statistical terms, college no longer was a rare experience.

More important, in emotional terms it also was far from the "sacramental experience" that Florence Kelley had undergone in 1875. Mid-century students did not let it be that, or did not know how to make it that. As they left home, they took along their domesticated attitudes. Most of them studied hard and played hard, but inside the boundaries of risk. Classrooms were quiet fields of neatly combed heads bent over spiral notebooks. "We *think* before we talk," a Smith student explained. Even when they talked, they moved on mental tiptoe. After an instructor challenged one student's opinion in a University of Wisconsin course, she meekly responded: "I take it back." The prevailing mood of passivity and caution drove many of their teachers wild. "It's almost as if they were painted on the wall," a literature professor exclaimed. "Goalkeepers," "listeners," "a generation of private seekers" were typical faculty snapshots of their students. "Are they really listening?" the poet Karl Shapiro wondered. "Their minds are as quiet as mice."[2]

The students themselves knew their own minds well enough. When asked to write a short essay describing how they expected to be living ten years later, forty-six of fifty sophomore women in 1955 outlined almost identical scenarios. They would be married to a successful professional man or junior executive, they wrote, chauffeuring three or more children around suburbia in a station wagon, while also participating in various civic organizations. In 1961 George Gallup was astonished to find that so many upper-middle-class women of college age not merely looked forward to owning lavish homes, but often specified their visions in terms of 1,250 square feet or built-in ovens with Formica counters thirty-four inches high. "Perhaps we are old-fashioned," the Smith College student newspaper commented in 1961, "but we feel that for the majority of women, their place is 'in the home.'" Marriage was a career all its own, the editors said. "Why don't we stop competing with the men, and instead cooperate with them?"

The sacramental experience of college had become a wedding. During the 1950s, when 15 percent of women were married even before graduation and as many as 75 percent within two years afterward, spinsterhood loomed like the spectre of failure. On a sociologist's questionnaire about future ambitions, a Smith student wrote simply: "Would like to be married to a Princeton graduate."[3]

The Princeton man welcomed the idea. When interviewed by *Time* in 1955, one senior on the eve of law school spoke for most of his classmates on other campuses.

> I'll belong to all the associations you can think of—Elks, V.F.W.'s Boy Scouts and Boys' Clubs, Y.M.C.A., American Legion etc. It will keep me away from home a lot. But my wife [a purely hypothetical wife] won't mind. She'll be vivacious and easy with people. And she will belong to everything in sight too—especially the League of Women Voters. I won't marry her until I'm twenty-eight, and so when I'm thirty-six we will have only two of the four children I hope for eventually. We'll be living in an upper-middle-class home costing about $20,000 by then, in a suburban fringe . . . We'll have two Fords or Chevvies when I'm thirty-six, so we can keep up the busy schedule we'll have. But in addition to this public social life, we'll have private friends who don't even live around Toledo—friends with whom we can be completely natural and relaxed. That's where Princeton friends will be very important.[4]

As men, however, he and his fellow collegians had to make the careers that their future wives hoped to sidestep. The statistics of enrollment in the various academic fields delineate their plans graphically. Of the male graduates in 1956, only one-third had majored in physical and biological sciences, mathematics, and the liberal arts. The rest had chosen fields of applied learning: agriculture, engineering, and, above all, business. A larger number of men were studying business and commerce than all the basic sciences and liberal arts together. And most of them wanted to join large corporations, preferring the security of working for someone else to being an individualistic entrepreneur or even to entering their fathers' businesses. According to William H. Whyte, there was "a generation of bureaucrats" marching soberly from the campus toward gray-flannel adulthood.[5]

PRESIDENT EISENHOWER WAS SPEAKING for most Americans in the 1950s when he asserted that "our government makes no sense unless it is founded in a deeply felt religious faith—and I don't care what it is." For a dissident few, however, it was not enough to say that the family should pray and play toward togetherness. They denounced positive thinking and domesticity as false faiths; they saw the pine-paneled family room and two-car garage as heathen temples. Americans were worshiping Moloch, Moloch, Moloch, chanted Allen Ginsberg, as he pointed out "the best minds of my generation destroyed by madness." While the children of domesticity walked down wedding aisles toward corporations and suburbias, Jack Kerouac was on the road, driving back and forth across the country in search of people "who never yawn or say a commonplace thing, but burn, burn, burn like fabulous yellow roman candles exploding like spiders across the stars." Ginsberg, Kerouac, and others proclaimed "the beat generation," a cluster of young artists enjoying sex and liquor and jazz while questing spiritual transcendence through orgasm and Zen. They offered a vibrant alternative and life style, a Whitmanesque revival.

Middle-class adults could not understand the Beatnik. "A model psychopath" was *Time*'s diagnosis. But the children of these adults did not really understand, either. When Kerouac came to give a speech at Brooklyn College, an eager crowd of students awaited him. As he began, they solemnly opened their notebooks and poised their pens. They did not vibrate to the incantations of Ginsberg and the Beats. Norman Mailer might celebrate the white hipster who won existential manhood through violence and sex, but most young people ignored or mocked that ferocious model. They found no answer in the hipster hero because they could not understand the question that he possessed and that possessed him. Like James Dean, he seemed to them a rebel without a cause. They would not live (or die) on the road.[6]

They did, nevertheless, have a question, a vague quest, but as "a generation of private seekers," they pursued it quietly and carefully. Their model was not the howling Ginsberg or the manly Mailer, but Holden Caulfield. *The Catcher in the Rye* was the favorite book of campus students because they identified with Caulfield's search for some authenticity beyond "phoniness." It was another in the long line of novels about rebellious male adolescents, yet Holden was untrue to form. He rebelled tenderly, compassionately, more feminine than masculine. When he undertook the standard initiation into manhood by bringing a prostitute to his hotel room, he couldn't go through with it. "Look, I don't feel very much like myself tonight . . . ," he told her. "I'll pay you and all, but do you mind very much if we don't do it?" He sought his identity, instead, through a female figure outside the realm of sexuality, namely, his ten-year-old-sister. "You'd like her," Holden told his audience. "I mean if you tell Phoebe something, she knows exactly what the hell you're talking about." To her he could confess his notion of becoming the catcher in the rye, the person who saved little kids from accidentally running over the cliff.[7]

If the young had a culture hero of their own, he was Holden Caulfield, the shy rebel, the rebel with a fragile cause of love. His story traced a faint line of generational division. Parents and children of the fifties were indistinguishable except on the matter of love and its corollary, sexuality. Here the young deviated. As with everything else, they made a modest rather than a brash break, but they nevertheless turned in a new direction, especially for men.

Approximately one-fourth of college women and between one-third and two-thirds of college men during the 1950s engaged in premarital intercourse. These rates did not substantially differ from those of earlier campus generations. The difference lay in young people's attitudes toward what they or their friends were doing. Whereas only one in five adults said it was all right for husband or wife to have had premarital sexual intercourse, during the 1950s an increasing majority of male college students and a rapidly increasing minority of females approved. And, more often, they were enjoying the experience without pangs of guilt.

By itself this statistical contrast proves little, because sociologists have found that the young liberal grows quickly conservative on premarital sex as soon as she or he has children. The graduates of the 1950s, however, did not conform to the usual pattern. By 1970, when they had entered parenthood and middle age, they remained as tolerant of premarital sex as they had been before marriage. Something significantly new occurred during the fifties, then—not a "revolution" in middle-class sexual behavior (that had taken place a half century before), but a convergence between behavior and attitudes. Young people's minds had finally caught up with their bodies.

When told in terms of gender roles, however, this story divides into two quite different stories. Although more college women approved of sexual intercourse, most of them restricted their approval either to a couple who were in love (what sociologist Ira Reiss calls "permissiveness with affection") or to a woman who loved the man (what Reiss calls "the transitional double standard"). Thus, the old self-image of woman as "the better half" still held sway within the new context of female sexuality. In this respect, daughters had not moved as far from their mothers as the statistics at first suggest. And they were even closer in the way they foresaw their husbands' roles, even their roles in bed, as loyal daughters of domesticity.

Young men, on the other hand, were substantially revising the traditional masculine role. During the fifties most of them discarded the Victorian principle of premarital chastity, but they also discarded its furtive opposite, "wild oats." Instead, they were endorsing, at a markedly increasing rate, the standard of "permissiveness with affection." The usual masculine separation of love and sex was becoming much less usual. The old Saturday-night story of the guys driving downtown to the whorehouse was a vintage tale; now they slept with women they knew and, sometimes, loved. As David Riesman observed in 1959:

> Young people are increasingly preoccupied with their capacity to love as well as be loved. And I have the impression that sexual relations themselves when they do occur come about less frequently from a desire on the part of the boys to present trophies to their own male vanity than to secure themselves against the anxiety that they may not be truly and deeply loved, or capable of love.

This development was occurring slowly, however, and secretively. Like Jack Nicholson in the film *Carnal Knowledge*, most college men of the fifties still wore the cynical mask of the cocksman; to lower it would expose them to comrades' wounding ridicule. For this reason, women believed that men were more chauvinistic than they really were. In fact, considerably fewer college men wanted to dominate marital decision-

making, and fewer portrayed the ideal woman with stereotyped "feminine" qualities, than women believed.[8]

For the first time, then, equalization of gender roles was occurring
on male initiative. But it was slight, gradual, almost imperceptible. Few
young men announced it, and few young women noticed it. And in any
case, what were they to do with these tentative new notions of human
relationship? At the end of *Catcher in the Rye*, we discover that Caulfield
has been narrating his search for authenticity from a mental institution. This was hardly an encouraging conclusion for students about to
graduate from their own mental institutions. But that was precisely the
point of their story. Many of the children of domesticity would have
liked to express moral vision and personal passion. But in the culture
of the fifties, they saw no adequate form for doing so. The Beats were
too "bohemian" for their middle-class values, the hipster was too ruth-
less for their sensibilities, and Holden Caulfield—well, in the end he
embraced his child sister and refused to grow up. To all students but
the most alienated, the last alternative was impossibly fanciful. So they
graduated into the adult world.

The culture awaiting them did not offer much promise of passionate, authentic self-fulfillment. For a table of cultural contents, one can
scan the 1953 list of nonfiction best-sellers. At the top for the second
consecutive year were the Revised Standard Version of the Bible and
The Power of Positive Thinking. In fourth, fifth, and sixth places were Dale
Evans Rogers's spiritual autobiography, *Angel Unaware*, Fulton J. Sheen's
Life is Worth Living, and Catherine Marshall's pious tribute to her husband, *A Man Called Peter*. Wedged in the middle was Kinsey's *Sexual Behavior of the Human Female*. It was a smug and phony world out there. It
was, according to *Look's* reporters in January 1960, "a pond of calm and
contentment," where almost everyone expected "a well-controlled,
manicured, safe, unspectacular existence of measured material realization."[9] But it was the only world that young people had. And so they
graduated into the pursuit of private happiness.

IN FEBRUARY 1960, ONE MONTH after *Look's* report, four black students from
North Carolina Agricultural and Technical College sat down at a Wool-
worth lunch counter in Greensboro. "We don't serve colored here," the
waitress told them, but they did not leave until closing time. Soon students were "sitting in" all over the South, northerners were marching
and raising funds in their support, and racially mixed groups were rid-

ing buses to segregated southern terminals and into the jeers and fists of angry white mobs. Meanwhile, the Student Nonviolent Coordinating Committee (SNCC) was organized in Raleigh, joined shortly after by its white ally, the Students for a Democratic Society (SDS).

Sit-ins, freedom rides, marches, picket lines—"the Movement" had begun, sending ripples, then shock waves, across that calm American pond. The sit-ins at lunch counters of the upper South became voter-registration drives in the Deep South, punctuated by imprisonment, beatings, and murders of the "outside agitators." Student demonstrations in San Francisco against the House Un-American Activities Committee's hearings in 1960 became the Free Speech Movement and a campus revolution at Berkeley in 1964. And then, on campuses throughout the country, students mobilized against ROTC, against faculty paternalism, against university investments in ghetto real estate, and against the Vietnam War. Thousands of Americans marched to Selma, Alabama; hundreds of thousands marched on Washington. In urban slums, SDS groups worked to organize the poor; in urban ghettos, the black masses erupted into violence.

"The times they are a'changin'," scowling Bob Dylan told Americans. Your sons and daughters are beyond your command, he warned, so please get out of the new road if you can't lend a hand. A new generation had abruptly appeared, as dissonant to established values as Dylan's voice sounded to adults' ears. "We are the people of this generation," the SDS Port Huron Statement announced in 1962, "bred in at least modest comfort, housed now in universities, looking uncomfortably to the world we inherit." They had grown up amid materialism, bureaucracy, racism, cold war, and apathy. But now these students of the sixties were posing radical questions: "What is really important? Can we live in a different and better way? If we wanted to change society, how would we do it?" They had not yet learned how the Movement should take them, but they knew where. "We would replace power rooted in possession, privilege, or circumstance by power and uniqueness rooted in love, reflectiveness, reason and creativity." They visualized a political and economic system in which all citizens shared in making decisions and a culture in which each individual sought "a meaning in life that is personally authentic."[10]

Holden Caulfield had broken out of his mental hospital into the open air, the Beats were on the road toward social justice, the rebels had found a cause. "We do not feel like a cool, swinging generation," a

Radcliffe student declared at her commencement ceremonies in 1968; "we are eaten up by an intensity we cannot name." No one hesitated to say it now: there was a younger generation decisively different from their elders. By the end of the decade, Kenneth Keniston discovered the emergence of a new stage of life, intervening between adolescence and adulthood, which he called "youth."[11]

But why? Even stunningly abrupt cultural shifts do not come from nowhere. Nor did this one. It began in the demographic cycle. Because of the depressed birthrate during the 1930s and the subsequent baby boom, in the 1960s young people formed the largest age group in the total population.* They not only were more numerous, but also felt more numerous, because they were collected by the thousands, even tens of thousands, on campuses. An unprecedented 25 percent of people aged twenty-one through twenty-four were still in school, forming what sociologists, borrowing from physics, call a "critical mass." They were there because their affluent parents could afford to keep them there and because the postindustrial economy increasingly required a college diploma as the passport to white-collar jobs. So they had an interlude between childhood dependence and adult responsibilities. For four years (and often, because of graduate school, for six or eight years) they were given "a psycho-social moratorium" during which to study, to play, and also to wonder where they wanted their lives to go.

And where was that? Their parents had a ready answer. "My son, the doctor," the proverbial Jewish mother said proudly, and Christians heaped upon their sons the same burdensome hopes for professional success. That expectation alone produced considerable anxiety. But the question of success contained an added anxious twist for the descendants of affluence. Because an unprecedented number of them had parents who themselves were college graduates, they could not feel the satisfaction of being "the first in the family to . . ." As the children of professionals, they could only do better what their fathers had already done well. Instead of breaking new paths, they were repaving established ones, with their parents ready to remind them of the standards for competence. In aspiring toward a career, then, they had smaller psychological space in which to explore.

---

*In 1960, persons aged fourteen to twenty-four made up 28% of the population, larger than any other ten-year cohort except the one right behind them, aged five to thirteen: Walter T. K. Nugent, *Modern America* (Boston, 1973), pp. 289–91.

During the fifties, most young men reacted to this situation by foreshortening their ambitions, graduating into secure niches offered by large corporations or universities. The young women, meanwhile, made the complementary choice of a domestic niche in suburbia. By 1960, however, their successors found it easier to consider riskier options. They not only could take for granted the economic security that their Depression-era parents had anxiously accumulated, but they also were surrounded by so many other "youth" who could share and validate the choice of risk. Economically as well as psychologically, they were well prepared for rebellion. They simply needed four black students in Greensboro and a hundred whites in San Francisco to break the silence of the fifties. After that, hundreds of thousands of others began shouting to one another what they had been quietly saying to themselves. They were still a small minority of their cohort, but they proclaimed themselves "the New Left" and then "the new generation."[12]

Almost immediately, their elders responded with alarmed cries of "generation gap" and "youth revolt," as if the marches and barricades and manifestoes signaled a war between the generations. The truth was not quite so melodramatically simple. Contrary to spokesmen on both sides, the insurgency did not seek to eradicate everything that "people over thirty" believed. To be sure, the young radicals were not moving into the places prepared by their parents, but neither had they leaped across a "generation gap" into some entirely new world of values. Rather, they were going in the direction that their own parents had pointed out to them. For their upbringing had included not only the injunctions to "work hard" and "find a good (job) (husband) (wife)," but also less cautionary advice. The echo chambers of their superegos resounded as well with parental voices saying "make up your own mind," "do what you think is right," and "we only want you to be happy." The offspring of Dr. Spock and familial democracy had been raised to take themselves seriously, to believe that their wants could and should "count."

Well, then, if expectations of professional success were burdensome, why not reject them? If black and poor Americans were oppressed, why not fight on their behalf? The young radicals were simply heeding the consciences that their parents had bred in them. As one antiwar organizer said, "I'm looking forward to really trying to explain to them the kinds of things I feel, that I am a very personal embodiment of what they are, what they created in a son, and what they brought me up to be." An underlying continuity of values linked the generations, making the parents inadvertent accomplices in their children's radicalism.

But the link was no more than underlying and inadvertent. Beyond that, there was indeed a significant difference between the young and the middle-aged—not in their principles, but in the way they chose to act on those principles.

Help those who are less fortunate than yourself, said the liberal and often religious parents. Yet many young radicals recalled:

> My father, unlike most businessmen—unlike all businessmen I have met—is probably the most sympathetic toward poor people. I mean he really understands the injustices. . . . But his point of view would be a very narrow, selfish one. He would say [about the things my friends and I are doing now]: "That's great, but let it happen after I'm dead. You guys can have your way then, but in the meantime I'm enjoying life."

Build a close, democratic family, the parents of togetherness had taught. But many young radicals recalled a home where Father was an occasional and shadowy figure. If they were born before 1945, he probably was absent in the armed services during the Second World War. Thereafter he was away at work during much of every week. When he came home, he was affectionate but often lacking in authority, an acquiescent rather than commanding figure.

> Some things about my father I like. Like . . . he did a lot of great things when he was younger. But it's clear that he cannot organize his own life, and that he shouldn't have married my mother. . . . My father is . . . gentle and loving, but he's also very weak in an interpersonal sense, though not in an intellectual sense. But he is a very submissive figure. I mean he always does whatever she wants.

They usually recalled Mother as the dominant figure of their childhood. She permeated the home with the strength of her nurturance and intelligence, busied herself with community activities and perhaps a part-time job, and instilled her children with ambitions to "make something of themselves." She provided a more effectual model than her husband and at the same time a confusing one. Even as her sons learned from her a strong sense of self-importance and social conscience, they also resented her overshadowing of their father.

The problem is that my mother is very dominant, very strong, very quick-tempered, quick to criticize.

The daughters, meanwhile, responded with their own sort of ambivalence, because they received mixed signals. On the one hand, Mother served as an example of individual competence struggling to surmount the tedious frustrations of housework; on the other hand, she told them that a woman's greatest happiness was marriage. Given such a confusing maternal heritage, the radical daughters were confused.

I think it's highly probable (and then again it's not) that I might end up living like my mother. It could go like that very easily. But on the other hand, the things I see are so cruddy. Every now and then the cruddiness comes through. . . . I don't think I want to live like that, but I don't know of anyone who has found any other model.

Many young radicals also described courageous and authoritative fathers, creative and satisfied mothers, parents who practiced as well as preached their principles. By no means all of their elders fitted the portraits of inconsistency. There were enough, though, to warrant Keniston's theory that young radicals were "living out expressed but unimplemented parental values." They discovered the compromises their parents had made, saw their parents as compromised persons. They did not therefore love them less. Rather, they directed their love into a determination to complete the half-kept promises of their parents' lives. They would not settle for the midway places where the older generation had stopped. Like Elaine Robinson in the wedding scene of *The Graduate*, when their parents cried, "It's too late," they shouted back, "Not for me!" and jumped on a bus toward some hopeful destination of their own.[13]

ON THEIR TELEVISION SCREENS and in their newspapers, Americans saw the Movement first of all as a political protest. But the activists were making a more profound kind of challenge because, in less visible ways, they were repudiating some basic cultural forms and values. In the beginning they questioned work and family. Ultimately they would question conventional gender roles.

Given the academic setting in which the radicals had spent their lives since the age of five, the most immediate meaning of work was schoolwork. Take Dave, for example, a New Left student at Harvard and the son of an Old Left professor at Antioch. "I'd always believed it was crucial for me to get my Harvard degree," he said, "—with high honors if possible—so I could go on to a good graduate school and fulfill my ambition to become a college professor." Two kinds of experience tore up his agenda. First, he joined SDS, writing leaflets, moderating an antiwar "teach-in," blocking Secretary of Defense Robert McNamara's car outside Quincy House, and living in a cooperative with political friends. Meanwhile, he continued his studies with extraordinary discipline and brilliance, but felt increasingly stifled as his thesis adviser narrowed his initial topic, "Imperialism and the State," to a technical analysis of international commerce between 1919 and 1939. "The more I got into it the less exciting it seemed," Dave recalled. "All the requirements about how it had to be written, how long it should be, when it had to be in, began to get to me. They just seemed irrelevant." Finally, after a week of agonizing doubts, he decided to drop it. "All of a sudden I felt a couple of chains fall off me, almost physically."[14]

Many other young men of the 1960s were repudiating the conventional form of work and success. They were not opting for laziness. Quite the contrary, they wanted to throw themselves into work, but literally so—wanted to put all of their selves into it, their moral and emotional impulses as well as their analytic and technical skill. They refused to be the Smiling Man gauging his accomplishment by the arrangement of file cabinets. They wanted to laugh and sing and feel, to mingle joy with achievement. To say "I am a historian" or an engineer or an executive was to say "I am less than myself." They were taking themselves seriously, which meant keeping their expressive and instrumental sides together. Rather than working toward the revolution, they wanted to live it here and now by enjoying themselves fully. So the Berkeley rebels sang satirical Christmas carols and the Pentagon demonstrators hung flowers on the bayonets of National Guardsmen.[15]

Their work involved more than fun. It involved personal risk. Eight hundred Berkeley students served prison terms of weeks or months; civil-rights workers went through jails, mobs, and constant fear; antiwar demonstrators faced the possibility of reprisals by university or government authorities, while draft resisters faced the certainty of imprisonment or expatriation. Their work brought risk as well as joy. Either way, it demanded wholehearted commitment. They were "putting themselves on the line," giving personal witness to their beliefs. Gerald Rosenfeld described "the exhilaration of feeling that you were, for once, really acting, that you were dealing directly with the things that affect your life, and with each other. You were for once free of the whole sticky cobweb that kept you apart from each other and from the roots of your existence, and you knew you were alive and what your life was all about." Unlike most of their parents, they did not commute between public and private compartments of their lives. In their work they kept their selves together.[16]

And they worked together with one another. At the heart of the Movement was "community," individuals in concert. Personal witness became first-person plural as the radicals joined hands and forces so that "we shall overcome" social inequality and create a participatory democracy for all. They renounced the competitive ethic and exploitative institutions of liberal capitalism, but they also renounced the Old Left's Marxist ideology and its strategy of coalition with established political-economic organizations. Institutions and ideology, whether on the left or in the center, contradicted the new radicals' commitment to a society where people would meet one another without formal rules, titles, or doctrines to differentiate and divide them. They refused to reach a communitarian goal by noncommunitarian means. In their own organizations, therefore, they consistently struggled against becoming too organized, resisting the temptation to adopt the efficiency of leaders and *Robert's Rules of Order*. They sought to overthrow the national power structure without being corrupted by ego-tripping and power-mongering in their own midst. They hoped, in short, to make a revolution by beginning it among themselves.[17]

"The revolution is about our lives," a radical manifesto declared in 1969. "We will create a soulful socialism. . . . We will find ways of taking care of each other as comrades. We will experiment with new ways of living together, such as communal families." When the rebels tried to merge the compartments of public and private, of doing and being, they created new forms of family. Open the front door of the Liberation News Service three-floor office building in 1967, and one beheld not only the electric typewriters and eight telephones befitting a journalistic enterprise, but also mattresses, bamboo curtains, posters of Mao and the Beatles, stereos playing the Stones, Bach, and Walt Disney's Greatest Hits, battered suitcases, half-eaten tuna-fish sandwiches, and eight residents, aged sixteen to thirty, who slept, ate, wrote poetry, made love, took dope, and were the LNS "work force." Like many other collectives, LNS more closely resembled a household than an office or political headquarters.[18]

More genuinely familial, though, were the thousands of communes that sprang up across the countryside and in urban houses during the later sixties. Here perhaps four, perhaps twelve, or even fifty people kept house for one another, pooled their belongings and incomes, tended the crops and livestock if they lived on the land, cared for the children if there were any. Most communes included some married couples, but usually the communal ethic permitted or encouraged extramarital relationships among any and all residents. "Make love, not war," they told the government and themselves. Everyone belonged to each other, in a family larger than the nuclear family. In the group marriage of Harrad West or of The Family, this was literally the case. Other communes let monogamy dissolve more informally, as members gave up private ownership not only of property, but also of another person's body and emotions. As a woman in an Oregon commune said, "We've learned how to be naked with one another—like a family." Thus the young radicals broke down yet another compartment of their lives.[19]

What did it all add up to? In the early years of the Movement, interpreters portrayed it in political terms, as the "New Left." Then as the radicals' redefinitions of work and family became more evident, the portrait broadened into "youth culture" or "counterculture." By the mid-sixties, the portrait became still more motley as developments ramified rapidly. On the one hand, Marxist factions took over SNCC and SDS, imposing the humorless ideological rigidity that the founders of the New Left had abhorred. On the other hand, thousands of young people hitchhiked on the Movement's momentum as "hippies," for whom social protest meant "dropping out" into the haphazard existence of psychedelic drugs, panhandling, casual sexuality, and "doing your own thing."[20]

Certainly the Movement added up to no compact conclusion. Instead, it kept evolving with disorderly spontaneity, a process of improvisation through experience. Having set out to complete the half-kept promise of their parents, the young radicals created a subculture that those parents had not intended and could not accept. But the radicals themselves produced consequences beyond their intentions—not only the hippies' trip and the Marxists' takeover, but Women's Liberation too. When women on the left began in 1967 to organize their movement within the Movement, they brought into the open the unnoticed fact that the radicals could not revise work and family without also revising the gender identities of males and females.

TO TELL THE STORY OF THE MODERN feminist movement, one must go back to 1960 and turn away temporarily from young radicals to older, liberal women working in professions. These career women did not intend to challenge the status quo, but they found themselves doing so, first in their behavior and then in their attitudes, exemplifying a process that social scientists label "relative deprivation."

Despite the image of Moms tending three or four youngsters all day in suburban yards, the fact was that an unprecedented proportion of middle-class wives and mothers were in the labor market. In 1960, just after the baby boom had crested, 31 percent of married women were employed (up from 24 percent in 1950), and, even more astonishing, almost 20 percent of mothers with children under the age of six (up from 13 percent in 1950). Few of them were disciples of a feminist "gospel of work." Like lower-class women in the Victorian era, they sought employment primarily because of economic necessity rather than self-fulfillment. And most of them flocked into boring jobs in traditionally female fields, especially as secretaries and sales clerks in the offices and shopping centers of affluent America, or as teachers in the schools of baby-boom America. Again like their Victorian ancestors, they were underpaid, earning only 61 percent of what men earned (down from 64 percent in 1955). But they accepted their lot. After all, most were working not as a career but as a supplement to their white-collar husbands' earnings. Forty-five percent of employed wives, in fact, were working only part-time. And in any case, what power did they have to change things?[21]

Women in the professions and business took a different perspective toward their work but not, it seemed, toward their rights. Having undergone years of specialized training, being engaged in work that interested them, and looking forward to a lifetime of development, they had invested a large part of themselves in their occupations. As career women, they took their work more seriously than did most employed women. Nevertheless, unlike so many Victorian career women, they did not talk like feminists. A senior vice-president at Macy's, for example, maintained that women were "equal-but-special," more emotional than men and not always as competent. The typical female executive, according to a *Fortune* survey, put her family ahead of her business, although she believed she could do both if she "wanted to badly enough." Many were doing just that. By 1960 close to half of female physicians, lawyers, natural scientists, and engineers were married, a marked contrast to the days when Carey Thomas and other aspiring professionals had had to "pray against" falling in love. And of course a college education no longer was a rare and bold achievement. By 1960, one of four women aged eighteen to twenty-one was enrolled (as compared to only one of ten in 1930 and one of thirty-five in 1900).* In keeping with this rise in education, the ranks of professional women swelled during the 1950s by more than 40 percent (faster than any occupational category except clerical).

Given these advantages, and surrounded by the domestic mystique, it is not surprising that professional women seemed to have forgotten the feminist faith. But their circumstances would not allow them to forget. Although more fortunate than their nineteenth-century predecessors as well as women in less skilled occupations, they too suffered discrimination in hiring, promotion, and pay. By the yardstick of other women, they had "never had it so good." By the yardstick of their male colleagues, it was not good enough. At this point the theory of "relative deprivation" enters the story. The better things become, the less good they will eventually seem if expectations outrace realities: that is why rebellions occur among the relatively deprived rather than the wholly deprived. Each female professional was well aware of the discrepancy between what she was capable of doing and what she had been given: the nontenured "adjunct professorship" in the English department; the salary equal to that of a man half her age; the assignment to the woman's page rather than to the city desk. These were the preconditions for a feminist ideology. The question was when attitudes would catch up with behavior. The question was when someone would declare that the obstacles faced by individual women added up to injustice done to womankind.[22]

The first such declaration came in 1963 from the President's Commission on the Status of Women. John F. Kennedy had been persuaded by prominent female Democratic party officials, shortly after his narrow victory in 1960, that he would win a lot of female votes if he appointed a group to investigate the "prejudices and outmoded customs" block-

*See the table on women in higher education in Appendix B.

ing the realization of women's basic rights. The commission's report two years later was hardly radical. It recommended equal-pay laws and government funding of day-care centers, for example, but opposed the Equal Rights Amendment and endorsed the traditional roles of women as homemakers, men as breadwinners. But the data in the report spoke for themselves, damningly loud. Most women worked to earn a living; their earnings and job status were lower than men's; their educational level was lower; and their legal status was inferior with regard to such matters as social-security taxes, wives' income, and jury service. Nor did the momentum end with the last page of the report. The federal commission spawned thirty-two state commissions, each of which unearthed the same kinds of damning facts within its local borders. In the process, the women who staffed these commissions produced not only documentation—ammunition for a potential war against gender injustice—but also a network of allies—potential generals and troops.[23]

At first, neither the legislators nor the media paid much attention. After all, the early 1960s already had an equal-rights movement which was struggling to overcome hideous discrimination against black Americans. Maybe women did not enjoy entirely equal rights, but surely one could not claim that they—a numerical majority, and mostly housewives supported by husbands—were an oppressed minority, could one? Yes, one could, and Betty Friedan did in a shrewd, angry book entitled *The Feminine Mystique* (1963). All those women who devoted themselves to suburban housekeeping, she argued, had been victimized by the seductive propaganda of advertisers, psychologists, and educators. Having exchanged individuality for security, they had trapped themselves in a mindless, unrewarded routine of laundry, casseroles, and baby talk. Home was a "comfortable concentration camp," Friedan said, and the only way for a woman to reclaim her power and her identity was to get an education and enter a profession. This was the message that reached the three million people who bought the book and the countless millions who read excerpts in *Ladies' Home Journal, McCall's, Mademoiselle*, and *Good Housekeeping*.[24]

The facts of inequality were being documented. The feelings of frustration were being dramatized. A momentum was developing, although as yet invisibly. Had Congressman Howard W. Smith of Virginia been aware of that momentum, for example, he would not have given it a huge push when he added two words, "or sex," to Title VII of the 1964 Civil Rights Act. Discrimination in employment based on "race, color, national origin or sex" would be prohibited. Smith, a racial segregationist, had hoped to defeat the bill with "my little amendment," but his tactic backfired. When the majority of congressmen voted for equal treatment of blacks, they extended the principle to women too. Employees who believed they had been mistreated because they were black or female (or both) were invited by the federal government to send their complaints to the Equal Employment Opportunity Commission (EEOC).

Facts and feelings and now official promises—even if the promises had been kept, this would have been an inflammatory combination. When they were not kept, it became explosive. During 1965 and 1966, the EEOC largely ignored or dismissed the thousands of complaints it received from women, until finally a small group of female activists, Betty Friedan among them, felt driven to retaliate. Meeting for lunch at a Washington hotel, they decided to create the National Organization for Women (NOW), which would (in the words that Friedan scribbled on a paper napkin and that soon became part of NOW's charter) "take the actions needed to bring women into the mainstream of American society, now, full equality for women, in fully equal partnership with men."[25] Whereas *The Feminine Mystique* addressed the plight of housewives, NOW addressed the other half of the situation—namely, the right of women to obtain equal access to education, professions, and political office. Like the civil rights movement for blacks, NOW wanted integration. Females should be brought into the masculine realm, commuting between work and family just as their husbands did, sharing the financial and social powers that their husbands enjoyed.

A historical revival was taking place. Back in 1919, the *Smith College Weekly* had declared, "We cannot believe . . . that a woman must choose between a home and her work." A half century later, Friedan (a graduate of Smith in 1942) led her new organization against the partition of sexual spheres. In its first official action, for example, NOW petitioned the EEOC to issue a long-delayed ruling on behalf of airline stewardesses, who were routinely fired when they reached the age of thirty or when they married, although pilots were allowed to fly long past middle age and fatherhood. Forty years after Charles Lindbergh flew alone across the Atlantic embodying the outdated hopes of manliness, thirty-nine years after Amelia Earhart was flown in the back seat across the Atlantic, NOW won its case. And that was just the beginning. Lobbying in legislatures, filing suits in court, and feeding publicity to the media,

NOW rapidly gained victories as well as members (1,000 in 1967, 3,000 in 1970, 40,000 in 1974).[26]

Here was a success story, but a success within certain limits. NOW primarily spoke for professional and business women and worked through established channels. Meanwhile a more radical, mass movement was emerging among college-age women, who wore blue jeans rather than skirts, who walked picket lines on dusty southern sidewalks and occupied campus administration buildings rather than lobbying legislatures. This feminist movement was born within the male-dominated New Left movement.

DURING THE SUMMER AFTER HER freshman year at Berkeley, Vivian Leburg was in Mississippi registering black voters by day, sleeping at night on a porch "next to a rifle which I didn't even know how to use." Sharon Jeffrey and Carol McEldowney were living in a Cleveland slum on a subsistence allowance from SDS, handing out leaflets, knocking on doors, and gradually organizing welfare mothers to fight for (and win) a free-lunch program in the public schools. Sue Thrasher—Tennessee-born, white, a graduate of a strongly Methodist college—hardly resembled a southern lady as she worked fourteen to eighteen hours a day in the Southern Student Organizing Committee headquarters, mimeographing civil rights newsletters, setting up interracial conferences, and ignoring phone calls by male voices threatening to harm her and the other "Communist agitators." Diana Oughton, daughter of a wealthy Illinois family and alumna of Bryn Mawr, broke windows and fought policemen before she was blown up by the dynamite bombs she was making for the Weathermen's terrorist campaign.[27]

Like the men of the Movement, women were "putting themselves on the line," taking direct action in ways that defied not only political norms, but also the norms of gender. Girls who had been brought up to be cheerleaders, literature majors, and wives were behaving in decidedly unfeminine fashion. At least that is how we perceive them in retrospect. The female activists themselves, even while acting in defiance of gender conventions, were not thinking in those terms—not at first. They had entered the Movement to fight against racism, poverty, and then the Vietnam War. Black and white, male and female, together we shall overcome. But all too soon it did not work out that way. By 1967 the blacks in SNCC had expelled the whites in the name of "black power." And before that, a few black and white women within SNCC met to discuss resentments at the ways they were being treated by male members: exclusion from decision-making groups, for example; assignment to clerical tasks; and being called "girls" while men were called "people." When these dissidents issued a blunt memo, "The Position of Women in SNCC," they drew little response except Stokely Carmichael's quip, "The only position for women in SNCC is prone."[28]

Like most jokes, it let out the truth. The Movement, especially in the north, was a masculine monopoly. Almost all the New Left leaders were men, most of whom had been intellectual and political stars in high school and college. In the Movement they continued to take charge, running meetings, drafting position papers, and speaking in public with an assured competence that others found hard to match. Needless to say, there were numerous women who also had great capabilities, but they directed them in other directions: toward cooperation instead of competition; toward feelings instead of rationality; toward the personal instead of the political. Although precisely these "feminine" values had given rise to the New Left ("power rooted in love," proclaimed the Port Huron statement), they quickly became submerged as SDS membership expanded and activities intensified. And the women became submerged with them. "I was so scared. I was so intimidated," Naomi Weisstein recalled, describing a New Haven CORE meeting where the men "were coming on very tough and I hadn't learned how to come on very tough yet." The women tended not to push their way into the male ranks of power, and the men did not offer them a helping hand. Female membership on the SDS Executive Committee, for example, rose to a high of 23 percent in 1963, then plunged to 6 percent in 1964. Women usually ended up at the mimeo machine or typewriter, in the kitchen, and often in their male comrades' beds. "We were . . . the movement secretaries and the shitworkers . . . ," as one woman put it; "we were the earth mothers and the sex-objects for the movement men." They were functionaries—used, enjoyed, and at best tolerated. "How many times," two women asked bitterly, "have you seen a woman enter the discussion only to have it resume at the exact point from which she made her departure, as though she had never said anything at all? How many times have you seen men get up and actually walk out of a room while a woman speaks?"[29]

To be treated as a second-class citizen within a movement attacking second-class citizenship in America—that flagrant inconsistency could not go long unnoticed. The same process of relative deprivation that affected women in the professions was operating even more force-fully among women on the Left. They had risked too many Ku Klux Klan nightriders and organized too many welfare mothers to let a Stokely Carmichael or Tom Hayden put them down. Having learned in personal action that they were as able as men, they would translate that lesson into attitudes and arguments and finally revolt.

In 1965, Casey Hayden and Mary King of SNCC wrote a long, angry essay titled "Sex and Caste," drawing parallels between the treatment of women and blacks. That same year, the national SDS conference scheduled a discussion of the "women's issue" during which men con-tributed shouts of "she just needs a good screw" and "she's just a cas-trating female." At the 1967 conference a "Women's Liberation Work-shop" challenged "our brothers" to deal with their "male chauvinism." But the brothers were not very sympathetic. Alongside its report of the proceedings, *New Left Notes* printed a cartoon of a girl—with earrings, polka-dot minidress, and matching visible panties—holding a sign: "We Want Our Rights and We Want Them Now."[30] When pushed, radical men revealed themselves to be conventional men, defending their power as adamantly as the "power elite" in Mississippi or the Pentagon. Some radical women now decided to reply in kind.

At the National Conference for a New Politics in the summer of 1967, the black caucus demanded 50 percent of all committee seats. The women's caucus, using the same moral arithmetic and claiming to represent more than half of the population, demanded 51 percent. When the conference leaders snubbed them, the women walked out—not just out of the conference, but out of the established New Left structure and into organizations of their own, into what their first memo called "a movement for women's liberation." Many radicals, male as well as female, objected that this emphasis on sexual equality was counterproductive because it distracted from the basic struggle against political and economic oppression. But the objection came too late. "Many of us now reject this view," Ellen Willis said. "We have come to see women's liberation as an independent revolutionary movement, potentially representing half the population. We intend to make our own analysis of the system and put our interests first, whether or not it is convenient for the (male-dominated) Left."[31] The radicals at the grass roots were putting into movement—into mass social movement—the ideas that NOW had begun to pursue through formal channels.

One hundred and twenty years after the Seneca Falls Convention, fifty years after the equal-suffrage amendment, the third feminist movement was born. But this was not a case of history repeating itself; rather, it was a case of history surpassing itself. As historian William Chafe has pointed out, the modern woman's movement differed from previous ones because it ran in tandem with social-economic trends and drew vital energy from them. Female employment, especially among middle-class wives, had been growing since World War II; the number of young women, especially college-educated women, was growing by leaps and bounds; and the birthrate began a steep downturn after the baby-boom peak in 1957. The objective and subjective dimensions were "in sync." This trio of trends formed a set of conditions that nurtured feminist attitudes far more strongly than Susan B. Anthony and her allies could count on in the nineteenth century.[32]

As a result, the movement grew like Topsy. By 1970 there were at least fifty liberation groups in New York City alone, thirty-five in San Francisco, countless others across the nation, bearing names like Redstockings, Bread and Roses, The Feminists, WITCH, and Cell 16. By 1973 a national woman's newsletter listed several thousand. There were also groups representing special kinds of female interests: the Professional Women's Caucus, the National Black Feminist Organization (2,000 members by 1974), the Coalition of Labor Union Women (3,000 members by 1973), the National Coalition of American Nuns, the Association for Women in Psychology, Women Artists for Revolution—the list goes on and on.[33]

This diversity bred confusion and contradiction. Many of the radical groups, for example, disparaged Betty Friedan as "the Martin Luther King of the feminist movement" because NOW sought reforms within a system that, they claimed, would not yield meaningful sexual equality without revolutionary overhaul. Friedan, in turn, rebuked the radicals. "We can change institutions," she said, "but it is a fantasy deviation from a really revolutionary approach to say that we want a world in which there will be no sex, no marriage, that in order for women to be free they must have a manless revolution and down with men." Meanwhile, radicals argued with one another about who or what was the enemy. Some indicted men as the force behind oppressive social institutions. The feminists' task, they declared, was to develop "a new dialectic of sex class—an analysis of the way in which sexual identity and institutions reinforce one another." Other radicals—known as the "politicos"—insisted that capitalism, not men, was the ultimate agent of oppression. Sexual inequality, they explained, was a by-product of a general economic inequality, which could be eradicated only by socialist revolution.[34]

The diversity also bred strength. Whereas late-nineteenth-century feminist leaders had focused primarily on the right to vote, modern feminists extended their protest to education, employment, marriage, birth control, and abortion. But the movement reached even further, beyond the realm of public rights to private experience—to consciousness, or female identity. Not merely an equal-suffrage movement or equal-rights movement, it was—boldly, inclusively—a women's movement. Not only professional women, black women, labor-union women, but women simply as women—daughters, sisters, wives, and mothers who came together not in terms of their public or political definitions, but in terms of their personal needs. And as it turned out the personal was also the political.

"The CR (consciousness-raising) group," some called it, or "support group," or just "our group." The most pervasive female liberation was taking place around the small circles of women meeting informally each week, in thousands of living rooms or churches or college dorms, to share feelings and ideas. These groups might include career women or housewives, fiancées or divorcées, teenagers or middle-agers, but always women. They talked about pregnancy, orgasms, diets, divorce, husbands, jobs, but the agenda was always their identities as persons born female. In the process of exchanging autobiographies, each discovered that she was not alone. She was not the only one afraid to look for a job after ten years of raising children, not the only one who fantasized about an extramarital affair or had bisexual feelings, not the only one who said, "In my home I always had a sense that my father and brother were more important than my mother and myself," not the only one to confess shamefully that she had stood up a (female) friend because a man had asked her for a date. Other women had done or felt the same. Many CR groups never went beyond "bitch sessions" or incoherent therapy, a blowing-off of steam. But many others became vehicles for feminism when their members discovered, in Jo Freeman's words, "that what was thought to be a personal problem has a social cause and a political solution." Growing into the solidarity of sisterhood, each of these women began to learn a new sense of who she was.[35]

If postwar social-economic trends formed the objective soil for the movement to take root, consciousness-raising groups were the seeds.

Then came the mass media, which broadcast feminist ideas throughout America—from the radical coastal regions into the moderate Midwest and genteel South, from SDS activists to housewives watching *All in the Family*—all this with breathtaking speed. In 1970, the *Ladies' Home Journal* editors surrendered to a radical sit-in at their offices and published a special section called "The New Feminism." That same year, Kate Millett, author of the polemical book *Sexual Politics*, stared sternly from the cover of *Time*. In 1971, Gloria Steinem and a few of her friends made history by publishing a national magazine by, of, and for women. Ms. was a communal product; the editors did not rank themselves in hierarchy but shared all the tasks, from typing manuscripts and selecting articles to making coffee and answering phones. They practiced the equality that their magazine would preach and that they had so often been denied in New Left organizations. "Ms. belongs to us all," they boasted. "All" turned out to include not only themselves and a clique of militant readers, but more than half a million people of all ages and all social-economic levels in every part of the country. The 300,000 copies of the preview issue sold out within eight days. Within weeks, 20,000 letters poured into the editors' one-room office, enthusiastic personal letters from women to "their" magazine. As the editors acknowledged with awe, they had "tapped an emerging and deep cultural change that was happening to us, and happening to our sisters."[36]

Events had gone far beyond the inner sanctum of NOW or the New Left. A mass movement was under way, translating women's personal indignations into a feminist ideology, which in turn was translated into dramatic changes almost anywhere one looked in the 1970s and 1980s.

Politics. The U.S. Department of Labor issued "affirmative action" guidelines for hiring women and other minorities, and Congress extended coverage of the 1963 Equal Pay Act to educational institutions. Meanwhile, the ERA suddenly triumphed, after enduring constant defeat throughout half a century. First, the League of Women Voters and the Women's Bureau did an about-face and endorsed the measure; then, in 1972, both houses of Congress passed it by overwhelming majorities. Fourteen states had already passed their own equal-rights laws, and, within a year, twenty-two ratified the federal amendment. At the same time, the Supreme Court was contributing its voice, banning "help wanted (male) or (female)" ads and, in *Roe v. Wade*, upholding women's right to abortion. Finally, female politicians began to be a less extraordinary, though hardly frequent, sight. There were twenty-four women in Congress by 1984, and fifty-three by 1992; almost a thousand in state legislatures, or 14 percent, by 1984; 1,535, or 24 percent, by 1994.[37]

Education. The increase in women earning college degrees was old news by the 1970s, but the huge jump in the number who earned professional degrees was startling (see Appendix B). In 1973, women made up 8 percent of law school graduates; in 1990, 42 percent. In 1977, women earned 16 percent of medical degrees; by 1994, 30 percent— and in eighteen medical schools females outnumbered males.[38]

Employment. As a result of this increase of women with professional degrees, male professions became somewhat more integrated. Whereas fewer than 5 percent of lawyers and judges had been women in 1970, more than 12 percent were in 1980 and 26 percent in 1995 (including one-fifth of state supreme court justices).[39] Between 1980 and 1995, the proportion of female physicians doubled, while women outnumbered men in accounting offices. Even the virtually all-male world of the army became a little less so, with one soldier in ten being a woman.[40]

Images and bodies. On television screens, Americans heard the evening news from Walter (Cronkite), Harry (Reasoner), and John (Chancellor), and also from Connie (Chung), Barbara (Walters), Diane (Sawyer), and Lesley (Stahl). On movie screens, they saw Jane Fonda exchanging her *Barbarella* bikini for the role of Lillian Hellman in *Julia*, while Jill Clayburgh responded to her husband's exit by finding work (in an art gallery) and love (with artist Alan Bates) and fulfillment by remaining an *unmarried* woman.[41] Sally Ride carried this self-assertion into outer space, orbiting the earth in 1983 as the first female astronaut.

That same year, Joan Benoit traveled only 26 miles, 385 yards, but it was no less a breakthrough, for she ran the Boston marathon in a record time of 2 hours, 22 minutes, 42 seconds. No woman had ever run a marathon that fast. Indeed, until 1972 no woman had been permitted to run in the Boston race. And when they had run, only once had a woman finished in less than three hours. Twelve years later, here was Benoit running an astounding thirty-seven minutes faster. Millions of uncelebrated women, meanwhile, were lifting weights in spas, jogging through city streets, and grunting on living-room floors in unison with Jane Fonda's workout tape.

In 1972, the federal government joined in with Title IX of the Educational Amendments Act. Unless schools and colleges raised their spending on female athletes to the level they spent on male athletes, they would lose federal funding. That threat had a marked impact. Within four years, the number of girls participating in high school sports rose from 7 to 19 percent of all high-school athletes. At the college level, the female participation rate made similar leaps, as did scholarships and spending for women's programs.[42]

Bodies and sexuality. "Experiences in the women's movement have drastically changed our thinking and feeling about our bodies," the Boston Women's Health Book Collective wrote in their best-selling *Our Bodies, Ourselves* (1973). In detailed chapters on reproductive anatomy, nutrition, venereal disease, childbearing, and other topics, the authors provided scientific information with which women could take control of their bodies and hence their lives. Anatomy is indeed destiny. But whereas Freud had belittled woman's sexual and psychic roles, William Masters and Virginia Johnson magnified it to awesome superiority. In *Human Sexual Response* (1966) and *Human Sexual Inadequacy* (1970), this team of sexologists reported that the typical woman attains the strongest orgasm by stimulation of the clitoris, not the vagina, which implies that she does not depend upon a man for sexual satisfaction. So much for the mid-twentieth-century cult of mutual orgasm. Not only does a woman not need a man, but she does it better than a man: During a limited period of time the male may be capable of more than one orgasm, but the female is capable of many orgasms, perhaps infinite orgasms. In short, the passionless Victorian lady became not simply an erotic partner but a sexual athlete who would go farther and faster than almost any man.[43]

While this revolutionary definition of female physiology was being produced in Masters and Johnson's laboratory, a revolution in sexual attitude and behavior was taking place among youth outside. In the early 1960s, only about 40 percent of college students thought it was all right for women as well as men to engage in premarital intercourse. At the end of the decade, almost 70 percent thought it was all right. During the 1970s the majority grew so large and unwavering (around 80 percent) that the interesting question was no longer what they thought about premarital sex, but what they did about it. Back in the early 1950s, four of five women had remained virgins throughout college; in the 1970s, four of five were *not* virgins by the time they graduated. What's more, only one of four "frequently" or "occasionally" felt guilt or regret about what she had done; half "never" had second thoughts. Attitudes as well as behavior had turned inside-out within less than a generation. Among the noncollegiate half of young Americans, the same shift occurred, though more slowly, so that by the late 1970s, six of every ten women had slept with at least one man before reaching the age of twenty. Premarital virginity had become the exception rather than the typical condition. "How has it happened," Yale sophomore Joyce Maynard asked in only somewhat laughing tones, "what have we come to, that the scarlet letter these days isn't A, but V?"[44]

Older Americans were less likely to laugh about the sexual revolution. While seven of ten college students in 1969 approved of premarital intercourse, seven of ten parents desperately disapproved. Wherever they looked, Eros seemed to be running loose: hair bouncing on male as well as female shoulders, women's breasts swaying braless under sweaters, miniskirts and see-through blouses and topless dance clubs, rock singers pleading "let's spend the night together" and "c'mon, baby, light my fire." At the corner newsstand, *Playgirl* cohabited with *Playboy* and *Cosmopolitan*'s centerfold opened to Burt Reynolds smiling in blissful nudity. Once there had been *The Joy of Cooking*; now there was *The Joy of Sex*. Chateau Martin wines asked, "Had any lately?" and the Noxzema shaving cream woman said, "Take it off; take it all off."

As the counterculture began to wane during the 1970s, however, so did public alarm. Indeed, gradually the revolution percolated upward into the ranks of older Americans. By 1978, not only did 52 percent of adults condone sexuality before marriage, but husbands and wives were having more of their own—more frequent intercourse, more varied techniques, and more enjoyable orgasms.[45]

"Women's liberation" nevertheless stirred up fears of sexual disorder, or, more basically, fears that the standard gender identities of masculine and feminine would melt into each other. Consider what took place during and especially after the Miss America Pageant in 1968. A group of feminists, in protest against reducing women to breasts, hips, and smiles, set up a "freedom trash can" for old bras, girdles, high-heeled shoes, women's magazines, and other "instruments of torture to women." The media, however, reported the event as "bra-burning" and thereby linked the antisexist movement with the sexy fashion of going braless. On the other hand, "libbers" were frequently labeled as frigid, castrating, and ugly (what nineteenth-century antis had called "unsexed"). Either way, critics indicted feminists for transgressing sexual propriety.

Victorian feminists had evaded this trap by identifying equal rights with social purity, a single standard of chastity for both sexes. The post-Victorians had rejected that position in favor of a single male standard. Feminists of the 1970s were divided about the meaning of "sexual freedom." The majority of them favored a woman's control ("ownership") of her body, by which they meant the right to have sex with a man but also to say no, the right to have an abortion, and freedom from sexual advances on the job.[46] A vociferous minority insisted that the issue was not simply sexuality, but gender; not a private matter of choice, but a political matter of oppression by patriarchal society. Freedom, they said, was to be found in lesbianism. "At the heart of women's liberation, and the basis for the cultural revolution," according to Rita Mae Brown, a founder of Radicalesbians, "is the primacy of women relating to women, of women creating a new consciousness of and with each other."[47] Like black-power advocates within the civil rights movement, lesbian-feminists wanted to define a social identity on their own terms. To quote the slogan on their T-shirts, "A Woman without a Man Is Like a Fish without a Bicycle."[48] So they eagerly set out in the 1970s to construct a woman-identified community—"Lesbian Nation," Jill Johnston called it—where not just lesbians but *all* women would find their authentic selves—in women's food co-ops, restaurants, health clinics, child-care centers, rape crisis centers. In women's auto-mechanics classes and garages. In women's journals, books, bookstores, and publishing houses. Perhaps most effectively, in women's music, music stars like Holly Near, and music festivals.[49]

For lesbians old enough to have experienced the furtiveness and oppression during the fifties, this was a giddy moment. "Suddenly there was women's music, which I'd never heard before, and it was performed in front of such huge audiences of proud lesbians," recalled a forty-five-year-old woman who had moved from the Midwest to New York. "There were all of those workshops. There were all-women dances at Columbia. There was a place in the Catskills where hundreds of women took over the entire hotel, running around bare, giving each other massages. . . . It was like I'd never lived before."[50]

The prevailing culture, not surprisingly, had a very different reaction. As lesbians turned sexual identity into a political weapon, so did the media. In August of 1970, *Time* put Kate Millett on its cover and praised *Sexual Politics* as a "remarkable book" providing a "coherent theory" for women's liberation. When Millett admitted her bisexuality four months later, though, *Time* warned that her confession "is bound to discredit her as spokeswoman for her cause, cast further doubt on her theories, and reinforce the views of those skeptics who routinely dismiss all liberationists as lesbians."[51]

Opposition came not only from "skeptics" but also from within the ranks of the women's movement. Many straight feminists were afraid that, just as *Time* had predicted, they would be stigmatized as "nothing but a bunch of man-hating dykes."[52] During the early seventies, nasty factional feuding took place until various leaders and organizations, including NOW, embraced the right to express one's sexual identity.

Family. Whenever feminists touched matters of sexuality, they thrummed a nerve of public opinion. When they criticized the family, they provoked seizures. For it was within the family that equality between the sexes would ultimately have to take place, and it was there that traditional identities remained entrenched. Men and women may have been feeling and behaving as equals in bed, but in the kitchen and living room they remained markedly unequal. The twentieth-century family had evolved from a patriarchy to a democratic team, but the average nonemployed wife still performed between fifty and fifty-six hours of family work per week, in contrast to her husband's seven to thirteen. That is why Friedan in the early 1960s called on housewives to escape their "comfortable concentration camp" at 8:00 A.M. and come home at 5:00 P.M. But even when a wife became employed and therefore presumably acquired more decision-making power, she still did at least twenty-eight hours of family work, while her husband did little more than before (and of course she earned only 60 percent of what he earned). And that is why the radical feminists of the late 1960s were calling on women to escape the home and not return—calling, in other words, for a basic transformation of the family.

"It's just not honest to talk about freedom for women," declared Ti-Grace Atkinson of the Redstockings, "unless you get the child rearing off their backs." Her solution was communal child-rearing. Shulamith Firestone's solution was artificial reproduction. And beyond children, there was the oppression of marriage. "In marriage a man has the sexual right to his wife: he can fuck her at will by right of law," said Andrea Dworkin. "It is through intercourse in particular that men express and maintain their power and dominance over women." And beyond marriage, a few radicals said, there was the oppression of love. "Love, in the context of an oppressive male-female relationship, becomes an emotional cement to justify the dominant-submissive relationship," a

New York women's group argued. "The man 'loves' the woman who fulfills her submissive ego-boosting role. The woman 'loves' the man she is submitting to—that is, after all, why she 'lives for him.'"[53]

These were the extreme positions and therefore, like lesbianism, they attracted disproportionate media attention. Most participants in the movement were content to advocate day-care centers and a fifty-fifty division of housework between spouses. Nevertheless, even moderate proposals for reforming the family aroused immoderate alarm. Feminists won federal laws requiring equal pay and equal subsidies of education, but federal money for day-care centers was another matter. That struck too close to home. President Nixon vetoed the appropriation bill in 1971 because "the vast moral authority of national government . . . must be . . . consciously designed to cement the family in its rightful position as the keystone of our civilization."[54] Just as it had in the Victorian era, "the home" stood as the sacred institution of society. Hearth, heart, and mother—this trio of symbols promised order and virtue in the world. To propose remodeling male and female domestic roles was to propose heresy.

Victorian feminists had sidestepped this land mine buried inside the "woman question" by accepting spinsterhood as the price of a career. Revised feminists of the 1920s, by contrast, wanted the opportunity to "have it all," both a family and a career, but they did not move very far before the Depression, the World War, and the baby boom canceled their hopes. Modern feminists of the 1960s and 1970s were mobilizing to bring those hopes back to life, reforming laws and institutions and consciousness so that women could enjoy the same choices as men. Within a short time they made astonishing progress, but as we will see in the fate of the ERA, they were vulnerable, perilously vulnerable, on the issue of the family.

ON AUGUST 26, 1970, WHILE 10,000 women marched along New York's Fifth Avenue in a "strike for equality," Mrs. Carolyn Malfa was shopping with her three young daughters in a suburban supermarket. "We're busy squeezing tomatoes like we do every day," she told a reporter. In a Brooklyn laundromat, Mrs. Barbara Sullivan was folding her infant daughter's diapers. "Women's liberation?" she said. "Never thought much about it, really."[55]

If women did think about it, they were at first less than enthusiastic. "Do you favor or oppose most of the efforts to strengthen and change women's status in society today?" Lou Harris's pollsters asked in 1970. A national cross section of women split evenly between pro (40 percent) and con (42 percent), while 17 percent were not sure which way they felt. Were these skeptics reacting against spectres of lesbianism and bra-burning? Some, no doubt. But there is reason to believe that most were speaking out of their own experience. Sixty percent of housewives, for example, told Gallup that they did not want a job, and only one in ten listed "lack of freedom" as her biggest complaint. Their main source of pride was not personal achievement, not material possessions, but "my children." After hearing these replies, one begins to wonder whether *The Feminine Mystique* (published seven years earlier) was social science or science fiction.[56]

Then one remembers that attitudes toward gender roles change slowly, a matter of decades rather than years, and all the more slowly as people become older. After thirty-five or forty-five years of growing up female through the era of domesticity, most women had learned their role too well to discard it easily for another. With a husband and children, they knew what they would lose in "liberation" and could only guess what they might gain. Listen to Lois Abramson, who was thirty-three years old, college-educated, wife of an insurance salesman, mother of two young children, living in a five-room apartment in New York City. "I have to admit it. I think life is boring," she said. Although "I have everything I wanted," she sometimes would become "terribly depressed" and then, in guilt "hate myself." But more free time was not the solution. "Free to do what?" she asked.

Pat Loud, a forty-five-year-old mother of four in California, could identify her malaise more specifically: Bill, her adulterous husband. After finding the heart-wrenching evidence in his office file—Kodachrome snapshots of smiling girl friends, credit card slips from fancy hotels and restaurants—she knew she should end the marriage, and at the same time she was too terrified to do so. Finding a job? Taking care of the kids? Living alone? "It wasn't that I didn't *want* life without Bill exactly, it was just that I couldn't even picture it." During the next five years, he remained faithful but their relationship grew emptier. "We just don't have any rapport at all any more," Pat complained to her brother and sister-in-law. "If, if we had any—well, if we had any sex life, you know, that would be kind of nice, but it's kind of like a courtesy. 'Thank you, ma'am.' And I'm too—too young for that. I'm too old for women's lib, but I'm a little young for that." So in the end she divorced Bill—she saw no tolerable alternative except to divorce him—and yet she said: "I've had a keen life, just a keen life." It seems a peculiarly cheery judgment. But then we understand. She *had* to say it, for otherwise she would have been dismissing all that she had so earnestly done for more than twenty years, deprecating the self-esteem she needed to carry her into a suddenly, terrifyingly open future.[57]*

These women belonged to an interim generation. While young people were calling for self-fulfillment and sexual equality, Pat Loud and Lois Abramson and Barbara Sullivan took a more ambivalent perspective. Having already made so many life investments, they found the prospect of "liberation" painfully difficult or altogether unimaginable. We can understand, then, why they would regard the feminist movement with mixed feelings and why the national polls reported such mixed opinions. In 1970 Gallup asked, "Which one of the alternatives on this list do you feel would provide the most interesting and satisfying life for you personally?" Thirty-two percent of women said that their ideal lifestyle was to be married with children and a full-time job; 44 percent chose marriage, children, and *no* job. More than any other factor, age drew the line between these two groups. Whereas most of those under thirty preferred employment, most in their thirties and forties and still more of those over fifty rejected it. College education also inclined women to favor employment. Judging by this arithmetic, then, Friedan's gospel of work was finding converts primarily among the young and the better-educated. As for radical critiques of the family, they won very little favor: although women divided on the issue of a job, 76 percent united in wanting marriage and children.[58]

When asked about the *kind* of marriage, however, they divided all over again. In 1977 another poll offered two choices: either a marriage in which both spouses shared the tasks of breadwinner and homemaker, or one in which the husband was the breadwinner and the wife the homemaker. Among all men and women, shared roles emerged the slight but surprising winner, 48 to 42 percent. But again, age made a huge difference. Among those over forty-five years old, a solid majority of 59 percent voted for traditional roles. It was younger people, particularly those in their twenties, who tipped the balance toward marital

---

*Pat Loud then moved to New York City, lived alone, and led an apparently contented life working for a literary agency. Bill Loud stayed in California, remarried, and also seemed content: "The Loud Family," Newsweek 90 (July 11, 1977): 6.

egalitarianism. The proverbial saying used to be "a woman's place is in the home," but two-thirds of college women dismissed it as "nonsense."[59]

The feminist movement was marching toward a generation gap. And depending upon the direction in which one looked, one could see it making rapid gains or recoiling in the 1970s. Let us first consider the progress. Whereas in 1970 only 40 percent of women favored efforts to strengthen female status, by 1980 a solid majority of 64 percent had gathered in favor (while 24 percent opposed and 11 percent were not sure). Among younger, college-educated, urban women, approval was higher yet. Meanwhile, the ERA was earning support by a massive ratio of two to one.[60]

But there is the other side of the story. Even though feminism advanced—or rather, precisely because it advanced—it collided with more and more resistance. By the mid-1970s, antifeminists had organized a powerful social movement of their own, mobilizing politicians, women, church groups, and mass media for a campaign to defeat the ERA and protect traditional womanhood. At first glance, it seems a rerun of history: suffragists against antis, New Woman against True Woman, with only the labels updated (the ERA instead of the vote). It turned out, however, to be less a rerun than a remake, featuring a much larger cast of characters and concepts as well as, of course, a different ending. For unlike woman's suffrage, the ERA failed to become part of the Constitution; in 1983, when its allotted time ran out, it still fell three states short of the three-fourths majority needed for ratification.

How could it go down to defeat when two of three Americans supported it? Much of the answer lies in the smoke-filled rooms of politicians, especially southern politicians. (Ten of the fifteen holdout states were in the South.) Equally much of the answer lies in the shrewd lobbying by Phyllis Schlafly's nationwide organization, STOP-ERA, with backing from the ministerial coalition calling itself the Moral Majority. Like Carrie Chapman Catt in the 1910s, Schlafly commanded her funds and troops expertly, calculating which states and which legislators would be most receptive to her message. In the end, she simply played politics better than the pro-ERA forces.

Much of the answer, though, goes beyond legislative maneuverings to the kinds of cultural values that Schlafly and her allies called forth. The fight over the ERA is less interesting as a political contest than as a morality play, which was staged not in statehouses but in the home (and in the shadow of the church). In the antis' scenario, two types of women confronted each other. On one side were the liberationists, "sharp-tongued, high-pitched, whining, bitter" unmarried women who preached a message of self-deprecation. The economic and social handicaps of being female, the inequity of being the only sex to bear babies, the rejection of feminine charm as merely socialization by a male-dominated society—these arguments for "equality," said Schlafly, began with a negative attitude toward women. Still worse, they ended with policies that, if put into practice, would hurt rather than benefit women. The ERA would include females in the military draft, for example. A more serious liability would fall upon housewives. Feminists might argue that the ERA would take away a husband's exploitative power, but the antis pointed out that it would also cancel his legal obligation to support his wife and would require both spouses to furnish equal financial support of the family. As a result, a wife would virtually be forced out of the home and into a job.

If she were a mother, the consequences would become still more dire. On the one hand, taxpayers would have to subsidize day-care centers for all those untended children. On the other hand, as Schlafly derisively noted, "since there is no way yet known to make the bearing of children equal between the sexes," the wife must carry more than half of the family burdens. In the name of equality would come inequality. Worse yet, said Schlafly (herself a lawyer), consider the implications of a court ruling under Pennsylvania's equal-rights law. The court voided a statute requiring the father of an illegitimate child to pay the support of the baby because the statute imposed a heavier obligation on the father than on the mother. "So," Schlafly concluded, "the woman bears the baby, and the man gets off scot-free." Given that prospect, many unmarried pregnant women would resort to abortion, and of course the principle of "equality" would require that the state provide them with medical services to kill their fetuses.[61]

On the other side of the anti-ERA morality play stood those women Schlafly labeled the "Christian Women," or the "Positive Women," those whom she summoned to do battle under the banner of STOP-ERA (Stop Taking Our Privileges). They had burdens to gain (employment and self-reliance) and privileges to lose (husband's support) from so-called liberation, she warned. But materialistic self-interest was not the main theme. Quite the contrary. In language that carried biblical as well as Victorian reverberations, Schlafly proclaimed: "A woman helps man to 'subdue' and take care of the earth by being a supportive, loving wife and a nurturing mother. Being a homemaker is a most honorable and valuable career"—not the demeaning role that feminists called it, but a means to fulfill herself, her husband, and also the social welfare. According to "the plan of the Divine Architect for the survival of the human race," a man must go out to earn the bread while a woman raises the family and gives him appreciation and admiration—"The Golden Rule with a simple male/female variation."[62] These were the ideals that North Carolina legislators were tangibly reminded of when each received a loaf of homemade bread baked by a STOP-ERA woman.[63]

Once again, as in the days of the suffrage crusade, the antis were mobilizing to save America from moral degeneration. They found allies among an increasingly vehement and numerous constellation of conservative activists known as the New Right. First and foremost were the antiabortion forces, led by the National Right to Life Committee and its chapters in almost every state. Then there were conservatives within the Republican party, who looked to Ronald Reagan to be their banner-carrier. Finally, and most influentially, there were evangelical Protestants, who founded a multitude of organizations such as the Christian Voice, Concerned Women of America, and the Moral Majority. The Rev. Jerry Falwell, Jimmy Swaggart, Jim and Tammy Faye Bakker, and other preachers reached millions of Americans through their weekly television programs. "It is time we come together," Falwell declared, "and rise up against the tide of permissiveness and moral decay that is crushing in on our society from every side."[64]

A cartoonist for the *Rocky Mountain News* in 1980 gleefully sketched two women reading the one-sentence text of the ERA. "That's all it says?" one of them asks in astonishment, to which her friend replies, "you have to read between the lines." "Okay," the first woman continues, "where's the passage about disassembling the family unit?" Pointing a finger, her friend says, "Right here after the sentence on enforced lesbianism. It helps if you squint." To the antis, however, it was no joke. The ERA seemed to them a symptom of a much wider corruption spreading through modern America. Indeed, here we come upon a surprising paradox. The same social-economic trends that were fostering feminism were also giving impetus to antifeminism. The rising employment of wives and mothers, the declining birthrate, the liberalization of sexual codes—one could read these as portents of female equality, but one could also read them as portents of the disintegration of family and, hence, of society. One woman's "liberation" was another woman's "anarchy." It depended on how she defined gender roles and, beyond that, on how she defined social order.

For those who founded their sense of order on a traditional family, the 1970s seemed an era of earthquake. In addition to mothers' employment and sexual liberalization—or, some argued, as a result of these trends—there were the 38 percent increase of unwed teenage mothers, the 52 percent climb in the divorce rate, and the nearly doubled number of households headed by a woman. These trends alarmed even those who supported women's rights. "Can the family survive?" Margaret Mead asked rhetorically. Psychologist Urie Bronfenbrenner had a gloomy answer: "America's families are in trouble—trouble so deep and pervasive as to threaten the future of our nation."[65]

IF THE WOMEN'S MOVEMENT FAILED to convert a significant portion of the gender that was supposed to be freed from oppression, what reaction could one expect from the ruling gender? Feminists in the early 1970s were pessimistic. "Maybe there's a faint ray of hope that someday, somewhere, a tiny group of men will be able to say 'We want to be human,'" remarked a member of a New York City liberation group. Then she sighed. "But I don't expect to have a real relationship with a man. Not in my lifetime." To which another woman in the room added, "Especially now, with every man you meet so insecure."[66]

The histories of men and women do not take place in isolation from each other. Even if one gender angrily withdraws, by its very opposition it remains involved with the other. Social roles and identities are interactional, shaped by and shaping the expectations and reactions of those "significant others" in one's life. As feminists began rewriting the feminine scripts, they necessarily implicated in their drama the men to whom they were daughters, colleagues, lovers, wives, or ex-wives. But they could not do all the rewriting on their own. Until men stopped classifying women in gendered terms, liberation would not go beyond a half-victory. Because of the dynamics of the interaction, though, men could not stop stereotyping women until they rewrote their own script of masculinity. And, in the early 1970s, the chances for that seemed unpromising.

Since the prime of the Victorian era, men had been in retreat. When the ladies jumped off their pedestals and invaded the male provinces of politics, higher education, employment, and sexuality, men grudgingly gave ground while clinging to whatever privileges they could claim. When the occupational world became increasingly bureaucratized, men still held to the notion of work as their primary source of self-esteem. When the wild West became buried under city streets and suburban lawns and when war was waged by computerized missiles, men still sought the strenuous life by turning the pages of James Bond's murderous exploits or watching twenty-two padded, helmeted athletes collide and tackle every Sunday on the television screen.[67]

The typical middle-class men of the 1970s were still playing the "manly" role they had inherited from their Victorian forefathers. The changes that occurred came from the outside, enforced either by women or social-economic circumstances. Men changed grudgingly, making no more than adjustments in order to preserve as much as possible of their privilege and supposed superiority. They reacted, in other words, as most elites do in response to insurgence: defensively rather than creatively, regarding innovation as a loss of power rather than as a gain of possibilities.

Even the radical young men within the New Left found it difficult to revise traditional masculine identity. In the early sixties, they fought nonviolently for civil rights, bending their heads beneath fists and clubs, and when drafted to fight in Vietnam, many chose to prove their courage in jail or exile. "Violence never does anything but destroy," Don Baty wrote from prison, "and love never does anything but build." In trespassing the boundaries between masculine and feminine, however, they had in mind the injustices of race and imperialism, not gender. Consequently, as the government kept escalating the war in Vietnam and the police intensified repression of dissidents at home, some New Left men reverted to old-fashioned masculinity—instead of nonviolence, street fighting and bombs; instead of love, class war. As one participant exclaimed after the 1968 uprising at Columbia University, "to be busted is to have balls—to come out on top."[68]

Lifelong socialization instilled deep and elusive needs that impeded a man's effort to revise his self-definition. He was born male, but he had to earn his manhood by struggling out of the weakness of boyhood and fighting, literally or figuratively, to win his standing in the world. A girl could grow up into marriage and motherhood by natural development, but a boy must *overcome* his boyishness and *achieve* his manhood—active verbs, transitive verbs. He engaged in a process of

earning and proving that was never completed. This sex-typed socialization inclined females and males into starkly contrasting stances.
When psychologist Carol Gilligan asked teenagers what dangers they
feared in their futures, she evoked tellingly different kinds of responses.
The girls worried about being out at the edge, stranded without a safety
net of friends; the boys worried about being impeded in climbing upward and alone.[69] Sharing versus competing. Safe versus coming out on
top. Carole King singing *Far Away* versus Jackson Browne *Running on
Empty*.

In reality, few men truly extinguished the need to be comforted, the
fear of loneliness, the anxiety of being inept or wrong or unloved. But
they had learned to hide those vulnerabilities behind tight lips and dry
eyes—the masculine armor. Control required, first of all, self-control.
Men wanted to sit in the driver's seat, but the price of power was that
they dared not fail or even ask for help. "No, Martha, we're not lost," he
would insist after twenty minutes of wandering along an unfamiliar
highway. "Goddamn it, Martha, I'm *not* going to ask directions at that
gas station," he would rage thirty minutes later, after two U-turns and
one dead end. Control required self-control, so the more he feared failing, the more tightly he must cling to the armor of self-sufficiency.
("Honey, you really tempt me, you know, the way you look so kind,"
sang Jackson Browne. "I'd love to stick around but I'm running behind.
You know, I don't even know what I'm hoping to find.")

If masculinity meant mastery—power in the world and over women
—it also meant proving the mastery and hiding the unmasterful parts
of oneself. With so much to lose or prove or hide, it's no surprise that
men greeted the women's movement with defensiveness. And when
the movement hit home, when their wives refused to pick up the dirty
laundry and quoted from Ms. magazine, the defensiveness mounted.
Even sympathetic husbands felt unsafe. Harry Boyte was a radical ac-
tivist committed to democracy both in society and at home, but he
found himself asking anxious questions when his wife joined a women's
group: "Would she discover secret angers? . . . Would Sara's widening
circle of women friends damage the closeness of our relationship?"[70]

To be sure, feminist wives were a minority. Most women above the
age of thirty preferred to stay home with children and be supported by
their husbands. But what the women's movement didn't accomplish,
the American economy did. A recession during the early seventies, followed by steeply rising unemployment and feverish inflation, abruptly

Reprinted with special permission of King Features Syndicate

punctured the postwar economic boom. After a quarter-century of growth, the average annual income of families stagnated. Whatever they preferred, more and more wives and mothers had to go out and earn money to pay the mortgage, the car loan, or the children's college tuition. By 1980, 51 percent of married women were gainfully employed, and an even higher proportion of women with children (see Appendix A).

A historic shift in public gender roles was taking place. But the impact upon domestic roles was not entirely what one would predict. Yes, employed women performed fewer hours of housework per week during the 1970s (for the first time in fifty years), while their husbands' contributions increased. But the division remained far short of fifty-fifty. In two-paycheck families, husbands performed on average only one-third of the domestic responsibilities (compared to one-fifth in the 1960s). Moreover, they typically took care of tasks that could be done at times of their choosing: yard work, repairs, and the like. Their wives' tasks—dish washing, preparing meals—had to be done every day. Indeed, women often were juggling two activities at once: writing checks and returning phone calls; folding laundry and tending the children.[71] Between paid employment, housework, and child care, mothers put in eighty-five-hour weeks, which were ten to twenty hours longer than their husbands'.[72]

This persistent inequity is unsurprising. What *is* surprising—and to a feminist, disturbing—is that only a minority of employed middle-class women wanted their husbands to do more of the housework and child care. In the late 1980s, two decades after the modern feminist wave began rolling across the American landscape, 63 percent of female professionals with preschool children said their husbands handled a "satisfactory amount" of domestic responsibilities. When they found fault, it more often was with themselves. "My house provides constant evidence of my shortcomings and inadequacies," one mother lamented. "No matter how hard I try, things at home are almost never as clean and orderly as I would like them to be."[73] And even more guiltily, they worried about neglecting their children and husbands. Conventional gender roles may have been stretched into new shapes by economic pressures, but gender identities—how people define themselves—proved more resistant: it was easier for a mother to be a feminist in her office than at home.[74] Instead of seeking equal treatment, most women struggled to be superwomen.

The male half of the family story, meanwhile, contained its own surprises. Husbands enjoyed a privileged position at home, but they too battled with internal tensions. "I work hard and take a full briefcase home most nights," said Chuck Powell, a forty-one-year-old comptroller for a leading corporation. "My life in the past five years has . . . become frenetic. . . . I feel a lot of pressure and I get more tired than I am willing to admit, even to myself." In the midst of chasing promotions, he took a rueful glance homeward and asked, "At sixty what am I going to tell my kids I did with my life? . . . I guess my personal and business values just don't click at times."[75]

There were a lot of Chuck Powells out there in the 1970s and 1980s, clambering the slippery skyscraper heights of the corporate economy. The days of rugged individualism were long gone: only one of ten men was self-employed, and three of ten nonagricultural employees worked for businesses with more than 500 people. Nevertheless, up-and-coming professional men worked as long as they would have worked in the nineteenth century: an average of fifty-seven hours per week in 1985, sixty-two by 1990.[76] They lived the strenuous life of the courtroom, the operating room, or the corporate boardroom, and along the way they succumbed to high blood pressure, heart attacks, and the kinds of nagging doubts that Chuck Powell voiced.

According to repeated surveys, one-third of married men felt that their jobs interfered with family life "somewhat" or "a lot." And family mattered to them. "What are the important things to you?" a sociologist asked two hundred executives in a large company. Sixty percent said "family"; fewer than 20 percent said "career." (As she was interviewing, this sociologist noticed on each executive's desk the color photographs of his wife and kids.) In 1979 the vast majority of men rated health, love, peace of mind, and family as being personally "very important"; work came in a distant fifth. In short, Superman wanted time off from fighting Lex Luthor and stopping runaway express trains. He wanted more opportunity to shed his uniform and become good old Clark Kent playing with Lois and their baby. As a United Auto Workers vice president put it, "Maybe we ought to stop talking about the work ethic and start talking about the life ethic."[77]

WHAT HAPPENED NEXT SEEMS INEVITABLE. Men began talking not only about a life ethic but also about male liberation—and not only talking, but taking collective action. If women had obvious reasons to call for freedom from oppression, in certain ways so did the ruling gender. Between the 1970s and the 1990s, five distinct "men's movements" emerged, although as we shall see, they disagreed on why men were oppressed and what was to be done about it.

The first was launched by veterans of the New Left who were deeply influenced by feminist ideas. "We, as men, want to take back our full humanity," proclaimed the Berkeley Men's Center in 1973. "We no longer want to strain and compete to live up to an impossible, oppressive masculine image—strong, silent, cool, handsome, unemotional, successful, master of women, leader of men, wealthy, brilliant, athletic, and 'heavy.'" In California and New York and in urban or academic oases between, some men were trying to break down the compartment of their social conditioning. They wanted to "affirm our strengths as men and at the same time encourage the creation of new space for men in areas such as child care, cooking, sewing, and other 'feminine' aspects of life." By the 1980s, thirty additional men's centers had opened, and several hundred men met each year in a national Conference on Men and Masculinity.[78]

What did it all add up to? One of the conference organizers exuberantly announced in 1977 "our own birth as a movement." The next year another promised "the not-quite-ready-for-prime-time revolution." Actually it was neither movement nor revolution, and far from ready for anything but hope. A network seems closer to the truth. In 1982 the network acquired strength and structure in the form of the National Organization of Changing Men (later renamed the National Organization of Men against Sexism), but it focused on changing consciousness more than laws or institutions. Male liberation was a personal more than a political matter, because middle-class men were not an oppressed minority. If they felt oppressed, it would be for interior rather than exterior reasons. Sexism rendered each man his own oppressor.[79]

"Straight/White/Male: Struggling with the Master Culture"—that was the theme for the 1977 meeting of the Conference on Men and Masculinity. The struggle was not about legal or economic discrimination but about gender identity. In the words of one button at the convention, "I am not a success object." And on a T-shirt, "Goodbye, John Wayne." At various "playshops," men joined in dance; instead of speeches and voting, they shared feelings about fathers, wife abuse, and homosexuality. When the participants took public action, they aimed at cultural rather than political enemies. During the 1979 conference at the University of Southern California, for instance, a squad of "antisexist merry pranksters" was dispatched to the Los Angeles Colosseum. On the field, the Rams were tackling, blocking, outrunning, and finally defeating the Minnesota Vikings. In the stands, the liberationists raised banners declaring, "Football is Ritualized Violence" and "NFL means No Family Life," until ushers hustled them away.[80]

The activity of profeminist men drew energy more from the trends in "personal growth" and humanistic psychology than from the civil rights movement. And therefore it took place primarily on such a nonpublic level and in such unideological forms that one could easily overlook it. Four Chicago men in their thirties cooked a potluck dinner in an apartment near Wrigley Field, greeting a latecomer with hugs, and then—as they did every Sunday—sat down to eat and talk. A group of fathers in Boston met once a month to discuss issues concerning their children and, inevitably, to reflect about their own issues as sons. Six middle-aged men in Chapel Hill, North Carolina, met every Monday evening to talk about anything and everything—last night's quarrel with a wife, a salary raise, high-school fantasies about success, what exactly constituted sexual harassment—but the underlying agenda was always support and intimacy. "With you I can let myself be known," said one member. The others nodded in agreement. "That's because we're all on each other's side."[81] These groups were not a lunch-hour basketball team playing to win. They were not a law-school study group or a moun-tain-climbing crew working to come out on top. Nor were they merely a bunch of guys shooting the bull and downing some brews at the bar. They were noncompetitive, noninstrumental, and self-disclosing—a homely rebellion against the masculine identity they had grown up with.

For one category of men, however, oppression had far more tangi-ble meaning. Homosexuals constituted a minority group who certainly were victimized. Unlike blacks, gay Americans could conceal their iden-tities, and until 1970 most chose to do so. The penalties for "coming out" were too severe: eviction by one's landlord, perhaps, or dismissal by one's employer, not to mention the intangible though no less dev-astating sheepishness or disgust or all-too-polite silence from ac-quaintances. Given these risks, many homosexuals led double lives—incognito by day in the straight culture, together by night in gay bars, where they found safety and identity in an underground subculture. But they were never really safe from the violence by "queerbashers," against which the police provided little protection, and from arrests by the po-lice themselves. In 1969, inspired by the protests of blacks and women, the patrons of a gay Greenwich Village bar decided to take their des-tinies into their own hands. When the police arrived to close down the place, the men threw beer cans, trash cans, and bricks. The next night, more than two thousand people fought with police. "I'm a faggot, and I'm proud of it," they shouted. "Gay Power!" At one point, an im-promptu chorus line of men danced in the middle of the street. "You know, the guys there were so beautiful," Allen Ginsberg exclaimed. "They've lost that wounded look that fags all had ten years ago."[82]

Within weeks, the Stonewall Inn riot triggered a national gay rights movement. "Say it loud, gay is proud," chanted thousands of men and women as they marched, openly and exuberantly, through New York, San Francisco, and other cities during the early 1970s. By the end of the decade, there were not hundreds but thousands of gay liberation groups, along with a thriving subculture of gay newspapers, magazines, churches, health clinics, even amateur sports leagues. Politicians, doctors, academic scholars, and TV reporters "came out," and some men organized caucuses against sexual discrimination within their profession. While all of this grassroots upheaval was occurring, authorities were granting legitimacy from above. More than half the states repealed their sodomy laws, the Civil Service Commission lifted its ban on hiring homosexuals, and the 1980 Democratic party platform endorsed gay rights. The American Psychiatric Association, meanwhile, changed its century-old position by removing homosexuality from its list of mental disorders.[83]

"We reject society's attempt to impose sexual roles and definitions on our nature," the Gay Liberation Front proclaimed. "WE ARE GOING TO BE WHO WE ARE."[84] But one's identity is not simply a "true self" waiting to "come out." It is formed by a lifelong process of give-and-take with others. To quote one historian of lesbianism, it is a process of "be-coming out."[85] Indeed, the personas homosexuals adopted in the seventies reflected more than they rejected the mainstream gender stereotypes. Lesbians turned to loving relationships and community—feminine values—albeit in work shirts and boots. Gay men turned to uninhibited sexuality, both public (bars and bath houses) and private (apartments). No limp wrists, no giggles and "camping," no fairies. Mustaches, leather pants, cowboy boots, and muscled bodies. "Hardness is in," said one gay observer.[86]

The emergence of AIDS in 1981 abruptly changed all this. When sex with a stranger might mean infection, horrible suffering, and inescapable death, gay men began choosing monogamous relationships. But for many men this choice came too late, because the HIV virus remains latent for years. Ten new cases of AIDS were reported every week in 1982, and 100 in 1984. By 1988, there were 62,000 cases in all, and half of the victims had died. A lethal epidemic was under way, killing more men than the Korean and Vietnam Wars combined.[87] In response, gay men mobilized politically, pressuring local and federal officials to provide more funds for medical care and research. They also formed an astounding array of volunteer service agencies: health clinics; meals-on-wheels groups with names such as "Chicken Soup Brigade" and "God's Love We Deliver"; support groups; and "buddy systems" pairing gay men with AIDS patients to provide legal advice, hot meals, or simple companionship. In cities throughout the nation, the so-called gay community really was a community now. What's more, lesbians were cooperating with gay men to meet the crisis, building a sexual culture in which, as historian John D'Emilio wrote, "some men and women could meet on ground that, if not common, was at least in the same neighborhood."[88]

Just as the women's movement had been born out of the civil rights movement and the New Left, the profeminist and the gay men's movements were descendants of all those three forebears. By this time, however, a backlash against "the sixties" was taking shape, not only in politics and religion, but also in gender. Among women there was Phyllis Schlafly's STOP-ERA campaign. Among men there would be three different movements, each critiquing feminism in a different way. Male indignation was predictable. After all, as sociologist R. W. Connell tartly remarked, a profeminist man "was easily defined as a fool, slightly mad, or a pervert. An easier answer to the sense of guilt was to deny the oppression of women; better still, to claim that men are equally oppressed."[89] These divisions among men underlined all the more forcefully that the meaning of masculinity was in flux.

"I am angry," declared a founder of the National Coalition of Free Men, "that in the name of eliminating sex-stereotyping, feminism has reinforced some of the most fundamental and devastating stereotypes of all: the man as predator . . . stalking . . . powerful . . . base and insensitive . . . exploitive and untrustworthy."[90] If women were victimized by sexism, men were being victimized by "the new sexism" promulgated by feminists. Men were being blamed for violence, racism, the environmental crisis, and other social evils. All this blame was based on "myths," these nonfeminists proclaimed in the titles of their articles and books: *The Myth of Male Power; The Myth of the Monstrous Male; The Myth of Masculine Privilege.* In reality, they said, American society imposed severe penalties upon most men: lifelong economic support of others; military service to the nation; "the self-destructive need to achieve." As a consequence, men displayed a higher incidence of alcoholism, crime, and disease, culminating in death ten years earlier than for women.[91] "Men are hurting more than women," said Warren Farrell. "That is, men are, in many ways, actually more powerless than women."[92]

Divorced fathers had the most specific complaints of discrimination. As one NCFM member wrote to President Clinton, "When an involuntarily unemployed man can be incarcerated for contempt of court due to his inability to pay child support, the legal system, aided and abetted by all levels of government, has reintroduced slavery." Even employed men were hard pressed. In New York City, most divorced men paid between 17 and 35 percent of gross income, which left middle-class fathers close to the financial edge. William B. Hess, a fifty-five-year-old architect who was briefly jailed for nonpayment, complained that "nobody monitors whether she spends the money on the children. It could be going to boyfriends, clothes, booze, whatever."[93] Even more heartfelt than child support was the issue of child custody. Numerous divorced fathers told stories of vindictive ex-wives, obstructive social workers, and callous judges. "I see my kid every weekend but it's become a nightmare. Lately, my six-year-old son acts terrified. My ex-wife has accused me, in front of him, of physically abusing him when I'm alone with him. Last time he threw up as soon as he got into the car."[94]

"Men need their own lobby . . . because we're really getting screwed, guys," said the author of *The Myth of the Monstrous Male*. "The only way to change is to organize, raise a few million consciousnesses, and start making with the squeaking wheel."[95] And organize they did. Approximately two hundred "fathers' rights" groups emerged in thirty-three states by 1981, and hundreds of others followed in the next few years. On the national level, meanwhile, nonfeminists formed two organizations, the Coalition of Free Men and Men's Rights Incorporated.[96]

As a squeaking wheel, they had some successes, notably the passage of joint-custody bills in forty-three states and an increased willingness of courts and legislatures to punish mothers who refused visits by fathers. Nevertheless, they aroused the consciousness of relatively few persons.[97] For the main problem surrounding divorced fathers was not discrimination against them but delinquency by them. Although mothers were awarded custody of children 70 percent of the time, that was because their husbands usually didn't ask for it—and when husbands did ask, most of them won custody. The unfortunate fact was that all too many fathers left their families in the lurch. Despite increasingly rigorous measures against "deadbeat dads" (such as taking away drivers' licenses and income tax refunds), one-fourth of all custodial mothers in 1991 were not receiving the child support their ex-husbands were supposed to pay, and many others were receiving far less than they were due. Even more fathers defaulted on personal contact. According to a study that followed one thousand children of disrupted families during 1976 through 1987, a full 42 percent had not seen their father at all during the previous year, and 80 percent had not slept in their father's house in the previous month.[98]

If a large segment of middle-class men felt deprived, theirs was not an economic or legal deprivation; it was emotional and spiritual. They were less concerned with demanding their rights as fathers than with healing their wounds as sons. And instead of exploding masculine myths, they were hungry to learn the mythology of masculine archetypes and rituals.

This is what emerged—or rather, poured out—in chants, tears, dancing, and the beating of drums as poet Robert Bly, storyteller Michael Meade, and Jungian psychologist James Hillman went around the country talking to gatherings of men. "We are living at an important and fruitful moment now," Bly wrote, "for it is clear to men that the images of adult manhood given by the popular culture are worn out; a man can no longer depend on them." The hard-working, tough man of the fifties, the feminist man of the sixties, the "soft" man of the seventies—each of these had been valuable. But men were feeling anguished and impotent because they hadn't experienced their deep, instinctual masculine energies.[99]

"It's a beautiful Saturday morning on the campus of the New Mexico School for the Deaf," wrote journalist Don Shewey,

> and 500 men fighting spring fever are lining up to enter the James A. Little Theater through the stage door. In the hallway, a shirtless man is dancing wildly and whooping; from behind him wafts the rumble of drumming. As we get closer to the entrance, a sense of chaos radiates, ever-stronger, from the other side. A tunnel of pine branches has been constructed as a sort of ritual birth canal. Just before I stoop to go through, the gatekeeper (a balding man in a flannel shirt and jeans) leans to whisper in my ear, "Let your movements be a blessing."
>
> In a flash I'm through. I stumble into bright lights, a thicket of drummers, men coming at me, the steady pulse of clapping. Where am I? Suddenly there's Bly, in my face, his blue eyes going all googly behind his steel-framed glasses, his long arms waving and wiggling like flapping wings. He's dancing like a big, silly silver-haired walrus in Tom Wolfe-white trousers and a blue brocade vest. I lock into his gaze and go into my own

basic boogaloo, and we dance together across what turns out to be the stage of the auditorium before he shakes my hand and points me down the stairs to the audience.[100]

The media found it easy to mock such goings-on. Feminists, both male and female, hastened to condemn them, at the least for ignoring women's inequities, at worst for endorsing the aggressive, misogynist, and homophobic sides of masculine identity.[101] Granted, some of the mythopoetic movement was either foolish or sexist or both, but we should also pay attention to what else lay behind the drumming and dancing.[102] "I think most men who come [to our programs] are yearning," said the president of the Men's Center of Raleigh, North Carolina, in 1989, after a crowd of two hundred attended a two-day Bly gathering. "There's a kind of piece missing. A lot of it has to do with father. Ninety-five percent of the men who come are feeling this distance, a disconnectedness, never having had the interaction with Dad."[103] Bly penetrated that chink in the emotional armor when he recounted growing up with an adoring mother and a forbidding, alcoholic father. He was a "soft" male, who embraced his feminine side and, in shame and anger toward his father, renounced his masculine side. Only in late-middle age did he see his father as a victim of social, especially female, expectations. Then Bly began to work out a relationship with him and, more generally, with his own masculine energy—what he called the Wild Man.[104]

Bly's story turned out to be the story of countless other men. "He really wasn't a very good father," went a typical lament. "He wasn't there physically as much as ideally he would [sic] have been, and when he was there, he was drunk or he was lying on the couch watching the football game on TV. . . . I was afraid of him, and I didn't like or respect him very much." After participating in a men's retreat, however, he stopped "demonizing" his father and realized "the problems weren't just because he was a man, which is what my mom would say. Now I know that I'm not necessarily doomed to be a fuck-up just because I also am a man."[105]

Such a testimonial could have come from AlAnon, a child-abuser's support group, or some other recovery program, but in one respect it was unique. This involved "men's work"—the recovery of gender identity. According to Bly, men couldn't do this work successfully in a culture in which fathers no longer taught sons a craft and women exercised undue influence. He was describing the same kind of crisis that middle-class men had experienced at the beginning of the century. Back then, they had turned to body building, Boy Scouts, Wild West fantasies, and ultimately, war. In the 1980s, Bly offered a remedy borrowed from mythology, anthropology, and Jungian psychology. The modern American male needed an older man—the king—to initiate him into manhood and help him exercise the power of the interior warrior. This was not destructive machismo, Bly emphasized; not murder or Cold War aggression. (Bly vehemently opposed both the Vietnam War and the Persian Gulf War.) It entailed claiming one's strength and autonomy while retaining love and sensibility—animus and anima, both halves of the whole self.[106]

At weekend gatherings around the country during the 1980s, Bly served as the king who fathered wounded sons through this rite of passage (fifty thousand between 1985 and 1989 alone). When he published *Iron John* in 1990, his charisma radiated even further. This intricate analysis of archetypes and historical trends stayed on the hardback bestseller list for more than a year, and Bill Moyers's PBS profile of Bly ("A Gathering of Men," 1990) sold twenty-seven thousand videocassette copies and ten thousand transcripts.[107] This was more than a one-man phenomenon, however. Although not a social movement, it certainly was a social and psychological stirring. By the mid-nineties, men could read twenty-four different mythopoetic journals and walk into more than forty men's centers. In the classified ads of *Wingspan: Journal of the Male Spirit* (circulation, 120,000), they were invited to attend the Gentle Warrior Retreat, at Shutesbury, Massachusetts; Canoeing with a Circle of Men, in New Hampshire; Exploring the Father/Son Wound in Lee Canyon, Nevada; and a dozen other gatherings. The experience could be transformative. After a New Warrior weekend, Daniel Garfield of Northampton, Massachusetts, took a more active role in caring for his children and proclaimed his commitment to his wife. "He left as a boy and came back as a man," she said. "He holds himself accountable for his actions now."[108]

The 1990s also witnessed the birth of yet another "men's movement"—the Promise Keepers—which espoused more religious ideas than the other four and was also more effectively structured. In 1990, former University of Colorado football coach Bill McCartney organized a local fellowship of seventy-two men in prayer, fasting, and discussion of the responsibilities that the Bible demanded of them. The truly

Christian man should take moral leadership in his family, honoring his wife and nurturing his children, exemplifying Christlike strength and sexual purity. "We're calling men of God to battle" against the promiscuity and permissiveness of modern America, McCartney said. He had discovered the right message at the right moment. Soon he was leading an evangelical revivalist crusade like Billy Graham's or Jerry Falwell's, but a crusade aimed at men. More than twenty thousand men gathered in the University of Colorado Folson Stadium in 1992, and fifty thousand a year later. By 1995, more than seven hundred thousand—almost all of them white and middle-aged—were paying fifty-five dollars each at thirteen sites around the country in what one journalist called "a combination Super Bowl game and revival meeting."[109]

By then McCartney had built an infrastructure of twenty-one state offices, thousands of congregations (eight hundred in Colorado alone), and teams of volunteers recruiting at the local level. Like the anti-ERA forces, the spokesmen for Promise Keepers criticized feminists for subverting the God-given family hierarchy. The first step toward becoming a spiritually pure man, Tony Evans advised, "is sit down with your wife and say something like this: 'Honey, I've made a terrible mistake. I've given you my role. . . . Now I must reclaim that role.' Don't misunderstand what I'm saying here," Evans continued. "I'm not suggesting that you *ask* for your role back, I'm urging you to *take* it back."[110] This sort of injunction found a receptive audience among conservative men. As a United Methodist minister remarked, "You don't come here and feel like you're losing your masculinity because of your faith."[111]

In one of his poems Robert Bly wrote:

It is a massive
masculine shadow,
fifty males sitting together
in hall or crowded room,
lifting something indistinct,
up into the resonating night.[112]

What did these various stirrings add up to? Not *a* movement—perhaps several movements at cross-purposes—but certainly a commotion. A remarkable number of middle-class men were raising large, often indistinct questions about themselves in the world. Prodded by the women's movement, gay liberation, and economic pressures, they were asking what it meant to "be a man." They had done the same a century earlier and had emerged with ambivalent answers: acknowledging "the new woman" while stigmatizing homosexuals as "inverts" and clinging to fantasies of the strenuous life. But the late-twentieth-century questions were not simply an episode of *déjà vu*. Amid traditional stereotypes and ambivalence one also saw men beginning to perforate the partition between "masculine" and "feminine" identity.

Manliness. A rash of films with muscular, violent heroes, epitomized by *Rambo*, signaled what Susan Jeffords called "the remasculinization of America" in reaction to the nation's defeat in Vietnam.[113] In the 1988 presidential campaign, Vice President George Bush anxiously shed his "wimp" image by hiring a consultant to help him eradicate his flitty gestures and proclaiming, "I'm a pit bull." His Republican rival, Senator Bob Dole, boasted, "I'm tough. You got to be tough." His Democratic rival, Governor Michael Dukakis, insisted, "I'm not squishy soft. I'm very tough," and posed for cameras riding a tank.[114]

The imagery offered by Hollywood and politicians didn't correspond, however, with what many men were wanting for themselves. "How would you rather be viewed by most people?" pollsters asked in 1991. A hefty majority of men, 71 percent, chose "sensitive and caring," and only 15 percent preferred "rugged and masculine."[115] In cities and towns across the country, middle-aged men were meeting in small groups every week or two, struggling (as the director of one men's center put it) to escape "a kind of gender blanket that we have been smothered under, one that tells us to be stoic, not to express pain, not be vulnerable." In nearly two hundred colleges, meanwhile, younger men were stepping back to re-examine gender premises in men's studies courses.[116]

Homosexuality. Within days of his inauguration, Bill Clinton triggered an explosion when he ordered the army to end its exclusion of homosexuals. Not only did the military force the commander in chief to back down; the gay issue became a substantial factor in turning white male voters against the Democratic party. In 1994 and again in 1996, the gender gap (Republican men versus Democratic women) grew to its widest since 1980.[117] Police harassment, vigilante "queer-bashing," and Christian campaigns against "homosexual rights" laws continued in the 1990s. Voters in Florida, Oklahoma, and Colorado, and in St. Paul and Wichita repealed their statutes that prohibited discrimination on account of sexual orientation. Two of three Americans believed that sexual relations between two consenting adults of the same sex were "always wrong."[118]

At the same time, gay and lesbian presence had never been so pervasive and accepted. More than 150 open homosexuals held political office, including eleven in state legislatures and three in the U.S. House of Representatives. At least a dozen cities and numerous corporations granted legal status to same-sex couples for health benefits, tax returns, and, in a few cases, even marriage. In those small towns where homosexuals once either had remained invisible or had fled, gay organizations, nightclubs, and bookstores were springing up.[119]

Family. "My strong, indeed passionate, intention was to be different from my father," declared Harry Boyte. "Which meant, simply, being available [to my son]." He was speaking for a great many of his fellow men. When Gail Sheehy interviewed professionals in their late twenties, she was astonished to hear them saying that the satisfaction they sought above all—more than work, money, success, or marital love—was children. Increasingly, men wanted to be good fathers, starting even before the birth of their children. As Lamaze classes proliferated during the 1970s and hospitals finally opened delivery rooms to husbands, millions of men coached their wives breath by breath, push by pelvic push, through the hours of struggle and pain until, together, mother and father, they witnessed their children entering the world. Houston Oilers tackle David Williams touched off a cultural firestorm when he missed a game to be with his wife during childbirth; he was fined $125,000. "It was no contest," Williams said, "and I'd do it again." Fatherhood was no longer simply the by-product of having planted sperm nine months earlier and of pacing off-stage in a hospital waiting room. It was a firsthand experience, a process of marital teamwork out of which men emerged feeling "bonded" with their children.[120]

There was a surge of interest in fatherhood during the 1980s and 1990s: support groups, workshops, programs, and books taught men (in a newly coined verb) *to parent.* It was startling to read in *Fortune* magazine, for example, that more fathers than mothers wanted companies to devise ways of combining responsibilities at home and work. A few men solved the problem on their own. Forty-six-year-old Burt Johnson of Winnetka, Illinois, for example, left his job as a civil engineer to take care of his two young daughters because, as he said, "my wife was making about six times my salary. It didn't make sense [to continue working] if we were going to give our children what we wanted them to have."[121]

Other evidence reminds us, alas, that the promise of wholehearted fatherhood often faltered in practice. In the typical middle-class two-career family, women still performed the major share of domestic duties, while their husbands "helped out." Whereas the average employed mom spent almost four hours a day with the children on workdays, dad spent only 2.6, and half of American men said they "never" vacuumed or did laundry.[122] Nor did men show much interest in family-leave programs enabling them to stay at home with their newborns. AT&T, for example, offered up to a full year without pay, but forty-nine of every fifty employees who took leave in the 1990s were women. At IBM, the ratio was more equal, but not by much. Even after the 1992 federal Family and Medical Leave Act required all companies with fifty or more employees to offer twelve unpaid weeks a year, only a handful of workers used it, and most of them were women. Indeed, only 5 percent took advantage of the less drastic option of part-time shifts.[123]

Given this discrepancy between promise and practice, it seems irresistible to hold men guilty of gross hypocrisy. That is part of the truth, but only part. Attitudes change slowly, after all, and attitudes toward something as basic as gender role and identity change with glacial slowness. Furthermore, men's occupational circumstances discouraged them from acting on what they promised.

If money were not a concern, one-third of men told pollsters, they would choose to work part-time. But of course the dictates of money could not be wished away. In fact, in the era of corporate downsizing, middle-aged breadwinners put in more hours than ever for fear of losing their jobs. "Unfortunately, there's the mentality that if you're here eight hours a day, you're a slacker," remarked thirty-eight-year-old Kendall Bodden, a middle manager at Storagetek in Colorado. In order to spend time with his wife and ten-month-old son in the evenings, then, he slept five hours a night, left home between three and five A.M., and worked ten to fourteen hours a day.[124] This was more than a rat race; it was a daily triathlon performed in suit and tie. Given this macho work culture, it's no wonder that few fathers dared to request family leave and be labeled "wimps." When companies were asked how long a leave was reasonable, 41 percent said *no* time.[125]

Men had to defy powerful social institutions and expectations if they wanted to revise the balance of work and family. But even if external forces relented, it wasn't clear to what extent men really wanted to change. More time at home, but how much greater a share of doing laundry? More time for family vacations, but with dad in the driver's seat of the van? Beneath the question of gender roles lay the question of gender identity. Were men too soft or too hard? Were they cowed by women or trapped inside their own armor? Would they find liberation among other men or in partnership with women or with their children? The heterogeneous answers of the so-called men's movements signaled the confusions and ambivalence felt by individual men as they struggled, in the postfeminist era, to define who they wanted to be. Gender identities were contested, in doubt.

8

The Children of the Women's Movement

In the Boston Museum of Fine Arts hangs a huge, mysterious painting by Paul Gauguin with the evocative title, "Where Do we Come From, Who Are we, Where Are we Going?" Most historians have the good sense not to assess the present, much less prophesy the future. What has happened cannot play the same tricks as what seems about to happen and then, more often than not, doesn't. But to stop here, one step short of the present, is to forfeit rich rewards of our study. As this book crosses the line between past and present, it brings us to the moment for drawing conclusions (prophecies of a modest kind). Indeed, unless we discern a few large patterns of meaning, we run the risk of leaving useful insights camouflaged among one hundred years and two hundred fifty pages of rapid details. So let us follow Gauguin.

WHERE DO WE COME FROM?

During most of this century, to be born into the middle class meant to travel a life course that divided into two lanes, each marked by a different gender sign. Males went to college, entered a white-collar occupation, married, and had children. Females went to college, married, and had children. A minority followed alternative routes, but paid a price for doing so: those women who entered careers and so had to give up marriage; and those men and women who chose same-sex relationships and had to remain hidden from public view. In the 1960s and 1970s, however, the equal rights movements opened up new paths, more options. Women commuted between work and family. Men gave more attention to fatherhood, home, and the feelings they found there. Gays and lesbians came out into the open. Instead of fitting themselves into rigid binary categories of masculine and feminine, more

Americans defined their roles and identities in flexible terms. But these innovations did not proceed smoothly. Not only did various groups and institutions defend traditional patterns and values; the innovators experienced confusion and ambivalence. It is hard, sometimes painfully hard, to replace the predictable with the open-ended and negotiable.

WHO ARE WE?

By the 1980s, the feminist movement had become history. Middle-aged veterans looked back with pride; young people with curiosity or condescension, sometimes scorn. History had revolved full cycle. Like the 1920s daughters of the suffrage movement, the 1980s and 1990s daughters (and sons) of the women's movement shied away from the "feminist" label. There would be none of that fist-waving and man hating for the younger generation. When Sarah Calian, a Brown University senior, heard the president of NOW speak on campus, she came away untouched. "I never felt so not a part of something. I don't know who she was talking to."[1] If you asked a hundred college students in the 1990s how many called themselves "feminists," at most fifteen raised their hands while a dozen others wanted to know what exactly you meant by that word. The backlash of the Reagan era had made its impact on this generation. The majority were afraid of feminism because it critiqued marriage and connoted lesbianism. And even those who had a less biased perspective remained indifferent to feminism, because it was political and they were not. Most young women in the eighties and nineties shaped their identities less in public life than in friendships and romantic relationships.[2]

But we should not be deceived by labels. If you asked those same hundred students how many believed in "equal rights for women," ninety-seven hands shot into the air.[3] As one journalist remarked, they were the "No, but . . ." generation.[4] No, they were not feminists, but they took for granted that they would have the same opportunities as men. Some of them, in fact, harshly criticized older feminists for harping on the abuses and disadvantages suffered by women, date rape being a prime example. This "victimism" not only distorted the facts of growing equality between the sexes, critics said; it cast females as fragile and passive creatures, neo-Victorian angels.[5]

Like Charlotte Perkins Gilman, Carrie Chapman Catt, and their fellow suffragists in the 1920s, the veterans of the seventies felt betrayed. But they needn't have given up hope. In an unmilitant, unideological fashion, the younger generation was living out the struggle for equality. They might take for granted the rights and opportunities that feminists had fought to acquire. The further they traveled into adulthood, though, the more they discovered that women still received less than equal treatment. The postfeminist story was a "Yes, but . . ." story: yes, progress had been made, but it remained short of the destination.

The lack of progress was evident in the realm of political power and legal rights. Women became an increasingly familiar presence in state legislatures, and on the national scene there were those three stars, Justices Sandra Day O'Connor and Ruth Bader Ginsburg and Secretary of State Madeleine Albright. But after rising steeply between 1970 and 1992, the number of women in Congress leveled out at 12 percent. Likewise, twenty years after Title IX ordered colleges to treat male and female athletes equally, the initial burst of compliance had expired. In 1997, women constituted more than half of all college students but only 37 percent of college athletes, receiving a disproportionately small fraction of recruiting expenses and athletic scholarships. Between 1992 and 1997, in fact, the overall operating expenditures for men's programs grew 60 percent faster than women's.[6] As for the right to abortion, it had been hedged by Congress, the states, and the Supreme Court itself; funding was canceled for poor women, and waiting periods and parental permission were required for teenagers. Meanwhile, right-to-life advocates created a physical kind of interference by demonstrating outside abortion clinics and harassing doctors by calling them "murderers." A woman who wanted an abortion often had to drive a hundred miles or more to the nearest clinic and then had to brave a gauntlet of shouting picketers at the entrance.

In the work world, it was the same story of limited advance. One can truthfully say both that "the sexes have never been so equal" and that "they remain unequal." Women made impressive inroads into hitherto all-male occupations—from bartending to engineering. Yet they continued to earn less than men. In 1960, women who were employed year-round and full-time earned an average of 61 percent of what men earned. In 1994, they earned 70 percent (lower than in almost all industrial countries except Japan).[7] Why this persistent gender gap?

Part of the explanation is that women often interrupt their careers for several months or years to raise their children and, when they return, have fallen behind male co-workers' earnings.[8] A larger part of the explanation is discriminatory treatment. Saleswomen, for example, increased their income during the 1980s at a much higher rate than did salesmen, yet in 1992 they still earned only 57 percent as much as men did, mainly because they were kept out of lucrative positions such as business-to-business sales.[9] Women numbered one-fourth of all lawyers, but earned an average of $17,000 less per year than did men.

To be sure, the gender gap was narrowing, so that younger women —and especially younger *college-educated* women—came close to male income levels. A woman fresh out of law school earned 95 percent as much as a male classmate. Still, as those newcomers looked up the career ladder, they faced the proverbial glass ceiling. In New York City law firms, the promotion rates for women, which were already lower than men's in the 1970s, dropped still further in the 1980s and early 1990s.[10] Likewise, in the business world, women occupied one-third of management positions but only 5 percent at the vice-presidential level and even fewer above that. In 1990, of the 4,012 highest paid officers and directors of major corporations, 19 were women. These rare females on the corporate heights earned less than their peers and worked as long (a median of sixty hours a week), and in order to do so, half of them remained childless. Marie Monet, who was an executive at a New York company, saw her husband, who was a general partner at a San Francisco securities firm, once a month. "I used to think I could work, get married and raise a family," she said. "I realize now it's hard enough just to do my job well. It was a rude awakening."[11]

When applied to family life, feminism contains an arithmetic flaw. We talk about 50-50, sharing the burdens and opportunities equally. In day-to-day reality for most middle-class couples, though, the arithmetic is 100-100, a full-time job for each. Then add children into the formula, and the numbers grow still heavier: 150-150, one full-time job and half the household responsibilities for each parent. Or, to put it another way, the two-career family is really a three-career family. "Doing it all" requires people to perform 150 percent of life's work, which is equality of an unfortunate kind, the equality of excess. It can be done; a few fathers and many mothers are doing it. But the price is high: personal exhaustion, for one thing, and not enough time to enjoy and care for one another as husbands, wives, and children (and also care for oneself).

Lisa Conte, chief executive of Shaman Pharmaceuticals in San Francisco, took her son, daughter, and nanny on business trips lasting longer than two nights. (Before his second birthday, her son had earned two cross-country frequent-flyer tickets.) "I do it for me," she said. "The time I get to spend on the plane with my children is the only time other than weekends." She was not unique. The number of business trips that included children rose by 63 percent during the early 1990s.[12] Other families devised less drastic solutions. Beverley Daniel (executive assistant to a college president) and her husband Warren (an architect) had bosses who let them work four long days a week, so one or the other was home with their two preschool daughters on Mondays and Fridays. "It's not easy," said Mrs. Daniel, "and we're pretty lucky."[13]

No wonder, then, as the director of the Institute for Women's Policy Studies regretfully put it, "People are saying that all feminism ever got us is more work."[14] It was easier in the not-so-old days. As recently as 1960, only 19 percent of wives with preschool children were gainfully employed, and most of these were employed part-time.[15] In the 1990s, the majority of women chose to "do it all"—marriage, children, and career. To pull off a triple play, a shortstop usually depends on good luck and two skillful teammates. The do-it-all woman had, at best, some luck and only one teammate.

Fathers, of course, have always "done it all," although they almost always delegated domestic tasks to their wives. In the 1990s, a growing number of middle-class men were committed to being more than absentee husbands and fathers. Part of the shift came by coercion—their wives were not staying home with vacuum cleaner and kids—but another part came from within the men themselves. If they didn't need a paycheck, 21 percent of men said they would prefer to stay home and care for their family.[16] Economic necessity dictated otherwise, of course. Nevertheless, two out of five did cut back on their working hours in order to spend more time with their children.[17]

These realignments of behavior amended rather than transformed gender roles, and even they came only with great difficulty. Still, they signaled that conventional categories were in flux. The Lamaze fathers and the corporation mothers belonged to a repertory company in which they played multiple parts. Indeed, given children's sore throats or a delayed airplane flight from Boston or some other of life's unfortunate surprises, members of the do-it-all family had to learn improvisational acting.

The flux went beyond roles to identities. *Who are we?* Gauguin's painting asked. In the aftermath of the women's movement as well as the men's movements, middle-class Americans were struggling to define how to live and, ultimately, who they were. It was a slow, unsteady process. On the one hand, the younger generation did not call themselves feminists; on the other hand, two out of three preferred a marriage in which husband and wife shared responsibilities at work and home. Furthermore, when college seniors were asked whether they expected to be the one who would miss an important meeting at work to stay home with a sick child, 54 percent of the college women and only 13 percent of the men said they would be the one.[18]

Masculine and feminine—with all their mutually exclusive connotations—function as one of our earliest and strongest markers of self-identification. It's understandable, then, that we have not erased those categories from our minds, even after a quarter-century of feminist crusading and even if we aspire to be nonsexist. The husband of a bank official, acting in loyalty to the "rules established by our two-career couplehood," readily agreed to move from Mexico City to Paris when she was offered a better job. After all, seven years earlier she had done the same when her husband had been transferred from New York. But his agreement gave way to second-guessing, then panic, then bickering, as he felt himself hostage to his wife's career, until finally, he said, "my worries about losing my self-worth or masculinity [were] offset by feeling courageous."[19]

People's behavior conflicted with their attitudes, and their attitudes conflicted with one another. These were the signs of change. All this wavering and confusion was eroding conventional gender categories. Americans could no longer presume what it meant to be a man or a woman. The meanings were becoming kaleidoscopic.

To conservatives, this trend meant social disorder, and, like Theodore Roosevelt at the turn of the century, they campaigned to save the family, the cornerstone of society. "Family values" became their rallying cry in the 1980s. But the family and familial values were thriving, albeit in unconventional arrangements.[20] Picture seven-year-old Warren Dill and his four-year-old brother, Graham, on a soccer field in suburban Yorktown Heights, New York, while their father, Douglas, coached from the sidelines. Then learn that Mr. Dill not only was a single father, who had adopted the boys as newborns in 1989 and 1992, but also was gay, openly and comfortably so. In a San Francisco suburb, meanwhile, Diane Dougherty and Audrey Covner, a lesbian couple in their early forties, were tending their two young daughters, cheerfully combining two careers with car seats and strollers.[21] Marriage between same-sex persons is legally recognized only in Hawaii, but gay and lesbian couples were setting down roots everywhere (one-third of them in the suburbs) and raising children (sometimes adopted, sometimes artificially inseminated, and sometimes inherited from a previous marriage of one or another partner).

Most Americans agreed that sexual relations between two adults of the same sex were "always wrong," or so they said when asked by pollsters.[22] In their day-to-day lives, however, they increasingly accepted the presence of gay men and lesbians. A kind of nationwide celebration took place, in fact, when Ellen DeGeneres, playing the main character on the TV series *Ellen*, came out as a lesbian. On that Wednesday evening in 1997, thousands of women gathered at public and private parties, and millions of other Americans sat in their nuclear family rooms, to watch the first openly homosexual character in a sitcom. It was a distinctly postmodern moment, this mingling of fictional and real Ellens, but it was symbolic of how much the culture had changed. Imagine Lucy in the fifties or Mary Richards in the seventies saying, "I'm gay." (Chrysler, Wendy's and other companies misread the culture, and timidly withdrew their ads from the show.)[23] Meanwhile, in nonfictional America, the AIDS epidemic had partly bridged the gap between the homosexual minority and the heterosexual majority. "There was no longer a need to kick [gay men], when they were already down," said Andrew Sullivan, gay former editor the *New Republic*. "I think this helps explain the change in the American psyche these last ten years from one of fearful stigmatization of homosexuals to one of awkward acceptance."[24]

Two-career couples with children or childless, househusbands, single fathers, same-sex parents—amid this diversification of social roles, Americans began thinking of gender identities more flexibly, placing themselves and others not in boxes but along a continuum. It was not a revolution overturning the old gender order. Rather, it was a cultural evolution—slow, incoherent, often invisible, but undeniable. As Vivian Gornick eloquently stated: "Feminism is a piece of consciousness that can't be gone back on. It has changed forever the way we think about ourselves. All over the country people who do not call themselves feminists see their lives differently." But we need to realize, Gornick added, that changed attitudes don't immediately produce changed behavior. As in psychoanalysis, insight is relatively easy, but extricating oneself from the old personality is slow and arduous work. "The insights of the Seventies are being assimilated in the slow unlovely way of social change: two steps forward, one step backward."[25]

WHERE ARE WE GOING?

American culture will continue to go where it has been going since the 1960s, perforating the boundaries of conventional gender roles and identities. That forecast is based on the impact of the women's movement and its offspring, the profeminist men's movements, and on demographic, economic, and cultural trends.

First, changes in the life cycle have restructured women's experience and therefore men's, too (see Figure 1, in Chapter 1, above). In contrast to her great-grandmother a century ago, the typical woman today has more options out of which to fashion herself. In early adulthood, she has college and perhaps professional school before she enters marriage and has children. Unlike her great-grandmother, though, she bears one or two children, not four, and combines family with paid employment. In later adulthood, she has fifteen "extra" years after her last child marries and before she dies. During the course of her life, then, the typical middle-class woman will play a variety of social roles, develop a correspondingly supple identity, and acquire the self-esteem and power that come with earning an income. All of this means, in turn, that her husband cannot be the patriarch his great-grandfather was. In short, marriage will become more and more egalitarian.

What demography permits, the economy compels. The decline of purchasing power since the early 1970s has compelled most married couples to find employment. But even apart from budgeting needs, women will continue to work because they want to, because they claim their identity as citizens of both the public and the private world.

What demography permits and the economy pushes, cultural values endorse. The prevailing ethic has shifted, in the course of a century, from duty to happiness. Instead of earnest reminders of "you ought," modern Americans hear enthusiastic cheers of "you can" and "you deserve." The nineteenth-century family hierarchy, in which everyone was assigned his or her complementary part, has been remodeled into an individualized team. Husband and wife go off to work, kids go off to day-care or school, and each pursues his or her own life all day until they reconvene at home and negotiate who should do what among their common tasks. Family ties are, more than ever, contractual rather than "naturally" or divinely given. (Victorians would say we have become selfish instead of selfless.)

Demographic, economic, and cultural trends merge into a broad current carrying us closer toward equal opportunity for those who are male or female, gay or straight, married or single, parents or childless. "Free to be you and me," as an antisexist children's song put it. It will be a long, fitful process, and not at all easy, arousing rancor, anxiety, confusion. There will be moments of doubt as to whether this is really change for the better. I think that the history of the past century offers a reassuring answer: yes.

Epilogue/
As We Are Becoming

[Paul Cowan and Rachel Brown met in Maryland during the summer of 1963 when, fresh out of college, they were working in the civil rights movement. Two years later, they married and went to Ecuador as Peace Corps Volunteers. In 1968 they returned to the United States, angered by the ineffectiveness of American liberal reform overseas, eager to promote social justice at home. Paul became a *Village Voice* journalist writing primarily about minority groups, while Rachel took up freelance photography. They also became involved with another kind of justice at home after Lisa was born in 1968 and then Matthew (called Mamu) in 1970. As feminists they believed in sharing their responsibilities equally; as parents they discovered this was even more difficult than they had expected. In the following paragraphs, spliced together from separate articles by Rachel in 1973 and Paul in 1975, they discussed the pleasures and problems of transcending conventional gender roles.][1]*

PAUL

Now, it seems clear to me that very few men in my generation were trained to accept the labor and emotional complexities of fatherhood. I know that I always assumed that my career would come first. When I imagined having kids (which I rarely did) I thought of them as pleasant distractions, part of a relaxed home, supervised by a thoroughly domesticated wife—which would permit me refuge from the turmoil of life.

It hasn't worked out that way. Rachel wasn't about to play the role of servant-wife-secretary. She was ambitious, too, and felt incomplete without her own career. And so, with great reluctance, I agreed to take on part of the housework; if Rachel was going to be a writer and pho-

*Reprinted with permission of the authors and the *Village Voice* © 1973, 1975.

tographer, then I'd have to become a part-time domestic. For a time it created considerable tension between us.

RACHEL

Paul and I wrestled with the problem of how to share child-care evenly. I wanted the kids to have a parent around part of every day—he was satisfied if they stayed with a sitter. He gave up work hours at night, on weekends, and on occasional mornings. For him it was a sacrifice, but it didn't help me with my basic conflict. I still wanted them to be with a parent during part of most days—forty hours of day care seemed too much when economic necessity didn't compel it.

Nevertheless, I spent a year ignoring my feelings that the children and I wanted to be together more. I felt that to relinquish work hours for family would be to compromise my feminism. I enjoyed the work I was doing, but I also felt guilty when I thought of doing it only part time. I was reacting to the signals I was perceiving from the women's movement. Most of the articles I read, or the discussions I heard, were about the dysfunctions of the nuclear family and the trap of motherhood. What was good for the children seemed irrelevant.

PAUL

I tried to talk, and even write, about the Zen-joys of fatherhood and housework. But it was largely a deceit. Though I only did a small portion of the housework, I still got terribly bored cleaning floors and changing diapers. I became angry when Rachel became so absorbed by an assignment that she was late for meals, though I never thought to deny myself that professional necessity. And I was frightened, too, since other writers always seemed more productive and potentially more successful than I.

RACHEL

Finally, I've recognized that for whatever reasons, Paul and I react differently to being parents. It's ridiculous for me to refuse to give up some of my work hours in order to have more time with the children just because he won't give up any more of his. I've decided I like both parts of my identity—the woman and the mother.

PAUL

Then, as our kids got older, I found my emotions changing. Suddenly, they were a vital presence, an essential part of my life, not two small bundles of incessant demands. As they grew old enough to begin school, Rachel and I both found time to work—our nerve-racking struggle for psychic space was eased. I still feel conflicts, but they are rooted in the complex experience of fatherhood now, not in the political theories of the women's movement.

RACHEL

Thus far feminism has not offered mothers much help in our struggle to unify our fractured selves. For the struggle is not one of making a choice between our children and our work—it is rather one of learning to live with and to understand our constant and relentless ambivalence.

One of the places where I feel that ambivalence about my identity most concretely is in the Museum of Natural History on weekday mornings. As Lisa, my four-year-old daughter, and I walk into the museum, I feel awkward, my huge body towers over its small satellite. What am I doing here when most people are working? I can't help but look at other women with their children as "just mothers," while I strain to exempt myself from the definition. Yet once we start our journey through the dark cavernous halls, I am as happy to be there as Lisa.

I have countless moments when I despair that I've cut myself permanently out of the world of achieving women. There are times when I resent the fact that it is more important to me than it is to Paul to spend extra time with the children. There are hours when I am bored, or when I feel absurd rattling on to two little kids. Sometimes I'm filled with such fury that I only wish I were three so I could hit them hard and tell them I'll never be their friend again.

But these times are balanced by the things I like about being a more involved mother. My life seems more harmonious than it used to. I like the way the intense personal relationships in my family and neighborhood blend with the briefer encounters with new people that come from my writing and photography.

PAUL

Between Chanukah and New Year's I spent most of my time with my kids. It was delightful. My son Mamu and I spent days pretending we were bears looking for Christmas instead of hibernating. My daughter Lisa and I learned to write Chinese characters; we played checkers, and compared grade-school experiences; we plotted Christmas surprises for Rachel and Mamu. I wouldn't trade those hours for anything, but still, often, I wondered what I was doing crawling around on my living room floor, devoting every ounce of my creative energy to my kids.

It seems to me wrenchingly simple. If you work hard you miss your kids. But if your main focus is on your kids, then you miss the part of yourself that you thought would accomplish something memorable in the adult world. That goes for women as well as men. You can't blame sexism for it. You can only say that life is more complicated than that.

Appendixes

A. THE FEMALE LABOR FORCE, 1890–1990

	Percentage of labor force who are women	Employed women as percentage of		Percentage of employed women who are married
		All women	Married women	
1890	16	18	5	14
1900	18	20	6	15
1910	21	24	11	25
1920	20	23	9	23
1930	22	24	12	29
1940	25	27	17	36
1950	29	31	25	52
1960	33	35	32	60
1970	38	43	41	63
1980	43	51	51	60
1990	45	58	58	54

SOURCES: U.S. Bureau of the Census, *Statistical Abstract of The United States: 1996* (Washington, D.C., 1996), pp. 394, 396, 399; U.S. Bureau of the Census, *Historical Statistics of the United States: Colonial Times to 1957* (Washington, D.C., 1961), pp.71, 72; U.S. Bureau of the Census, *Fifteenth Census of the United States: 1930—Population,* vol. 4, *Occupations* (Washington, D.C., 1933), p. 69; Joseph A. Hill, *Women in Gainful Occupations,* 1870–1920, Census Monographs 9 (Washington, D.C., 1929), pp. 52, 76; Sophonisba P. Breckinridge, *Women in the Twentieth Century: A Study of Their Political, Social, and Economic Activities* (New York, 1933), pp. 116, 117.

B. HIGHER EDUCATION, 1870–1990

	Thousands of women in college	Percentage of undergraduates who are women	Undergraduate students as percentage of all persons aged 18–21
1870	11	21	2
1880	40	32	3
1890	56	35	3
1900	85	35	4
1910	140	39	5
1920	283	47	8
1930	481	43	12
1940	601	40	14
1950	806	31	27
1960	1,339	36	31
1970	3,284	41	44
1980	6,223	52	26*
1990	7,535	54	32*

SOURCES: Patricia Graham, "Expansion and Exclusion: A History of Women in American Higher Education," *Signs* 3 (Summer 1978): 766, table 1; Mabel Newcomer, *A Century of Higher Education for American Women* (New York, 1959), p. 46, table 2; U.S. Bureau of the Census, *Statistical Abstract of the United States: 1965* (Washington, D.C., 1965), p. 129, and *Statistical Abstract of the United States: 1984* (Washington, D.C., 1983), p. 161. National Center for Education Statistics, Digest of Education Statistics (Washington, D.C., 1996), p. 182.

*1980 and 1990 data cover 18- to 24-year-olds.

Notes

I have deleted most of the redundant citations that appeared in the first edition. Readers interested in fuller documentation may consult that edition, which is out of print but in most libraries.

ABBREVIATIONS

Annals	*Annals of the American Academy of Political and Social Science*
LC	Library of Congress
LHJ	*Ladies' Home Journal*
SEP	*Saturday Evening Post*
SHC	Southern Historical Collection, University of North Carolina at Chapel Hill
SL	Schlesinger Library on the History of Women in America, Radcliffe College
WHC	*Woman's Home Companion*

PREFACE TO THE THIRD EDITION

1. See R. W. Connell, *Gender and Power: The Person and Sexual Politics* (Cambridge, 1987), pp. 47, 140, as well as his review in *Signs* 19 (Autumn 1993): 282. Also Helena Z. Lopata and Barrie Thorne, "On the Term 'Sex Roles,'" *Signs* 3 (Spring 1978): 718–21.

2. John P. Hewitt, *Dilemmas of the American Self* (Philadelphia, 1989), pp. 116–17, 164–66, 152–53, and chap. 5 passim.

PREFACE TO THE FIRST EDITION

1. Robert W. White, *Lives in Progress: A Study of the Natural Growth of Personality*, 2d ed. (New York, 1966), pp. 122–25; Jerold Heiss, ed., *Family Roles and Interaction: An Anthology* (Chicago, 1968), pp. 1–27; Shirley Angrist, "The Study of Sex Roles," *Journal of Social Issues* 25 (1969): 215–32.

2. Norman B. Ryder, "The Cohort as a Concept in the Study of Social Change," *American Sociological Review* 30 (December 1965): 843–61. Also, Bennett

M. Berger, "How Long Is a Generation?" (1960), reprinted in Berger, *Looking for America: Essays on Youth, Suburbia, and Other American Obsessions* (Englewood Cliffs, N.J., 1971), pp. 20–37; Karl Mannheim, "The Sociological Problem of Generations," in *Essays on the Sociology of Knowledge*, ed. Paul Kecskemeti (New York, 1953), pp. 276–322; Alan B. Spitzer, "The Historical Problem of Generations," *American Historical Review* 78 (December 1973): 1353–85.

3. David Riesman, "Styles of Response to Social Change," *Journal of Social Issues* 1 (1961): 81. For a useful definition of classes, see Melvin L. Kohn, *Class and Conformity: A Study in Values* (Homewood, Ill., 1969), pp. 11–12.

4. White, *Lives in Progress*, esp. pp. 243–49; White, "Motivation Reconsidered: The Concept of Competence," *Psychological Review* 66 (1959): 297–333; Gordon W. Allport, *The Person in Psychology: Selected Essays* (Boston, 1968), chaps. 1, 6; Kenneth Keniston, *Young Radicals: Notes on Committed Youth* (New York, 1968), esp. app. B; Abraham Maslow, *Toward a Psychology of Being* (Princeton, N.J., 1962).

PROLOGUE: AS THEY WERE

1. I have written these letters and the journal entry as a historical recreation, a fiction drawn from empirical evidence. The situation, the attitudes, and many of the actual words are taken from several sources, particularly Sara Norton and M. A. DeWolfe Howe, eds., *Letters of Charles Eliot Norton*, 2 vols. (Boston, 1913), 1:19–22; Arthur S. Link, ed., *The Papers of Woodrow Wilson* (Princeton, N.J., 1966), 1:50, 250–51, 254–55, 258–59, 345, 441; Elting E. Morison, *Turmoil and Tradition: A Study of the Life and Times of Henry L. Stimson* (Boston, 1960), chaps. 1–2 and pp. 27, 40; Anne Firor Scott, *The Southern Lady: From Pedestal to Politics, 1830–1930* (Chicago, 1970), chap. 3, pp. 60, 73, and passim. On the Victorian house and housework, see Robert W. Smuts, *Women and Work in America* (New York, 1959), pp. 6–19, and Russell Lynes, *The Domesticated Americans* (New York, 1963), pt. 2, esp. chaps. 8 and 12.

1. WOMEN AND THE WORLD

1. William J. Goode argues that women's domestic role changed as a consequence of changes in their public roles: Goode, *World Revolution and Family Patterns* (New York, 1963), pp. 55–56.

2. *Philadelphia Public Ledger and Daily Transcript*, quoted in Arthur W. Calhoun, *A Social History of the American Family from Colonial Times to the Present*, 3 vols. (Cleveland, 1917–19), 2:84–85. On Victorian values, see Walter E. Houghton, *The Victorian Frame of Mind, 1830–1870* (New Haven, 1957).

3. For a general description, see Barbara Welter, "The Cult of True Womanhood: 1820–1860," *American Quarterly* 18 (Summer 1966): 151–74, and Carl Degler, *At Odds: Women and the Family in America from the Revolution to the Present* (New

York, 1980), chaps. 2–3. Madeleine Wallin to George Sykes, 1882, is quoted by Ellen Rothman, *Hands and Hearts: A History of Courtship in America* (New York, 1984), p. 247. For firsthand observations during 1850–1900, see Oscar Handlin, ed., *This Was America* (Cambridge, Mass., 1949), pp. 221, 239, 304–6; Calhoun, *Social History of the American Family*, 2:112, and Arthur M. Schlesinger, *Learning How to Behave: A Historical Study of American Etiquette Books* (New York, 1946), pp. viii–ix. Nineteenth-century school textbooks reproduced the same "ideal type," as did fiction in popular magazines: Ruth Miller Elson, *Guardians of Tradition: American Schoolbooks of the Nineteenth Century* (Lincoln, Neb., 1964), pp. 301–2; Donald R. Makosky, "The Portrayal of Women in Wide-Circulation Magazine Short Stories, 1905–1955" (Ph.D. diss., University of Pennsylvania, 1966), pp. 148–49.

4. For the farm population, see Andrew Sinclair, *The Better Half: The Emancipation of the American Woman* (New York, 1965), p. 207. Lacking precise data for 1900, I have adapted those furnished by a federal survey of 10,000 farm families in the North and West in 1920: Mary Sumner Boyd, "Department of Agriculture Extension Work with Women," *Woman Citizen* 5 (April 2, 1921): 1128–29. For housework, see Robert W. Smuts, *Women and Work in America* (New York, 1959), pp. 6–19. For prejudice against canning, see Robert Lynd and Helen M. Lynd, *Middletown: A Study in American Culture* (New York, 1929), pp. 155–56. On leisure activity, see Sophonisba P. Breckinridge, *Women in the Twentieth Century: A Study of Their Political, Social, and Economic Activities* (New York, 1933), pp. 70–77.

5. On appliances, see Susan Strasser, *Never Done: A History of American Housework* (New York, 1982), pp. 38–45, 78; Mary Sherman, "The Small-Town Woman Speaks," WHC 53 (June 1926): 28, 58–60; idem, "The Home Equipment Survey," WHC 53 (November 1926): 15, 111–13 and idem, "Heat and Light in America's Homes," WHC 54 (January 1927): 4, 94. On the prewar household, see Harvey Green, *The Light of the Home: An Intimate View of the Lives of Women in Victorian America* (New York, 1983), chaps. 1–3.

6. I have adapted the housework time from a survey by the U.S. Bureau of Home Economics of urban families in the 1920s: *Recent Social Trends in the United States: Report of the President's Research Committee on Social Trends* (New York, 1933), 1:669. A survey of sixty (unsystematically chosen) urban middle-class families in 1912–14 reports the same times for housework and child care: John B. Leeds, *The Household Budget: With a Special Inquiry into the Amount and Value of Household Work* (Germantown, Pa., 1917), pp. 67–68. Likewise, see the sixty-hour week recorded in 1918 by Marion Woodbury, the wife of a university professor and mother of three small children, cited by Ruth Schwartz Cowan, *More Work for Mother: The Ironies of Household Technology from the Open Hearth to the Microwave* (New York, 1983), p. 157.

7. Laura C. Phillips to Cornelia P. Spencer, February 20, 1892, quoted by Daniel E. Sutherland, *Americans and Their Servants: Domestic Service in the United States from 1800 to 1920* (Baton Rouge, La., 1981), p. 16. On the number of ser-

vants, ibid., pp. 46–50, and David Katzman, *Seven Days a Week: Women and Domestic Service in Industrializing America* (New York, 1978), pp. 56–58. These two books provide excellent surveys.

8. Anne L. Vrooman, "The Servant Question in Social Evolution," *Arena* 24 (June 1901): 645. See also "Martyrdom of the Housewife" (editorial), *Nation* 77 (October 22, 1902): 317; "A Vanishing Relation" (editorial), *Independent* 61 (August 23, 1906): 466–67; *New York Times*, January 23, 1913, 10:5.

9. *New York Times*, August 12, 1906. On wage rates, see Mary E. Trueblood, "Housework Versus Shop and Factories," *Independent* 54 (November 13, 1902): 2691–93. On income and cost of living, see Douglas C. North, *Growth and Welfare in the American Past: A New Economic History* (Englewood Cliffs, N.J., 1966), p. 163, table 19; Paul H. Douglas, *Real Wages in the United States, 1890–1926* (Boston and New York, 1930), p. 211, table 77; Richard Hofstadter, *The Age of Reform: From Bryan to F.D.R.* (New York, 1960), p. 168.

10. Mary Hamilton Talbott, "The Servantless Home," *Good Housekeeping* 52 (April 1911): 469. On the apartment hotel, see Russell Lynes, *The Domesticated Americans* (New York, 1963), pp. 51–52, and Dolores Hayden, *The Grand Domestic Revolution: A History of Feminist Designs for American Homes, Neighborhoods, and Cities* (Cambridge, Mass., 1981), pp. 72–77, 195–205.

11. On life cycle, see Robert V. Wells, "American Demographic Change," *Journal of Interdisciplinary History* 2 (Autumn 1971): 273–82; Paul C. Glick, "Updating the Life Cycle of the Family," *Journal of Marriage and Family* 39 (February 1977): 5–13; idem, *American Families* (New York, 1957), p. 55. On the birthrate, see Rowland Berthoff, *An Unsettled People: Social Order and Disorder in American History* (New York, 1971), p. 406. On family size, see Paula S. Fass, *The Damned and the Beautiful: American Youth in the 1920s* (New York, 1977), pp. 59–61; Richard Sennett, *Families against the City: Middle-Class Homes of Industrial Chicago, 1872–1890* (Cambridge, Mass., 1970), pp. 78–80. On infant mortality, see U.S. Bureau of the Census, *Historical Statistics of the United States: Colonial Times to 1957* (Washington, D.C., 1960), p. 26; Sam Shapiro, Edward R. Schlesinger, and Robert E. L. Nesbitt, Jr., *Infant, Perinatal, Maternal, and Childhood Mortality in the United States* (Cambridge, Mass., 1968), pp. 3–4.

12. Bureau of the Census, *Historical Statistics*, p. 24. Life-expectancy data before 1900 are available only for Massachusetts. Note, in addition, that expectancy at ages forty and sixty was no higher in 1900 than in 1850.

13. Wilson to Ellen Axson, March 25, 1885, Axson to Wilson, March 29, 1885, and Ellen Axson Wilson to Woodrow Wilson, February 6, 1894, in *The Priceless Gift: The Love Letters of Woodrow Wilson and Ellen Axson Wilson*, ed. Eleanor Wilson McAdoo (New York, 1962), pp. 126–27, 185.

14. Almira MacDonald Journal, 1885, quoted by Green, *Light of the Home*, pp. 60, 78; Charlotte Perkins Stetson quoted by Mary A. Hill, *Charlotte Perkins Gilman: The Making of a Radical Feminist, 1860–1896* (Philadelphia, 1980), p. 126. On duti-

fulness, see, for example, John Mack Faragher, *Women and Men on the Overland Trail* (New Haven, Conn., 1979), pp. 174–78.

15. Mary Helen Smith to John Jewell Smith, August 24, 1893, in Hilda Worthington Smith Papers, SL, folder 348; Leon Edel, ed., *The Diary of Alice James* (New York, 1964), p. 66. Also Jean Strouse, *Alice James: A Biography* (New York, 1980), provides insight. For background on female health and illness, see John S. Haller, Jr., and Robin M. Haller, *The Physician and Sexuality in Victorian America* (Urbana, Ill., 1974), chap. 1, and Page Smith, *Daughters of the Promised Land: Women in American History* (Boston, 1970), chap. 9. For contemporary views, see John K. Mitchell, "Self Help for Nervous Women," *Harper's Bazar* 25 (May–October 1901): 25–27, 120–22, 382–84, 409–11, 546–48; "My Grandmother, Myself, and My Girl Friends," LHJ 28 (October 1911): 15; Annie Payson Call, "'What Is It That Makes Me So Nervous?'" LHJ 28 (June 1911): 14; Bertha M. Terrill, *Household Management* (Chicago, 1911), p. 73.

16. Acton is quoted in Steven Marcus, *The Other Victorians: A Study of Sexuality and Pornography in Mid-Nineteenth-Century England* (New York, 1966), pp. 31–32. On Acton's influence in the United States, see Nathan G. Hale, Jr., *Freud and the Americans: The Beginnings of Psychoanalysis in the United States, 1876–1917* (New York, 1971), pp. 36–37. On advice, see Emma F. A. Drake, *What a Young Wife Ought to Know*, rev. ed. (Philadelphia). Quotations come from Charles Rosenberg and Carroll Smith-Rosenberg, "The Female Animal: Medical and Biological Views of Woman and Her Role in Nineteenth-Century America," *Journal of American History* 60 (September 1973): 335, 340, 336. On corsets, see Haller, *Physician*, pp. 146–74.

17. Mabel Todd Journal, September 10 and 11, 1879, quoted by Peter Gay, *The Bourgeois Experience, Victoria to Freud: Education of the Senses* (New York, 1984), p. 84. Mosher respondents quoted ibid., pp. 139–40. See Degler, *At Odds*, chap. 11, and Nancy F. Cott, "Passionlessness: An Interpretation of Victorian Sexual Ideology, 1790–1850," *Signs* 4 (Winter 1978): 219–36.

18. On visiting and friendship, see Carroll Smith-Rosenberg, "The Female World of Love and Ritual," *Signs* 1 (Autumn 1975): 1–29. On club membership, see William L. O'Neill, *Everyone Was Brave: The Rise and Fall of Feminism in America* (Chicago, 1969), pp. 84–85, and Mary I. Wood, *The History of the General Federation of Women's Clubs for the First Twenty-two Years of Its Organization* (New York, 1912), esp. pp. 49, 76, 131, 154.

19. Quoted in Wood, *History of the General Federation*, p. 375.

20. For club activities, see Louis B. Wright, *Culture on the Moving Frontier* (Bloomington, Ind., 1955), pp. 226–30; Wood, *History of the General Federation*, pp. 46, 134–35, 234–35, 252–61; Martha E. D. White, "The Work of the Woman's Club," *Atlantic Monthly* 93 (May 1904): 614–23; "As to Women's Clubs," ibid. 103 (January 1909): 135; William Theodore Doyle, "Charlotte Perkins Gilman and the Cycle of Feminist Reform" (Ph.D. diss., University of California, 1960), pp.

12, 14–16; Julia Magruder, "The Typical Woman of the New South," *Harper's Bazar* 33 (November 3, 1900): 1685–87; Rheta Childe Dorr, *What Eight Million Women Want* (Boston, 1910), pp. 28–35.

21. On suffrage and political power, see S. M. Franklin, "The Biennial of Women's Clubs," *Life and Labor* 4 (August 1914): 228–29; A. Elizabeth Taylor, "The Last Phase of the Woman Suffrage Movement in Georgia," *Georgia Historical Quarterly* 43 (March 1959): 14; Doyle, "Charlotte Perkins Gilman," p. 126; *Boston Journal*, June 26, 1915, and *Boston Post*, June 26, 1915, clippings in Maud Wood Park Papers, SL, scrapbooks, vol. 1. Political focus, see Wood, *History of the General Federation*, p. 383, and Lynd, *Middletown*, pp. 290–91. On role, see Sallie Southall Cotten to Bruce Cotten, May 15, 1904, in Cotten Papers, SHC, Box 1. Similarly, "The Best Thing Our Club Ever Did," *Harper's Bazar* (June 1909): 615; Winnifred Harper Cooley, "The Future of the Woman's Club," *Arena* 27 (April 1902): 380. For an unusually egalitarian view, see "As to Women's Clubs," p. 135.

22. "The Woman Who is Tied Down" (editorial), LHJ 28 (October 1911): 6; "A Plea for Long Skirts" (editorial), *Harper's Bazar* 33 (December 8, 1900): 2066; Gertrude Lynch, "The Art of Coquetry," *Cosmopolitan* 36 (March 1904), 603–10; Margaret Deland, "The Change in the Feminine Ideal," *Atlantic Monthly* 105 (March 1910): 290.

23. Schlesinger, *Learning How to Behave*, p. 39; *New York Times*, January 2, 1908, 3:6; January 10, 1908, 2:5; January 12, 1908, 1:4; January 22, 1908, 4:5; January 23, 1908, 4:1; January 24, 1908, 6:4; May 3, 1908, 11:1; and Edward A. Steiner, *The Immigrant Tide: Its Ebb and Flow* (New York, 1909), pp. 16–17.

24. Anna A. Rogers, "Why American Marriages Fail," *Atlantic Monthly*, September 1907, p. 296.

25. William R. Leach, "Transformations in a Culture of Consumption: Women and Department Stores, 1890–1925," *Journal of American History* 71 (September 1984): 319–42; Winifred D. Wandersee, *Women's Work and Family Values, 1920–1940* (Cambridge, Mass., 1981), chap. 1.

26. Caroline Ticknor, "The Steel-Engraving Lady and the Gibson Girl," *Atlantic Monthly* 88 (July 1901): 105–8.

27. Mary Thomas to M. Carey Thomas, early 1870s, quoted in Edith Finch, *Carey Thomas of Bryn Mawr* (New York, 1947), p. 46 (also chaps. 1–3 for biographical information); Maud Nathan, *Once upon a Time and Today* (New York, 1933), p. 25; Mary Dewson to "Hick" (Lorena Hickok), November 21, 1952, typed copy, in Dewson Papers, SL, folder 1; Rheta C. Dorr, *A Woman of Fifty* (New York, 1924), pp. 3–7; Margaret Sanger, *An Autobiography* (New York, 1938), pp. 25–26; Mary Anderson Boit Diary, June 27, 1891, and similarly August 31, 1891, in Hugh Cabot Family Papers, SL, box 10, vol. 17.

28. Jane Addams, *Twenty Years at Hull House* (New York, 1910), pp. 72–73, 77; Addams to Ellen Gates Starr, February 7, 1886, quoted in Christopher Lasch,

The New Radicalism in America, 1889–1963: The Intellectual as a Social Type (New York, 1965), p. 23.

29. Addams to Starr, January 29, 1880, quoted in Lasch, *The New Radicalism*, p. 9; Mary A. Boit Diary, August 28, 1891, in Cabot Family Papers, box 10, vol. 17. For a remarkably parallel expostulation, but with sexual desire more prominent, see Harriet Burton Diary, February 27, 1890, in Harriet Burton Laidlaw Papers, SL, folder 4.

30. For critiques of the "new girl," see Gertrude Atherton, "Woman Will Cease to Love," *Harper's Bazar* 46 (November 1912): 538, 571; "The Loss of Respect for Woman" (editorial), LHJ 28 (August 1911): 3; "The Passing of the Old Lady," *Atlantic Monthly* 99 (June 1907): 874; Eliot Gregory, "Our Foolish Virgins," *Century Magazine* 63 (November 1901): 1–15. For ambivalence, see Katherine G. Busbey, *Home Life in America* (London, 1910), pp. 75–76: American Mother [pseud.], "What the American Girl Has Lost," LHJ 17 (May 1900): 17; Florida Pier, "Man's New Humility," *Harper's Weekly* 53 (December 18, 1909): 27. For approval, see Mary Roberts Coolidge, *Why Women Are So* (New York, 1912), pp. 97–98; Dorothy Dix, "The Girl of Today," *Good Housekeeping* 62 (March 1916): 291. For apotheosis of girls, see Ruth Cranston, "The European Idea of the American Girl," *Independent* 67 (September 9, 1909): 593–97; Calhoun, *Social History of the American Family*, 3:148; Busbey, *Home Life*, pp. 75–76.

31. [Phyllis Blanchard], "The Long Journey," *Nation* 124 (April 27, 1927): 472–73; [Lorine Pruette], "The Evolution of Disenchantment," *Nation* 124 (February 2, 1927): 113–15. Both Blanchard and Pruette did eventually marry, but without giving up their careers and without having children. See also [Kate L. Gregg], "One Way to Freedom," *Nation* 124 (February 16, 1927): 165–67; Hilda Worthington Smith, "The Remembered Way," 1936, pp. 3–4, 468, typescript, Smith Papers, SL.

32. [Crystal Eastman], "Mother-Worship," *Nation* 124 (March 16, 1927): 283–84; Virginia Gildersleeve, *Many a Good Crusade* (New York, 1954), pp. 200, 204.

33. On role of fathers, see James R. McGovern, "Anna Howard Shaw: New Approaches to Feminism," *Journal of Social History* 3 (Winter 1969–70): 135–53; Robert E. Riegel, *American Feminists* (Lawrence, Kans., 1963), p. 189; Smith, *Daughters of the Promised Land*, p. 120. Contrary to the tendency to ignore the mother's role, Beatrice M. Hinkle (a psychiatrist) stresses it in "Why Feminism?" *Nation* 125 (July 6, 1927): 8–9.

34. Doris Stevens, address to Eastern Regional Conference of National Woman's Party, Atlantic City, N.J., June 16, 1946, in Jane Norman Smith Papers, SL, folder 124. Stevens herself contradicts her formula and says she was "more fortunate" in having a father who encouraged her sense of rights and independence. Indeed, he even supported her decision, as a college freshman, to give a public speech for suffrage in their home town.

35. [Elizabeth Stuyvesant], "Staying Free," *Nation* 124 (March 30, 1927):

339–41; Sanger, *An Autobiography*, pp. 16–17, 23; David M. Kennedy, *Birth Control in America: The Career of Margaret Sanger* (New Haven, 1970), p. 3. Kennedy also notes much ambivalence in Sanger's feelings about her father. Harriet Taylor Upton, "Random Recollections," 1927, chap. 5, p. 3, chap. 11, pp. 1–4, chap. 21, p. 2, mimeographed, in SL. Similarly, see [Ruth Pickering], "A Deflated Rebel," *Nation* 124 (January 5, 1927): 11–12; [Victoria McAlman], "Free for What?" *Nation* 124 (May 11, 1927): 522–24; Mary Kenney O'Sullivan, "Autobiography," c. 1930, pp. 2, 8, 9, typescript, in SL; Mary Dewson, "As I Remember My Mother," c. 1945, esp. pp. 1–2, 8, 22, typescript, in Dewson Papers, SL; James P. Louis, "Mary Garret Hay," in *Notable American Women, 1607–1950: A Biographical Dictionary*, ed. Edward T. James, 3 vols. (Cambridge, Mass., 1971), 2:163.

36. Alice Foote MacDougall, *The Autobiography of a Business Woman* (Boston, 1928), pp. 28, 39, and passim; Mildred Aldrich, "Confessions of a Breadwinner," 1926, esp. pt. 1, pp. 58, 64, 82, 156–57, typescript, SL.

37. Smuts, *Women and Work*, pp. 49–50; Busbey, *Home Life*, p. 92; Nathan, *Once upon a Time*, p. 27; Mabel Newcomer, *A Century of Higher Education for Women* (New York, 1959), p. 46, table 2; U.S. Office of Education, *Biennial Survey of Education in the United States, 1950–1952* (Washington, D.C., 1955), chap. 1, p. 22, table 15, and p. 40, table 33. On Thomas, see her 1907 address, "Present Tendencies in Women's College and University Education," reprinted in *Up from the Pedestal: Selected Writings in the History of American Feminism*, ed. Aileen Kraditor (Chicago, 1968), p. 92. On Dewson, see her letter to "Hick" (Lorena Hickok), November 21, 1952, Dewson Papers, SL.

38. Newcomer, *Century of Higher Education*, p. 46, table 2; Laurence R. Veysey, *The Emergence of the American University* (Chicago, 1965), p. 272; Willystine Goodsell, *The Education of Women* (New York, 1923), p. 26; Kelley, in *Survey Graphic*, February 1, 1927, p. 559, quoted in Josephine Goldmark, *Impatient Crusader: Florence Kelley's Life Story* (Urbana, Ill., 1953), p. 11.

39. Newcomer, *Century of Higher Education*, pp. 27, 190–91; Dorothy Gies McGuigan, *A Dangerous Experiment: One Hundred Years of Women at the University of Michigan* (Ann Arbor, Mich., 1970), epigraph on title page, pp. 32–33, 98; Helen R. Olin, *The Women of a State University* (New York, 1909), pp. 252–54; Edwin E. Slosson, *Great American Universities* (New York, 1910), pp. 132–33, 167, 274, 308–9; Frederick Rudolph, *The American College and University: A History* (New York, 1962), pp. 322–23; Veysey, *Emergence of the American University*, p. 272.

40. Olin, *Women of a State University*, pp. 225, 232–33, 246; McGuigan, *Dangerous Experiment*, chap. 9; Marion Talbot, *The Education of Women* (Chicago, 1910), chap. 17; Lulu Holmes, *A History of the Position of Dean of Women in a Selected Group of Co-educational Colleges and Universities in the United States* (New York, 1939), chap. 2 and p. 24; Calvin B. T. Lee, *The Campus Scene, 1900–1970: Changing Styles in Undergraduate Life* (New York, 1970), pp. 1–11.

41. Mary Caroline Crawford, *The College Girl of America and the Institutions Which*

Make Her What She Is (Boston, 1904), pp. 46–50, 65, and passim; *Smith College Weekly* 22 (March 16, 1932): 1, 6.

42. Newcomer, *Century of Higher Education*, pp. 55, 82–83, 87; Rudolph, *American College*, pp. 317–18; Thomas Woody, *A History of Women's Education in the United States*, 2 vols. (New York, 1929), 2:181–82, 220; *New York Times*, January 28, 1900, 11:2.

43. Smith, "The Remembered Way," pp. 201–2, 302–3, Smith Papers, SL; similarly, Aldrich, "Confessions of a Breadwinner," pt. 1, p. 148, SL; Addams, *Twenty Years*, pp. 72–73, 77; Lasch, *New Radicalism*, pp. 38–39, 51–52, 60; Margaret Mead, ed., *An Anthropologist at Work: Writings of Ruth Benedict* (Boston, 1957), p. 135.

44. Ethel Puffer to her mother, May 4, 1896, in Ethel Puffer Howes Papers, SL, folder 140; Agnes E. Meyer, *Out of These Roots: The Autobiography of an American Woman* (Boston, 1953), p. 65.

45. Mary Van Kleeck, "A Census of College Women," *Journal of the Association of Collegiate Alumnae* 11 (May 1918): 577–78; Goodsell, *Education of Women*, pp. 36–38; Marion Florence Lansing, "The Tabulated College Woman," *Independent* 72 (May 23, 1912): 1111–12; Paul H. Jacobson, *American Marriage and Divorce* (New York, 1959), tables 7 and 8, pp. 34–35, and table A6, p. 159.

46. U.S. Bureau of the Census, *Proportion of the Sexes in the United States*, Bulletin no. 14 (Washington, D.C., 1904), pp. 10–13, 19. On coeds' marriage rate, see Goodsell, *Education of Women*, pp. 38, 42–44, 48.

47. Contributor to Wellesley Classbooks, 1907 and 1910, quoted by Joyce Antler, "'After College, What?' New Graduates and the Family Claim," *American Quarterly* 32 (Fall 1980): 429; letters to Harriet Burton, 1905, quoted by Ellen Rothman, *Hands and Hearts*, pp. 252–53. Also Edith Rickert, "What Has the College Done for Girls?" *LHJ* 29 (March 1912): 16; "Why Educated Women Do Not Marry," *Independent* 67 (November 25, 1909): 1193–94; Finch, *Carey Thomas*, p. 79; Alice Stone Blackwell to Kitty Barry Blackwell, January 14, 1883, in Blackwell Family Papers, SL, folder 165; Inez Haynes Gillmore, "Confessions of an Alien, I: The Double Standard," *Harper's Bazar* 46 (April 1912): 170–71, 210; Lasch, *New Radicalism*, pp. 67–68.

48. On marriage and child-rearing rates, see note 45, and Smuts, *Women and Work*, pp. 50–51. On happiness, see Katharine Bement Davis, *Factors in the Sex Life of Twenty-two Hundred Women* (New York, 1929), chap. 5 and p. 274, table 13(b). On bachelor women, see Mary Gay Humphreys, "Women Bachelors in New York," *Scribner's Magazine* 20 (November 1896): 626–36; Rafford Pyke, "What Women Like in Men," *Cosmopolitan* 31 (July 1901): 303–7; Anna Garlin Spencer, "The Day of the Spinster," *Forum* 47 (February 1912): 194–210.

49. Statistics and other information come from Joseph A. Hill, *Women in Gainful Occupations*, 1870–1920, Census Monographs, 9 (Washington, D.C., 1929), pp. 52, 76, 83; Smuts, *Women and Work*, pp. 19–20, 23–24, 51–55; Breckinridge, *Women in the Twentieth Century*, table 7, p. 116, and table 8, p. 126; John D. Durand,

The Labor Force in the United States, 1890–1960 (New York, 1948), table 2, p. 40, and table A-6, pp. 208–9. Elizabeth Faulkner Baker, *Technology and Woman's Work* (New York, 1964), provides a convenient survey. Smuts, pp. 40–42, 93, 98, describes workers' enjoyment of their jobs, but exaggerates it. Contrast Mary McEnemey, "The Woman on the Pedestal," *Life and Labor* (August 1913): 227, and Rose Schneidermann, "The Woman Movement and the Working Woman," ibid. 5 (April 1915): 65 (whom I've quoted in the text).

50. Hill, *Women in Gainful Occupations*, table 32 (p. 42), table 33 (p. 45), and table 57 (p. 83); Breckinridge, *Women in the Twentieth Century*, table 34, p. 190, and table 6, p. 172; Gerda Lerner, "Changes in the Status of Women: 1800–1840" (Paper delivered at the American Historians' Association convention, 1966); MacDougall, *Autobiography of a Business Woman*; Woody, *History of Women's Education*, 1:105–6; *New York Times*, September 14, 1914, 5:1; McGiuigan, *Dangerous Experiment*, p. 88; Slosson, *Great American Universities*, p. 358. On discrimination toward lawyers, see *Woman Citizen* 7 (October 7, 1922): 23, and *New York Times*, January 19, 1900, 1:6.

51. Robert H. Wiebe, *The Search for Order, 1877–1920* (New York, 1967), pp. 120–21; Smuts, *Women and Work*, pp. 19–20, 49–50, 81, 90–91; Hill, *Women in Gainful Occupations*, table 32, p. 42, and table 57, p. 83. On Howes, see *Smith Alumnae Quarterly*, February 1951; on Salmon, see McGuigan, *Dangerous Experiment*, pp. 73–74; on Thomas, see Finch, *Carey Thomas*, and O'Neill, *Everyone Was Brave*, pp. 110–13.

52. On wage rates, see Smuts, *Women and Work*, pp. 90–91; Breckinridge, *Women in the Twentieth Century*, table 39, p. 218. On unions, see O'Neill, *Everyone Was Brave*, pp. 98–102, 154; National Women's Trade Union League of America, *Proceedings of the Third Biennial Convention*, Boston, June 12–17, 1911, p. 19. Eleanor Flexner, *A Century of Struggle: The Woman's Rights Movement in the United States* (Cambridge, Mass., 1959), pp. 217–19, 259, claims that the suffrage movement won working women's support after 1890. But most of the evidence indicates absence of support or even of interest among the economic rank and file: "A Poll of Women on the Suffrage," *Outlook* 104 (June 7, 1913): 268–69; Schneidermann, "The Woman Movement," p. 65; Aileen S. Kraditor, *Ideas of the Woman Suffrage Movement, 1890–1920* (New York, 1965), pp. 260–61.

53. Breckinridge, *Woman in the Twentieth Century*, table 34, p. 190; Edward Gross, "Plus Ça Change . . . ? The Sexual Structure of Occupations over Time," *Social Problems* 16 (Fall 1968): 198–208.

54. Flexner, *Century of Struggle*, pp. 229–30; Smuts, *Women and Work*, pp. 5–6; *Recent Social Trends*, 1:279; *New York Times*, April 1, 1900, 24:3, and February 6, 1908, 14:5; Ida Husted Harper, *The Life and Work of Susan B. Anthony*, 3 vols. (Indianapolis, 1898–1903), 2:1004–12, and reprinted in Kraditor, *Up from the Pedestal*, pp. 162–63.

55. On suffrage campaigns, see Kraditor, *Ideas of Woman Suffrage Movement*,

pp. 4–6, and Janet Zollinger Giele, "Social Change in the Feminine Role: A Comparison of Woman's Suffrage and Woman's Temperance, 1870–1920" (Ph.D. diss., Radcliffe, 1961), p. 288. On early public attitudes, see T. A. Larson, "Woman Suffrage in Western America," *Utah Historical Quarterly* 38 (Winter 1970): 8; Susan B. Anthony and Ida Husted Harper, eds., *The History of Woman Suffrage*, vol. 4, 1883–1900 (Rochester, N.Y., 1902), p. xxii; *New York Times*, January 5, 1908, sec. 4, p. 2, February 28, 1908, 7:3, and April 28, 1908, 2:5; Mary Lee Marquis (president of Albert Lea College) to Maud C. Stockwell, March 6, 1908, in Maud Wood Park Papers, SL, folder 698.

56. On "unsexed" women, see *Votes for Men* (New York, 1918), pp. 9–11, 13–15, 18–19; *New York Times*, February 27, 1900, 6:5, March 23, 1908, 6:5, May 12, 1913, 2:4, and July 28, 1913, 1:2. On "freak legislation," see N.C. State Senator T. T. Speight in 1915, quoted in A. Elizabeth Taylor, "Woman Suffrage Movement in North Carolina," *North Carolina Historical Review* 38 (January 1961): 58–59, and *The Case against Woman Suffrage: A Manual for Speakers, Debaters, Writers, Lecturers, and Anyone Who Wants the Facts and Figures* (New York, 1915), p. 5. On family, see untitled address to 1894 N.Y. State Constitutional Convention, Brooklyn Auxiliary of New York State Association Opposed to the Extension of the Suffrage to Women, quoted in Degler, *At Odds*, p. 353; Alice J. George, *The Case against Woman Suffrage* (Massachusetts Anti-Suffrage Committee, 1915), pp. 15–16, in Grace A. Johnson Papers, SL, folder 153; Henry T. Finck, "Are Womanly Women Doomed?" *Independent* 53 (January 31, 1901): 267–71.

57. On spheres and function, see Lyman Abbott, "Why Women Do Not Wish the Suffrage," *Atlantic Monthly* 92 (September 1903): 290–91; Grace Duffield Goodwin, "The Non-Militant Defenders of the Home," *Good Housekeeping* 55 (July 1912): 77; Emily P. Bissell, A *Talk to Women on the Suffrage Question* (New York, 1909), p. 3; Jessie Atkinson McGriff, "Before the American Woman Votes," LHJ 27 (April 1910): 56. See also the discussion by Degler, *At Odds*, pp. 347–55, which I have found very illuminating.

58. Quotations come from Inez Haynes Irwin to Maud Wood Park, December 7, 1910, in NAWSA Papers, LC, box 10; Anna Howard Shaw to Lucy E. Anthony, Lincoln, Neb., January (?), 1913, Shaw to Anthony, Kansas City Railroad Station, n.d., Shaw to Anthony, St. Joseph, Mo., [1913], Shaw to Anthony, Montgomery, Ala., February 6, 1915, and Shaw to Anthony, Austin, Texas, March 27, 1915, all copies, in Shaw Papers, SL, folder 426; Frances M. Björkman, Easton, N.Y., February 25, [1915], and Glens Falls, N.Y., n.d., in Björkman Papers, SHC, Box 6, folder 81. On membership, see Giele, "Social Change in Feminine Role," p. 288.

59. The best source on suffragists' arguments is Kraditor, *Ideas of Woman Suffrage Movement*, esp. pp. 43–44, 54–69. On women as moral voters, see Ida Husted Harper, "Would Woman Suffrage Benefit the State, and Woman Herself?" *North American Review* 178 (March 1904): 362–74; Anthony and Harper, *History of Woman Suffrage*, 4:36–37, 39, 120, 135, 356. On men's endorsements,

see *Current Literature* 51 (December 1911): 596–97; "The Necessity of Woman Suffrage" (editorial), *North American Review* 183 (October 5, 1906): 689–90; Taylor, "The Woman Suffrage Movement in North Carolina," p. 56; William Watts Ball to Major J.F.J. Caldwell, January 6, 1919, in Ball Papers, Duke University. On referendum voting patterns, see Giele, "Social Change in the Feminine Role," p. 288. On good housekeeping, see Mary Holland Kinkaid, "The Feminine Charms of the Woman Militant," *Good Housekeeping* 54 (February 1912): 146–55. On maternal voters, see Maud Wood Park, quoted in *Manchester Union*, January 11, 1915, clipping in Park Papers, SL, scrapbooks, vol. 1. The New York State Woman Suffrage Party flyer quoted is in Ethel E. Dreier Papers, Sophia Smith Collection, Smith College, box 4.

2. WOMEN AND THE HOME

1. *Congressional Record*, 63d Cong., 2d sess., 51 (May 7 and 8, 1914): 8233, 8276. For exemplary comments on family breakdown, see Arthur W. Calhoun, *A Social History of the American Family from Colonial Times to the Present*, 3 vols. (Cleveland, 1917–19), 3:166–68, 173; "The Educated Mother" (editorial), *Independent* 53 (December 5, 1901): 2911–12: Chauncey J. Hawkins, *Will the Home Survive? A Study of Tendencies in Modern Literature* (New York, 1907), pp. 7–10, 13–14; Julia E. Johnson, ed., *Selected Articles on Marriage and Divorce* (New York, 1925), p. 39. Also David M. Kennedy, *Birth Control in America: The Career of Margaret Sanger* (New Haven, 1970), pp. 49–50.

2. Paul H. Jacobson, *American Marriage and Divorce* (New York, 1959), table 42, p. 90, and table 2, p. 21; Langdon Mitchell, *The New York Idea*, quoted in Donald N. Koster, *The Theme of Divorce in American Drama, 1871–1939* (Philadelphia, 1942), p. 59; Edward Alsworth Ross, "The Significance of Increasing Divorce," *Century Magazine* 78 (May 1909): 149–52. For examples of dismay, see Hawkins, *Will the Home Survive*, pp. 9–10; editorial, *New York Times*, May 24, 1904, 8:3; Margaret Deland, "The Change in the Feminine Ideal," *Atlantic Monthly* 105 (March 1910): 289–302; for a general discussion, see William L. O'Neill, *Divorce in the Progressive Era* (New Haven, 1967), esp. chaps. 2–3 and pp. 254–55.

3. For birthrates, see U.S. Bureau of the Census, *Historical Statistics of the United States: Colonial Times to 1957* (Washington, D.C., 1960), p. 24. For Roosevelt's phrase and other data, see Kennedy, *Birth Control*, pp. 42–44.

4. On cooking, see *New York Times*, January 20, 1908, 6:6, and June 28, 1908, sec. 5, 10:5. On employment, see Ida M. Tarbell, "The Uneasy Woman," *American Magazine* 73 (January 1912): 259–62; idem, "Making a Man of Herself," ibid. 73 (February 1912): 427–30; Hutchinson address, 1895, quoted in Larzer Ziff, *The American 1890s: Life and Times of a Lost Generation* (New York, 1966), p. 280; Mrs. A. J. George, *Woman's Rights vs. Woman Suffrage* (New York, [1913?]), pp. 12–13; Mrs. Gilbert E. Jones, "Some Impediments to Woman Suffrage," *North American Review*,

190 (August 1909): 158–169. On suffrage, see *The Case against Woman Suffrage: A Manual for Speakers, Debaters, Writers, Lecturers, and Anyone Who Wants the Facts and Figures* (New York, 1915), pp. 29–30; *Votes for Men* (New York, 1913), pp. 55–56. On education, see G. Stanley Hall, quoted in Thomas Woody, *A History of Women's Education in the United States*, 2 vols. (New York, 1929), 2:274; Margaret Bisland, "The Curse of Eve," *North American Review* 177 (July 1903): 112–13, 117.

5. Quoted in Mark H. Haller, *Eugenics: Hereditarian Attitudes in American Thought* (New Brunswick, N.J., 1963), p. 79. On values, see Henry F. May, *The End of American Innocence: A Study of the First Years of Our Own Time, 1912–1917* (New York, 1959).

6. Anna A. Rogers, "Why American Marriages Fail," *Atlantic Monthly* 100 (September 1907): 289–98; on notoriety of this article, "Is Woman to Blame for the Present Marital Unrest?" *Current Literature* 43 (November 1907): 535; Lyman Abbott, "The Spirit of Democracy: In the Family—the Hebrew Ideal," *Outlook* 95 (July 9, 1910): 522–26; Bisland, "The Curse of Eve," p. 121.

7. Robert Sunley, "Early Nineteenth-Century American Literature on Child Rearing," in *Childhood in Contemporary Cultures*, ed. Margaret Mead and Martha Wolfenstein (Chicago, 1955); Willystine Goodsell, *Problems of the Family* (New York, 1928), pp. 429–30; Orville G. Brim, Jr., *Education for Child Rearing* (New York, 1959), pp. 326, 328–30; Bernard Wishy, *The Child and the Republic: The Dawn of Modern American Child Nurture* (Philadelphia, 1968), chaps. 11–12; L. Emmett Holt, *The Care and Feeding of Children: A Catechism for the Use of Mothers and Children's Nurses*, 8th ed. (New York, 1916).

8. Mary Boit Cabot Journal, January 18, 1906, in Hugh Cabot Family Papers, SL, vol. 20. See, generally, Katherine G. Busbey, *Home Life in America* (London, 1910), pp. 12–13; *New York Times*, January 13, 1913, 11:3; "The American Girl" (editorial), LHJ 25 (May 1908): 5; "Mothers of Yesterday and To-day" (editorial), *Harper's Bazar* 33 (January 13, 1900): 26; Mary L. Read, *The Mothercraft Manual* (Boston, 1916). On effects of child-care advice, see Gerald R. Leslie and Kathryn P. Johnson, "Changed Perceptions of the Maternal Role," *American Sociological Review* 28 (December 1963): 919–28.

9. On changing advice, see Clark E. Vincent, "Trends in Infant Care Ideas," *Child Development* 22 (September 1951): 204–5. On Ruth Ashmore, see Edward W. Bok, *The Americanization of Edward Bok: The Autobiography of a Dutch Boy Fifty Years After* (New York, 1922), pp. 169–71.

10. [Lyman Abbott], "Home Making the Woman's Profession" (editorial), *Outlook* 99 (December 16, 1911): 909.

11. Elizabeth M. Bacon, "The Growth of Household Conveniences in the United States from 1865 to 1900" (Ph.D. diss., Radcliffe, 1944), pp. 66–68, 75; William Theodore Doyle, "Charlotte Perkins Gilman and the Cycle of Feminist Reform" (Ph.D. diss., University of California, 1960), pp. 60–66; Woody, *History of Women's Education*, 2:52–64; Brim, *Education*, pp. 326–28; [Abbott], "Home Making

the Woman's Profession," p. 909; William Hard, *The Women of Tomorrow* (New York, 1911), pp. 96–97, 102–8; similarly, Bertha M. Terrill, *Household Management* (Chicago, 1911), pp. 3, 5; Christine Frederick, *The New Housekeeping: Efficiency Studies in Home Management* (Garden City, N.Y., 1913), p. 22; *Proceedings of the Lake Placid Conference on Home Economics*, 3d conference, 1901, pp. 101–2; Lucy M . Salmon, "Recent Progress in the Study of Domestic Service," *Atlantic Monthly* 96 (November 1905): 635; Mary Woolley, "The Woman's Club Woman." *Good Housekeeping* 50 (May 1910): 559–65; Elizabeth Barber Young, *A Study of the Curricula of Seven Selected Women's Colleges of the Southern States* (New York, 1932), pp. 206–7; Edith Rickert, "What Has the College Done for Girls? III: Where the College Has Failed with Girls," *LHJ* 29 (March 1912): 15–16; Ethel Puffer Howes, "The Place of Music and Art in the Curriculum of a Cultural College," *Smith Alumnae Quarterly*, November 1913, p. 7, in Howes Papers, SL, folder 151.

12. Quoted in Hard, *Women of Tomorrow*, pp. 96–97.

13. Frances M. Björkman to Edwin A. Björkman, August 2, |1914|, in Björkman Papers, SHC. box 6, folder 82, Anna Howard Shaw to Clara Osborn, August 19, 1902, copy, in Shaw Papers, SL, folder 424; Edith Finch, *Carey Thomas of Bryn Mawr* (New York, 1947), pp. 78, 82; Alice Stone Blackwell to Kitty Blackwell, January 14, 1883, in Blackwell Family Papers, SL, folder 165; A.B.M., letter to *New York Times*, April 7, 1908.

14. Katharine Bement Davis, *Factors in the Sex Life of Twenty-two Hundred Women* (New York, 1929), esp. pp. 248–54, 257, 298, 307; Alfred C. Kinsey et al., *Sexual Behavior in the Human Female* (Philadelphia, 1953), pp. 461–62 and table 134, p. 495; Mervin B. Freedman, *The College Experience* (San Francisco, 1967), pp. 97–98; Alice Stone Blackwell to Kitty Barry Blackwell, March 22, 1873, June 14, 1874, March 14, 1879, November 2, 1879, and November 30, 1884, in Blackwell Papers, folders 161, 162, 164, 165; on Marks and Woolley, Lillian Faderman, *Surpassing the Love of Men: Romantic Friendship and Love between Women from the Renaissance to the Present* (New York, 1981), p. 228; on Addams, Allen Davis, *American Heroine: The Life and Legend of Jane Addams* (New York, 1973), pp. 84–89; Anna Howard Shaw to Lucy Anthony, March 6, 1891, |no month| 1910, and |undated, 1911|, all copies, in Shaw Papers, folders 421, 425, 426. My perspective on nineteenth-century lesbianism has been influenced by Helen Lefkowitz Horowitz, *Alma Mater: Design and Experience in the Women's Colleges from their Nineteenth-Century Beginnings to the 1930s* (New York, 1984), pp. 188–91. For a different perspective, see Blanche Wiesen Cook, "Female Support Networks and Political Activism: Lillian Wald, Crystal Eastman, and Emma Goldman," in *A Heritage of Her Own: Toward a New Social History of American Women*, ed. Nancy F. Cott and Elizabeth H. Pleck (New York, 1979), pp. 412–44.

15. Alice Stone Blackwell in *Woman's Journal*, January 3, 1891, quoted in Aileen S. Kraditor, *Ideas of the Woman Suffrage Movement, 1890–1920* (New York, 1965), p. 116; Susanne Wilcox, "A Wider Morality for American Women," *Inde-*

pendent 72 (January 20, 1912): 1363; Ida Husted Harper, "Women Ought to Work," ibid. 53 (May 16, 1901): 1125; Louise Collier Willcox, "Woman's Place in the World," *Delineator* 94 (May 1919): 39. On divorce, see Susan B. Anthony's address to National Council of Women, in *New York Times*, April 15, 1905, 1:5; Elizabeth Cady Stanton, "Divorce Versus Domestic Warfare," *Arena* 1 (April 1890): 560–69; Ida Husted Harper, "Changing Conditions of Marriage," *Independent* 61 (December 6, 1906): 1329; Kraditor, *Ideas of Woman Suffrage Movement*, pp. 115–16.

16. Alva Murray (Smith) Vanderbilt Belmont Memoir, in Matilda Young Papers, Duke University, pp. 151–54; Henry F. Harris, "Marriage and Divorce," *Arena* 29 (February 1903): 167–73; Henry Gaines Hawn, "The Divorce Problem: A Suggestion," *Arena* 33 (March 1905): 262–66; *New York Times*, June 5, 1905, 9:2; "The Ex-Married Confess," *Scribner's Magazine* 87 (April 1930): 380–81; O'Neill, *Divorce*, pp. 255–57; Koster, *Theme of Divorce*, pp. 107–8; Kennedy, *Birth Control*, p. 49; Elizabeth Cady Stanton, testimony before Senate Committee on Woman Suffrage, February 20, 1892, quoted in Susan B. Anthony and Ida Husted Harper, *The History of Woman Suffrage*, vol. 4, 1883–1900 (Rochester, N.Y., 1902), pp. 189–90.

17. Anthony and Harper, *History of Woman Suffrage*, p. xxii; Harriet Taylor Upton to Catharine McCulloch, September 30, 1911, in McCulloch Papers, SL, folder 201; Ella Harrison to "Pa," April 4, 1897, New Albany, Miss., in Harrison Papers, SL; Anna Howard Shaw to Lucy E. Anthony, November 1, 1910, en route to Belle Fourche, S. Dak., copy, in Shaw Papers, folder 425.

18. M. Carey Thomas, "Present Tendencies in Women's College and University Education," in *Publications of the Association of Collegiate Alumnae* (February 1908), quoted in *Up from the Pedestal: Selected Writings in the History of American Feminism*, ed. Aileen Kraditor (Chicago, 1968), pp. 90–92.

19. *New York Times*, March 10, 1913, 20:3; Margaret Sanger Journal, [November 4, 1914], in Sanger Papers, Sophia Smith Collection, Smith College, box 29. On women as a class, see Helena Hill Weed, "4,000,000—Even at That," *Suffragist* 4 (March 11, 1916): 4; "Is Suffrage a National Issue?" ibid. 3 (March 20, 1915): 6. On Socialists, see Theresa S. Malkiel, "Where Do We Stand on the Woman Question?" *International Socialist Review* 10 (August 1909): 160–62, and John Spargo, "Women and the Socialist Movement," ibid. 8 (February 1908): 450–51, both quoted in Sara Evans Boyte, "An Uneasy Home: Women in the Socialist Party, 1901–1915" (Seminar paper, University of North Carolina, 1971), pp. 3, 5. On Shaw, see Anna Howard Shaw to Lucy Anthony, [undated, 1912], February 5, 1903, and [no month] 1908, all copies, in Shaw Papers, folders 424, 425, 426. Similarly, Rheta C. Dorr, *A Woman of Fifty* (New York, 1924), p. 83.

20. On Shaw and men, see James R. McGovern, "Anna Howard Shaw: New Approaches to Feminism," *Journal of Social History* 3 (Winter 1969–70): 145. On impatience, see Inez Haynes Irwin to Maud Wood Park, March 14, 1921, and July 29, 1938, in NAWSA Papers, LC, box 17; Harriot Stanton Blatch and Alma Lutz, *Challenging Years: The Memoirs of Harriot Stanton Blatch* (New York, 1940), p. 109;

Olive Mills Belcher to Grace A. Johnson, February 2, 1916, Johnson Papers, SL, folder 134; Eleanor Flexner, A Century of Struggle: The Woman's Rights Movement in the United States (Cambridge, Mass., 1959), p. 250. English militants are discussed in Flexner, p. 251, and William L. O'Neill, ed., The Woman Movement: Feminism in the United States and England (Chicago, 1971), pp. 83–85. On new tactics and Woman's Party, see Flexner, pp. 250, 252–53, 263–69; Loretta Ellen Zimmerman, "Alice Paul and the National Woman's Party, 1912–1920" (Ph.D. diss., Tulane, 1964), pp. 82–83. On Alice Paul's leadership, see Zimmerman, pp. 87, 92–98; Mrs. Medill McCormick to Harriet Vittum, July 31, 1914, quoted in Zimmerman, p. 36; Inez Haynes Irwin, The Story of the Woman's Party (New York, 1921), pp. 15–16, 19–24. For a rare expression of affection, in which she confessed to missing Maud Younger and closed the letter "With a great deal of love to you," see Alice Paul to Maud Younger, March 6, 1920, copy, in National Woman's Party Papers, LC, tray 29, box 3. On sex-bloc strategy generally, see Irwin, Story of Woman's Party, esp. pt. 1, chaps. 9–10, and pt. 2, chaps. 5–7; also "Hearing before the House Judiciary Committee," Suffragist 3 (December 25, 1915): 5–7; "Conference of Officers of the Congressional Union" and "Suffrage in the Next Election," ibid. 4 (April 15, 1916): 4–7; "Policy of the National Woman's Party," ibid. 4 (September 30, 1916): 6. Typical critiques of this strategy appear in Carrie Chapman Catt to Sue White, May 6, 1918, in White Papers, SL, folder 21; "Three 'Little Scares'" (editorial), Woman Citizen 2 (December 15, 1917): 46. On need to attack, see Ethel Adamson to Abbie Scott Baker, August 20, 1916, in Woman's Party Papers, tray 28, box 2.

21. Ethel Puffer to her mother, December 3, [1895], in Howes Papers, folder 140; Inez Haynes Gillmore, "Confessions of an Alien, I: The Double Standard," Harper's Bazar 46 (April 1912): 170–71, and "Why I Am Glad I Am a Woman," ibid. 46 (August 1912): 384.

22. Carrie Chapman Catt, address to Congress of International Woman Suffrage Alliance, Amsterdam, June 15, 1908, copy, in Catt Papers, Sophia Smith Collection, Smith College, box 1; Catt to Mrs. George Gellhorn, Mrs. Richard E. Edwards, and Miss Elizabeth Hauser, February 17, 1921, in League of Women Voters Papers, LC, box 3.

23. See the following by Charlotte Perkins Gilman: "On Ellen Key and the Woman Movement," Forerunner 4 (February 1913): 36; "As to 'Feminism,'" ibid. 5 (February 1914): 45; "Do We Want a Political Party for Women?" ibid. 6 (November 1915): 285; The Man-Made World: On Our Andocentric Culture (New York, 1911), p. 132; "The Woman's Party," Forerunner 2 (November 1911): 291; and ibid. 1 (October 1910): 12.

24. For expressions of "humanist feminism," see Maud Wood Park, in unidentified newspaper clipping, October 26, 1910, and Teresa A. Crowley, in Boston Herald, January 24, 1914, both in Park Papers, SL, scrapbooks, vol. 1; Alice Stone Blackwell, Objections Answered (New York, 1913), pp. 2–3; Rose Young,

"Men, Women, and Sex Antagonism," *Good Housekeeping* 58 (April 1914): 490. For Gilman's exaltation of woman's influence, see "The Woman's Party," *Forerunner* 2 (November 1911), and "The Humanness of Women," ibid. 1 (January 1910).

25. On hardships, see Maud Wood Park's itineraries for 1907, and Park to [?], March [?] 1912, on train from Cincinnati to Lawrence, Kans., in Park Papers, folders 697, 654; Ella Harrison to "Pa," April 4, 1897, New Albany, Miss., in Harrison Papers. Shaw's conflicting feelings are expressed in Shaw to Harriet B. Laidlaw, June 10, 1914, in Laidlaw Papers, folder 115. On work, see Shaw quoted in Ida Husted Harper, *The History of Woman Suffrage*, 5 (n.p., 1922): 230; Charlotte Perkins Gilman, *Human Work* (New York, 1904), p. 182, quoted in Carl Degler's introduction to Gilman, *Women and Economics* (New York, Harper Torchbooks, 1966), p. xxix; Carrie Chapman Catt to Anna Howard Shaw, n.d., in Shaw Papers, folder 461; Martha Bensley Bruere, "Home vs. Family," *Independent* 86 (April 3, 1916): 15; Harriet Taylor Upton, "Random Recollections" (1927), chap. 6, p. 8, mimeographed, in SL; Molly Dewson, "Should Women of the Leisure Class Follow Gainful Occupations?" typed ms. of speech, [1925], in Dewson Papers, SL, folder 2.

26. Carrie Chapman Catt to Maud Wood Park, August 30, 1916, Park Papers, folder 735; Clara B. Arthur to Park, April 24, 1908, Park Papers, folder 698; Mary Beard to Jane N. Smith, June 23, 1916, New Milford, Conn., in Smith Papers, SL, folder 55. Also Beard to Smith, January 17, [1917?], New York City, in Smith Papers, folder 55; Beard to Lucy Burns, June 8, [1915], and Beard to Alice Paul, April 30, 1916, in National Woman's Party Papers, tray 29, box 4. Beard's resignation is related in Alice Paul to Mrs. William Kent, November 3, 1915, copy, in Woman's Party Papers, tray 29, box 2; similarly, see Mrs. Harvey Wiley to Paul, March 10, 1913, in Woman's Party Papers, tray 29, box 5. On Mrs. Darrow, see Anna Howard Shaw to Lucy Anthony, September 19, [1914], Bismarck, N.Dak., copy, in Shaw Papers, folder 426.

27. On birth control, see Kennedy, *Birth Control*, p. 45. For a defense of childlessness and the ensuing controversy, see Childless Wife [pseud.], "Why I Have No Family," *Independent* 58 (March 23, 1905): 654–59, and "The Family," ibid. 58 (April 13, 1905): 830–38. On marital status of suffragists, see Janet Zollinger Giele, "Social Change in the Feminine Role: A Comparison of Woman's Suffrage and Woman's Temperance, 1870–1920" (Ph.D. diss., Radcliffe, 1961), table 17, p. 153.

28. Ethel Puffer Howes to her mother, c. 1910, in Howes Papers, folder 143; James Lees Laidlaw to Harriet Burton Laidlaw, c. 1910–16, and James to Harriet, [1915], in Laidlaw Papers, folder 14; for his expressions of love, James to Harriet, August 19, 1905, and elsewhere, in Laidlaw Papers, folder 13; Ethel E. Dreier to H. Edward Dreier, c. 1915–20, in Dreier Papers, Sophia Smith Collection, Smith College, box 1. For another example of a suffragist's mollification of her husband, see Frances M. Björkman to Edwin A. Björkman, November 9,

1914, en route to Troy, N.Y., and letter dated "Sunday eve," [1914], Gloversville, N.Y., in Björkman Papers, box 6, folder 80. Although the Laidlaws and Dreiers remained happily married, the Björkmans eventually got divorced: Frances M. to Edwin A. Björkman, February 13, 1926, in Björkman Papers, box 6, folder 82.

29. Quotations come from Charlotte Perkins Gilman, *The Home: Its Work and Influence* (New York, 1910; orig. ed., 1903), pp. 13, 302. She states her premises, among many other places, in *The Home*, pp. 10, 320–21; in *Women and Economics*, pp. 222–23, 267–68; and in Anthony and Harper, *History of Woman Suffrage*, 4:278. On freeing of women, see *Women and Economics*, pp. 74–75, 136–45, 257. On the ideal home, see *Women and Economics*, pp. 242–47. On her socialism, see William L. O'Neill, *Everyone Was Brave: The Rise and Fall of Feminism in America* (Chicago, 1969), pp. 132–33.

30. On precedents for Gilman's program, see Bacon, "Growth of Household Conveniences," pp. 129–30. On Gilman's reception, see Ada May Krecken, "The Passing of the Family," *Mother Earth* 7 (October 1912): 258–66; A. L. Mearkle, "The Higher Education of Women," *Arena* 23 (June 1900): 666; Sarah Louise Arnold, "The Ideal Suburban Home of the Near Future," *Good Housekeeping* 55 (October 1912): 501–2; Martha Bensley Bruere, "Twentieth-Century Housekeeping," ibid. 58 (March 1914): 387–92; Susanne Wilcox, "The Unrest of Modern Woman," *Independent* 67 (July 8, 1909): 62–66; *New York Times*, January 24, 1915, sec. 5, p. 9, and April 6, 1913, sec. 5, 8:1. On ranking, see "Woman's Growing Revolt against 'Coercive Marriage,'" *Current Opinion* 56 (February 1914): 132.

31. On nurseries, see Mary Dabney Davis, *Nursery Schools: Their Development and Current Practices in the United States* (Washington, D.C., 1933), pp. 1, 19, 25, and William Carl Jordan, "The History, Scope and Prospects for the Future of the Nursery School Movement" (Ph.D. diss., Harvard, 1950), p. 84. For mention of a few communal experiments, see Calhoun, *Social History of the American Family*, 3:185–86. The quotation from Gilman is in her *Women and Economics*, p. 205. On suffragists' views, see Kraditor, *Ideas of Woman Suffrage Movement*, pp. 120–21; Flora McDonald Thompson, "The Work of Wives," *Arena* 27 (January 1902): 68–75, and the unnamed suffragist quoted by Gilman, *The Living of Charlotte Perkins Gilman* (New York, 1935), p. 198.

32. Krecken, "Passing of the Family," 259.

33. Quotation from Gilman comes from her *Women and Economics*, p. 300. On Henrietta Rodman, see interview with her by George MacAdam, "Feminist Apartment House to Solve Baby Problem," *New York Times*, January 24, 1915, sec. 5, p. 9. On socialists, see Boyte, "An Uneasy Home," pp. 8–10 (including quotation from Kate Richards O'Hare).

34. Gilman's views are exemplified in "Humanness," *Forerunner* 4 (September 1913): 247; editorial, ibid. 5 (July 1919): 196; "Birth Control," ibid. 6 (July 1915): 179. For advocacy of free love, see Krecken, "Passing of the Family"; John R. Coryell, "Marriage and the Home," *Mother Earth* 1 (April 1906): 23–30; Emma

Goldman, *Anarchism and Other Essays*, 2d rev. ed. (New York, 1911), pp. 241–43. Quotations on prudery come from Alice Stone Blackwell to Kitty Barry Blackwell, March 1, 1912, in Blackwell Papers, folder 169 Inez Haynes Irwin Diary, June 13, 1891, in Irwin Papers, SL.

35. Jane Addams, "As I See Women," LHJ 32 (August 1915): 11.

36. On the ages of suffragists, see Lois Bannister Merk, "The Early Career of Maud Wood Park," *Radcliffe Quarterly* 32 (May 1948): 11; *New York Times*, November 16, 1902, 25:1; Anthony and Harper, *History of Woman Suffrage*, 4:271. On leaders' reactions, see Anthony and Harper, p. 350; Anna Howard Shaw to Harriet Burton Laidlaw, October 29, 1916, in Laidlaw Papers, folder 133; Olympia Brown to Ida H. Harper, as quoted by Harper to Brown, 1917, cited in Charles B. Neu, "Olympia Brown and the Woman's Suffrage Movement," *Wisconsin Magazine of History* 43 (Summer 1960): 284. On newcomers' attitudes, see Winnifred Harper Cooley, "The Younger Suffragists," *Harper's Weekly* 58 (September 27, 1913): 7–8.

37. Carrie Chapman Catt to Margaret Sanger, November 24, 1920, quoted by Sheila M. Rothman, *Woman's Proper Place: A History of Changing Ideals and Practices, 1870 to the Present* (New York, 1978), p. 196; Dorothy Kirchwey to LaRue Brown, October 4 and 17, 1915, quoted by Ellen Rothman, *Hands and Hearts: A History of Courtship in America* (New York, 1984), p. 262; Milholland quoted in Zimmerman, "Alice Paul and the National Woman's Party," p. 59. On attitudes toward contraception see Linda Gordon, *Woman's Body, Woman's Right: A Social History of Birth Control in America* (New York, 1976), chap. 5. For an interesting index of the changed sexual attitudes between the 1890s and the 1910s, compare the responses by Mary Roberts Coolidge to the Mosher Survey, the first in 1892 during her first marriage, when she found sex "agreeable" but often leaving her unfulfilled and with "great nervousness," the second in 1912 during her second marriage, when she was far more desirous and satisfied: see Rosalind Rosenberg, *Beyond Separate Spheres: Intellectual Roots of Modern Feminism* (New Haven, 1982), pp. 179–83, 195–96, and James MaHood and Kristine Wenburg, eds., *The Mosher Survey: Sexual Attitudes of Forty-five Victorian Women* (New York, 1980), pp. 22–26.

38. Finch, *Carey Thomas*, p. 79. Margaret Sanger Journal, November 4, 1914. On petting, see Kinsey et al., *Sexual Behavior in the Human Female*, pp. 242–43. Data on premarital sex differ on specifics, but agree that a steady increase occurred, especially sharp among women born after 1900. According to Kinsey, pp. 298–99, 14 percent of women born before 1900 and unmarried at age twenty-five had engaged in premarital intercourse, 36 percent of those born during 1900–1909. Studies of college women report that 7 percent in the early 1900s had done so, although 20 percent condoned it. During 1915–25 the incidence doubled or tripled: Davis, *Factors in the Sex Life*, pp. 19, 250–51; Freedman, *College Experience*, pp. 108–9. A study of middle-class wives in 1938 reported premarital intercourse by 13 percent of those born before 1890, most with their fu-

ture husbands only. The rate doubled for wives born in the 1890s, and then leaped to 49 percent for those born during 1900–1909 (still primarily with future husbands only): Lewis M. Terman, *Psychological Factors in Marital Happiness* (New York, 1938), table 113, p. 321. For sardonic comments by the younger generation on the older generation's views of virginity and illegitimacy, see David Graham Phillips, *Susan Lenox: Her Fall and Rise* (New York, 1930; orig. ed., 1917), 1:33–34. On love affairs, birth control, and marriage, see Dorr, *A Woman of Fifty*, p. 50; [Wanda Gag], "A Hotbed of Feminists," *Nation* 124 (June 22, 1927): 693; "Marriage Looking Up" (editorial), *Independent* 74 (March 27, 1913): 676–77; Robert Herrick, *One Woman's Life* (New York, 1913), p. 167; Dorothy Dix, "The Girl of Today," *Good Housekeeping* 62 (March 1916): 290–91; "Our Young People and Marriage" (editorial), LHJ 28 (August 1911): 4; Hutchins Hapgood, *A Victorian in the Modern World* (New York, 1939), p. 395. In his short story, Gilbert Seldes is much less sanguine than Hapgood about the consequences of free love: Seldes," Emancipated," *Forum* 51 (June 1914): 899–910.

39. Walter Lippmann, *Drift and Mastery* (New York, 1914), pp. xvii–xviii, chap. 11.

40. Margaret Anderson, *My Thirty Years' War: An Autobiography* (New York, 1930), pp. 18–19 and passim; Gilman, *The Living*, chap. 8 and pp. 163, 190, 242, 248, 291 (her marriage is mentioned on pp. 281 and 326); Margaret Sanger, *An Autobiography* (New York, 1938), esp. pp. 119–20, 136, 181–82, 355–57; Kennedy, *Birth Control*, chap. 1; Frances M. Björkman to Edwin A. Björkman, February 13, 1926, New York City, in Björkman Papers, box 6, folder 82.

41. Mary Dewson to Sue White, October 13, 1939, in White Papers, folder 8.

42. Margaret Mead, ed., *An Anthropologist at Work: Writings of Ruth Benedict* (Boston, 1957), pp. 119–20, 130–32, 139, 143, 145–46, 155. On her poetry, see pp. 71, 91–94. Donald Fleming, "Ruth Benedict," in *Notable American Women, 1607–1950: A Biographical Dictionary*, ed. Edward T. James, 3 vols. (Cambridge, Mass., 1971), 1:128–31, is also helpful.

43. Mildred Aldrich, "Confessions of a Breadwinner" (1926), pt. 1, pp. 179–82, 209, typescript, in SL. Similarly, "How Love Passed Me By: The Confessions of a Business Woman," *Harper's Bazar* 46 (June 1912): 277; "Should the Woman Choose?" *Delineator* 94 (May 1919): 36; Hilda Worthington Smith, "The Remembered Way" (1936), p. 279, typescript, in Smith Papers, SL.

44. Lotte Bailyn, "Career and Family Orientation of Husbands and Wives in Relation to Marital Happiness," *Human Relations* 23 (1970): 97–114,

3. MEN AND MANLINESS

1. Albert J. Beveridge, *The Young Man and the World* (New York, 1923; orig. ed., 1905), p. 12; Theodore Roosevelt, *The Strenuous Life: Essays and Addresses* (New York, 1900), pp. 113–24; Abraham L. Kellogg, quoted in *Up from the Pedestal: Se-*

lected Writings in the History of American Feminism, ed. Aileen Kraditor (Chicago, 1968), p. 197; Senator Joseph E. Brown, quoted in Susan B. Anthony and Ida Husted Harper, eds., The History of Woman Suffrage, vol. 4, 1883–1900 (Rochester, N.Y., 1902), p. 94; Alexander Lewis, Manhood-Making: Studies in the Elemental Principles of Success (Boston, 1902), pp. 24–25; "College Courses and Marriage" (editorial), Harper's Bazar 33 (August 25, 1900): 1089; Sylvanus Stall, What a Young Husband Ought to Know (Philadelphia, 1907; orig. ed., 1899), p. 3; Thomas Walton Galloway, Sex and Life: A Message to Undergraduate Men (New York, 1919), pp. 2–3; Albert Shaw, The Outlook for the Average Man (New York, 1907), p. 17. For a portrait of English manliness, see Walter E. Houghton, The Victorian Frame of Mind, 1830–1870 (New Haven, 1957), pp. 196–203.

2. The quotations are from Sergeant Kendall to Frank and Elizabeth Kendall, August 12, 1882, and Richard Cabot to Ella Lyman, September 12, 1889, quoted by E. Anthony Rotundo, "Manhood in America: The Northern Middle Class, 1770–1920" (Ph.D. diss., Brandeis University, 1982), pp. 299, 314; Beveridge, Young Man, p. 157. Likewise, Mary Roberts Coolidge, Why Women Are So (New York, 1912), pp. 329–30; Robert N. Willson, The Social Evil in University Life: A Talk with the Students of the University of Pennsylvania (Pamphlet reprinted from Medical News, January 16, 1904). For instructive historical interpretations, see David M. Kennedy, Birth Control in America: The Career of Margaret Sanger (New Haven, 1970), pp. 62–63; Steven Marcus, The Other Victorians: A Study of Sexuality and Pornography in Mid-Nineteenth-Century England (New York, 1966), pp. 28–32; and esp. Rotundo, American Manhood: Transformations in Masculinity from the Revolution to the Modern Era (New York, 1993).

3. Roosevelt, Strenuous Life, p. 1.

4. On versions of the strenuous life, see George M. Fredrickson, The Inner Civil War: Northern Intellectuals and the Crisis of the Union (New York, 1965), chap. 14. On magazine heroes, see Theodore P. Greene, America's Heroes: The Changing Models of Success in American Magazines (New York, 1970), pp. 110–15, 153; quotations on p. 127.

5. Quoted in Greene, America's Heroes, pp. 156–58.

6. Quotations from Shaw, Outlook for the Average Man, pp. 2, 12, 17. Likewise, Lewis, Manhood-Making, pp. 190–91; and Saturday Evening Post 177 (January 7, 1905): 10, quoted in Greene, America's Heroes, p. 191. For business leaders' denials, see Edward W. Bok, "Problems of Young Men," LHJ 12 (January 1895): 12; "About Opportunities," World's Work 11 (January 1906): 7034–35; and Irvin G. Wyllie, The Self-Made Man in America: The Myth of Rags to Riches (New Brunswick, N.J., 1954), pp. 164–65.

7. Sam B. Warner, Jr., The Private City: Philadelphia in Three Periods of Its Growth (Philadelphia, 1968), pp. 162–68; Robert H. Wiebe, The Search for Order, 1877–1920 (New York, 1967), chap. 5; C. Wright Mills, White Collar: The American Middle Classes (New York, 1956), esp. chaps. 4 and 10.

8. Russell Sage, quoted in Wyllie, *Self-Made Man*, p. 43; David Graham Phillips, quoted in James R. McGovern, "David Graham Phillips and the Virility Impulse of Progressives," *New England Quarterly* 39 (September 1966): 341, 344; and Joseph Henry Dubbs, *Conditions of Success in Life: An Address . . .* (Philadelphia, 1870), p. 16. See also the comment in Phillips's novel, *Susan Lenox: Her Fall and Rise* (New York, 1930; orig. ed., 1917), 2:455–56. On the desire to work, see Daniel T. Rodgers, *The Work Ethic in Industrial America, 1850–1920* (Chicago, 1978); also Elting E. Morison, *Turmoil and Tradition: A Study of the Life and Times of Henry L. Stimson* (Boston, 1960), pp. 4–5. On nervousness and breakdowns, see Rotundo, *American Manhood*, pp. 185–93; also Nathan G. Hale, Jr., *Freud and the Americans: The Beginnings of Psychoanalysis in the United States, 1876–1917* (New York, 1971), pp. 232–35.

9. Roosevelt, *Strenuous Life*, p. 115; Richard Weiss, *The American Myth of Success: From Horatio Alger to Norman Vincent Peale* (New York, 1969), pp. 97–98, 118; Wyllie, *Self-Made Man*, pp. 86–87; *The Autobiography of Andrew Carnegie* (New York, 1920), esp. chaps. 1–3.

10. "Editor's Easy Chair," *Harper's Magazine* 103 (November 1901): 1004–8; "The Marriage Question," *Independent* 67 (December 9, 1909): 1305. On women, see Flora McDonald Thompson, "Retrogression of the American Woman," *North American Review* 171 (November 1900): 750–51; *New York Times*, January 7, 1900, 27:6, February 17, 1901, 19:1, April 20, 1908, 6:4, and May 6, 1908, 6:5; Ella Wheeler Wilcox, "The Restlessness of the Modern Woman," *Cosmopolitan* 31 (July 1901): 314–17; Anna A. Rogers, "Why American Marriages Fail," *Atlantic Monthly* 100 (September 1907): 289–98; Margaret Deland, "Change in the Feminine Ideal," ibid. 105 (March 1910): 289–302.

11. On muscular Christianity and the YMCA, see David I. Macleod, *Building Character in the American Boy: The Boy Scouts, YMCA, and Their Forerunners, 1870–1920* (Madison, Wis., 1983), chap. 4, and Benjamin Rader, *American Sports: From the Age of Folk Games to the Age of Spectators* (Englewood Cliffs, N.J., 1983), pp. 151–56. Gulick, Athletic League Letters, June 1901, is quoted by Rader, p. 155. On success, see George W. Perkins, *The Modern Corporation* (1908), quoted in Moses Rischin, ed., *The American Gospel of Success: Individualism and Beyond* (Chicago, 1965), p. 117; Josiah Strong, *The Times and Young Men* (New York, 1901), pp. 32–38; Shaw, *Outlook for the Average Man*, pp. 12–14; William A. McKeever, *Training the Boy* (New York, 1913), p. 308; Greene, *America's Heroes*, chap. 6, esp. pp. 234, 268–72, 274–76.

12. "The Man and the Woman" (editorial), LHJ 32 (October 1915): 7.

13. Greene, *America's Heroes*, pp. 310–14.

14. Webster to Bingham, February 11, 1800, October 26, 1801, and April 3, 1804, quoted in E. Anthony Rotundo, *American Manhood: Transformations in Masculinity from the Revolution to the Present Era* (New York, 1993), pp. 78–79.

15. Blake diary, December 27, 1851, and July 10, 1851, quoted in ibid., p. 80.

16. George Chauncey, *Gay New York: Gender, Urban Culture, and the Making of the Gay Male World,* 1890–1940 (New York, 1994), pp. 13–15, 46–50; Jonathan Katz, *Gay American History: Lesbians and Gay Men in the U.S.A.: A Documentary Anthology* (New York, 1976), pp. 4, 30, 44–49; John Higham, "The Reorientation of American History," in *Writing American History: Essays on Modern Scholarship* (Bloomington, Ind., 1970), p. 79. Note that, according to Chauncey, pp. 12–14 and 27, this division between homosexual and heterosexual emerged in working-class culture only in the 1930s and thereafter.

17. In this discussion I've relied heavily on Rotundo, *Manhood,* pp. 276–78. "The woman within" is his felicitous phrase.

18. "Rapid Transit and Home Life," *Harper's Bazar* 33 (December 1900): 200, quoted in Peter J. Schmitt, *Back to Nature: The Arcadian Myth in Urban America* (New York, 1969), p. 20.

19. Robert Sunley, "Early-Nineteenth-Century American Literature on Child Rearing," in *Childhood in Contemporary Cultures,* ed. Margaret Mead and Martha Wolfenstein (Chicago, 1955), p. 152; Mrs. M.E.W. Sherwood, *Amenities of Home* (New York, 1881), p. 106; D. Collin Wells, "Some Questions Concerning the Higher Education of Women," *American Journal of Sociology* 14 (May 1909): 732–33; Arthur W. Calhoun, *A Social History of the American Family from Colonial Times to the Present,* 3 vols. (Cleveland, 1917–19), 3:157–58, 161; Harold L. Ickes, *The Autobiography of a Curmudgeon* (New York, 1943), p. 8. On working and commuting time, see Sebastian de Grazia, *Of Time, Work, and Leisure* (New York, Anchor ed., 1964), pp. 62–67, 419, 454; U.S. Bureau of the Census, *Historical Statistics of the United States: Colonial Times to 1957* (Washington, D.C., 1969), pp. 90–91; Warner, *The Private City,* pp. 169, 196–97, and *Streetcar Suburbs: The Process of Growth in Boston, 1870–1900* (Cambridge, Mass., 1962).

20. Orville G. Brim, Jr., *Education for Child Rearing* (New York, 1959), p. 326; Willystine Goodsell, *Problems of the Family* (New York, 1928), pp. 429–30; "Mothers of Yesterday and To-day" (editorial), *Harper's Bazar* 33 (January 13, 1900): 26; Katherine G. Busbey, *Home Life in America* (London, 1910), pp. 32–33; Richard Sennett, *Families against the City: Middle-Class Homes of Industrial Chicago, 1872–1890* (Cambridge, Mass., 1970), p. 53.

21. Calhoun, *Social History of the American Family,* 3:158; on Roosevelt and Hale, Rotundo, "Manhood in America," pp. 334–41; Ethel Adamson to Abby Scott Baker, March 8, 191[?], in National Woman's Party Papers, LC, tray 29, box 2. Likewise, Morison, *Turmoil and Tradition,* p. 5; Wilson's essay, "One Duty of a Son to His Parents," [October 8, 1876], and diary, November 7, 1876, in Arthur S. Link, ed., *The Papers of Woodrow Wilson* (Princeton, N.J., 1966), 1:205–7, 222.

22. Catton is quoted by Macleod, *Building Character in the American Boy,* p. 8. On fathers' relationships with children, see Rotundo, "Manhood in America,"

pp. 334–56; Wanda C. Bronson, Edith S. Katten, and Norman Livson, "Patterns of Authority and Affection in Two Generations," *Journal of Abnormal and Social Psychology* 58 (1959): 143–56.

23. Arthur M. Schlesinger, *The Rise of the City, 1878–1898* (New York, 1933), pp. 355, 360; E. M. Jellinek, "Recent Trends in Alcoholism and in Alcohol Consumption," *Quarterly Journal of Studies on Alcohol* 8 (July 1947): 8, 20. U.S. Public Health Service, *Syphilis: A Synopsis,* PHS Publication no. 1660 (Washington, D.C., 1968), p. 13; Henry H. Hazen, *Syphilis: A Treatise on Etiology, Pathology, Diagnosis, Prophylaxis, and Treatment* (St. Louis, 1919), p. 522; Taliaferro Clark, "Some Public Health Aspects of Syphilis," *Venereal Disease Information* 12 (May 20, 1931): 209; Thomas Parran, Jr., Willard C. Smith, and Selwyn D. Collins, "Venereal Disease Prevalence in Fourteen Communities," ibid. 9 (February 20, 1928): 50–53. On prostitution, see Harold Underwood Faulkner, *The Quest for Social Justice, 1898–1914* (New York, 1931), pp. 159–61; Roy Lubove, "The Progressives and the Prostitute," *Historian* 24 (May 1962): 308–30; Ruth Rosen, *The Lost Sisterhood: Prostitution in America, 1900–1918* (Baltimore, 1982), chap. 3.

24. Nina Baym, *Woman's Fiction: A Guide to Novels by and about Women in America, 1820–1870* (Ithaca, 1978), esp. pp. 17–20; Helen Waite Papashvily, *All the Happy Endings: A Study of the Domestic Novel in America . . .* (New York, 1956), esp. pp. xvi–xvii; Leslie Fiedler, *Love and Death in the American Novel,* rev. ed. (New York, 1969), p. 74.

25. David Jay Pivar, "The New Abolitionism: The Quest for Social Purity, 1876–1900" (Ph.D. diss., University of Pennsylvania, 1965), esp. chaps. 1, 8–9, and pp. 332–34. See also Anna Garlin Spencer, "A World Crusade," *Forum* 50 (August 1913): 182–95; Paul S. Boyer, *Purity in Print: The Vice-Society Movement and Book Censorship in America* (New York, 1968), pp. 5–25.

26. Andrew Sinclair, *Era of Excess: A Social History of the Prohibition Movement* (New York, Harper Colophon ed., 1964), chaps. 2–3; Frances Willard, *Glimpses of Fifty Years: The Autobiography of an American Woman* (Chicago, 1889), pp. 396, 401; Faulkner, *Quest for Social Justice,* pp. 222–26; James H. Timberlake, *Prohibition and the Progressive Movement, 1900–1920* (Cambridge, Mass., 1963), pp. 146–52 and chaps. 5–6; Joseph R. Gusfield, *Symbolic Crusade: Status Politics and the American Temperance Movement* (Urbana, Ill., 1963), esp. chap. 5.

27. *American Issues,* Oklahoma ed., June 1912, quoted in Peter H. Odegard, *Pressure Politics: The Story of the Anti-Saloon League* (New York, 1928), p. 42.

28. Mrs. J. J. Ansley, *History of the Georgia Woman's Christian Temperance Union from 1883 to 1907* (Columbus, Ga., 1914), p. 102, and Belle Kearney, *A Slaveholder's Daughter* (New York, 1900), p. 117, both quoted in Anne Firor Scott, *The Southern Lady: From Pedestal to Politics, 1830–1930* (Chicago, 1970), pp. 148–49.

29. Jon M. Kingsdale, "The 'Poor Man's Club': Social Functions of the Urban Working-Class Saloon," *American Quarterly* 25 (December 1973): 472–89.

30. Andrew Sinclair, *The Better Half: The Emancipation of the American Woman*

(New York, 1965), chap. 20; Janet Zollinger Giele, "Social Change in the Feminine Role: A Comparison of Woman's Suffrage and Woman's Temperance, 1870–1920" (Ph.D. diss., Radcliffe, 1961), pp. 67–69, 190–205; Gusfield, *Symbolic Crusade*, esp. pp. 80–81, 129–31; Aileen S. Kraditor, *Ideas of the Woman Suffrage Movement, 1890–1920* (New York, 1965), p. 57.

31. Alice Stone Blackwell to Kitty Barry Blackwell, December 24, 1882, in Blackwell Family Papers, SL, folder 164.

32. Galloway, *Sex and Life*, pp. 43–45; Mortimer A. Warren, *Almost Fourteen: A Book Designed to Be Used by Parents in the Training of Their Sons and Daughters for Present Modesty and Nobility, and for Future Fatherhood and Motherhood* (New York, 1897); W. F. Robie, *Rational Sex Ethics: A Physiological and Psychological Study of the Sex Lives of Normal Men and Women, with Suggestions for a Rational Sex Hygiene* (Boston, 1916), p. 106; G. Stanley Hall, *Adolescence: Its Psychology and Its Relations to Physiology, Anthropology, Sociology, Sex, Crime, Religion, and Education* (New York, 1904), p. 435; *The Autobiography of William Allen White* (New York, 1946), p. 75; Lewis Atherton, *Main Street on the Middle Border* (Bloomington, Ind., 1954), p. 91.

33. Quoted in Carleton Putnam, *Theodore Roosevelt: The Formative Years, 1858–1886* (New York, 1958), 1:141.

34. E.g., Stall, *What a Young Husband Ought to Know*, pp. 48–49; Bernarr Macfadden, *Marriage a Lifelong Honeymoon: Life's Greatest Pleasures Secured by Observing the Highest Human Instincts* (New York and London, 1903), pp. 147–48; Sinclair, *Better Half*, p. 133. Robie, *Rational Sex Ethics*, p. 95, a liberal physician, found from an unsystematic survey of several hundred middle-class persons that most believed intercourse should occur two to four times a week. On continence, see *Survey* 29 (March 8, 1913): 801, and Rabbi Rudolph I. Coffee, "Pittsburgh Clergy and the Social Evil," ibid., p. 815.

35. For one of the rare male confessions of the double standard, see Chester T. Crowell, "The Worm Turns: An Indictment of Women and a Defense of Men," *Independent* 67 (January 12, 1914): 68–69.

36. The Wharton episode is taken from R.W.B. Lewis, *Edith Wharton: A Biography* (New York, 1975), p. 53. On precedents see, Edmund S. Morgan, "The Puritans and Sex," *New England Quarterly* 15 (December 1942): 591–607; John Demos, *A Little Commonwealth: Family Life in Plymouth Colony* (New York, 1970), pp. 96–97, 158; Maurice J. Quinlan, *Victorian Prelude: A History of English Manners, 1700–1830* (New York, 1941); Houghton, *Victorian Frame of Mind*, pp. 353–59. On pornography, see Marcus, *Other Victorians*. On ideals and practice, see Barbara Welter, "The Cult of True Womanhood: 1820–1860," *American Quarterly* 18 (Summer 1966): 151–74; Sinclair, *Better Half*, chaps. 10–11; and Peter Gay, *The Bourgeois Experience, Victoria to Freud: Education of the Senses* (New York, 1984), esp. chaps. 2 and 3.

37. *Congressional Record*, 56th Cong., 1st sess., 33, pt. 2 (January 24, 1900): 1132, 1145. Similarly, pp. 1147, 1190. For background, see p. 1178.

38. Alan P. Grimes, *The Puritan Ethic and Woman Suffrage* (New York, 1967).

39. Statement in *New York World*, November 1899, quoted in Ida Husted Harper, *The Life and Work of Susan B. Anthony*, 3 vols. (Indianapolis, 1898–1903), 3:1152.

40. Childless Wife [pseud.], "Why I Have No Family," *Independent* 58 (March 23, 1905): 655. On the "purity revolt," see also Pivar, "New Abolitionism," chap. 3.

41. Quotations are in O. Edward Janney, *The White Slave Traffic in America* (New York, 1911), pp. 5–8, 22–23. Also see Janney, p. 24; Lubove, "Progressives and the Prostitute"; Phillips, *Susan Lenox*; Vern L. Bullough, *The History of Prostitution* (New York, 1964), chap. 11.

42. Vice Commission of Chicago, *The Social Evil in Chicago: A Study of Existing Conditions* (Chicago, 1911), p. 26.

43. Harriet Laidlaw, a leader in the campaign, admonished: "Remember, it is more important to be aroused than accurate": Laidlaw, "The A.B.C. of the Question," typed ms. of article, [1912], Laidlaw Papers, SL, folder 149. For contemporary data and views, see "The Traffic in Women," *Literary Digest* 25 (August 23, 1902): 231; *Current Literature* 47 (December 1909): 594–98; Janney, *White Slave Traffic*, pp. 122–24; "National Merger to Fight White Slavery," *Survey* 27 (March 30, 1912): 1991, and 30 (May 3, 1913): 162–64. For a skeptical historical analysis, see Lubove, "Progressives and the Prostitute." By contrast, Ruth Rosen offers evidence and reasons to support the existence of white slavery: *The Lost Sisterhood: Prostitution in America, 1900–1918* (Baltimore, 1982), esp. pp. 3, 118, and chap. 6.

44. Quoted in *Current Opinion* 56 (February 1914): 129.

45. Kai Erikson, *Wayward Puritans: A Study in the Sociology of Deviance* (New York, 1966), pp. 137–59.

46. "Sex O'Clock in America," *Current Opinion* 55 (August 1913): 113–14; "The Man's Hand in Dancing" (editorial), LHJ 31 (February 1914): 6; Busbey, *Home Life*, p. 79; Schlesinger, *Rise of the City*, pp. 122–23; "Confessions of a Co-ed," *Independent* 63 (October 10, 1907): 873; Helen R. Olin, *The Women of a State University* (New York, 1909), pp. 209–12; Florence M. Fitch, "What Are Our Social Standards?" *Journal of Social Hygiene* 1 (September 1915): 546–48; Alice Stone Blackwell to Kitty Barry Blackwell, March 25, 1883, in Blackwell Papers, folder 165; James R. McGovern, "The American Woman's Pre-World War I Freedom in Manners and Morals," *Journal of American History* 55 (September 1968): 326n.

47. *Nation* 94 (March 14, 1912): 260–62; Spencer, "A World Crusade," pp. 183–95; "Dramatizing Vice," *Literary Digest* 47 (October 4, 1913): 577–78; "Sex O'-Clock in America," pp. 113–14; Maurice A. Bigelow, *Sex-Education: A Series of Lectures Concerning Knowledge of Sex in Its Relation to Human Life* (New York, 1916), p. 206; Henry, "The Vice Problem from Various Angles," p. 144; Hornell Hart, "Changing Social Attitudes and Interests," in *Recent Social Trends in the United States: Report of the President's Research Committee on Social Trends* (New York, 1933), 1:414 (table 16) and 418. On the intellectuals, see William L. O'Neill, *Divorce in*

the Progressive Era (New Haven, 1967), chaps. 4–5 and pp. 198–203; Henry F. May, *The End of American Innocence: A Study of the First Years of Our Own Time, 1912–1917* (New York, 1959), pp. 307–10.

48. The two quotations come from an editorial in *Survey* 31 (February 28, 1914): 683, and Brand Whitlock, "The White Slave," *Forum* 51 (February 1914): 195. For background, see *Survey* 27 (October 14, 1911): 991, and 27 (November 11, 1911): 1177–88; A. H. Finn, "Detroit Sex Hygiene Campaign," *Survey* 25 (December 17, 1910): 400–401; Irving W. Wolf, letter to editor, *Survey* 30 (May 10, 1913): 227; Editha Phelps, "Sex Hygiene in the Schools," *Life and Labor* 4 (February 1914): 55–57. For opposition, see Vivian Hadley Harris, "The Status of Sex Education in Public Educational Institutions," *Journal of Social Hygiene* 7 (April 1921): 167–77; Corinne Marie (Tuckerman) Allen Papers, SL, esp. "What Should Be Taught to Children Concerning the Sex Relation," December 4, 1912, ms., folder 10; *New York Times*, September 21, 1913, 14:6. On puritanism, see Bigelow, *Sex-Education*, p. 228; Vice Commission of Chicago, *Social Evil*, p. 253; Ethel Sturges Dummer to B. S. Steadwell, November 11, 1921, in Dummer Papers, SL, folder 375.

49. Vice Commission of Chicago, *Social Evil*, pp. 46–47; Bigelow, *Sex-Education*, p. 165; "The Livingston Case," *Woman Voter* (191?), pp. 17–18, in Laidlaw Papers, folder 152; Chicago Society of Social Hygiene, "Education against Venereal Disease a Need of the State," c. 1907, in Allen Papers, folder 30; Rose Woodallen Chapman, *The Moral Problem of the Children* (New York, 1909), pp. 39–40. For more valid statistics, see note 23.

50. Anne Heslit to "Editor *American*," November 26, 1910, copy, in Walter Rauschenbusch Papers, American Baptist Historical Society, Rochester, N.Y. I wish to thank Ralph Luker for showing this letter to me.

51. Macfadden, *Marriage a Lifelong Honeymoon*, pp. 98, 197–98; Marcus, *Other Victorians*, pp. 28, 32; G. J. Barker-Benfield, *The Horrors of the Half-Known Life: Male Attitudes toward Women and Sexuality in Nineteenth-Century America* (New York, 1976), chaps. 14–16. Quotations are from Cass Gilbert to Julia Finch, March 29, 1887, and Frank Lillie to Frances Crance, September 24, 1894, in Ellen Rothman, *Hands and Hearts: A History of Courtship in America* (New York, 1984), p. 187.

52. Quotations are from Ida Husted Harper, *The History of Woman Suffrage*, 5 (n.p., 1922): 588, and *New York Times*, January 21, 1913, 8:1.

53. Joseph F. Kett, *Rites of Passage: Adolescence in America, 1790 to the Present* (New York, 1977), p. 173.

4. IN TIME OF WAR

1. Roderick Nash, ed., *The Call of the Wild (1900–1916)* (New York, 1970), pp. 240, 320; Joe B. Frantz and Julian Ernest Choate, Jr., *The American Cowboy: The Myth & the Reality* (Norman, Okla., 1955), pp. 156–58, 171–74; Leslie A. Fiedler, *Love and Death in the American Novel*, rev. ed. (New York, 1969), pp. 254–55.

2. Foster Rhea Dulles, A History of Recreation: America Learns to Play, 2d ed. (New York, 1965), pp. 182–91, 244–46; Addington H. Bruce, "Baseball and the National Life," Outlook 104 (May 1913): 104–7, reprinted in Nash, Call of the Wild, pp. 294–300.

3. Quotations come from Ernest Thompson Seton, Boy Scouts of America: A Handbook of Woodcraft, Scouting, and Life-Craft (New York, 1910), p. 3, and William A. McKeever, Training the Boy (New York, 1913), p. 112. The best study is David I. Macleod, Building Character in the American Boy: The Boy Scouts, YMCA, and Their Forerunners, 1870–1920 (Madison, Wis., 1983) esp. chaps. 9 and 15 and p. 278. See also William D. Murray, The History of the Boy Scouts of America (New York, 1937).

4. Turnover figures are in Macleod, Building Character, pp. 154 and 280. See also Peter J. Schmitt, Back to Nature: The Arcadian Myth in Urban America (New York, 1969), p. 112. In harmony with the Victorian sexual "spheres," the Girl Scouts was founded in 1912 as a counterpart, but a distinctively feminine counterpart, to the Boy Scouts. The Girl Scouts offered physical activity of a sociable sort (dancing and coeducational hikes, for example) and gave badges for domestic achievements like homemaking and laundering. Whereas BSA leaders worried about boys being restless, Girl Scout leaders worried about their troops being melancholy. "Be happy" was the final law of the Camp Fire Girls. See Macleod, Building Character, pp. 50–51.

5. "Tom," LHJ 34 (October 1917): 7.

6. Quotations from Charles V. Genthe, American War Narratives, 1917–1918: A Study and Bibliography (New York, 1969), p. 29; Arthur C. Train, The Earthquake (New York, 1918), p. 279.

7. George Weston, "The Feminine Touch," Saturday Evening Post (1918), reprinted in War Stories, ed. by Roy J. Holmes and A. Starbuck (New York, 1919), pp. 299–321.

8. E.g., The Autobiography of William Allen White (New York, 1946), pp. 49–50; William G. McAdoo, Crowded Years: The Reminiscences of William G. McAdoo (Boston, 1931), p. 25.

9. "To Joyce Kilmer" (editorial), Delineator 94 (January 1919): 3.

10. Norman Springer, "A Recruit," Saturday Evening Post 190 (November 10, 1917): 15–18, 98–105.

11. Ira E. Bennett, Editorials from the "Washington Post," 1917–1920 (Washington, D.C., 1921), p. 197. See also Genthe, American War Narratives, pp. 29, 68–69.

12. Train, Earthquake, p. 201.

13. Russell G. Pruden Papers, Sterling Library, Yale University; James M. Merrill, ed., Uncommon Valor: The Exciting Story of the Army (New York, 1964), pp. 312, 327–42.

14. Arthur Guy Empey, "Over the Top" (New York, 1917), pp. 279–80; Sgt. Thomas R. Cole to Mrs. J. W. Elliott, with the AEF in France, July 24, 1918, in Cole Papers, SHC; letter from Albert Angier, June 5, 1918, in On the Field of Honor:

A *Collection of War Letters of Three Harvard Undergraduates Who Gave Their Lives in the Great Cause*, ed. Paul B. Elliott (Boston, 1920), p. 22; Alan Seeger to his mother, October 17, 1914, in *Letters and Diary of Alan Seeger* (New York, 1917), p. 8. See also Genthe, *American War Narratives*, pp. 40–45, 87.

15. Genthe, *American War Narratives*, pp. 25–26.

16. Dos Passos to Arthur K. McComb, August 26, 1916, and July 31, 1917, both quoted in Melvin Landsberg, *Dos Passos' Path to U.S.A.: A Political Biography, 1912–1936* (Boulder, Colo., 1972), pp. 48, 56; Dos Passos to McComb, spring 1917, quoted in Landsberg, p. 52, and in Daniel Aaron, *Writers on the Left: Episodes in American Literary Communism* (New York, Avon ed., 1965), pp. 358–59; Dos Passos Notebook, August 26, [1917], reprinted in introduction to Dos Passos, *One Man's Initiation: 1917* (Ithaca, N.Y., 1969), p. 22.

17. Letter from Francis Reed Austin, August 16, 1918, in Elliott, *On the Field of Honor*, p. 62; Charles Bernard Nordhoff, "More Letters from France," *Atlantic Monthly* 121 (January 1918): 123.

18. Albert N. Depew, *Gunner Depew* (New York, 1918), p. 159, quoted in Genthe, *American War Narratives*, p. 80; Frank Freidel, *Over There: The Story of America's First Great Overseas Crusade* (Boston, 1964), pp. 197, 290.

19. Frank Parker Stockbridge, "The Cleanest Army in the World," *Delineator* 93 (December 1918): 8; Kate Waller Barrett, head of the Florence Crittenton movement for unwed mothers, quoted in Paul S. Boyer, *Purity in Print: The Vice-Society Movement and Book Censorship in America* (New York, 1968), pp. 63–64; M. J. Exner, introduction to *Sex and Life: A Message to Undergraduate Men*, by Thomas Walton Galloway (New York, 1919), p. x; B. S. Steadwell, "Modern Campaign against Venereal Disease," *Light*, January–February 1920, in Ethel Sturges Dummer Papers, SL, folder 403.

20. William F. Snow, "Social Hygiene and the War," *Journal of Social Hygiene* 3 (July 1917): 420–22; Rachelle S. Yarros, "'Shall We Finish the Fight?'" *Life and Labor* 9 (January 1919): 19–20; Harold Hersey, quoted in Boyer, *Purity in Print*, pp. 55–57.

21. Stanley Cooperman, *World War I and the American Novel* (Baltimore, 1967), pp. 117, 132–34; Genthe, *American War Narratives*, pp. 44–45; Floyd Gibbons, "And They Thought We Wouldn't Fight" (New York, 1918), pp. 93, 272; Luther H. Gulick, *Morals and Morale* (New York, 1919), p. 43.

22. Quoted in Snow, "Social Hygiene and the War," p. 499; letter from Albert Edgar Angier, June 5, 1918, in Elliott, *On the Field of Honor*, pp. 22–23.

23. Stephen Longstreet, ed., *Nell Kimball: Her Life as an American Madam: By Herself* (New York, 1970), p. 279; Eugene A. Hicken to Grace A. Johnson, September 22, 1917, in Johnson Papers, SL, folder 119; *Report of the Surgeon General, U.S. Army, to the Secretary of War* (Washington, D.C., 1920), fig. 44, p. 181, and (1918), pp. 196–97, 200–201.

24. *Report of the Surgeon General* (1919), pp. 1312, 1634; P. M. Ashburn, *A History of the Medical Department of the United States Army* (Boston, 1929), pp. 336–37;

Freidel, *Over There*, pp. 80–81; Victor Hicken, *The American Fighting Man* (New York, 1969), p. 302.

25. Maude Radford Warren, "War and the Woman," *Delineator* 92 (January 1918): 5.

26. Boyer, *Purity in Print*, p. 57; Raymond E. Fosdick to Ethel Sturges Summer, September 20, 1917, and *Committee on Protective Work for Girls* (Washington, D.C., n.d.), both in Dummer Papers, folder 377; B. B. Howell, "Record of Investigation at Rockford, Illinois," typescript and "Report of the Committee on Protective Work for Girls, October 1, 1917, to April 1, 1918," typed carbon copy, in Dummer Papers, folders 380, 381: Dixon Wecter, *When Johnny Comes Marching Home* (Boston, 1944), p. 330.

27. Maurice Rickards, *Posters of the First World War* (New York, 1968), poster no. 120: Joseph S. Smith, *Over There and Back in Three Uniforms: Being the Experiences of an American Boy in the Canadian, British, and American Armies at the Front and through No Man's Land* (New York, 1918), pp. 50–51.

28. E.g., A.H.S., letter to the editor, *New Republic* 11 (June 16, 1917): 189–90; "The Woman's Committee of the United States Council of National Defense," LHJ 34 (August 1917): 3; Ida C. Clarke, *American Women and the World War* (New York, 1919), esp. pt. 2.

29. Margaret Spaulding Gerry, "The Flag Factory," LHJ, 1917, reprinted in Holmes and Starbuck, *War Stories*, pp. 126–35.

30. *New York Times*, January 12, 1918, 16:4, and January 13, 1918, sec. 1, 4:1; "Female Labor Arouses Hostility and Apprehension in Union Ranks," *Current Opinion* 64 (April 1918): 292–93. Statistics of female wartime employment are not precise: see *New York Times*, March 30, 1918, 18:8, and William Henry Chafe, *The American Woman: Her Changing Social, Economic, and Political Roles, 1920–1970* (New York, 1972), pp. 50–53.

31. Esther Harney, "Boston's Shine Girls," *Life and Labor* 7 (December 1917): 186–88.

32. Quotation is from Mabel Potter Daggett, *Women Wanted: The Story Written in Blood Red Letters on the Horizon of the Great World War* (New York, 1918), p. 87. On employment, see *New York Times*, July 29, 1917, sec. 2, 11:2; August 27, 1917, 5:3; September 6, 1917, 4:4; November 18, 1917, 7:6, 10:4; December 23, 1917, sec. 5, 8:3; December 30, 1917, sec. 7, 6:1. "Where Girls Are Really Doing Men's Jobs," LHJ 34 (November 1917): 83.

33. *New York Times*, October 6, 1918, sec. 8, p. 3; "Women's Wages," *Nation* 108 (February 22, 1919): 270–71.

34. "Men and Women" (editorial), *Woman Citizen* 3 (November 23, 1918): 625.

35. *New York Times*, August 6, 1914, quoted in *Up from the Pedestal: Selected Writings in the History of American Feminism*, ed. Aileen Kraditor (Chicago, 1968), p. 287.

36. E.g., Kraditor, *Up from the Pedestal*, p. 287; Elizabeth Selden Rogers memo, [1915 or 1916], in National Woman's Party Papers, LC, tray 29, box 6;

Anna Howard Shaw to "Dear friend," form letter, January 5, 1915, in Harriet Burton Laidlaw Papers, SL, folder 119.

37. William L. O'Neill, *Everyone Was Brave: The Rise and Fall of Feminism in America* (Chicago, 1969), pp. 173–78; Clarke, *American Women and the World War*, chap. 2; "Suffrage Service in Wartime," *Woman Citizen* 1 (June 30, 1917): 80.

38. *New York Times*, February 9, 1917, 11:1; Grace A. Johnson to Mrs. Joseph Fels, April 23, 1917, carbon copy, Ethel Lorenz Halladay to Johnson, March 7, 1917, and Johnson to Halladay, March 9, 1917, in Johnson Papers, folder 116; Lois D. Parker to Johnson, March 12, 1917, folder 119; Zara du Pont to Johnson, April 16, 1917, folder 136; Loretta Ellen Zimmerman, "Alice Paul and the National Woman's Party, 1912–1920" (Ph.D. diss., Tulane, 1964), pp. 243, 250–52.

39. For public admiration, see A. Elizabeth Taylor, "The Last Phase of the Woman Suffrage Movement in Georgia," *Georgia Historical Quarterly* 43 (March 1959): 15–16; "Pouring Sand in the Bearings" (editorial), *Saturday Evening Post* 190 (December 29, 1917): 22; Alice Stone Blackwell, "As a War Measure," *Woman Citizen* 2 (April 27, 1918): 432; also, *Woman Citizen* 2 (January 26, 1918): 167, and 3 (July 27, 1918): 167. For antis, see editorial, *New York Times*, November 6, 1917, 12:2, and *New York Times*, November 23, 1917, 5:1.

40. *New York Times*, June 21, 1917, 1:5, and June 23, 1917, 9:5.

41. For public reaction, see Rose Young to Helen H. Gardener, December 4, 1917, carbon copy, in Maud Wood Park Papers, SL, folder 745. For NAWSA's views, see Anna Howard Shaw to Robert N. Lewis (son of Mrs. Lawrence Lewis, a Woman's Party executive who was jailed for picketing), November 28, 1917, in National Woman's Party Papers, tray 29, box 6; *New York Times*, August 31, 1917, 18:1; Ethel M. Smith to Carrie Chapman Catt, June 26, 1917, typed copy, in Park Papers, folder 735; *New Republic* 13 (December 8, 1917): 135.

42. Zara du Pont to Grace A. Johnson, April 16, 1917, and Johnson to du Pont, April 27, 1917, copy, in Johnson Papers, folders 136, 139.

43. On Rankin, see, e.g., letters from Gertrude Atherton and Elizabeth Newport Hepburn, *New York Times*, November 5, 1917, 14:7, 8. The editorial in the General Federation *Magazine* 16 (June 1917): 5–6, is quoted in O'Neill, *Everyone Was Brave*, p. 216.

44. O'Neill, *Everyone Was Brave*, p. 223.

45. Isaac F. Marcosson, "The After-the-War Woman," LHJ 35 (June 1918): 13, 90–93; "Shall Women Lose Their New Jobs?" *Literary Digest* 55 (January 11, 1919): 14–15; "Us Girls!" (editorial), *Delineator* 95 (August 1919): 1.

5. NEW GENERATIONS

1. Quotations are from A. Elizabeth Taylor, *The Woman Suffrage Movement in Tennessee* (New York, 1957), p. 84, and Mercedes M. Randall, *Improper Bostonian: Emily Greene Balch* (New York, 1964), p. 282. See also "'Every Woman Has Her

Principle'" (editorial), *Woman Citizen* 2 (January 12, 1918): 129; "'To the Victors Belong the Spoils'" (editorial), *Good Housekeeping* 71 (November 1920): 6; Vivian Pierce to Alice Paul, March 30, 1919, and Susan Quackenbush to Alice Paul, July 11, 1919, in National Woman's Party Papers, both quoted in Loretta Ellen Zimmerman, "Alice Paul and the National Woman's Party, 1912–1920" (Ph.D. diss., Tulane, 1964), pp. 323–24.

2. Carrie Chapman Catt, "The Next Contest," *Woman Citizen* 5 (November 20, 1920): 677; William Henry Chafe, *The American Woman: Her Changing Social, Economic, and Political Roles, 1920–1970* (New York, 1972), p. 34; Maud Wood Park, presidential address, April 25, 1922, in *Proceedings of the Third Annual Convention of the National League of Women Voters*, p. 92; *New York Times*, November 21, 1920, sec. 7, 2:1.

3. Alice Paul to Jane Norman Smith, August 30, 1921, in Smith Papers, SL, folder 110; *New York Times*, May 1, 1923, 1 :4, and September 24, 1923, 5:2. Paul's statement is from the *New York Times*, August 17, 1924, 1:4.

4. Mrs. Gifford Pinchot to Maud Wood Park, March 4, 1920, in League of Women Voters (LWV) Papers, LC, series I, box 49; Pinchot, address at 1923 LWV convention, box 12; Alice Stone Blackwell, "'Nervous Prognostication,'" *Woman Citizen* 5 (May 21, 1921): 1241; "Woman Candidates" (editorial), ibid. 6 (October 8, 1921): 13; "No Sex Line-up" (editorial), ibid. 7 (June 3, 1922): 13; Mary Garrett Hay, "The Future of Women in Politics," ibid. 7 (January 27, 1923): 20–21; "A Women's Bloc?" *Nation* 119 (September 3, 1924): 230.

5. For succinct samples of this long, verbose debate, see Alice Paul to Jane Norman Smith, November 29, 1921, in Smith Papers, folder 110; Ethel M. Smith, "What Is Sex Equality?" *Century Magazine* 118 (May 1929): 96–106; Felix Frankfurter, letter, *New Republic* 41 (November 26, 1924): 20; Elsie Hill and Florence Kelley, "Shall Women Be Equal before the Law?" *Nation* 114 (April 12, 1922): 419–21; Harriot Stanton Blatch, "Wrapping Women in Cotton-wool," *Nation* 116 (January 31, 1923): 115–16; Clara Mortenson Beyer, "What Is Equality?" *Nation* 116 (January 31, 1923): 116; Doris Stevens, "Suffrage Does Not Give Equality," *Forum* 72 (August 1924): 145–52; *New York Times*, March 17, 1924, 15:3. A perceptive synopsis is in Chafe, *American Woman*, chap. 5, esp. pp. 114, 122–24, 126. Also useful is William L. O'Neill, *Everyone Was Brave: The Rise and Fall of Feminism in America* (Chicago, 1969), pp. 274–93, and Sheila M. Rothman, *Woman's Proper Place: A History of Changing Ideals and Practices, 1870 to the Present* (New York, 1978), p. 163. Kelley's quotation is from her letter to Newton D. Baker, June 3, 1921, copy, in National Consumers League Papers, LC, box 54.

6. Chafe, *American Woman*, pp. 27–29. For typical local league work, see Avis Carlson, *The League of Women Voters in St. Louis: The First Forty Years, 1919–1959* (St. Louis, 1959), pp. 34–37. On group quarrels, see Carrie Chapman Catt to Maud Wood Park, February 18, 1922, and Gladys Harrison to Mrs. James Morrison, October 12, 1925, in LWV Papers, boxes 3, 21. On ERA clash, see Chafe, pp. 118–20; Jane Norman Smith to Alice Paul, December 4, 10, and 16, 1922, and

January 7, 1923, copies, in Smith Papers, folders 110, 111; Anne Martin, "Feminists and Future Political Action," *Nation* 120 (February 18, 1925): 185–86; Jane Norman Smith to Anne Martin, February 13, 1925, copy, in Smith Papers, folder 62; Florence Kelley to Mrs. Katherine Edson, January 28, 1926, in Consumers League Papers, box 54. On broken friendships, see Kelley to Maud Younger, October 19, 1921, in Consumers League Papers, box 54; Mary Beard to Jane Norman Smith, [1922], and Smith to Elizabeth Gifford, December 3, 1928, in Smith Papers, folders 60, 70.

7. Sophonisba P. Breckinridge, *Women in the Twentieth Century: A Study of Their Political, Social, and Economic Activities* (New York, 1933), pp. 267–68, 289–90, 323–25, 336; Chafe, *American Woman*, p. 38. Nellie Ross's statement in *New York Times*, April 24, 1925, 21:8. The *Woman Citizen* quotation comes from an editorial, "How Shall We Put Women in Office?" 7 (November 18, 1922): 14.

8. On educational function, see Subcommittee on Possible Extension of Scope, "Report on Scope and Policy," April 12, 1921, in LWV Papers, box 4; [Mrs. Richard E. Edwards?] to Carrie Chapman Catt, February 27, 1922, copy of unsigned letter, box 3; Maud Wood Park, address at Fifth Annual Convention, April 25, 1924, box 40, esp. pp. 12, 14; Belle Sherwin, presidential address at National Convention, April 30, 1930, box 142. For Sherwin on women voters see *New York Times*, April 30, 1928, 20:8, and her address to the Sixth Annual Convention, April 17, 1925, in LWV Papers, box 41. In 1923–24 there were 607 local leagues in 346 congressional districts; in 1930 there were approximately 600 locals in 267 districts: "Summary Report of the Regions, 1923–24," in LWV Papers, box 18; various reports to the National Board, 1930, box 199; card from 1930 Convention, box 142. Estimate of one-tenth is from Chafe, *American Woman*, p. 37. Budgets come from LWV, *Proceedings of the Second Annual Convention*, 1920–21, pp. 84–85, and Ninth Annual Convention, 1929–30, pp. 98–99. For Woman's Party membership, see Chafe, p. 114.

9. Chafe, *American Woman*, pp. 30–32, 36–37; O'Neill, *Everyone Was Brave*, pp. 261–62; Eleanor Brannon to Belle Sherwin, October 6, 1922, in LWV Papers, box 57; Anne Martin, "Woman's Inferiority Complex," *New Republic* 27 (July 20, 1921): 211. For activists' attitudes, see Elizabeth Green, "I Resign from Female Politics," *New Republic* 42 (April 22, 1925): 233–35; Ruth B. McIntosh to the Organization Department, LWV, August 27–28 and September 1–9, 1925, in LWV Papers, box 66; Emily Newell Blair, "Are Women a Failure in Politics?" *Harper's Magazine* 151 (October 1925): 513–22; "Is Woman Suffrage Failing?" *Woman Citizen* 8 (March 22, 1924): 7–9, 29; Sue Shelton White to Mary Dewson, November 23, 1928, in White Papers, SL, vol. 1.

10. Chafe, *American Woman*, pp. 54–57; Clarke A. Chambers, *Seedtime of Reform: American Social Service and Social Action, 1918–1933* (Minneapolis, 1963), pp. 62–63; Mary Elizabeth Pidgeon, *The Employed Woman Homemaker in the United States: Her Responsibility for Family Support*, Women's Bureau Bulletin no. 148

(Washington, D.C., 1936), pp. 6–7. Quotation is from Florence Guy Woolston, "The Cooks of Yesterday," *New Republic* 31 (August 9, 1922): 302–4.

11. Breckinridge, *Women in the Twentieth Century*, tables 26–27 (pp. 172–73), table 29 (p. 176), and tables 32–33 (pp. 188–89); also, Chafe, *American Woman*, pp. 57–58, 89.

12. On law, see *Woman Citizen* 7 (October 7, 1922): 23. On medicine, see Alice Stone Blackwell, "Sex Prejudice among the Doctors" ibid. 6 (July 2, 1921): 15; Carson C. Hathaway, "Woman's Demand for Man's Full Civil Rights," *Current History* 17 (January 1923): 645; Carol Lopate, *Women in Medicine* (Baltimore, 1968), pp. 21–22. (By 1934 "only" 43% of hospitals had never employed a woman doctor, and only 38% of medical schools had never graduated one.) On ministry, see "Woman Defying Paul's Decree," *Literary Digest* 68 (February 5, 1921): 32–33; also, "Woman's Progress toward the Pulpit," ibid. 67 (October 23, 1920): 34; *New York Times*, April 13, 1920, 24:4. On teaching and earnings, as well as other data, see Chafe, *American Woman*, pp. 61, 89–91, and Willystine Goodsell, "The Educational Opportunities of American Women—Theoretical and Actual," *Annals* 143 (May 1929): esp. 12. In lower education, women constituted 80% of the teachers but fewer than 2% of school superintendents. On business, see *New York Times*, June 18, 1920, 17:2, and December 21, 1921, 22:5; "Woman's Place Not in the Bank," *Literary Digest* 64 (March 13, 1920): 141–43 (quotation from p. 143).

13. U.S. Bureau of Census, *Fifteenth Census of the United States: 1930—Population*, vol. 4, *Occupations, by States* (Washington, D.C., 1933), p. 69; *Recent Social Trends in the United States: Report of the President's Research Committee on Social Trends*, 2 vols. (New York, 1933), 1:666; *New York Times*, October 10, 1925, 14:4; David W. Peters, *The Status of the Married Woman Teacher* (New York, 1934), p. 23. A study of 687 women listed in the 1927 edition of *American Men* [!] *of Science* discovered that only 72 were married: Mary Jo Huth, "A Comparative Study of Women Listed in the 1900 and 1950 Editions of *Who's Who in America*" (M.A. thesis, Indiana University, 1951), pp. 17–18. For quotations of attitudes, see *New York Times*, May 20, 1923, sec. 8, 1:7, and December 16, 1928, sec. 10, 6:2; also Lorine Pruette, *Women and Leisure: A Study of Social Waste* (New York, 1924), pp. 100–101. On wives' employment, Winifred D. Wandersee, *Women's Work and Family Values, 1920–1940* (Cambridge, Mass., 1981), p. 305.

14. For enrollment and degrees, see U.S. Office of Education, *Biennial Survey of Education in the United States, 1950–1952* (Washington, D.C., 1955), chap. 1, table 33, p. 40. For marriage and employment statistics, see Mary Levy Meyer, "To See Ourselves," *Mount Holyoke Alumnae Quarterly*, Summer 1962; annual reports of the Appointment Bureau, Mount Holyoke; *New York Times*, February 21, 1926, 12:2; January 31, 1927, 21:5; May 27, 1928, sec. 5, p. 11; also *Smith College Weekly* 13 (February 21, 1923): 3; Bernice Kenyon, "Girl Graduates—Ten Years Out," *Scribner's Magazine* 89 (June 1931): 640–43; Agnes Rogers, *Vassar Women: An*

Informal Study (Poughkeepsie, N.Y., 1940), pp. 113, 151–53; Chafe, *American Woman*, p. 102.

15. Vassar graduate, quoted in *New York Times*, May 27, 1923, sec. 4, 7:1; Chase Going Woodhouse, "Married College Women in Business and the Professions," *Annals* 143 (May 1929): 327–29. For parallel survey results, see Cecil Tipton LaFollette, *A Study of the Problems of 652 Gainfully Employed Married Women Homemakers* (New York, 1934), pp. 28–29.

16. Quotation on generational split comes from Dorothy Dunbar Bromley, "Feminist—New Style," *Harper's Magazine* 155 (October 1927): 552. See also editorial, *Smith College Weekly* 11 (October 6, 1920): 2; Alyse Gregory, "The Changing Morality of Woman," *Current History* 19 (November 1923): 295–99; "The Passing of 'The Giants' in the Women's Movement," *Literary Digest* 77 (May 5, 1923): 46–50; Elizabeth Breuer, "Feminism's Awkward Age," *Harper's* 150 (April 1925): 545–51; Elizabeth Vincent, book review, *New Republic* 42 (March 25, 1925): 135; Anne O'Hagan, "The Serious-Minded Young—If Any," *Woman Citizen* 13 (April 1928): 5–7, 39; Lillian Symes, "Still a Man's Game," *Harper's* 158 (May 1929): 678–86; Elizabeth Onativia, "Give Us Our Privileges," *Scribner's Magazine* 87 (June 1930): 593–98; Elmer Davis, "The New Eve and the Old Adam," *Delineator* 116 (March 1930): 9; Hilda Worthington Smith, "The Remembered Way" (1936) pp. 273–74, typescript, in Smith Papers, folders 274–94. For typical historians' views, see O'Neill, *Everyone Was Brave*, chap. 7 ("the woman movement as a whole was dead": p. 263), and Robert W. Smuts, *Women and Work in America* (New York, 1959), p. 143.

On combining work with home, see "We Both Had Jobs," WHC 52 (August 1925): 4; "The Filth Uplifters" (editorial), LHJ 41 (August 1924): 20. Harriet Abbott, "What the Newest New Woman Is," LHJ 37 (August 1920): 154, succinctly illustrates the revised feminism. Her argument seems confused until one realizes that she is fumbling not toward old values (family), but in fact toward new ones (family and work). Throughout the early 1920s, LHJ printed numerous laudatory articles about working women: e.g., Mary Roberts Rinehart, "A Home or a Career," 38 (April 1921): 25, 53–54 (in which Rinehart also notes the passing of the "parasite woman"); Alice Ames Winter, "Careering Mothers," 44 (November 1927): 35, 120–21.

On college women, see editorial, *Smith College Weekly* 10 (December 3, 1919): 2. Also see a survey of Vassar women, *New York Times*, January 3, 1923, sec. 8, 1:6 in which 28% said marriage and career were incompatible, 19% disagreed, and 33% were uncertain. If forced to choose, a large majority chose marriage over career, but when not forced, 90% looked toward marriage and one-half also toward a career. Similarly, Pruette, *Women and Leisure*, pp. 112–24, 131, reported that 39% of her respondents (median age, 16) wanted to be wife or mother, the rest some kind of career woman; but, in a forced choice, 64% preferred home to career. For Des Moines high-school girls, see *New York Times*, June 8, 1923, 14:3. In "Accepting the Universe," *Atlantic Monthly* 129 (April 1922): 444–53, Ethel Puffer Howes stated matter-of-factly that "of course" women's colleges no longer assume that women who choose careers must be celibate.

17. Editorial, *Smith College Weekly* 10 (December 3, 1919): 2.

18. On housework times, see *Recent Social Trends*, 1:669; Mirra Komarovsky, *Women in the Modern World: Their Education and Their Dilemmas* (Boston, 1953), p. 111; Mary Elizabeth Pidgeon, *Women in the Economy of the United States of America: A Summary Report*, Women's Bureau Bulletin no. 155 (Washington, D.C., 1937); LaFollette, *Study of Women Homemakers*, chap. 6. For international comparisons, see *New York Times*, August 24, 1930, sec. 2, 1:4. For an invaluable wealth of data on appliances from which I have taken only a few samples, see Mary Sherman, "The Housewife in the Big City," WHC 53 (May 1926): 32, 36, "The Small-Town Woman Speaks," 53 (June 1926): 28, 58–60, "The Home Equipment Survey," 53 (November 1926): 15, 111–12, "Heat and Light in America's Homes," 54 (January 1927): 4, 94, and "Where the American Family Finds Its Recreation," 54 (February 1927): 32, 78; also, Mary Sumner Boyd, "Department of Agriculture Extension Work with Women," *Woman Citizen* 5 (April 2, 1921): 1128–30.

On servants, see Robert Lynd and Helen Lynd, *Middletown: A Study in American Culture* (New York, 1929), pp. 169–71, and *Middletown in Transition: A Study in Cultural Conflicts* (New York, 1937), p. 197.

19. Elsie M. Hill to Jane Norman Smith, March 10, 1925, in Smith Papers, folder 62. For her later party work, see Hill to Smith, March 14, 1933, folder 82. On wifehood and wife-ing it, see Anne Herendeen, "Wife-ing It," *Woman Citizen* 13 (November 1928): 12. According to a poll of all married women listed in *Who's Who*, four-fifths were successfully combining careers and marriage: "Can a Woman Run a Home and a Job, Too?" *Literary Digest* 75 (November 11, 1922): 40. Margaret F. Dunaway Journal, vol. 1, pt. 2, April 26, 1929, and [February 1929], and Journal, vol. 1, pt. 1, December 6, 1928, in Dunaway Papers, SL. Edith Clark, "Trying to Be Modern," *Nation* 125 (August 17, 1927): 153–55. For frequency of phasing of career and motherhood, see LaFollette, *Study of Women Homemakers*, pp. 36–37, and Woodhouse, "Married College Women," pp. 325–338.

20. Mary Alden Hopkins, "Fifty-Fifty Wives," *Woman Citizen* 7 (April 7, 1923): 13.

21. "The Home-Plus-Job Woman," *Woman Citizen* 10 (March 1926): 15–16, 45; E. Davenport, "When Father Helps with the Wash," LHJ 38 (June 1921): 83, 98; Joseph Morschauser, "Divorce," WHC 52 (January 1925): 24, 90; *New York Times*, July 29, 1926, 21:4, Ruth La Y'La, "Should Husbands Do Housework?" *Good Housekeeping* 82 (January 1926): 18–19, 101; Ira S. Wile and Mary Day Winn, *Marriage in the Modern Manner* (New York, 1929), pp. 47–48.

On fifty-fifty marriages, see Eleanor Gilbert, "Why I Hate My Independence," LHJ 37 (March 1920): 139–40; "We Both Had Jobs," WHC 52 (August 1925): 4, 34; Frances Duncan Manning, "Charting the Sea of Matrimony," WHC

53 (January 1926): 4, 44; "The Fifty-Fifty Husband," WHC 55 (April 1928): 31, 130. For a fictional account, see Katharine Brush, *Young Man of Manhattan* (New York, 1930).

On survey of housework allocation, see LaFollette, *Study of Women Homemakers*, chap. 6. Because sociologists made only a few studies of household relationships in the 1920s, the evidence is sparse. But it parallels the results of studies after the Second World War, e.g., F. Ivan Nye and Lois Wladis Hoffman, *The Employed Mother in America* (Chicago, 1963), pp. 222–23, 236–37, 244–45.

22. Alice Ames Winter, "What Is Your Market Value, Madam?" WHC 50 (January 1923): 18, 82; Ethel Puffer Howes and Myra Reed Richardson, "We Women," WHC 50 (February 1923): 15–16; Anna Steese Richardson, "What about the Children?" WHC 58 (January 1931): 21–22; *Smith College Weekly* 10 (December 3, 1919): 2; Alice Beal Parsons, *Woman's Dilemma* (New York, 1926), pp. 217–48; letters, *Woman Citizen* 5 (August 7, 1920): 252–53; William Carl Jordan, "The History, Scope, and Prospects for the Future of the Nursery School Movement" (Ph.D. diss., Harvard, 1950), pp. 84, 90; Mary Dabney Davis, *Nursery Schools: Their Development and Current Practices in the United States*, U.S. Office of Education Bulletin no. 9, 1932 (Washington, D.C., 1933), pp. 1, 19, 25, 31. In a letter to W. I. Thomas, April 28, 1920, Ethel Sturges Dummer notes that her daughter and son-in-law were forced by inflation to give up their plan for "a cooperative housing scheme with central kitchen and heating": Dummer Papers, SL, folder 785. Contrary to O'Neill, *Everyone Was Brave*, p. 325, I do not believe that "an audience for their [Gilmanite] message no longer existed."

For examples of traditional child-care advice, see Vera L. Connolly, "Parents, Wake Up!" *Good Housekeeping* 77 (July 1923): 67, 168–74, and Arthur H. Sutherland, "Your Child's Emotions," WHC 53 (February 1926): 4, 170. For new advice, see Mary B. Mullett, "Are You This Woman?" WHC 53 (March 1926), 4, 77–83; Dorothy Dunbar Bromley, "This Maternal Instinct," *Harper's Magazine* 159 (September 1929): 423–33; *New York Times*, November 23, 1929, 22:5; M. K. Wisehart, "What Is a Wife's Job Today?" *Good Housekeeping* 91 (August 1930): 34–35, 166–73; Ernest R. Groves, *The Drifting Home* (Boston and New York, 1926), p. 82. On fathers, see Frederick Arnold Kummer, "The Father in Child Training," *Good Housekeeping* 75 (July 1922): 27, 147–51; *New York Times*, November 1, 1925, sec. 9, 10:1; Grace Nies Fletcher, "Bringing Up Fathers," LHJ 44 (September 1927): 35, 199–203. On mothers' attitudes, see Dorothy Canfield Fisher, "Aren't You Glad You're Not Your Grandmother?" *Good Housekeeping* 74 (April 1922): 169; Lynd, *Middletown*, pp. 143, 147, 149–50; *The Nursery School as Social Experiment: Conference Called by the Institute for the Co-ordination of Women's Interests at Smith College's Commencement*, June 17, 1927 (Northampton, Mass., 1928), p. 29.

23. *New York Times*, November 1, 1925, sec. 9, 6:1; Ethel Puffer Howes, "The Progress of the Institute for the Co-ordination of Women's Interests," *Report at Alumnae Conference*, October 12, 1928 (Northampton, Mass., 1928), esp. pp. 7–9,

13–18, 20, in Smith College Archives. See also Howes, "The Meaning of Progress in the Woman Movement," Annals 143 (May 1929): 17–20. Chafe, American Woman, pp. 100–101, 103, capsulates the institute's history but misinterprets Howes's view of home economics. On the School of Euthenics, see Chafe, pp. 103–4; New York Times, May 23, 1926, sec. 9, 8:1, and May 5, 1929, sec. 5, p. 21; Mildred Adams, "The Whole Family Studies 'Euthenics,'" Woman Citizen 11 (September 1926): 5–7, 40.

24. The specific reasons for the institute's demise are not clear. According to an executive of the Laura Spelman Rockefeller Memorial Foundation, which funded and then defunded it, Smith faculty members disdained its interests and thus canceled it: Lawrence K. Frank to Thomas Mendenhall, January 8, 1960, in Smith Archives. But the Depression may also have been the reason.

Quotations come from Mount Holyoke News, February 21, 1931, quoted in Arthur C. Cole, A Hundred Years of Mount Holyoke College: The Evolution of an Educational Ideal (New Haven, 1940), p. 333; anonymous letter, Smith College Weekly 22 (March 2, 1932): 2. Also see letters in response, Smith Weekly 22 (March 9, 1932): 2. On home economics, see Louise Stanley, "Home-Making Education in the Colleges," Annals 143 (May 1929): 361–67; New York Times, May 1, 1932, sec. 5, p. 21; Mabel Newcomer, A Century of Higher Education for Women (New York, 1959), p. 58.

For male views, see President Henry Nobel MacCracken of Vassar in New York Times, May 23, 1926, sec. 9, 8:1; President Charles Richmond of Skidmore, New York Times, November 17, 1925, 24:8, "Why I Am Glad I Married a College Girl," WHC 52 (February 1925): 25–26, 52; "Beginning 1930" (editorial) LHJ 47 (January 1930): 22; Chafe, American Woman, pp. 104–6. On polls, see New York Times, April 6, 1930, sec. 2, 3:2, Phyllis Blanchard and Carlyn Manasses, New Girls for Old (New York, 1930), pp. 174–75.

25. Quotations are from Mary Lathrop in New York Times, August 19, 1930, 16:3 and Mildred Adams, "Woman Sets a Pace for Busy New York," ibid., October 12, 1930, sec. 5, p. 5. On the double burden, Symes, "Still a Man's Game," pp. 678–86. Likewise, Onativia, "Give us Our Privileges," pp. 597–98; Blanchard and Manasses, New Girls, p. 175; Jane Allen, "You May Have My Job," Forum 87 (April 1932): 228–31; editorial, New York Times, September 13, 1929, 28:4; Margaret Banning, "The Future of Marriage: A Socratic Dialogue," Forum 86 (August 1931): 76.

26. Charlotte Perkins Gilman: "The New Generation of Women," Current History 18 (August 1923): 735–36; "His Religion and Hers, II: What Her Religion Will Do for the World," Century Magazine 105 (April 1923): 859; "Toward Monogamy," Nation 118 (June 11, 1924): 672; "Parasitism and Civilized Vice," in Woman's Coming of Age, ed. V. F. Calverton and S. D. Schmalhausen (New York, 1931), p. 125.

27. Fitzgerald, quoted in Frederick J. Hoffman, The Twenties: American Writing

in the Postwar Decade (New York, 1955), p. 89; Helen Bullitt Lowry, "Mrs. Grundy and Miss 1921," *New York Times*, January 23, 1921, sec. 3, p. 1; Ellen Welles Page, "A Flapper's Appeal to Parents," *Outlook* 132 (December 6, 1922): 607; Warner Fabian, *Flaming Youth* (New York, 1923); Groves, *Drifting Home*, pp. 111–12, 118–19; Martha P. Falconer, "The Girl of To-day," *Journal of Social Hygiene* 8 (October 1922): 369–73; Gertrude Atherton, *Black Oxen* (New York, 1923), p. 44. For other samples of this "generation" theme, see Lucian Cary, "Is Flapperism Making Our Colleges Unsafe for Youth?" *McCall's* 50 (October 1922): 5, 40–52; Fletcher, "Bringing Up Fathers," pp. 35, 199–203; John F. Carter, Jr., "'These Wild Young People,'" *Atlantic Monthly* 126 (September 1920): 301–4.

28. On the concept of "generation," see Bennett Berger, "How Long Is a Generation?" *British Journal of Sociology* 11 (1960): 553–68. On prewar youth, see the discussion in Chapter 2. On Middletown mores, see Lynd, *Middletown*, pp. 138–39. For an explanation in terms of war, see, e.g., Fletcher, "Bringing Up Fathers," pp. 35, 199–203; Gregory, "Changing Morality of Woman," p. 298; Gene Stratton-Porter, "Educating Mother," *McCall's* 51 (July 1924): 2, 39–40, 77; Carter, "'These Wild Young People,'" pp. 301–4.

29. On literature, movies, and theater, see Paul S. Boyer, *Purity in Print: The Vice-Society Movement and Book Censorship in America* (New York, 1968), pp. 89–90; editorial, *New Republic* 33 (February 14, 1923): 306; "The Woman Theatre Public" (editorial), *Woman Citizen* 11 (April 1927): 29; Catherine Beach Ely, "Life in the Raw," *North American Review* 226 (November 1928): 566–69; Hugh L. McMenamin, "Evils of Woman's Revolt against the Old Standards," *Current History* 27 (October 1927): 30–32; Lillian Symes, "The New Masculinism," *Harper's Magazine* 161 (June 1930): 98–107. On boxing, see *New York Times*, October 2, 1922, 8:5. On drinking, see *New York Times*, March 15, 1922, 12:3; Margaret Culkin Banning, "Lit Ladies," *Harper's* 160 (January 1930): 162; "This Moderate Drinking," ibid. 162 (March 1931): 426. For examples of blame of women, see Frank Crane, "The Flapper," *Collier's* 74 (October 11, 1924): 23; *New York Times*, January 10, 1924, 7:1, and January 31, 1924, 6:4.

The discussion of smoking is voluminous. Quotations come from editorial, *New York Times*, July 17, 1925, 14:5; February 14, 1922, 8:3; June 23, 1921, 19:4; July 10, 1925, 6:1. On male attitudes, see *New York Times*, March 28, 1922, 1:6, and June 21, 1921, 1:4. For views of etiquette authorities, see Arthur M. Schlesinger, *Learning How to Behave: A Historical Study of American Etiquette Books* (New York, 1946), pp. 52–53, 55–56. For attempts to prohibit smoking, see e.g., *New York Times*, June 25, 1920, 10:6; March 6, 1924, 1:5; October 17, 1929, 1:7. For spread of smoking, see *New York Times*, January 29, 1920, 9:3; May 7, 1930, 6:4; "Women, Religion, and Cigarets," *Literary Digest* 96 (January 28, 1928): 28–29; Harry Burke, "Women Cigarette Fiends," LHJ 39 (June 1922): 19, 132; Frances Perkins, "Can They Smoke Like Gentlemen?" *New Republic* 62 (May 7, 1930): 319–20.

Smoking on college campuses was an especially heated issue, and as late as 1933 the students (usually by their own rulings) in leading women's and co-educational colleges were permitted to smoke only in restricted areas or not at all. For example, see (re Smith) *New York Times*, December 19, 1926, sec. 2, 7:3; *Smith College Weekly* 22 (May 11, 1932): 3; (Mount Holyoke) *New York Times*, November 20, 1925, 43:1; (Goucher) *New York Times*, May 18, 1924, sec. 8, 2:7; (Bryn Mawr) *New York Times*, November 24, 1925, 1:6; (Swarthmore) *New York Times*, January 19, 1930, sec. 2, 6:7; (Northwestern) *New York Times*, March 29, 1930, 4:6; (Salem and other North Carolina colleges) *Raleigh News and Observer*, September 8, 1931, p. 1.

30. Fabian, *Flaming Youth*, preface; *New York Times*, February 17, 1922, 1:2.

31. Alfred C. Kinsey et al., *Sexual Behavior in the Human Female* (Philadelphia, 1953), pp. 242–43, 298–99; Lewis H. Terman, *Psychological Factors in Marital Happiness* (New York, 1938), pp. 320–21; Mervin B. Freedman, *The College Experience* (San Francisco, 1967), pp. 108–9; Blanchard and Manasses, *New Girls*, chap. 5; Duke *Chronicle*, April 25, 1923, quoted by Paula Fass, *The Damned and the Beautiful: American Youth in the 1920s* (New York, 1977), p. 264. I have found Fass's book, esp. pp. 262–79, to be extremely helpful.

32. "'My Children, Too!'" *Woman Citizen* 11 (March 1927): 13–14, 38. For other feminists' horror, see Anna Garlin Spencer to Edith Houghton Hooker, December 18, 1920, typed copy, in Dummer Paper, SL, folder 403; Catt and Addams, quoted in *New York Times*, January 17, 1926, 20:1, and June 30, 1926, 12:1; Mary Gray Peck to Carrie Chapman Catt, December 5, 1928, in NAWSA Papers, LC, box 24; Harriet B. Laidlaw, review of Sherwood Eddy's *Sex and Youth*, in *Birth Control Review* (September 1929), copy, in Laidlaw Papers, SL, folder 27.

33. Quotations come from Gregory, "Changing Morality of Woman," p. 299, and *Ohio State Lantern*, January 9, 1922, quoted by Fass, *Damned and Beautiful*, p. 307. On "sentimentality," see Dorothie Sharp, "'Flappers and Philosophers,'" *McCall's* 50 (May 1923): 24; Aldrich, "Confessions of a Breadwinner," pt. 2, pp. 3–4; "Ten Years after the Divorce," *Harper's Magazine* 165 (August 1932): 318. On "puritanism," see Clement Wood, "Modern Sex Morality," *New Republic* 36 (September 12, 1923): 68–70; Vincent, book review, ibid. 42 (March 25, 1925): 135; Ex-feminist [pseud.], "The Harm My Education Did Me," *Outlook*, 147 (November 30, 1927): 397; G. V. Hamilton and Kenneth MacGowan, *What Is Wrong with Marriage* (New York, 1929), pp. 49–50; O'Hagan, "The Serious-Minded Young," p. 40; Frances Woodward Prentice, "The Confused Generation," *Scribner's Magazine* 91 (January 1932): 50–51; Edna Ferber, *The Girls* (Garden City, N.Y., 1921), esp. pp. 187, 254.

34. The preceding paragraphs are a composite from the following sources: Gregory, "Changing Morality of Woman," pp. 295–99; Adele Clark, "New Voters and an Old Cause," *Woman Citizen* 11 (October 1926): 30; O'Hagan, "The Serious-Minded Young," pp. 5–7, 39; Julia Adams, "The 'Serious Young' Speak Up,"

Woman Citizen 13 (May 1928): 8–9; Elinor Rowland Wembridge, "The Girl Tribe—An Anthropological Study," *Survey* 60 (May 1, 1928): 156–59, 197–99; Breuer, "Feminism's Awkward Age," pp. 545–51; Bromley, "Feminist—New Style," pp. 552–60. Also, *New York Times*, March 17, 1923, 10:3, and July 2, 1922, sec. 7, 3:6; Ruth Hooper, "Flapping Not Repented Of," *Times*, July 16, 1922, sec. 3, 13:1; "The Toleration of Unconventional Opinions about Sex," *New Republic* 36 (October 10, 1923): 168–70; Isabel Leavenworth, "Virtue and Women," *Nation* 119 (July 9, 1924): 42–44; Lorine Pruette, "Should Men Be Protected," *Nation* 125 (August 31, 1927): 200–201; Rheta C. Dorr, A *Woman of Fifty* (New York, 1924), pp. 446–48.

35. For a convenient synopsis, see Edwin O. Smigel and Rita Seiden, "The Decline and Fall of the Double Standard," *Annals* 376 (March 1968): 7–17.

36. On public reaction to the novel, see Mark Schorer, *Sinclair Lewis: An American Life* (New York, 1961), pp. 268–72. Quotations come from Sinclair Lewis, *Main Street: The Story of Carol Kennicott* (New York, 1920), pp. 195, 422, 425, 439, 442.

37. Schorer, *Sinclair Lewis*, pp. 207–9, 428, 430, 431, 486, 488, 503, 538, 576, 629, 744; Vincent Sheean, *Dorothy and Red* (Boston, 1963), pp. 33–34, 296, 298, 299–300.

38. F. Scott Fitzgerald, *The Great Gatsby* (New York, 1925), p. 133; John Dos Passos to Arthur McComb, May 7, 1918, quoted in Melvin Landsberg, *Dos Passos' Path to U.S.A.: A Political Biography, 1912–1936* (Boulder, Colo., 1972), pp. 57–58. See also Hoffman, *The Twenties*, pp. 58–60. On soldiers' silence and quotation from diary, Dixon Wecter, *When Johnny Comes Marching Home* (Boston, 1944), pp. 315–20; also, on effect of war, see Stanley Cooperman, *World War I and the American Novel* (Baltimore, 1967), pp. 47–48, 63–64, 72; James G. Dunton, ed., *C'est la Guerre: The Best Stories of the World War* (Boston, 1927), p. xii and passim; Parkhurst Whitney, "Brothers in Arms," *American Legion Monthly* 4 (March 1929): 16–17.

39. Quotation from Philip Curtiss, "Is Fame Becoming Extinct?" *Harper's Magazine* 140 (May 1920): 849–52. Likewise, Reinhold Niebuhr, "Heroes and Hero Worship," *Nation* 112 (February 13, 1921): 293. Polls are in "The Boys' Leading Hero," *Literary Digest* 96 (February 11, 1928): 31–32, and Dixon Wecter, *The Hero in America: A Chronicle of Hero-Worship* (New York, 1941), p. 434.

40. On manhood and sports, see "Football as Our Greatest Popular Spectacle," *Literary Digest* 75 (December 2, 1922): 52–57; "The Greatest of All Sport Years," ibid. 76 (January 13, 1923): 58; "Sport Is Elected" (editorial) *Nation* 119 (September 17, 1924): 278; John W. Heisman, "Here Are Men," *Collier's* 87 (November 16, 1929): 25, 44–46; Grantland Rice, "The Stuff Men Are Made Of," ibid. 76 (October 25, 1925): 27; Walter Camp, "What Makes a Champion," ibid. 72 (September 29, 1923): 9–10; "How Football Fosters Fair Play and Clean Living," *Literary Digest* 87 (October 31, 1925): 57–58; "Football or Baseball the National Game?" ibid. 83 (December 6, 1924): 66; "The Big Game," *Outlook* 126 (November 24, 1920): 541–42; George Marvin, "The Big Business of Football," ibid. 135

(October 3, 1923): 183–87. On death, see Edith Wyschogrod, "Sport, Death, and the Elemental," in *The Phenomenon of Death: Faces of Mortality*, ed. Wyschogrod (New York, 1973). On commercialism, see "Football—the Frankenstein of Athletics," *Literary Digest* 79 (December 1, 1923): 52–56; "Shall Intercollegiate Football Be Abolished?" ibid. 87 (October 10, 1925): 68–76; "Football under Fire," *Outlook* 141 (December 16, 1925): 588–89; John R. Tunis, "The Great God Football," *Harper's Magazine* 157 (November 1928): 742–52; Tunis, "American Sports and American Life," *Nation* 130 (June 25, 1930): 729–30.

41. All quotations come from John W. Ward, "The Meaning of Lindbergh's Flight," *American Quarterly* 10 (1958): 3–16. On the Scout *Handbook*, see Wecter, *Hero in America*, p. 433.

42. On occupational data, see Breckinridge, *Women in the Twentieth Century*, table 27 (p. 173), table 29b (p. 176), and table 33 (p. 189); also, Bureau of Census, *Historical Statistics*, p. 74; Daniel R. Miller and Guy E. Swanson, *The Changing American Parent: A Study in the Detroit Area* (New York, 1958), table 2-1, p. 45 and p. 48. On attitudes, see Victor H. Vroom, *Work and Motivation* (New York, 1964), pp. 129–45; Nancy S. Morse and Robert S. Weiss, "The Function and Meaning of Work and the Job," *American Sociological Review* 20 (April 1955): 191–98; Edward Earle Purinton, "Making Workers Like Their Work," *Independent* 99 (September 20, 1919): 408, 427–42; Charles Merz, "Smoke-Stacks in Eden," *Century Magazine* 106 (May 1923): 116–23. The higher death rate for middle-aged men than for women in Chicago during the 1920s suggests the price of the male "struggle for existence": "Middle Life Is Hard on Men," *Survey* 65 (November 15, 1930): 216.

43. Grocery executive is quoted in "Motion Is Money, Says This Man, Who Has Plenty of Both," *Literary Digest* 66 (July 10, 1920): 79; factory manager, in Alfred J. Lotka, "Why Men Work," *Independent* 99 (July 12, 1919): 55. For Standard Oil executive and other information, see James Warren Prothro, *Dollar Decade: Business Ideas in the 1920s* (Baton Rouge, La., 1954), pp. 28–29, 66–67, and Christine Frederick, "Man's Business and the Woman's," *Outlook* 148 (February 1, 1923): 168, 188–89.

44. Prothro, *Dollar Decade*, p. 73; William E. Leuchtenburg, *The Perils of Prosperity* (Chicago, 1958), pp. 198–99; Irvin G. Wyllie, *The Self-Made Man in America: The Myth of Rags to Riches* (New Brunswick, N.J., 1954), pp. 168–70; Merle Curti, *The Growth of American Thought*, 3d ed. (New York, 1964), p. 680; Bruce Barton, *The Man Nobody Knows: A Discovery of the Real Jesus* (Indianapolis, 1925), p. 140 and passim; Lynd, *Middletown*, pp. 80–81. For a Rotarian's comment on Jesus that was identical with Barton's see Lynd, p. 304n.

45. For a rare statement of discontent, with dreams of wild oats and South Seas, see letter from "A Husband," *Nation* 124 (January 12, 1927): 39.

46. Charles F. Marden, *Rotary and Its Brothers: An Analysis and Interpretation of the Men's Service Club* (Princeton, N.J., 1935), esp. pp. 4–5, 10, 82–83; Lynd, *Middletown*, pp. 304–6.

47. Quotations come from Lynd, *Middletown*, pp. 177–78; Pruette, "Should Men Be Protected?" p. 200; Belle Squire, "Love and the Law," *Collier's* 66 (September 4, 1920): 12, 23–24. On family breakdown, see Whiting Williams, "What's on the Working Woman's Mind?" *Scribner's Magazine* 85 (April 1929): 460–66; Thomas Woody, *A History of Women's Education in the United States*, 2 vols. (New York, 1929), 2:50; Groves, *Drifting Home*, pp. 2–3, 41–42, 185; *New York Times*, March 23, 1925, 16:4, and February 6, 1926, 18:1; Willystine Goodsell, *Problems of the Family* (New York, 1928), pp. v, 420, 435; Kathleen Norris, "Home: The Center of the World," *Pictorial Review* 30 (February 1929): 14–15, 74. On partnership, see *New York Times*, June 3, 1923, sec. 8, 1:6; "—'and Obey,'" *Literary Digest* 86 (September 26, 1925): 33–34; [Lou Rogers], "Lighting Speed through Life," *Nation* 124 (April 13, 1927): 395–97; Margaret F. Dunaway Journal, vol. 1, pt. 1, December 8, [1928], in Dunaway Papers; Corinne Roosevelt Robinson, "Is Divorce the Way Out?" *North American Review* 226 (July 1928): 41; Wile and Winn, *Marriage in Modern Manner*, pp. 47–48, 123; Davis, "The New Eve and the Old Adam," pp. 9, 79–80; Wisehart, "What Is a Wife's Job Today?" p. 35; references on fifty-fifty marriages in note 21.

48. Quotations come from Gwen Warren, letter to *New York Times*, September 11, 1926, 14:7, and Fletcher, "Bringing Up Fathers," p. 35. On housewives' wages, see *New York Times*, January 21, 1921, 15:7; William Johnson, "The Best Job for a Girl," *Good Housekeeping* 78 (June 1924): 215; editorial, *Nation* 118 (March 19, 1924): 297; Doris Stevens, "Wages for Wives," *Nation* 122 (January 27, 1926): 81–83; Elizabeth J. Hecker, "Wages for Wives," *Nation* 122 (April 14, 1926): 400–401.

49. Quotation from Bent, "Woman's Place Is in the Home," p. 212.

50. Quotations come from Merle Farmer Murphy, "Poor Dad," *Independent* 114 (January 31, 1925): 127, 129; Henry R. Carey, "The Two-headed Monster—the Family," *Harper's Magazine* 156 (January 1928): 169; "Have I Stolen My Husband's Birthright?" WHC 54 (August 1927): 4, 57. See also Will Durant, "The Modern Woman," *Century Magazine* 113 (February 1927): 422; Donald R. Makosky, "The Portrayal of Women in Wide-Circulation Magazine Short Stories, 1905–1955" (Ph.D. diss., University of Pennsylvania 1966), pp. 217–18, 244–50. For sociological data, see *Recent Social Trends*, 1:700–701; Hamilton and MacGowan, *What Is Wrong with Marriage*, p. 807.

51. Quotations from Fabian, *Flaming Youth*, pp. 143–44, 152, and Lindsey, *Companionate Marriage* (1927), cited in Charles Larsen, *The Good Fight: The Life and Times of Ben B. Lindsey* (Chicago, 1972), pp. 170–71. For traditional male view see Eugene Lyman Fisk, "'Our Girls!'" *Good Housekeeping* 72 (May 1921): 170; "Woman and the Weed," pp. 31–32; *New York Times*, August 14, 1927, sec. 2, 7:2, and January 22, 1923, sec. 3, 5:7; E. W. Howe, "These Women!" *Forum* 83 (April 1930): 245–46. On orgasm, see Kinsey et al., *Sexual Behavior in the Human Female*, pp. 356–57, and table 97, p. 397. For suggestive data on frequency of female adultery, see Hamilton and MacGowan, *What Is Wrong with Marriage*, p. 285. On sexu-

ality, see "Today's Morals and Manners: The Side of 'the Girls,'" *Literary Digest* 70 (July 9, 1921): 34–42; Parsons, "Changes in Sex Relations," pp. 551–53; Joseph Collins, "The Foundering of the Good Ship Matrimony," *Bookman* 64 (February 1927): 697; Pruette, "Should Men Be Protected?" p. 201; Wile and Winn, *Marriage in Modern Manner*, p. 28; Blanchard and Manasses, *New Girls*, p. 196; Banning, "The Future of Marriage," pp. 76–77.

52. On birth control, see Parsons, "Changes in Sex Relations," p. 552; Ernest R. Groves and William Fielding Ogburn, *American and Family Relationships* (New York, 1928), pp. 54–55; Paul Popenoe, *Modern Marriage: A Handbook* (New York, 1925), pp. 162–68; Lynd, *Middletown*, p. 123; James Reed, *From Private Vice to Public Virtue: The Birth Control Movement and American Society since 1830* (New York, 1978), pp. 43–45, 123–25; Katharine Bement Davis, *Factors in the Sex Life of Twenty-two Hundred Women* (New York, 1929), p. 14; David M. Kennedy, *Birth Control in America: The Career of Margaret Sanger* (New Haven, 1970), pp. 136–37, 140–41. On marital roles, see Michael Gordon and M. Charles Bernstein, "Mate Choice and Domestic Life in the Nineteenth-Century Marriage Manual," *Journal of Marriage and the Family* 32 (November 1970): 671; Michael Gordon and Penelope J. Shankweiler, "Different Equals Less: Female Sexuality in Recent Marriage Manuals," ibid. 33 (August 1971): 460–461; Beatrice M. Hinkle, "Women and the New Morality," *Nation* 119 (November 19, 1924): 541; idem "Chaos of Marriage," *Harper's Magazine* 152 (December 1925): 1–13; Smiley Blanton and Woodbridge Riley, "Shell Shocks of Family Life," *Forum* (November 1929): 282–89; Frederick, "Man Problem," pp. 8, 21; Hamilton and MacGowan, *What Is Wrong with Marriage*, pp. 23, 57, 278. On male inadequacy fears, see Charles E. Rosenberg, "Sexuality, Class, and Role in Nineteenth-Century America," *American Quarterly* 25 (Summer 1973): 149.

53. On Lindsey controversy, see Larsen, *Good Fight*, pp. 162, 174–76. Wife's complaint is quoted by Lynd, *Middletown*, pp. 118–19. On marital relationship, see Wile and Winn, *Marriage in Modern Manner*, p. 235; Wood, "Modern Sex Morality," p. 69; Hamilton and MacGowan, *What Is Wrong with Marriage*, p. 57; Norris, "Home," p. 15; Florence Guy Woolston, "The Sheltered Sex," *New Republic* 34 (April 4, 1923): 161–63.

54. *Michigan Daily*, May 11, 1920, quoted in Dorothy Gies McGuigan, *A Dangerous Experiment: One Hundred Years of Women at the University of Michigan* (Ann Arbor, Mich., 1970), p. 110.

55. Quoted in Nancy Milford, *Zelda* (New York, 1971), p. 320.

6. THE LONG AMNESIA: DEPRESSION, WAR, AND DOMESTICITY

1. John Burke, *Winged Legend: The Story of Amelia Earhart* (New York, 1970), pp. 96–97; Eunice Fuller Barnard, "Feminism Now Battles on a New Front," *New York Times*, July 3, 1932, sec. 6, p. 11. For feminist interpretations of female aviation,

see Vera L. Connolly, "Daughters of the Sky," *Delineator* 115 (August 1929): 9, 81–83; "The Women's Air Derby," *Literary Digest* 102 (September 7, 1929): 9; Margery Brown, "Flying Is Changing Women," *Pictorial Review* 31 (June 1930): 30, 108–9.

2. Quotations come from William Henry Chafe, *The American Woman: Her Changing Social, Economic, and Political Roles, 1920–1970* (New York, 1972), pp. 107–8, and *New York Times*, June 4, 1939, 7:1. For polls, see Hadley Cantril, ed., *Public Opinion, 1935–1946* (Princeton, N.J., 1951), p. 1044. For prohibitions, see *New York Times*, May 21, 1937, 11:4; July 3, 1937, 13:3; March 29, 1939, 25:7; also David W. Peters, *The Status of the Married Woman Teacher* (New York, 1934), p. 23; "Marriage and Teaching," *Newsweek* 12 (August 1, 1938): 28; *Life and Labor* 10 (March 1940): 3; *New York Times*, April 14, 1940, sec. 2, 6:1; Mary Anderson, *Woman at Work: The Autobiography of Mary Anderson as Told to Mary N. Winslow* (Minneapolis, 1951), pp. 155–56; Edith Valet Cook, *The Married Woman and Her Job* (Washington, D.C., 1936), pp. 5–6, in Maud Wood Park Papers, SL, folder 744. For protests, see *New York Times*, June 22, 1939, 25:5, and July 12, 1939, 1:2; "Should Wives Work?" (editorial) LHJ 58 (January 1941): 4, 35; "Working Wives" (editorial) WHC 66 (October 1939): 2; Peters, *Status of Woman Teacher*, p. 13.

3. On reactions to fascism, see *New York Times*, May 3, 1935, 21:4; July 17, 1935, 21:8; July 19, 1935, 10:1; also, Alice Paul to Jane Norman Smith, November 7, 1934, Geneva, in Smith Papers, SL, folder 116. On unemployment, see Mary Elizabeth Pidgeon, *Trends in the Employment of Women, 1928–1936*, Women's Bureau Bulletin no. 159 (Washington, D.C., 1938); Elizabeth D. Benham, *The Woman Wage Earner: Her Situation Today*, Women's Bureau Bulletin no. 172 (Washington, D.C., 1939), pp. 48–49; Chafe, *American Woman*, p. 270, n. 20; S. A. Stouffer, P. F. Lazarsfeld, and A. J. Jaffee, *Research Memorandum on the Family in the Depression*, Social Science Research Council Bulletin no. 29 (1937), p. 28. Quotation on single women comes from Mary Simkhovitch, quoted in Lorena A. Hickok Report, October 2–12, [1933], New York City, in Harry L. Hopkins Papers, Franklin D. Roosevelt Library, box 61. On dependents, see Mary Elizabeth Pidgeon, *Women in the Economy of the United States of America: A Summary Report*, Women's Bureau Bulletin no. 155 (Washington, D.C., 1937), pp. 80, 82; *New York Times*, December 2, 1934, sec. 2, 1:7, and March 6, 1938, sec. 6, 5:2. On displacement of men, see Pidgeon, *Women in the Economy*, p. 44, and Chafe, *American Woman*, p. 271, n. 22.

4. Quotations come from Hickok Report, December 4, 1933, Sioux City, Iowa, in Hopkins Papers, box 61. See *New York Times*, August 3, 1933, 16:5; on poll data, Cantril, *Public Opinion*, p. 1044.

5. Chafe, *American Woman*, pp. 58–59 and 270, n. 20; *New York Times*, March 13, 1932, sec. 9, 5:1; Benham, *Woman Wage Earner*, p. 50; Ishbel Ross, "Girls Must Work," LHJ 53 (June 1936): 32–33, 91–96; National Manpower Council, *Womanpower* (New York, 1957), table 13, p. 169.

6. On LWV, see Chafe, *American Woman*, p. 115; *New York Times*, August 22, 1937, 7:2. On Woman's Party, see Jane Norman Smith to Alice Paul, January 13, 1934, and February 26, 1933, carbon copies, in Smith Papers, folders 116, 155; Sarah Pell to Smith, July 27, 1937, in Smith Papers, folder 91; Gretta Palmer, "A Truce with Men," SEP 209 (June 5, 1937): 12. On political office-holding, see Chafe, *American Woman*, pp. 40–44; *New York Times*, December 22, 1940, sec. 2, 5:2. For poll on woman president, see Cantril, *Public Opinion*, p. 1052.

7. *New York Times*, April 20, 1940, 13:7.

8. In creating this composite portrait of a typical middle-class family, I have drawn upon a variety of sources, particularly Mirra Komarovsky, *The Unemployed Man and His Family: The Effect of Unemployment upon the Status of the Man in Fifty-nine Families* (New York, 1940); E. Wight Bakke, *Citizens without Work: A Study of the Effects of Unemployment upon the Workers' Social Relations and Practices* (New Haven, 1940), pp. 111–19, 183, 198–99, and passim; Caroline Bird, *The Invisible Scar* (New York, 1966), esp. pp. 59–62, 274–75; Robert Lynd and Helen Lynd, *Middletown in Transition: A Study in Cultural Conflicts* (New York, 1937); and my own conversations with a myriad of middle-aged and elderly North Carolinians in the spring of 1973: see Peter Filene, "Recapturing the Thirties: History as Theater," *Change: The Magazine of Higher Learning* 6 (February 1974): 40–44.

9. Quotations from Hickok Report, May 4, 1934, Phoenix, Ariz., in Hopkins Papers, box 61; Komarovsky, *Unemployed Man*, pp. 80–81.

10. Komarovsky, *Unemployed Man*, pp. 43, 44, 86, 98, Bakke, *Citizens without Work*, pp. 10–14, 115, 184–85, 199, 202; Bird, *Invisible Scar*, pp. 50, 59–60. On intercourse, see Komarovsky, pp. 28, 130–33; Roger Campbell, "The Attrition of the Male Image during the Great Depression" (M.A. thesis, Stetson, 1968), pp. 31–32.

11. "Man at the Fireside," *Harper's Magazine* 166 (May 1933): 750–58; David Allen Bates, "A Husband Turns Housewife," *Forum* 101 (January 1939): 8–10; Dorothy Cole Randolph, "I Support My Husband," WHC 64 (March 1937): 24, 144; James H. S. Bossard, "Children in a Depression Decade," *Annals* 212 (November 1940): 80–81.

12. Arthur M. Schlesinger, Jr., *The Age of Roosevelt: The Coming of the New Deal* (Boston, 1959), pp. 269, 272–73; Bird, *Invisible Scar*, pp. 130–34, 198, 274; William E. Leuchtenburg, *Franklin D. Roosevelt and the New Deal* (New York, 1963), pp. 120–30; Lynd, *Middletown in Transition*, chap. 4.

13. Quotation comes from Leuchtenburg, *Roosevelt*, p. 119.

14. Komarovsky, *Unemployed Man*, pp. 23, 54, 68, 106 (quotation on p. 56); Ruth Shonle Cavan and Katherine Howland Ranck, *The Family and the Depression: A Study of One Hundred Chicago Families* (Chicago, 1938), pp. 72–73, 116–17; Bakke, *Citizens without Work*, esp. pp. 215–42; Stouffer et al., *Research Memorandum*, p. 99.

15. Quoted in Lynd, *Middletown in Transition*, p. 142.

16. For information on popular culture, see Russel B. Nye, *The Unembarrassed Muse: The Popular Arts in America* (New York, 1970), esp. pp. 45–46, 224–29,

253–56, 382–83; Dixon Wecter, *The Hero in America: A Chronicle of Hero-Worship* (New York, 1941), pp. 461–69; William O. Aydelotte, "The Detective Story as a Historical Source," *Yale Review* 39 (September 1949): 92–94; George Grella, "The Gangster Novel: The Urban Pastoral," in *Tough Guy Writers of the Thirties*, ed. David Madden (Carbondale and Edwardsville, Ill., 1968), p. 188.

17. For vital statistics, see Paul H. Jacobson, *American Marriage and Divorce* (New York, 1959), table 2 (p. 21), table 7 (p. 34), and table 42 (p. 90); also, Wilson H. Grabill, Clyde V. Kiser, and Pascal K. Whelpton, *The Fertility of American Women* (New York, 1958), table 12, p. 28; Bird, *Invisible Scar*, p. 51.

18. For opinion polls on family size, see Henry F. Pringle, "What Do the Women of America Think about Birth Control?" *LHJ* 55 (March 1938): 14–15, 94–97; Cantril, *Public Opinion*, p. 206. For demographic data, see Grabill et al., *Fertility*, p. 329 and table 96, p. 287. On birth control, see Pringle, "What Do Women Think?" pp. 14–15; Norman C. Himes, "A Decade of Progress in Birth Control," *Annals* 212 (November 1940): 88–96; James West, *Plainville, U.S.A.* (New York, 1945), p. 165; Ronald Freedman, Pascal K. Whelpton, and Arthur A. Campbell, *Family Planning, Sterility, and Population Growth* (New York, 1959), p. 6; "The Single Woman's Dilemma," *Harper's Magazine* 167 (October 1933): 552; David M. Kennedy, *Birth Control in America: The Career of Margaret Sanger* (New Haven, 1970), pp. 140–41. For the Chases, see J. C. Furnas, *How America Lives* (New York, 1941), pp. 49–54.

19. Leuchtenburg, *Roosevelt*, p. 124; Lynd, *Middletown in Transition*, pp. 242–46, 406, 409, 447 (quotation on pp. 496–97); Ernest R. Groves, Edna L. Skinner, and Sadie J. Swenson, *The Family and Its Relationships* (Philadelphia and Chicago, 1932), pp. 120, 122; Groves, *Marriage* (New York, 1933), pp. 327–28; Bates, "Husband Turns Housewife," 8–10; Cecile Tipton LaFollette, *A Study of the Problems of 652 Gainfully Employed Married Women Homemakers* (New York, 1934), pp. 147, 149, 150–51, and chap. 9. For opinion polls, see Henry F. Pringle, "What the Men of America Think about Women," *LHJ* 56 (April 1939): 95; George H. Gallup, *The Gallup Poll: Public Opinion, 1935–1971*, 3 vols. (New York, 1972), 1:131.

20. *New York Times*, November 27, 1938, sec. 2, 4:1; "Razzberries for Housewives," *Time* 38 (November 17, 1941): 65; *New York Times*, November 15, 1936, sec. 2, 5:2; Joseph Kirk Folsom, *The Family and Democratic Society* (New York, 1943), pp. 616–17. Similarly, Toni Taylor, "Class of '41," *McCall's* 68 (June 1941): 24–25; Theodore Newcomb, "Recent Changes in Attitudes toward Sex and Marriage," *American Sociological Review* 2 (October 1937): 665; *New York Times*, December 26, 1937, sec. 2, 5:2, and June 11, 1938, 19:1.

21. Quotation comes from Bakke, *Citizens without Work*, p. 198. On housework, see surveys reported in *New York Times*, February 26, 1939, sec. 2, 5:1; Zella Dague Forsyth and F. Howard Forsyth, "Trend toward Sex Equality in Homemaking," *Journal of Home Economics* 31 (April 1939): 249–57. Poll data are in Henry F. Pringle, "What Do the Women of America Think about the Double Standard?"

LHJ 55 (November 1938): 22–23, 48–52; Mary Cookman, "What Do the Women of America Think about Men?" LHJ 56 (January 1939): 19, 63–64. For a complex experiment on inconsistency of female self-definition, see Clifford Kirkpatrick, *The Family as Process and Institution* (New York, 1955), pp. 150–51, 163–65.

22. Pearl S. Buck, "America's Medieval Women," *Harper's Magazine* 177 (August 1938): 225; Rose Wilder Lane, "Woman's Place Is in the Home," LHJ 53 (October 1936): 96; Dorothy Thompson, "It's a Woman's World," LHJ 57 (July 1940): 25. Similarly, Margaret Mead, "Sex and Achievement," *Forum* 94 (November 1935): 301–3; Rose Heylbut, "When Love Comes My Way," *Good Housekeeping* 103 (August 1936): 34–35, 140–42; Sidonie Matsner Gruenberg, *We, the Parents: Our Relationship to Our Children and to the World Today* (New York, 1939), pp. 281–82; Inez Haynes Irwin, "Women Should Be People," LHJ 58 (December 1941): 6. On marriage as partnership, see Ruth M. Ziegler, "Occupation: Housewife," WHC 67 (October 1940): 101–2; *New York Times*, September 29, 1935, sec. 4, 9:2; Margaret Culkin Banning, "Brought Up to Do Something," LHJ 52 (November 1935): 18; Olga Knopf, "Marriage and a Job," LHJ 58 (March 1941): 96; Betty Friedan, *The Feminine Mystique* (New York, Dell ed., 1963), p. 119.

23. *Smith College Weekly* 10 (December 3, 1919): 2; 29 (November 2, 1938): 2; 29 (November 9, 1938): 3. Samuel A. Stouffer et al., *The American Soldier*, 4 vols. (Princeton, N.J., 1949), 1:437–38, 449; 2:131.

24. On women in armed services, see "Stepsister Corps," *Time* 41 (May 10, 1943): 55–56; "Hobby's Army," *Time* 43 (January 17, 1944): 57–62; "Miss Mac," *Time* 45 (March 12, 1945): 20–23; "Army's Most Unusual Rookies Are 'Processed' into WAACS," *Newsweek* 20 (July 27, 1942): 29–30; advertisement in *Newsweek* 20 (November 16, 1942): 1; "WAAC Whispers," *Newsweek* 21 (June 14, 1943): 34–36; "WAAC Rumors," *Newsweek* 21 (June 21, 1943): 46; Frank U. McCoskrie, "I Learned about Women from Them," *American Magazine* 136 (November 1943): 17, 112–14; Ernest O. Hauser, "Those Wonderful G.I. Janes," SEP 217 (September 9, 1944): 26–27, 60, 63; polls in Cantril, *Public Opinion*, p. 1052.

25. In the following pages I've relied on Allan Bérubé, *Coming Out under Fire: The History of Gay Men and Women in World War Two* (1990; New York, 1991). Quotation comes from p. 256.

26. Ibid., pp. 100, 102.

27. John D'Emilio, *Sexual Politics, Sexual Communities: The Making of a Homosexual Minority in the United States, 1940–1970* (Chicago, 1983), p. 30; Lillian Faderman, *Odd Girls and Twilight Lovers: A History of Lesbian Life in Twentieth-Century America* (New York, 1991), p. 127.

28. Quoted by Bérubé, *Coming Out under Fire*, p. 114.

29. Ibid., pp. 188–89.

30. Quoted by John D'Emilio and Estelle B. Freedman, *Intimate Matters: A History of Sexuality in America* (New York, 1988), p. 290.

31. Quoted by Bérubé, *Coming Out under Fire*, pp. 36–37, 55.

32. Ibid., chap. 5.

33. On living conditions, see Richard R. Lingeman, *Don't You Know There's a War On? The American Home Front, 1941–1945* (New York, 1970), pp. 68–70, 80–84, 244–52; Edmund N. Bacon, "Wartime Housing," *Annals* 229 (September 1943): 128–37; Chafe, *American Woman,* pp. 139–40, 163.

34. Chafe, *American Woman,* pp. 137–38, 140–41, 144–49; *Women Workers in Ten War Production Areas and Their Postwar Employment Plans,* Women's Bureau Bulletin no. 209 (Washington, D.C., 1946), pp. 3–4, 7, and passim; Margaret Culkin Banning, "A New Heroine in Literature," *Saturday Review of Literature* 26 (May 15, 1943): 22; Harold L. Ickes, "Watch Out for the Women," *SEP* 215 (February 20, 1943): 19, 79. Norman Rockwell's famous portrait of Rosie the Riveter is on the *SEP* cover of May 29, 1943.

35. Chafe, *American Woman,* pp. 136–37, 141–42, 148; "Fortune Management Poll," *Fortune* 27 (February 1943): 143; Pennsylvania Railroad advertisement on inside front cover of *Newsweek* 22 (August 30, 1943). See also Steve King, "Danger! Women at Work," *American Magazine* 134 (September 1942): 40, 117–18; advertisements in *Newsweek* 23 (April 24, 1944): 51, and *Time* 41 (June 7, 1943): 35.

36. On discrimination, see Chafe, *American Woman,* pp. 156–58. On resentment, see "Women and Machines," *Time* 39 (May 11, 1942): 62–64; Virginia Snow Wilkinson, "From Housewife to Shipfitter," *Harper's Magazine* 187 (September 1943): 335–37; King, "Danger!" pp. 40, 117–18 (quotation from p. 118). On sweaters, see King, "The Margin Now Is Womanpower," *Fortune* 27 (February 1943): 99–103, 222–24; "Sex in the Factory," *Time* 40 (September 14, 1942): 21 (including sign quoted).

37. Chafe, *American Woman,* pp. 162–70, 176; *Women during the War and After: Summary of a Comprehensive Study by the Carola Woerishoffer Graduate Department of Social Economy and Social Research* (Bryn Mawr, Pa., 1945), p. 23; Willard Waller, "The Family and Other Institutions," *Annals* 229 (September 1943): 108; "Eight-Hour Orphans," *SEP* 115 (October 10, 1942): 20–21, 105–6;" Margin Is Womanpower," p. 224; J. Edgar Hoover, "Mothers . . . Our Only Hope," *WHC* 71 (January 1944): 20; James Madison Wood, "Should We Draft Mothers?" *WHC* 71 (January 1944): 21, 69.

38. *Vogue* quoted in "The Ladies!" *Time* 39 (January 26, 1942): 61. On attitudes to day care, see Chafe, *American Woman,* pp. 164–65, and Richard Polenberg, *War and Society: The United States, 1941–1945* (Philadelphia, 1972), p. 149. According to a Gallup poll in 1943, only 29% of American women would take a job if their children were cared for in a day nursery without cost; 56% said they would not. Quotations comes from King, "Danger," p. 118.

39. *Women Workers in Ten Areas;* Cecil Brown, "What's Going to Happen to Our Women Workers?" *Good Housekeeping* 114 (December 1943): 42, 78–83 (quotation from pp. 78, 80); Mary Parker, "What Are Career Girls Made Of?" *WHC* 72 (January 1945): 88–89; Chafe, *American Woman,* pp. 176, 178–79.

40. Chafe, *American Woman*, p. 182; F. Ivan Nye and Lois Wladis Hoffman, *The Employed Mother in America* (Chicago, 1963), pp. 8–11.

41. On songs, see Lingeman, *Don't You Know*, pp. 218–19. On marriage, see Jacobson, *American Marriage*, table 2, p. 21; Grabill et al., *Fertility*, table 96, p. 287, and pp. 186, 188; Robert W. Smuts, *Women and Work in America* (New York, 1959), p. 65; Paul C. Glick, *American Families* (New York, 1957), pp. 54, 131–32; *New York Times*, January 1, 1947, 6:6, and June 23, 1947, 20:6; John Willig, "Class of '34 (Female) Fifteen Years Later," *New York Times Magazine*, June 12, 1949, pp. 10, 51–53. Poll is in Joseph Veroff and Sheila Feld, *Marriage and Work in America: A Study of Motives and Roles* (New York, 1970), p. 72.

42. Grabill et al., *Fertility*, fig. 6, p. 35, and pp. 217, 386–87, 390–91; Pascal K. Whelpton, Arthur A. Campbell, and John E. Patterson, *Fertility and Family Planning in the United States* (Princeton, N.J., 1966), table 12, p. 34, and pp. 302–4. For male and female views of ideal family size, see *Public Opinion News Index*, report no. 69 (March 1971), p. 17. See also Will Herberg, *Protestant—Catholic—Jew*, rev. ed. (New York, 1960), p. 61; Mabel Newcomer, *A Century of Higher Education for Women* (New York, 1959), pp. 212–13. Quotation is from Betty Hannah Hoffman, "We Live by the Journal," *LHJ* 68 (November 1951): 190.

43. "They Think of the Moment," *Time* 45 (February 26, 1945): 18; "How to Be Marriageable," *LHJ* 71 (March 1954): 47.

44. Quoted by Bérubé, *Coming Out under Fire*, p. 250.

45. D'Emilio, *Sexual Politics*, pp. 41–51. Quotations on pp. 41 and 42.

46. Letter from Jane S. Hill to editors, *LHJ* 68 (November 1951): 187.

47. "They Think of the Moment," p. 18; "Working Wives," *Life* 34 (January 5, 1953): 76.

48. Chafe, *American Woman*, pp. 218–19; 1960 *Handbook on Women Workers*, Women's Bureau Bulletin no. 275 (Washington, D.C., 1960), table 15, p. 96; *Part-Time Employment for Women*, Women's Bureau Bulletin no. 273 (Washington, D.C., 1960); Smuts, *Women and Work*, pp. 36–37, 63–64.

49. Marion G. Sobol, "Commitment to Work," in Nye and Hoffman, *Employed Mother*, esp. pp. 44, 49, 53; "Women in America," *Fortune* 34 (August 1946): 10; Robert S. Weiss and Nancy M. Samuelson, "Social Roles of American Women: Their Contribution to a Sense of Usefulness and Importance," *Marriage and Family Living* 20 (November 1958): 338–66. See also Mildred W. Weil, "An Analysis of the Factors Influencing Married Women's Actual or Planned Work Participation," *American Sociological Review* 26 (February 1961): 91–96; Ward S. Mason, Robert J. Dressel, and Robert K. Bain, "Sex Role and the Career Orientations of Beginning Teachers," *Harvard Educational Review* 29 (Fall 1959): 370–83; Smuts, *Women and Work*, p. 148; Dael Wolfle, *America's Resources of Specialized Talent: A Current Appraisal and a Look Ahead* (New York, 1954), pp. 234–35. On occupational data, see F. Ivan Nye and Lois Wladis Hoffman, "The Socio-Cultural Setting," in Nye and Hoffman, *Employed Mother*, table 1:1, p. 8. For a subtle and

somewhat divergent view of women's motivations, see Chafe, *American Woman*, pp. 191–92.

50. On the debate about work, see "Women in America," p. 8; public opinion polls in 1952 (Minn. no. 100) and 1953 (Minn. no. 121), both furnished to me by the Roper Public Opinion Research Center, Williamstown, Mass.; "It's Too Late to Send the Working Woman back to the Kitchen" (editorial) SEP 231 (January 24, 1959): 10; Chafe, *American Woman*, pp. 214–15. On education, see Newcomer, *Century of Higher Education*, table 2, p. 46. Quotations come from "The Plight of the Young Mother," LHJ 73 (February 1957): 62; "The Eighty-Hour Week," *Life* 39 (August 15, 1955): 93, 95. For attitudes toward housework, see a 1957 poll (Minn. no. 157), Roper Center; "Do Men or Women Lead the Harder Life?" LHJ 64 (May 1947): 44–45, 152; letter from Evalyn F. Thomas to editors, LHJ 73 (March 1956): 6–7; Herbert J. Gans, *The Levittowners: Ways of Life and Politics in a New Suburban Community* (New York, 1967), pp. 228–29; Friedan, *Feminine Mystique*.

51. Elaine Tyler May, *Homeward Bound: American Families in the Cold War Era* (New York, 1988). Quotation is from p. 11.

52. Quoted in ibid., p. 183.

53. Quoted in George Gallup and Evan Hill, "The American Woman," SEP 235 (December 22, 1962): 18. On nurseries, see Sidonie Matsner Gruenberg, *We the Parents*, rev. ed. (New York, 1948), chap 12.

54. On motives and attitudes, see Veroff and Feld, *Marriage and Work*, p. 286; Frederick Herzberg et al., *Job Attitudes: Review of Research and Opinion* (Pittsburg, 1957), fig. 3, p. 44, and p. 48; William H. Whyte, Jr., *The Organization Man* (New York, 1956), pp. 68–71, 143–44, 146–47, 321–26; John R. Seeley, R. Alexander Sim, and Elizabeth W. Loosley, *Crestwood Heights: A Study of the Culture of Suburban Life* (New York, 1956), pp. 126, 131; Paul Harvey, "What Are Fathers Made Of?" *Parents' Magazine* 25 (October 1950): 28; William Attwood, "The American Male: Why Does He Work So Hard?" *Look* 22 (March 4, 1958): 70–75. On hours, see Whyte, *Organization Man*, p. 144; Sebastian de Grazia, *Of Time, Work, and Leisure* (New York, Anchor ed., 1964), pp. 124–25 and table 15, p. 454. On income, see U.S. Bureau of the Census, *Statistical Abstract of the United States: 1965* (Washington, D.C., 1965), p. 340.

55. Quotation comes from Seeley et al., *Crestwood Heights*, p. 152. The term "social ethic," as well as much of my analysis, comes from Whyte, *Organization Man*, esp. pts. 1 and 4. See also Daniel R. Miller and Guy E. Swanson, *The Changing American Parent: A Study in the Detroit Area* (New York, 1958), pp. 52–54. On job satisfaction, see Veroff and Feld, *Marriage and Work*, pp. 228–29, 282; Herzberg et al., *Job Attitudes*, pp. 3–4, 20, 23, 44, 48, 72; Robert Blauner, "Work Satisfaction and Industrial Trends in Modern Society," in *Class, Status, and Power*, ed. Reinhard Bendix and Seymour Martin Lipset, 2d ed. (New York, 1966), pp. 475, 477; Melvin L. Kohn, *Class and Conformity: A Study in Values* (Homewood, Ill., 1969), pp.

166, 169, 171. On alienation, see Walter S. Neff, *Work and Human Behavior* (New York, 1968), p. 35; Irene Taviss, "Changes in the Form of Alienation: The 1900's vs. the 1950's," *American Sociological Review* 34 (February 1969): 46–57.

56. Mabel McNeil Hages, "Families That Play Together Stay Together," *Parents' Magazine* 29 (February 1954): 119; Kathleen Doyle, "Everybody Works at Our House," ibid. 27 (March 1952): 43, 66; Dorothy Dowdell, "We Almost Failed as a Family," ibid. 27 (June 1952): 35, 70–72; *New York Times*, July 2, 1956, 25:3; Friedan, *Feminine Mystique*, pp. 42–44.

57. Edward A. Strecker, "Pops and Popism," *Parents' Magazine* 22 (May 1947): 99; Dorothy Barclay, "What Every Father Should Know," *New York Times Magazine*, June 11, 1950, p. 47; Ruth Wall, "Let Daddy Take Over," *Parents' Magazine* 26 (June 1951): 36–37, 56; Hilda Cole Espy, "Men Make Wonderful Mothers," LHJ 63 (October 1946): 260, 262; *New York Times*, February 16, 1950, 27:6; April 28, 1950, 17:3; July 22, 1952, 28:6. On fathers' participation in parenting, see 1949 poll in *Gallup Poll*, p. 808; *New York Times*, July 29, 1950, 16:8; Robert O. Blood, Jr., and Donald M. Wolfe, *Husbands and Wives: The Dynamics of Married Living* (New York, 1960), table 16, p. 50; Marvin E. Olsen, "Distribution of Family Responsibilities and Social Stratification," *Marriage and Family Living* 22 (February 1960): 60–65; William G. Dyer and Dick Urban, "The Institutionalization of Equalitarian Family Norms," ibid. 20 (February 1958): 53–58; Gallup and Hill, "American Woman," p. 28; Catherine Mackenzie, "Schools for Fathers," *New York Times Magazine*, January 4, 1948, p. 24; Mackenzie, "When Fathers Help," ibid., August 29, 1948, p. 30; Sidonie Matsner Gruenberg, "Why They Are Marrying Younger," ibid., January 30, 1955, p. 38; C. B. Palmer, "Life With Father (1955 Model)," ibid., January 23, 1955, p. 15; Rita B. Marshall, "Father's in the Kitchen," *Parents' Magazine* 26 (June 1951): 52; *New York Times*, September 10, 1956, 29:5; Wanda C. Bronson, Edith S. Katten, and Norman Livson, "Patterns of Authority and Affection in Two Generations," *Journal of Abnormal and Social Psychology* 58 (March 1959): 148, 150; Kohn, *Class and Conformity*, pp. 112, 115, 125; "The New American Domesticated Male," *Life* 36 (January 4, 1954): 42–45.

58. On comics, see Gerhart Saenger, "Male and Female Relations in the American Comic Strip," *Public Opinion Quarterly* 19 (Summer 1955): 200. On fathers in television plays, see Norman Podhoretz, "Our Changing Ideals, as Seen on TV," in *The Scene before You: A New Approach to American Culture*, ed. Chandler Brossard (New York, 1955), pp. 95–96, 98–99. For advice, see O. Spurgeon English and Constance J. Foster, "Father's Changing Role," *Parents' Magazine* 26 (October 1951): 44–45, 153–56; Robert Coughlan, "Changing Roles in Modern Marriage," *Life* 41 (December 24, 1956): 108–18 (quotation on p. 116); Benjamin Powell, "Father on the Other 364 Days," *New York Times Magazine*, June 15, 1952, p. 18; M. Robert Gomberg, "Father as a Family Man," ibid., September 6, 1953, p. 34; Dorothy Barclay, "Rights of Man around the House," ibid., October 2, 1955, p. 48; *New York Times*, March 14, 1956, 29:6, and November 19, 1959, 40:2;

Samuel Withers, "The 364 Other Days with Father," *Times Magazine*, June 16, 1963, p. 56; *Times*, November 5, 1960, 17:1; Dan Gillmor, "The Care and Feeding of Spock-Marked Fathers," *Parents' Magazine* 29 (July 1954): 36, 92–93. For a perceptive comment on the confusion between masculinity and manhood, see Margaret Mead, "The Job of the Children's Mother's Husband," *New York Times Magazine*, May 10, 1959, pp. 66–67.

59. On marital attitudes, see Blood and Wolfe, *Husbands and Wives*, pp. 150, 166–67, 222–23; J. Richard Udry, "Sex and Family Life," *Annals* 376 (March 1968): 27, 30–31; "Shaping the '60's . . . Foreshadowing the '70's," LHJ 79 (February 1962): 124; Gallup and Hill, "American Woman," pp. 16, 26–27; Sanford Brown, "'May I Ask You a Few Questions about Love?'" SEP 239 (December 31, 1966): 24. On female sexuality, see Michael Gordon, "From an Unfortunate Necessity to a Cult of Mutual Orgasm: Sex in American Marital Education Literature, 1830–1940," in *Studies in the Sociology of Sex*, ed. James M. Henslin (New York, 1971), pp. 67–70; Michael Gordon and Penelope J. Shankweiler, "Different Equals Less: Female Sexuality in Recent Marriage Manuals," *Journal of Marriage and the Family* 33 (August 1971): 459–66; Robert R. Bell, "Some Emerging Sexual Expectations among Women," in *The Social Dimension of Human Sexuality*, ed. Robert R. Bell and Michael Gordon (Boston, 1972), pp. 158–65; Max Lerner, *America as a Civilization: Life and Thought in the United States Today* (New York, 1957), pp. 684–85; Margaret Mead, *Male and Female: A Study of the Sexes in a Changing World* (New York, 1949), pp. 284–95. On premarital sex, see E. Lowell Kelly, "The Reassessment of Specific Attitudes after Twenty Years," *Journal of Social Issues* 17, no. 1 (1961): 29–37; Robert R. Bell and Jack V. Buerkle, "Mother and Daughter Attitudes to Premarital Sexual Behavior," *Marriage and Family Living* 23 (November 1961): 389–92; Daniel Scott Smith, "The Dating of the American Sexual Revolution: Evidence and Interpretation," in *The American Family in Social-Historical Perspective*, ed. Michael Gordon (New York, 1973), pp. 328–31.

60. Blood and Wolfe, *Husbands and Wives*, pp. 40–41, 156, 159, 169, 191; Veroff and Feld, *Marriage and Work*, p. 108; Dorothy Barclay, "How to Live with Father's Job," *New York Times Magazine*, July 23, 1961, pp. 48–49; J.H.S. Bossard and E. S. Boll, "Marital Unhappiness in the Life Cycle of Marriage," *Marriage and Family Living* 17 (February 1955): 10–14; E. A. Walkening and Denton E. Morrison, "A Comparison of Husband and Wife Responses Concerning Who Makes Farm and Home Decisions," ibid. 25 (August 1963): 349–51; Leland J. Axelson, "The Marital Adjustment and Marital Role Definitions of Working and Nonworking Wives," ibid. 25 (May 1963): 189–95; Jan E. Dizard, "The Price of Success," in *The Future of the Family*, ed. Louise Kapp Howe (New York, 1972), pp. 194–97; S. M. Miller, "Confusions of a Middle-Class Husband," in Howe, pp. 106–7. According to Dizard, the wife's employment increased marital satisfaction. But contrary evidence is reported in F. Ivan Nye, "Marital Interaction," in Nye and Hoffman, *Employed Mother*, pp. 267–70. For the poll of Chicago wives,

see Helena Znaniecki Lopata, *Occupation: Housewife* (New York, 1971), pp. 91–94. For a significant critique of the methodology of "marital happiness" studies, see Judith Long Lee, "A Feminist Review of Marital Adjustment Literature: The Rape of the Locke," *Journal of Marriage and the Family* 33 (August 1971): 483–516.

61. Veroff and Feld, *Marriages and Work*, pp. 155, 334–35; Miller and Swanson, *Changing American Parent*, pp. 203–4. For a lyrical account of "immortality" through children, see Phyllis McGinley, "Women Are Wonderful," *Life* 41 (December 24, 1956): 76.

7. THE CHILDREN OF DOMESTICITY

1. Elizabeth Douvan and Joseph Adelson, *The Adolescent Experience* (New York, 1966), esp. pp. 32–33, 36–37, 45–47, 78, 107–8, 113, 194–95, table 2:1, pp. 233–34, and pp. 363–66; Robert W. Smuts, *Women and Work in America* (New York, 1959), p. 151; Lamar T. Empey, "Role Expectations of Young Women Regarding Marriage and a Career," *Marriage and Family Living* 20 (May 1958): 152–55; "Twenty-Year-Olds' Ideal," *Life* 41 (December 24, 1956): 143; John R. Seeley, R. Alexander Sim, and Elizabeth W. Loosley, *Crestwood Heights: A Study of the Culture of Suburban Life* (New York, 1957), pp. 102–17; James S. Coleman, *The Adolescent Society: The Social Life of the Teenager and Its Impact on Education* (New York, 1961), chaps. 2, 5, 6; Dale B. Harris, "Sex Differences in the Life Problems and Interests of Adolescents, 1935 and 1957," *Child Development* 30 (1959): 453–59; Edgar Z. Friedenberg, *The Vanishing Adolescent* (New York, 1959). On teenage marriage, see Wilson H. Grabill, Clyde V. Kiser, and Pascal K. Whelpton, *The Fertility of American Women* (New York, 1958), table 96, p. 287; Barbara Lang, "The Teen-Age Marriage: Love Finds a Way," LHJ 82 (June 1965): 68–69, 100–102 (quotation on p. 102); Mildred Gilman, "Why They Can't Wait to Wed," *Parents' Magazine* 33 (November 1958): 46, 86; Margaret Parton, "Why Do They Marry So Young?" LHJ 75 (November 1958): 163–65, 172–78. On premarital pregnancies, see Daniel Scott Smith, "The Dating of the American Sexual Revolution: Evidence and Interpretation," in *The American Family in Social-Historical Perspective*, ed. Michael Gordon (New York, 1973), pp. 323–27.

2. On college attendance, see Christopher Jencks and David Riesman, *The Academic Revolution* (Garden City, N.Y., 1968), pp. 94–96, 100–103. On the campus mood, see "The Younger Generation," *Time* 58 (November 5, 1951): 45, 48; David Boroff, *Campus U.S.A.: Portraits of American Colleges in Action* (New York, 1961), passim (quotations from pp. 35, 144); "The Careful Young Men," *Nation* 184 (March 4, 1957): 199–214.

3. On sophomores, see Douvan and Adelson, *Adolescent Experience*, p. 235; for Gallup, "Shaping the '60's . . . Foreshadowing the '70's," LHJ 79 (January 1962): 31. Newspaper quotation is from "Is Marriage a Career?" *Smith Sophian* 10 (November 21, 1961): 2. On marriage rates, see U.S. Bureau of Census, *Statisti-*

cal Abstract of the United States: 1965 (Washington, D.C., 1965), p. 129; Mary Levy Mayer, "To See Ourselves," *Mount Holyoke Alumnae Quarterly*, Summer 1962. Smith student is quoted by Boroff, *Campus*, p. 145. Similarly, see Betty Friedan, *The Feminine Mystique* (New York, Dell ed., 1963), pp. 143–48.

4. David Riesman, "The Found Generation" (1956), in his *Abundance for What? and Other Essays* (Garden City, N.Y., 1964), p. 318.

5. William H. Whyte, Jr., *The Organization Man* (New York, 1956), pp. 68–72, 80–81.

6. Eisenhower quoted in Will Herberg, *Protestant—Catholic—Jew* (New York, Anchor ed., 1960), p. 84; Allen Ginsberg, *Howl and Other Poems* (San Francisco, 1956); Jack Kerouac, *On the Road* (New York, 1957), p. 8; *Time* 71 (June 9, 1958): 98; Boroff, *Campus*, p. 102; Norman Mailer, "The White Negro: Superficial Reflections on the Hipster" (1957), in his *Advertisements for Myself* (New York, 1959), pp. 337–58. For background, see Bruce Cook, *The Beat Generation* (New York, 1971). For general assessment and the public's reaction, see James F. Scott, "Beat Literature and the American Teen Cult," *American Quarterly* 14 (Summer 1962): 150–60; *Smith Sophian*, quoted in Boroff, *Campus*, p. 145.

7. J. D. Salinger, *The Catcher in the Rye* (New York, Bantam ed., 1964; orig. ed., 1951), quotations from pp. 96, 67. On campus popularity of the novel, see "Careful Young Men," *Nation* 184 (March 4, 1957): 199, 200, 210; Jack Newfield, *A Prophetic Minority* (New York, New American Library ed., 1966), p. 42. For background on the genre, see W. Tasker Witham, *The Adolescent in the American Novel, 1920–1960* (New York, 1964), esp. pp. 85–86.

8. The most useful sources on premarital attitudes and practice are Edwin O. Smigel and Rita Seiden, "The Decline and Fall of the Double Standard," *Annals* 376 (March 1968): 12–14; Ira L. Reiss, *The Social Context of Premarital Sexual Permissiveness* (New York, 1967), esp. pp. 25–27, 142–43; Joseph Katz et al., *No Time for Youth: Growth and Constraint in College Students* (San Francisco, 1968), pp. 54–55; Mervin B. Freedman, *The College Experience* (San Francisco, 1967), pp. 84–85, 98–100; Smith, "Dating of the Sexual Revolution," pp. 328–30; *New York Times*, December 30, 1967, 1:3; Morton Hunt, "Sexual Behavior in the 1970's," *Playboy* 20 (October 1973): 198–200; *Public Opinion Quarterly* 30 (Winter 1966–67): 673. Riesman's comment is in "Permissiveness and Sex Roles," *Marriage and Family Living* 21 (August 1959): 212. On images of male and female roles, see Katz, *No Time for Youth*, pp. 58–59; John P. McKee and Alex C. Sheriffs, "Men's and Women's Beliefs, Ideals, and Self-concepts," *American Journal of Sociology* 64 (January 1959): 356–63.

9. On Caulfield as eternal boy, see Leslie A. Fiedler, *Love and Death in the American Novel* (New York, Laurel ed., 1966), pp. 286–87. On best-sellers, see Alice P. Hackett, *Sixty Years of Best Sellers, 1895–1955* (New York, 1956), p. 205. Quotation comes from William Attwood, "How America Feels as We Enter the Soaring Sixties," *Look* 24 (January 5, 1960): 15. On the alienated minority, see

Kenneth Keniston, *The Uncommitted: Alienated Youth in American Society* (New York, 1965).

10. "The Port Huron Statement," in *The New Radicals*, ed. Paul Jacobs and Saul Landau (New York, 1966), pp. 150, 153, 154, 155.

11. Quotation is from Kathy Mulherin, "Memories of a (Latter-day) Catholic Girlhood," *Commonweal*, March 6, 1960, reprinted in *The Movement toward a New America: The Beginnings of a Long Revolution*, ed. Mitchell Goodman (New York, 1970), p. 634. Kenneth Keniston, *Youth and Dissent: The Rise of a New Opposition* (New York, 1971), p. 7. See also Bennett M. Berger, "Student Unrest and the Crisis in the Universities" (1969), reprinted in Berger, *Looking for America: Essays on Youth, Suburbia, and Other American Obsessions* (Englewood Cliffs, N.J., 1971), pp. 99–117.

12. It is impossible to state precisely how many people belonged to the New Left or to the youth culture. According to a Gallup poll in 1969, 28% of college students said they had participated in some kind of demonstration: *New York Times*, May 25, 1969, 68:3. Other surveys report that in the mid-1960s 5 to 15% of students were activists, and in 1968 5% of them indicated "strongly agree" on the need for "a mass revolutionary party": Kirkpatrick Sale, SDS (New York, 1973), pp. 293, 457. For demographic data, see Walter T. K. Nugent, *Modern America* (Boston, 1973), pp. 289–91; Richard Flacks, *Youth and Social Change* (Chicago, 1971), p. 10. For the concept of "moratorium," see Erik Erikson, "Youth: Fidelity and Diversity," *Daedalus* 91 (Winter 1962): esp. 7, 11–12. Also see Jencks and Riesman, *Academic Revolution*, pp. 42–43. I gratefully credit Riesman for suggesting to me the idea about second-generation college students. I also gained rich insight from Kenneth Keniston's "Faces in the Lecture Room" (1966), reprinted in his *Youth and Dissent*, esp. pp. 111–13. For statistical documentation, see Mabel Newcomer, *A Century of Higher Education for Women* (New York, 1959), pp. 132–33.

13. Quotations come from Kenneth Keniston, *Young Radicals: Notes on Committed Youth* (New York, 1968), pp. 35, 39, 56, 58, 59, 309. The general analysis derives largely from Keniston, chap. 2, pp. 111–20, and app. B. See also J. Anthony Lukas, *Don't Shoot: We Are Your Children* (New York, Dell ed., 1972), pp. 421–36; Richard E. Flacks, "The Liberated Generation: An Exploration of the Roots of Student Protest," *Journal of Social Issues* 23 (1967): 52–75; Robert Liebert, *Radical and Militant Youth: A Psychoanalytic Inquiry* (New York, 1971), pp. 120–21; Christopher Jencks, "Is It All Dr. Spock's Fault?" *New York Times Magazine*, March 3, 1968, pp. 27, 76–94; Berger, "Student Unrest" and "Self-hatred and the Politics of Knocks" (1966), both reprinted in *Looking for America*, pp. 99–118, 130–35.

14. Lukas, *Don't Shoot*, pp. 42–43, 45, 47–48, 51–53.

15. Michael Rossman, "Barefoot in a Marshmallow World" (1966), reprinted in his *The Wedding within the War* (New York, Anchor ed., 1971), p. 125; "F.S.M.'s Joy to U.C.: Free Speech Carols" and Mario Savio, "An End to History,"

in Jacobs and Landau, *New Radicals*, pp. 206–8, 233–34; Keniston, *Young Radicals*, pp. 97–101; Paul Goodman, "The New Reformation," *New York Times Magazine*, September 14, 1969, p. 33; Raymond Mungo, *Famous Long Ago: My Life and Hard Times with the Liberation News Service* (Boston, 1970), pp. 150, 188.

16. Gerald Rosenfeld, "Generational Revolt and the Free Speech Movement," *Liberation* (December 1965–January 1966), reprinted in Jacobs and Landau, *New Radicals*, p. 215.

17. Newfield, *Prophetic Minority*, esp. pp. 121, 126; Paul Potter, "The Intellectual and Social Change" (1964), and Thomas Hayden, "Student Social Action: From Liberation to Community" (1962), in *The New Student Left: An Anthology* (Boston, 1966), pp. 16–21, 270–88; Jacobs and Landau, *New Radicals*, esp. pp. 29–38, 74–81; Keniston, *Young Radicals*, pp. 160–73; Mungo, *Famous Long Ago*, pp. 18–20, 156.

18. The manifesto was published in *Leviathan*, Summer 1969, and reprinted in Goodman, *The Movement toward a New America*, p. 513. On the Liberation News Service, see Mungo, *Famous Long Ago*, chap. 3.

19. On communes, see "Communes, U.S.A.," *Modern Utopia* 5, nos. 1–3 (1971); Rosabeth Moss Kantor, *Commitment and Community: Communes and Utopia in Sociological Perspective* (Cambridge, Mass., 1972), esp. pp. 22, 43–47, 165–75; Bennett M. Berger, Bruce M. Hackett, and R. Mervyn Millar, "Child Rearing in Communes," in *The Future of the Family*, ed. Louise Kapp Howe (New York, 1972), pp. 164–67; Robert Houriet, *Getting Back Together* (New York, 1971); *New York Times*, June 1, 1967, 39:5. Quotation from Houriet, *Getting Back Together*, p. 95.

20. Theodore Roszak, *The Making of the Counter Culture: Reflections on the Technocratic Society and Its Youthful Opposition* (New York, 1967); Bennett M. Berger, "Hippie Morality" (1967), reprinted in *Looking for America*, pp. 119–30; Goodman, *Movement toward New America*; Hunter S. Thompson, "The 'Hashbury' Is the Capital of the Hippies," *New York Times Magazine*, May 14, 1967, pp. 28–29, 120–24.

21. On wives and mothers, see U.S. Bureau of the Census, *Statistical Abstract: 1975* (Washington, D.C., 1975), p. 347. On occupations and earnings: U.S. Bureau of Labor Standards, *Perspectives on Working Women: A Databook* (Washington, D.C., 1980), Bulletin 2080, pp. 10, 52. On part-time workers: *Part-Time Employment for Women*, Women's Bureau Bulletin no. 273 (Washington, D.C., 1960), p. 3, and 1960 *Handbook on Women Workers*, Women's Bureau Bulletin no. 275 (Washington, D.C., 1960), p. 40. In 1958, there were 28,700,000 women employed, of whom 12,200,000 were wives, of whom 5,430,000 were working part-time. Looking at the situation from another angle, 60% of part-time female workers were married in 1958, of whom 37% had children aged 6 to 17 and 36% had children under the age of 6: 1960 *Handbook*, pp. 10–11.

22. Quotations from Katherine Hamill, "Women as Bosses," *Fortune* 53 (June 1956): 106–7, 209, cited in Sara Evans, *Personal Politics: The Roots of Women's Liberation in the Civil Rights Movement and the New Left* (New York, 1979), p. 10. On

marriage of professionals, see Cynthia Fuchs Epstein, *Woman's Place: Options and Limits in Professional Careers* (New York, 1970), table 8, p. 97. On college see Newcomer, *Century of Higher Education*, table 2, p. 46. On numbers of professionals, see Bureau of Labor Standards, *Perspectives on Working Women*, p. 10. On relative deprivation, see Jo Freeman, *The Politics of Women's Liberation: A Case Study of an Emerging Social Movement and Its Relation to the Policy Process* (New York, 1975), pp. 15–17, 28–36, and James C. Davies, "The J-Curve of Rising and Declining Satisfactions as a Cause of Some Great Revolutions and a Contained Rebellion," in *Violence in America: Historical and Comparative Perspectives*, ed. Hugh Davis Graham and Ted Robert Gurr (New York, Signet ed., 1969), pp. 671–709. I have been influenced by the analysis of William H. Chafe, "The Paradox of Progress: Social Change since 1930," in *Paths to the Present: Interpretive Essays on American History since 1930*, ed. James T. Patterson (Minneapolis, 1975), pp. 8–25, and idem, *Women and Equality: Changing Patterns in American Culture* (New York, 1977), chap. 5.

23. Judith Hole and Ellen Levine, *Rebirth of Feminism* (New York, 1971), pp. 18–24, 433–38; Margaret Mead and Frances Balgley Kaplan, eds., *American Woman: The Report of the President's Commission on the Status of Women* (New York, 1965).

24. Friedan, *The Feminine Mystique*. On circulation, see Friedan, *It Changed My Life: Writings on the Women's Movement* (New York, 1976), p. 19.

25. Quotations from Friedan, *It Changed My Life*, p. 83. For a general background see ibid., pp. 75–85, as well as Hole and Levine, *Rebirth*, pp. 30–44.

26. *Smith College Weekly* 10 (December 3, 1919): 2; Friedan, *it Changed My Life*, pp. 92–95, 141; Nancy Woloch, *Women and the American Experience* (New York, 1984), p. 514.

27. Evans, *Personal Politics*, pp. 72, 157–58; Lukas, *Don't Shoot*, pp. 157–58 and chap. 4; Thomas Powers, *Diana: The Making of a Terrorist* (Boston, 1971), pp. 1–5, 152, 155, and passim.

28. Evans, *Personal Politics*, chap. 4, provides the best analysis.

29. Weisstein, quoted in Evans, *Personal Politics*, p. 115; Beverly Jones and Judith Brown, *Toward a Female Liberation Movement* (1968), quoted in Hole and Levine, *Rebirth*, p. 111; Sale, SDS, p. 526. For background, see Evans, *Personal Politics*, pp. 108–15 and 156–76.

30. Evans, *Personal Politics*, pp. 190–92, and Hole and Levine, *Rebirth*, p. 112.

31. Willis, quoted in Hole and Levine, *Rebirth*, p. 134.

32. Chafe, *Women and Equality*, pp. 119–23.

33. Ibid., p. 125; Woloch, *Women and American Experience*, p. 522; Hole and Levine, *Rebirth*, pp. 346, 366, 391.

34. Lynne Powell, *National Guardian*, November 4, 1967, p. 7; Friedan "Ideological Traps for New Feminists to Avoid" (Speech at Cornell University, 1969), in *It Changed My Life*, p. 116; Martha Weinman Lear, "The Second Feminist Wave," *New York Times Magazine*, March 10, 1968, p. 58; "Politics of the Ego: A Manifesto for New Radical Feminists," in Hole and Levine, *Rebirth*, pp. 442–45.

35. Quotations from Boston Women's Health Book Collective, *Our Bodies, Ourselves* (New York, 1971), p. 6, and Freeman, *Politics*, p. 118. For a fine account of the CR process, see Vivian Gornick, "Consciousness," *New York Times Magazine*, January 10, 1971, pp. 22–23, 77–82.

36. "The New Feminism," LHJ 87 (August 1970): 64–71; cover of *Time* 96 (August 31, 1970); "The Women Who Know Their Place," *Newsweek* 76 (September 7, 1970): 16–18; "Women Arise," *Life* 69 (September 4, 1970): 18–19; Francine Klagsbrun, ed., *The First Ms. Reader* (New York, 1973), pp. 262–72; "A Personal Report," *Ms.* 1 (July 1972). Despite *Ms.*'s success, 77% of women in 1980 still preferred addressing women as "Miss" or "Mrs.": Roper Organization, *The 1980 Virginia Slims American Women's Poll: A Survey of Contemporary Attitudes* (n.p., n.d.), p. 23.

37. *Statistical Abstract*, 1996, pp. 279, 283.

38. Joyce Jacobsen, *The Economics of Gender* (Cambridge, 1994), p. 222; *Raleigh News & Observer*, May 31, 1995, 5A:1.

39. *Raleigh News & Observer*, February 23, 1997, 7A:1; *Statistical Abstract*, 1996, p. 405.

40. Department of Defense, *Selected Manpower Statistics*, 1988 (Washington, D.C., 1989), pp. 100–101.

41. Gender typecasting in the media didn't disappear, though. According to a 1996 analysis of top-rated movies, TV shows, and music videos, men not only greatly outnumbered women, but were shown working half again as often as females. It's not surprising, then, that the ten people on TV most admired by a national sample of teenage boys were all males, and that eight of the ten named by teenage girls were male (except for Oprah Winfrey and Rosie O'Donnell): *New York Times*, May 1, 1997, A17:1.

42. On high schools, Jane Longman, "How the Women Won," *New York Times Magazine*, June 23, 1996, p. 47, and Benjamin Rader, *American Sports: From the Age of Folk Games to the Age of Spectators* (Englewood Cliffs, N.J., 1983), p. 341. On college, *New York Times*, June 6, 1997, A1:2, C18:1.

43. Boston Women's Health Book Collective, *Our Bodies, Ourselves*, quotation from p. 12. For a brilliant analysis of Masters and Johnson, see Paul Robinson, *The Modernization of Sex* (New York, 1976), chap. 3. On Freud and women, see Jean Strouse, ed., *Women and Analysis: Dialogues on Psychoanalytic Views of Femininity* (New York, 1975), pp. 17–26, 32–48, 57–69. In saying "anatomy is destiny," Freud was in fact not referring to the womb and female destiny, but the phrase has since become (mis)quoted: Strouse, p. 67.

44. Smigel and Selden, "Decline and Fall of the Double Standard," pp. 12–14; Morton Hunt, *Sexual Behavior in the 1970s* (New York, 1974), pp. 115–17, 148–50; *New York Times*, September 14, 1969, 69:2, and September 8, 1974, 68:3; Daniel Yankelovich, *The New Morality: A Profile of American Youth in the Seventies* (New York, 1974), chaps. 8–9; Melvin Zelnik et al., "Probabilities of Intercourse

and Conception among U.S. Teenage Women, 1971 and 1976," *Family Planning Perspectives* 11 (1979): 177–84; "A Look at the Opposite Sex," *Newsweek on Campus*, April 1984, p. 21; Joyce Maynard, *Looking Back: A Chronicle of Growing up Old in the Sixties* (New York, 1973), p. 138.

45. For advertisements, see *New York Times*, May 8, 1966, sec. 3, 16:4. On adults, see *Public Opinion* 3 (December–January 1980): 28; Hunt, *Sexual Behavior*, pp. 21, 212, 215.

46. For a convenient survey, see Estelle Freedman and John D'Emilio, *Intimate Matters: A History of Sexuality in America* (New York, 1988), pp. 311–15.

47. Quoted in Wandersee, *On the Move: American Women in the 1970s* (New York, 1985), p. 65.

48. Lillian Faderman, *Odd Girls and Twilight Lovers: A History of Lesbian Life in Twentieth-Century America* (New York, 1991), pp. 202–9. Slogan is quoted on 208.

49. Ibid, 218–35. Also Arlene Stein, *Sex and Sensibility: Stories of a Lesbian Generation* (Berkeley, 1997), pp. 35–46.

50. Quoted by Faderman, *Odd Girls*, p. 210.

51. Hole and Levine, *Rebirth*, pp. 123, 229–30; Robin Morgan, "Lesbianism and Feminism: Synonyms or Contradictions?" *Second Wave* 2, no. 4 (1973): 22; *Time* 96 (August 31, 1970): 16, and 96 (December 14, 1970); 50. See also Friedan, *It Changed My Life*, pp. 158–59.

52. Faderman, *Odd Girls*, pp. 209–13.

53. For housework times, which vary slightly according to different studies, see Joseph H. Pleck, "Husbands' Paid Work and Family Roles: Current Research Issues," in *Research on the Interweave of Social Roles*, vol. 3 *Families and Jobs: A Research Annual*, ed. Helen Z. Lopata and Joseph H. Pleck (Greenwich, Conn., 1983), pp. 256–59, and table 7, p. 281; Heidi Hartmann, "Family as the Locus of Gender, Class, and Political Struggle: The Example of Housework," *Signs* 6 (Spring 1981): 377–79; William R. Beer, *Househusbands: Men and Housework in American Families* (New York, 1983), pp. 26–27. Atkinson, quoted in Lear, "Second Feminist Wave," p. 58; Shulamith Firestone, *The Dialectic of Sex: The Case for Feminist Revolution* (New York, Bantam ed., 1971), pp. 238–39; Andrea Dworkin, *Right-Wing Women* (New York, 1983), pp. 77, 83; "Politics of the Ego," quoted in Hole and Levine, *Rebirth*, p. 442.

54. Nixon quoted by Carole Joffe, "Child Care: Destroying the Family or Strengthening It?" in *Future of the Family*, ed. Howe, p. 261.

55. *New York Times*, August 27, 1970, 30:8.

56. Roper, 1972 *Virginia Slims Poll*; *Gallup Poll: Public Opinion*, 1972–1977 3 vols. (Wilmington, Del., 1978), 3:2260; and "What Women Really Think about Their Marriages," *Family Circle*, February 1968, pp. 34, 94.

57. Lyn Tornabene, "The Bored Housewife," LHJ 83 (November 1966): 97–99, 155; Pat Loud, *Pat Loud: A Woman's Story* (New York, 1974), p. 84; Anne Roiphe, "Things Are Keen But Could Be Keener," *New York Times Magazine*, Feb-

ruary 18, 1973, p. 50. The Louds were portrayed in an extraordinary twelve-hour nationwide TV documentary, "An American Family," in 1973.

58. *Gallup Poll*, 2:697–700.

59. *New York Times*, November 27, 1977, 75:2; Chafe, *Women and Equality*, p. 139.

60. Roper, 1972 *Virginia Slims Poll*, p. 2, and 1980 *Virginia Slims Poll*, p. 17; *Gallop Report No.* 190, July 1981, p. 24.

61. *The Phyllis Schlafly Report*, no. 5 (February 1972), and no. 8 (July 1975); Schlafly, *The Power of the Christian Woman* (Cincinnati, 1981), pp. 17–18, 92–94; Edith Mayo and Jerry Frye, "ERA: Post Mortem of a Failure in Political Communication," *Organization of American History Newsletter*, August 1983, pp. 21–24. For typologies of antis and feminists, see Kent L. Tedin et al., "Social Background and Political Differences between Pro- and Anti-ERA Activists," *American Politics Quarterly* 5, no. 3 (1977): 395–408, and Joan Huber, Cynthia Rexroat, and Glenna Spitze, "A Crucible of Opinion on Women's Status: ERA in Illinois," *Social Forces* 57 (December 1978): 549–65.

62. Schlafly, *The Power of a Positive Woman* (New Rochelle, N.Y., 1977), pp. 14, 62–63, 94.

63. For an excellent analysis, see Donald Mathews and Jane De Hart, *Sex, Gender and the Politics of ERA: A State and a Nation* (New York, 1990).

64. Quotation from Jerry Falwell, *Listen, America!* (Garden City, N.Y., 1980), p. 7. For background, see Steve Bruce, *The Rise and Fall of the New Christian Right: Conservative Protestant Politics in America, 1978–1988* (New York, 1988), chap. 8; Connie Page, *The Right to Lifers: Who They Are, How They Operate, Where They Get Their Money* (New York, 1983), esp. pp. 51–64; Robert Wuthnow, *The Restructuring of American Religion, Society, and Faith since World War Two* (Princeton, 1988), esp. pp. 195, 203–7; James Davison Hunter, *American Evangelicalism: Conservative Religion and the Quandary of Modernity* (New Brunswick, N.J., 1983), chap 7.

65. Quotations from *Time* 96 (December 28, 1970): 34. The rate of births to unwed teenagers increased abruptly in the late 1960s: from 15.3 per 1,000 women aged 15–19 (1960) to 17.0 (1965) to 22.4 (1970). Thereafter it rose to 27.6 (1980) and 42.5 (1990): U.S. Bureau of Census, *Statistical Abstract: 1984* (Washington, D.C., 1983), p. 70, and *Statistical Abstract: 1994* (Washington, D.C., 1993), p. 80. For female-headed households, *Statistical Abstract: 1984*, p. 47. On divorce, *Statistical Abstract: 1983* (Washington, D.C., 1982), p. 84, and Arthur J. Norton and Paul C. Glick, "Marital Instability in America: Past, Present, and Future," in *Divorce and Separation: Context, Causes, and Consequences*, ed. George Levinger and Oliver C. Moles (New York, 1979), pp. 6–19. These trends affected blacks more than whites, and people in lower classes more than those in the middle class.

66. Quoted in Jane Kramer, "Founding Cadre," *New Yorker* 46 (November 28, 1970): 84–85.

67. On Bond's popularity, see "Spectacular Cult of Ian Fleming," SEP 236

(June 22, 1963): 66–68. On football, see Richard Schickel, "On Pro Football," *Commentary* 147 (January 1969): 66–68.

68. Baty quoted in Lukas, *Don't Shoot*, p. 307. Columbia student quoted in Robert Liebert, *Radical and Militant Youth: A Psychoanalytic Inquiry* (New York, 1971), p. 157. On violence within the New Left, see Sale, SDS, pp. 374–89, 425–28, 503–4, 512–13, 632–35, 652–53.

69. Jeffrey P. Hantover, "The Social Construction of Masculine Anxiety," in *Men in Difficult Times: Masculinity Today and Tomorrow*, ed. Robert Lewis (Englewood Cliffs, N.J., 1981), pp. 87–98; Carol Gilligan, *In a Different Voice: Psychological Theory and Women's Development* (Cambridge, Mass., 1982), esp. pp. 42–49, 62.

70. Harry Boyte, "In Movement," in *Men in the Middle: Coping with the Problems of Work and Family in the Lives of Middle-Aged Men*, ed. Peter Filene (Englewood Cliffs, N.J., 1981), pp. 42–43. Likewise, Jack Lietwka, "The Socialized Penis," in *For Men against Sexism: A Book of Readings*, ed. Jon Snodgrass (Albion, Calif., 1977), p. 30; Robert E. Gould, "Some Husbands Talk about Their Liberated Wives," *New York Times Magazine*, June 18, 1972, pp. 10–11, 46–52.

71. On decline of women's hours, Winifred D. Wandersee, *On the Move: American Women in the 1970s* (Boston, 1985), p. 145. On husbands' contribution, Pleck, "Husbands' Paid Work," pp. 255–68; Pleck, "The 'Family Supportive' Employer Policies Relevant to Men," in *Men, Work, and Family*, ed. Jane Hood (Newbury Park, Calif., 1993), pp. 219–22; Arlie Hochschild, *The Second Shift: Working Parents and the Revolution at Home* (New York, 1989), p. 8 and passim. On stress, see Niall Bolger et al., "The Microstructure of Daily Role-Related Stress in Married Couples," in *Stress between Work and Family*, ed. John Eckenrode and Susan Gore (New York, 1990), pp. 95–115.

72. Two studies in 1983 and 1985 cited in Hochschild, *Second Shift*, p. 272.

73. In the mid-seventies, 34 to 42 percent of a national sample of employed women were satisfied with the division of housework: Pleck, "Husbands' Paid Work," p. 278. In the late eighties, 24 percent of a small sample of female professionals with preschool children were satisfied: Carol-Ann Emmons et al., "Stress, Support, and Coping among Women Professionals with Preschool Children," in *Stress Between Work and Family*, ed. Eckenrode and Gore, pp. 61–93. Quotation is on pp. 85–86.

74. Jessie Bernard, *Women, Wives, Mothers: Values and Options* (Chicago, 1975), p. 189.

75. Powell is quoted in Barrie S. Greiff and Preston K. Munter, "Tradeoffs," *Harvard Magazine*, May–June 1980, p. 48C.

76. For employment data, Bureau of the Census, *Statistical Abstract, 1982–1983* (Washington, D.C., 1982), p. 385, and Rosabeth Moss Kanter, *Men and Women of the Corporation* (New York, 1977), pp. 15–16. For working hours, *Time* 125 (January 14, 1985): 55; and Bradley K. Googins, *Work/Family Conflicts: Private*

Lives—Public Responses (New York, 1991), p. 111. One-third of CEOs worked longer than sixty hours; 30 percent of men with children under the age of fourteen worked more than fifty hours: Juliet Schor, *The Overworked American: The Unexpected Decline of Leisure* (New York, 1992), pp. 19–20.

77. On work preference, Joseph Veroff, Elizabeth Douvan, and Richard Kulka, *The Inner American: A Self-Portrait from 1957 to 1976* (New York, 1981), p. 292; U.S. Department of Commerce, *Social Indicators: 1976—Selected Data on Social Conditions and Trends in the United States* (Washington, D.C.), p. 389; *Public Opinion* 4 (August–September 1981): 31. Men's preferences on working have held steady since at least the 1950s: Nancy S. Morse and Robert S. Weiss, "The Function and Meaning of Work and the Job," *American Sociological Review* 20 (April 1955): 191–98. The UAW vice president is quoted in "Is the Work Ethic Going Out of Style?" *Time* 100 (October 30, 1972): 97.

78. Berkeley Men's Center, "Manifesto," January 1973, in Schlesinger Library on the History of Women in America, Radcliffe College; Alan E. Gross and Ronald Smith, "The Men's Movement: Personal versus Political," in *Social Movements of the Sixties and Seventies*, ed. Jo Freeman (New York, 1983), pp. 71–81.

79. Quotations from Sam Julty, "Creating a Movement for Change" (Keynote address, Fourth Conference on Men and Masculinity, St. Louis, Mo., November 25, 1977), reprinted by *The Malebox* (Ann Arbor, Mich.), and Perry Garfinkel, "The Men's Movement: The Not-Quite-Ready-for-Prime-Time Revolution," *Boston Real Paper*, January 20, 1979, p. 1. Also *Men's Studies Newsletter* 1, no. 1 (January 1984), published by the Men's Studies Task Group of the National Organization for Men, and Robert Brannon, "Inside the Men's Movement," *Ms.* 10 (October 1982): 40–44.

80. Carol Kleiman, "'Good-bye, John Wayne'? Three Days at a Men's Conference," *Ms.* 6 (April 1978): 45–47, 77; Garfinkel, "Men's Movement"; Gross and Smith, "Men's Movement."

81. *Chicago Sun-Times*, October 15, 1979, p. 43; my personal conversations with men, and my experiences in men's groups since 1973.

82. John D'Emilio, *Sexual Politics, Sexual Communities: The Making of a Homosexual Minority in the United States, 1940–1970* (Chicago, 1983), p. 232; Dennis Altman, *Homosexual: Oppression and Liberation* (New York, 1993; orig. ed., 1971), p. 127.

83. D'Emilio, *Sexual Politics*, esp. chaps. 2–3, 12; Toby Marotta, *The Politics of Homosexuality* (Boston, 1981), pp. 32–37, 48, 66, 71–76, 87–89; *New York Times*, June 9, 1970, 1:6, and August 24, 1970, 1:7.

84. Quoted by Altman, *Homosexual*, p. 130.

85. Arlene Stein, *Sex and Sensibility: Stories of a Lesbian Generation* (Berkeley, 1997), esp. pp. 60–67.

86. In general, see D'Emilio, *Making Trouble*, p. 258. On "camp," see Esther Newton, *Cherry Grove, Fire Island: Sixty Years in America's First Gay and Lesbian Town*

(Boston, 1993), esp. pp. 296–98. On seventies macho style, Seymour Kleinberg, "The New Masculinity of Gay Men," in *Alienated Affections: Being Gay in America* (New York, 1980), pp. 145–50. Quotation on p. 146.

87. Mirko D. Grmek, *History of* AIDS: *Emergence and Origin of a Modern Pandemic* (Princeton, 1990), pp. 32, 41; Institute of Medicine, National Academy of Science, *Confronting* AIDS: *Update* 1988 (Washington, D.C., 1988), p. 51.

88. On community groups, National Research Council, *Social Impact of* AIDS *in the United States,* Jeff Stryker and Albert R. Jonsen (Washington, D.C., 1993), pp. 160–65; Lewis Katoff and Susan Ince et al., "Supporting People with AIDS: The GMHC Model," in *The* AIDS *Reader: Social, Political, and Ethical Issues,* ed. Nancy F. McKenzie (New York, 1991), pp. 551–53; Katherine Boo, "What Mother Teresa Could Learn in a Leather Bar," *Washington Monthly* 23 (June 1991): 34–40. Also D'Emilio, *Making Trouble,* pp. 263–65 (quotation on p. 265).

89. R.W. Connell, *Gender and Power: The Person and Sexual Politics* (Cambridge, 1987), p. 235.

90. Richard Haddad, "Concept and Overview of the Men's Liberation Movement," in *Men Freeing Men: Exploding the Myth of the Traditional Male,* ed. Francis Baumli (Jersey City, N.J., 1985), pp. 285–86.

91. Ibid., 281–88; Herb Goldberg, *The Hazards of Being Male: Surviving the Myth of Masculine Privilege* (New York, 1976); John Gordon, *The Myth of the Monstrous Male—And Other Feminist Fables* (New York, 1982); Warren T. Farrell, *The Myth of Male Power: Why Men Are the Disposable Sex* (New York, 1993).

92. Quoted by Susan Faludi, *Backlash: The Undeclared War Against American Women* (New York, 1991), p. 300. See also Warren Farrell, *Why Men Are the Way They Are* (New York, 1986).

93. Dave Guthrie to Bill Clinton, World Wide Web, June 1997. Also George Ritchey to NCFM members, World Wide Web, June 1997. I thank Lou Lipsitz for bringing this correspondence to my attention. On New York fathers, see *New York Times,* September 8, 1995, B4:3. Hess quoted in ibid., April 26, 1995, A1:2.

94. Quoted in Robert L. Griswold, *Fatherhood in America: A History* (New York, 1993), p. 262.

95. John Gordon, "I Have a Fantasy," in *Men Freeing Men,* ed. Baumli, p. 279.

96. Tom Williamson, "A History of the Men's Movement," in ibid., pp. 320, 323; For a critical but balanced overview by an outsider, see Kenneth Clatterbaugh, *Contemporary Perspectives on Masculinity: Men, Women, and Politics in Modern Society,* 2d. ed. (Boulder, Colo., 1997), chap. 4.

97. On successes, see ibid., p. 86, Griswold, *Fatherhood,* pp. 260–61, and *New York Times,* April 26, 1995, A1:2. As of 1990, there were eight thousand members in the National Organization for Men, two thousand in the Coalition for Free Men: Daniel Gross, "The Gender Rap," *New Republic* 202 (April 16, 1990): 11–14.

98. On payments, U.S. Bureau of the Census, "Child Support for Custodial Mothers and Fathers: 1991," *Current Population Reports, Consumer Income,* P60–187

(Washington, D.C., 1995); *New York Times*, November 28, 1985, A8:1, and September 8, 1995, B1:2. On custody and fathers' contact, Griswold, *Fatherhood*, pp. 232, 260–61.

99. Robert Bly, *Iron John: A Book about Men* (Reading, Mass., 1990), p. ix. Also Robert Moore and Douglas Gillette, *King, Warrior, Magician, Lover: Rediscovering the Archetypes of the Mature Masculine* (San Francisco, 1991).

100. Don Shewey, "Town Meeting in the Hearts of Men," *Village Voice*, February 11, 1992, pp. 36–42, 45–46 (quotation on p. 38), reprinted as "An Exercise in Sacred Space," in *The Politics of Manhood: The Mythopoetic Men's Movement and the Mythopoetic Leaders Answer*, ed. Michael S. Kimmel (Philadelphia, 1995), pp. 333–54.

101. For example, Jon Tevlin, "Of Hawks and Men: A Weekend in the Male Wilderness," *Utne Reader*, November-December 1989, pp. 50–54; Kay Leigh Hagan, ed., *Women Respond to the Men's Movement: A Feminist Collection* (San Francisco, 1992); Faludi, *Backlash*, pp. 304–12; E. Anthony Rotundo, *American Manhood: Transformations in Masculinity from the Revolution to the Modern Era* (New York, 1993), pp. 287–89; Michael Schwalbe, *Unlocking the Iron Cage: The Men's Movement, Gender Politics, and American Culture* (New York, 1996), pp. 142–44, 189.

102. For examples of antifeminist, misogynist, and homophobic attitudes, see Moore and Gillette, *King, Warrior, Magician, Lover*, pp. 155–56; quotation in Schwalbe, *Unlocking the Iron Cage*, p. 112; and Shewey, "Exercise in Sacred Space," p. 347.

103. Quoted in David Guy, "Are Men Changing?" *North Carolina Independent*, Feb. 9–22, 1989, pp. 8–9.

104. For deft portraits of Bly, see Ted Solotaroff, "Captain Bly," *Nation*, September 9, 1991, 270–74, and Lance Morrow, "The Child Is Father of the Man," *Time* 138 (August 19, 1991): 52–54.

105. Quoted in Schwalbe, *Unlocking the Iron Cage*, pp. 20–21. On the basis of three years of participant observation as a sociologist, Schwalbe estimates that nearly all participants were white, middle or upper-middle class, and heterosexual. One-third had been in an alcoholic or abuse recovery program: pp. 19, 23.

106. Bly, *Iron John*, pp. 26–27 and chap. 6. On the Gulf War, Shewey, "Exercise in Sacred Space," p. 353. For a helpful introduction to Jungian archetypal analysis, see Schwalbe, *Unlocking the Iron Cave*, chap. 2. For other influential mythopoetic books, see Moore and Gillette, *King, Warrior, Magician, Lover*, and Sam Keen, *Fire in the Belly: On Being a Man* (New York, 1991).

107. David Gelman, "Making It All Feel Better," *Newsweek* 116 (November 26, 1990): 66–68; Faludi, *Backlash*, p. 307.

108. For centers and journals, see Christopher Harding, ed., *Wingspan: Inside the Men's Movement* (New York, 1992), pp. 253–60. For gatherings, *Wingspan* 6 (October-December 1992): 14–15. Mrs. Garfield in quoted in *Boston Globe*, August 13, 1995, 34:3.

109. David Van Bieman, "Full of Promise," *Time* 146 (November 6, 1995): 62–63. Also Clatterbaugh, *Contemporary Perspectives on Masculinity*, pp. 178, 181.

110. Tony Evans, *Seven Promises of a Promise Keeper* (Colorado Springs, 1994), p. 79, quoted by Clatterbaugh, *Contemporary Perspectives on Masculinity*, p. 185.

111. Quoted by William R. Mattox, Jr., "Christianity Goes to the Playoffs: Is Something Stirring in the Promise Keepers Movement?" *American Enterprise* 6 (November/December 1995): 41.

112. Robert Bly, "Fifty Males Sitting Together," in *Loving a Woman in Two Worlds* (New York, 1985), p. 3.

113. Susan Jeffords, *The Remasculinization of America* (Bloomington, Ind., 1989).

114. "Bush Battles the 'Wimp Factor,'" *Newsweek* 110 (October 19, 1987): 29; *Los Angeles Times*, February 28, 1988, I, 1:2. Also Bruce Curtis, "The Wimp Factor," *American Heritage* 40 (November 1989): 40–50; Maureen Dowd, "Of Knights and Presidents," *New York Times*, October 10, 1992, 1:1, 9:3.

115. *American Enterprise* 4 (September/October 1993): 89. For similar responses from a self-selected group of male and female readers, see Sam Keen and Ofer Zur, "Who Is the New Ideal Man?" *Psychology Today* 23 (November 1989): 54–60.

116. Quoted by Michael Marriott, "It's a Cold, Cruel World, and Guys Need to Talk," *New York Times*, April 7, 1997, B7:1. On courses, Daniel Gross, "The Gender Rap," *New Republic* 202 (April 16, 1990): 11–14.

117. *New York Times*, November 11, 1994, 1:1, 11:1; October 6, 1996, 1:4, 14:1.

118. Barry D. Adam, *The Rise of a Gay and Lesbian Movement*, rev. ed. (New York, 1995), pp. 110–13; Bennett L. Singer and David Deschamps, eds., *Gay and Lesbian Stats: A Pocket Guide of Facts and Figures* (New York, 1994), p. 57.

119. Adam, *Rise of a Gay and Lesbian Movement*, pp. 138–43; *New York Times*, January 4, 1994, A6:1, November 14, 1994, A9:1, and January 21, 1996, 9:1.

120. Boyte, "In Movement," in *Men in the Middle*, ed. Filene, p. 44; Gail Sheehy, "Introducing the Postponing Generation: The Truth about Today's Young Men," *Esquire* 92 (October 1979): 25–31; "New Science of Birth," *Newsweek* 88 (November 15, 1976): 60; "A New Kind of Life with Father," ibid. 98 (November 30, 1981): 93. Williams quoted in *Raleigh News & Observer*, April 17, 1994, A17:1, A19:1.

121. Griswold, *Fatherhood*, pp. 224, 247–49, 263; *New York Times*, October 29, 1995, 14:2. Johnson quoted in ibid., February 12, 1995, sec. 3, 23:1.

122. *New York Times*, November 12, 1995, sec. 3, 9:1; *American Enterprise* 4 (September/October 1993): 93; "The Myth of Quality Time," *Newsweek* 129 (May 12, 1997): 62–69.

123. Fleck, "'Family Supportive' Employer Policies," in *Men, Work, and Family*, ed. Hood, pp. 226–27; "Taking Baby Steps toward a Daddy Track," *Business Week*, April 15, 1991, p. 90; *New York Times*, July 31, 1994, III, 19:3; Arlie Russell

Hochschild, "There's No Place Like Home," *New York Times Magazine*, April 20, 1997, p. 52.

124. Poll on working part-time: *Raleigh News & Observer*, May 11, 1995, 7C:3, 8C:5. Bodden quoted in *New York Times*, June 18, 1995, sec. 3, 1:6, 12:1.

125. Fleck, "'Family Supportive' Employer Policies," in *Men, Work, and Family*, ed. Hood, pp. 228–31.

8. THE CHILDREN OF THE WOMEN'S MOVEMENT

1. Claudia Wallis, "Onward, Women," *Time* 134 (December 4, 1989): 81.

2. See Lisa Maria Hogeland, "Fear of Feminism," *Ms.* 5 (November–December, 1994): 18–21; and Dorothy C. Holland, *Educated in Romance: Women, Achievement, and College Culture* (Chicago, 1990).

3. I am relying on my classroom polls at the University of North Carolina, Chapel Hill. According to a poll of 514 female students at sixteen universities in 1989, 16 percent "definitely" considered themselves feminists, 47 percent "probably," 27 percent "probably not," and 8 percent "definitely not." Among *all* American women, 33 percent considered themselves feminists, 58 percent did not, and 9 percent were not sure: *American Enterprise* 2 (November/December 1991): 92.

4. Wallis, "Onward, Women," *Time* 134 (December 4, 1989): 81.

5. For example, Katie Roiphe, *The Morning After: Sex, Fear, and Feminism on Campus* (Boston, 1993); Rene Denfield, *The New Victorians: A Young Woman's Challenge to the Old Feminist Order* (New York, 1995); Christina Hoff Sommers, *Who Stole Feminism? How Women Have Betrayed Women* (New York, 1994). On the other side, Faludi, *Backlash*; Naomi Wolf, *The Beauty Myth: How Images of Beauty Are Used against Women* (New York, 1992).

6. *Raleigh News & Observer*, April 29, 1997, C1:1; *New York Times*, April 29, 1997, C23:5, and June 16, 1997, C18:1.

7. *Statistical Abstract: 1996* (Washington, D.C., 1996), p. 471. On international comparison, *Wall Street Journal*, July 2, 1993, A6:4.

8. *New York Times*, October 9, 1994, sec. 3, 1:1, 6:3.

9. *Wall Street Journal*, March 29, 1994, A1:5 and January 24, 1995, B1:3.

10. On young women, *Statistical Abstract: 1996*, p. 471. On lawyers, *New York Times*, January 8, 1996, A12:1; and Diane Harris, "How Does Your Pay Stack Up?" *Working Woman*, February 1996, p. 33. On glass ceiling, *New York Times*, March 16, 1996, C22:1. For background, see Nancy F. Rytina, "Earnings of Men and Women: A Look at Specific Occupations," *Monthly Labor Review*, April 1982, 25–31. For useful interpretations, see Andrea H. Beller, "Trends in Occupational Segregation by Sex and Race, 1960–1981," and Mary Corcoran et al., "Work Experience, Job Segregation, and Wages," in *Sex Segregation in the Workplace: Trends,*

Explanations, Remedies, ed. Barbara F. Reskin (Washington, D.C., 1984), pp. 11–26, 171–91; Barbara F. Reskin and Irene Padavic, *Women and Men at Work* (Thousand Oaks, Calif., 1994), p. 118.

11. *Wall Street Journal*, March 29, 1994, A1:6; Jaclyn Fierman, "Why Women Still Don't Hit the Top," *Fortune* 122 (July 30, 1990): 40 (Monet is quoted on p. 58). At the current pace, women won't achieve parity with male managers before at least the year 2015. For a detailed portrait of female executives in 1984, see *Wall Street Journal*, October 25, 1984, p. 35, and October 30, 1984, pp. 33, 35.

12. *New York Times*, November 12, 1995, sec. 3, 1:2.

13. Daniel is quoted in Anita Shreve, "Careers and the Lure of Motherhood," *New York Times Magazine*, November 21, 1982, p. 50.

14. Heidi Hartman, quoted in *New York Times*, December 15, 1996, sec. 4, 5:1.

15. Bureau of Labor Standards, *Female–Male Earnings Gap*: A, p. 6. Review of Employment and Earnings Issues, *Report*. No. 673 (September 1982), p. 9.

16. Lou Harris poll in *Wall Street Journal*, May 11, 1995, B1:3.

17. Robert L. Griswold, *Fatherhood in America: A History* (New York, 1993), p. 224.

18. On marital roles, *Gallup Poll: Public Opinion* (1995), p. 255; Roper Organization, 1985 *Virginia Slims American Woman's Opinion Poll: A Survey of Contemporary Attitudes*, p. 68; ibid. (1989) cited in *American Enterprise* 4 (September/October 1993): 92. On college students, Arlie Hochschild, *The Second Shift: Working Parents and the Revolution at Home* (New York, 1989), p. 266, and Beth Willinger, "Resistance and Change: College Men's Attitudes toward Family and Work in the 1980s," in *Men, Work and Family*, ed. Jane C. Hood (Newbury Park, Calif., 1993), pp. 108–30.

19. Gordon Mott, "Following a Wife's Move," *New York Times Magazine*, April 14, 1985.

20. See Stephanie Coontz, *The Way We Never Were: American Families and the Nostalgia Trap* (New York, 1992), and *The Way We Really Are: Coming to Terms with America's Changing Families* (New York, 1997).

21. *New York Times*, May 16, 1996, B1:6, B6:1.

22. National Opinion Research Center polls, 1993 and earlier, in *Gay and Lesbian Stats: A Pocket Guide of Facts and Figures*, ed. Bennett L. Singer and David Deschamps (New York, 1994), pp. 56–57.

23. *New York Times*, May 1, 1997, A17:1. On ads, James B. Stewart, "Coming Out at Chrysler," *The New Yorker* 73 (July 21, 1997): 48.

24. Andrew Sullivan, "When Plagues End," *New York Times Magazine*, November 10, 1996, p. 56.

25. Vivian Gornick, "Who Says We Haven't Made a Revolution?" ibid., April 15, 1990, pp. 52–53.

EPILOGUE: AS WE ARE BECOMING

1. Rachel Brown Cowan and Jane Lazarre, "I Can Be, I Tell Myself, I Will Be Both a Feminist and a Good Mother," *Village Voice*, October 25, 1973, pp. 29–32; Paul Cowan, "Can Men Really Be Feminists?" ibid., February 17, 1975, p. 33. For biographical background, see Paul Cowan, *The Making of an Un-American* (New York, 1970), and *An Orphan in History* (New York, 1982).

Essay on Sources

While writing this book about sex roles I sometimes felt that I was writing about almost everything since 1890. So much of American culture, after all, was involved in the ways that middle-class Americans thought and behaved as males and females. To "exhaust" the pertinent sources, one would have to possess the stamina of a marathon scholar. I did not go that far, but as the notes indicate, I went far and wide.

In my explorations I used several conceptual categories as guidelines. For women there were *feminism* and *suffrage*, of course, but also *education*, *child rearing*, *family*, *employment*, *marriage*, and *sexuality*. For men the categories had to be more indirect, because indexes almost never refer to *men* or *masculinity*. So I pursued them via *fatherhood*, *success*, *work*, *violence*, *heroes*, and *sports*.

The references in the following pages provide what I hope is a convenient and informative introduction to these diverse topics. In each case I have cited the titles that synthesize the greatest amount of material or offer the most incisive interpretations or are particularly representative of a theme or viewpoint. Anyone who wants to investigate a topic more thoroughly should consult the source notes in these books or the notes to my own chapters.

PERIODICALS AND NEWSPAPERS

The *Readers' Guide to Periodical Literature* directed me to the most extensive and illuminating evidence about what middle-class opinion leaders (and also, I infer, their followers) were thinking and doing. Much of what I read was narrow, much also trivial, and most soon became redundant, as the sixteenth article on race suicide or coeducation or suffrage rehearsed the clichés of the previous fifteen. Triviality and repetition pave the cultural historian's route, however, for reaching a generalization about the "climate (or cliché) of the times."

Good Housekeeping, *Ladies' Home Journal*, *Woman's Home Companion*, and *Ms.* were particularly helpful. I also learned a lot from the following: *The American Magazine*, *The Arena*, *The Atlantic Monthly*, *The Bookman*, *The Century Magazine*, *Collier's*, *Cosmopolitan*, *Current History*, *Current Literature*, *Current Opinion*, *The Delineator*,

The Forerunner, Fortune, Forum, Harper's Bazar, Harper's Magazine, Harper's Weekly, The Independent, Journal of Home Economics, Journal of Social Hygiene, Life, Life and Labor, The Literary Digest, McCall's Magazine, The Nation, The New Republic, Newsweek, The North American Review, The Outlook, The Parents' Magazine, Pictorial Review, The Saturday Evening Post, Scribner's Magazine, The Suffragist, The Survey, Time, The Woman Citizen, and *The World's Work.*

Another rich source of data on popular culture is the *New York Times*, conveniently accessible through its *Index.*

For technical articles, many of which, unfortunately, also were trivial and redundant, I made good use of these two guides: *The Social Sciences and Humanities Index* and *International Bibliography of Research in Marriage and the Family, 1900–1964*, edited by John Aldous and Reuben Hill. The most interesting and reliable studies have appeared in *American Journal of Sociology, American Sociological Review, Annals of the American Academy of Political and Social Science, Journal of Social Issues, Journal of Social Psychology, Marriage and Family Living* (later *Journal of Marriage and the Family*), *Public Opinion Quarterly,* and *Social Forces.*

PUBLIC OPINION POLLS

After 1935, polls provide invaluable clues to the public state of mind. Hadley Cantril's compilation, *Public Opinion, 1935–1946* (Princeton, N.J.: Princeton University Press, 1951), is a good place to begin, followed by the more recent compilations, *The Gallup Poll: Public Opinion, 1935–1971*, 3 vols. (New York: Random House, 1972), *The Gallup Poll, 1972–1977*, 3 vols. (Wilmington, Del., 1978), and the monthly *Gallup Report.* The Roper *Virginia Slims American Woman's Poll* (1972, 1980, 1985, and 1989) has been invaluable. Also see the periodical *Public Opinion* and its successor, *The American Enterprise.*

PERSONAL HISTORIES

I found considerable guidance in the quantitative generalities offered by the opinion polls and also by the surveys of sexual behavior and attitudes cited below. But I gained a real sense of the past from the qualitative singularities of individuals' lives. Letters, diaries, and private journals often (though not always) described vividly their authors' inner or outer experience. Of the following manuscript collections that I read, I have marked with asterisks the ones that were most revealing:

Corinne Marie (Tuckerman) Allen Papers, SL; William Watts Ball Papers, Duke University; Alva Murray (Smith) Vanderbilt Belmont Memoir, in Matilda Young Papers, Duke University; *Edwin A. Björkman Papers, SHC; *Blackwell Family Papers, SL; Hugh Cabot Family Papers, SL; *Carrie Chapman Catt Papers, LC; Carrie Chapman Catt Papers, Sophia Smith Collection, Smith College;

Thomas Reid Cole Papers, SHC; *Sallie Southall Cotten Papers, SHC; *Mary W. Dewson Papers, SL; Mary W. Dewson Papers, Franklin D. Roosevelt Library; *Ethel D. Dreier Papers, Sophia Smith Collection, Smith College; *Ethel Sturges Dummer Papers, SL; *Margaret Fowler Dunaway Papers, SL; Ella Harrison Papers, SL; *Lorena A. Hickok Reports, in Harry L. Hopkins Papers, Franklin D. Roosevelt Library; *Ethel Puffer Howes Papers, SL; Inez Haynes Irwin Papers, SL; Grace A. Johnson Papers, SL; *Harriet Burton Laidlaw Papers, SL; *League of Women Voters of the United States Papers, LC; Catharine Waugh McCulloch Papers, SL; Mothers' Discussion Club Papers, SL; *National American Woman Suffrage Association Papers, LC; National Consumers League Papers, LC; *National Woman's Party Papers, LC; National Women's Trade Union League Papers, LC; Maud Wood Park Papers, SL; Russell G. Pruden Papers, Sterling Library, Yale University; *Margaret Sanger Papers, Sophia Smith Collection, Smith College; *Anna Howard Shaw Papers, SL; *Hilda Worthington Smith Papers, SL; *Jane Norman Smith Papers, SL; Helen Hunt West Papers, SL; and *Sue Shelton White Papers, SL.

Autobiographies are more guarded or contrived than letters or diaries, but they too provided enormously useful information. Here I list the ones that served me best, including some especially perceptive biographies. The order is roughly chronological.

Three unpublished autobiographies, available in typescript at the Schlesinger Library, Radcliffe College, contain a wealth of detail: Harriet Taylor Upton, "Random Recollections" (1927); Hilda Worthington Smith, "The Remembered Way" (1936); and Mildred Aldrich, "Confessions of a Breadwinner" (1926). The lives of five dissident women also are instructive: Rheta C. Dorr, A Woman of Fifty (New York: Funk & Wagnalls, 1924); Jane Addams, Twenty Years at Hull House (New York: Macmillan, 1910); Charlotte Perkins Gilman, The Living of Charlotte Perkins Gilman (New York: Appleton-Century, 1935); Margaret Anderson, My Thirty Years' War: An Autobiography (New York: Covici Friede, 1930); and Margaret Sanger, An Autobiography (New York: W. W. Norton, 1938). For excellent biographical studies, see Allen F. Davis, American Heroine: The Life and Legend of Jane Addams (New York: Oxford University Press, 1973); Mary A. Hill, Charlotte Perkins Gilman: The Making of a Radical Feminist, 1860–1896 (Philadelphia: Temple University Press, 1980); and Jean Strouse, Alice James: A Biography (Boston: Houghton Mifflin, 1980). Also worth reading are Edith Finch, Carey Thomas of Bryn Mawr (New York: Harper, 1947), and Josephine Goldmark, Impatient Crusader: Florence Kelley's Life Story (Urbana: University of Illinois Press, 1953). For another kind of career story, see Alice Foote MacDougall, The Autobiography of a Business Woman (Boston: Little, Brown, 1928).

Three outstanding autobiographies by Victorian men are Hutchins Hapgood, A Victorian in the Modern World (New York: Harcourt, Brace, 1939); The Autobiography of William Allen White (New York: Macmillan, 1946); and The Autobiography *of Lincoln Steffens*, 2 vols. (New York: Harcourt, Brace, 1931). For sensitive recreations of patrician lives, see Elting E. Morison, *Turmoil and Tradition: A Study of the Life and Times of Henry L. Stimson* (Boston: Houghton Mifflin, 1960; Carleton Putnam, *Theodore Roosevelt: The Formative Years, 1858–1886* (New York: Scribner's, 1958); and Edmund Morris, *The Rise of Theodore Roosevelt* (New York: Coward, McCann & Geoghegan, 1979). Two biographies that are sensitive to questions of manliness are Justin Kaplan, *Lincoln Steffens: A Biography* (New York: Simon and Schuster, 1974), and Nick Salvatore, *Eugene V. Debs: Citizen and Socialist* (Urbana: University of Illinois Press, 1982).

Among twentieth-century women there are, as yet, fewer autobiographies. Ruth Benedict is superbly portrayed in Margaret Mead's combination of Benedict's paper and Mead's commentary, *An Anthropologist at Work: Writings of Ruth Benedict* (Boston: Houghton Mifflin, 1957). Mead portrays herself vividly in *Blackberry Winter: My Earlier Years* (New York: Simon and Schuster, 1972). For a rich, evocative biography of Zelda Fitzgerald and, indirectly, of Scott, read Nancy Milford, *Zelda* (New York: Avon, 1971). More superficial, but very helpful, is Vincent Sheean's study of another literary couple, *Dorothy and Red* (Boston: Houghton Mifflin, 1963). Elaine Showalter has edited an interesting set of essays, originally published in *The Nation: These Modern Women: Autobiographical Essays from the Twenties* (New York: The Feminist Press, 1978).

The personae of more recent history are still too young to have produced many autobiographies. Out of the New Left have come some revealing personal accounts, however: Michael Rossman, *The Wedding within the War* (New York: Doubleday Anchor, 1971); Paul Cowan, *The Making of an Un-American: A Dialogue with Experience* (New York: Viking Press, 1970), and a sequel *An Orphan in History* (New York: Doubleday, 1982); Raymond Mungo, *Famous Long Ago: My Life and Hard Times with the Liberation News Service* (Boston: Beacon Press, 1970). Useful first-person reflections on men's lives since the 1950s can be found in *Men in the Middle: Coping with the Problems of Work and Family in the Lives of Middle-Aged Men*, ed. Peter Filene (Englewood Cliffs, N.J.: Prentice-Hall Spectrum, 1981). The women's movement has produced innumerable testimonials. Those that I found most illuminating are Sally Kempton, "Cutting Loose: A Private View of the Women's Uprising," *Esquire* 84 (July 1970): 54–57, reprinted in *The American Sisterhood: Writings of the Feminist Movement from Colonial Times to the Present*, ed. Wendy Martin (New York: Harper & Row, 1972); several of the essays by Robin Morgan in *Going Too Far: The Personal Chronicle of a Feminist* (New York: Random House, 1977); and Betty Friedan, *It Changed My Life: Writings on the Women's Liberation Movement* (New York: Random House, 1976).

An invaluable reference book is Edward T. James, ed., *Notable American Women, 1607–1950: A Biographical Dictionary*, 3 vols. (Cambridge: Harvard University Press, 1971), and its sequel, Barbara Sicherman and Carol Hurd Green, eds.,

Notable American Women: The Modern Period (Cambridge: Harvard University Press, 1980).

FICTIONAL HISTORIES

Somewhere between "objective" social science and subjective autobiography is the novel. A good social novelist brings into her or his fiction as much empirical accuracy as any historian or sociologist, and more lifelikeness. Many of the following novels are hardly literary masterpieces, but they gave me vivid re-creations of past places and perspectives.

The best introduction to middle-class Victorian New England is by William Dean Howells, especially *A Modern Instance* (1881) and *The Rise of Silas Lapham* (1885). Somewhat later, and equally vivid in its social rendering, is the fiction of Winston Churchill, of which *A Modern Chronicle* (1910) is a fine example. Kate Chopin's novel of a woman's secret passion, *The Awakening* (1899), is a superb piece of fiction. Second-rate by comparison, but useful, are many of Dorothy Canfield's novels. I found *The Bent Twig* (1916) to be particularly vivid. Two other social novelists have also helped to keep the prewar era alive for our retrospect: Robert Herrick, particularly in *One Woman's Life* (1913), and David Graham Phillips, particularly in *Susan Lenox: Her Fall and Rise* (1917).

The classic novel of the 1920s, and also the most useful for social historians, is Sinclair Lewis's *Main Street* (1920). But one must read, too, the haunting, extraordinary *Great Gatsby* (1925), by F. Scott Fitzgerald. Of surprisingly good quality is the sensation of its time, *Flaming Youth* (1923), by Warner Fabian, which is the pseudonym chosen by Samuel Hopkins Adams. Of lesser quality but very interesting are Gertrude Atherton, *Black Oxen* (1923); Dorothy Canfield, *The Home-Maker* (1924), which treats role reversal by husband and wife; Margaret Culkin Banning, *Women of the Family* (1926), focusing on women's lives in the flapper era, more sympathetic to the young than is Atherton's reprimand; and Katharine Brush, *Young Man of Manhattan* (1930), about a dual-career marriage.

I have found the most memorable and representative works from the fifties to be J. D. Salinger, *The Catcher in the Rye* (1951), Herman Wouk, *Marjorie Morningstar* (1955), Philip Roth, *Goodbye Columbus* (1959) and William Styron, *Lie Down in Darkness* (1951).

GENERAL HISTORIES

Masculinity

Historians have finally begun to study men and masculinity, and the number of studies has multiplied at a gratifying rate. A good place to begin is

Michael Kimmel, *Manhood in America: A Cultural History* (New York: Free Press, 1996) and an earlier survey by Joe Dubbert, *A Man's Place: Masculinity in Transition* (Englewood Cliffs, N.J.: Prentice-Hall Spectrum, 1979). Also see E. Anthony Rotundo's thoughtful, instructive study focusing on the nineteenth century: *American Manhood: Transformations in Masculinity from the Revolution to the Present Era* (New York: Basic Books, 1993). A thorough and much needed overview, *Fatherhood in America: A History* (New York: Basic Books, 1993), is provided by Robert L. Griswold.

Four exceedingly helpful collections of articles are: Mark C. Carnes and Cluyde Griffen, eds., *Meanings for Manhood: Constructions of Masculinity in Victorian America* (Chicago: University of Chicago Press, 1990); J. A. Morgan and James Walvin, eds., *Manliness and Morality: Middle-Class Masculinity in Britain and America, 1800–1940* (New York: St. Martin's Press, 1987); Harry Brod, ed., *The Making of Masculinities: The New Men's Studies* (Boston: Allen and Unwin, 1987); and Elizabeth H. Pleck and Joseph H. Pleck, eds., *The American Man* (Englewood Cliffs, N.J.: Prentice-Hall Spectrum, 1980).

One can assess manliness indirectly by studying heroism and success. The best sources I have found are Theodore P. Greene, *America's Heroes: The Changing Model of Success in American Magazines* (New York: Oxford University Press, 1970), and Richard Weiss, *The American Myth of Success: From Horatio Alger to Norman Vincent Peale* (New York: Basic Books, 1969).

Historians have given a lot of attention to the crisis of manliness at the turn of the century. Two good examples are Gail Bederman, *Manliness and Civilization: A Cultural History of Gender and Race in the United States, 1890–1917* (Chicago: University of Chicago Press, 1995), and Kevin White, *The First Sexual Revolution: The Emergence of Male Heterosexuality in Modern America* (New York: New York University Press, 1993). I also received enormous benefit from John Higham, "The Reorientation of American Culture in the 1890s," in his collection, *Writing American History: Essays on Modern Scholarship* (Bloomington: Indiana University Press, 1970), 73–102; James R. McGovern, "David Graham Phillips and the Virility Impulse of Progressives," *New England Quarterly* 39 (September 1966): 334–55; and Roderick Nash, ed., *The Call of the Wild 1900–1916* (New York: Braziller, 1970).

For more recent eras, see two provocative interpretations: on the post–World War II years, Barbara Ehrenreich, *The Hearts of Men: American Dreams and the Flight from Commitment* (New York: Doubleday Anchor, 1983); and on the 1970s and 1980s, Susan Jeffords, *The Remasculinization of American Gender and the Vietnam War* (Bloomington: Indiana University Press, 1989).

There has been a flurry of recent books on the various men's movements since 1970. For an efficient introduction, see Kenneth Clatterbaugh, *Contemporary Perspectives on Masculinity: Men, Women and Politics in Modern Society*, 2nd ed.

(Boulder, Colo.: Westview Press, 1997) and Michael A. Messner, *Politics of Masculinities: Men in Movements* (Thousand Oaks, Calif.: Sage, 1997). Michael Schwalbe provides a superb analysis of the mythopoetic movement in *Unlocking the Iron Cage: The Men's Movement, Gender Politics, and American Culture* (New York: Oxford University Press, 1996). And for the arguments pro and con, consult the valuable collection of articles edited by Michael S. Kimmel, *Politics of Manhood: Profeminist Men Respond to the Mythopoetic Men's Movement* (Philadelphia: Temple University Press, 1995).

Women's Movements

Among the many surveys of women's history, I have benefited the most from the following: William H. Chafe, *The Paradox of Change: American Women in the 20th Century* (New York: Oxford University Press, 1991), which is a revision of *The American Woman* (1972); Nancy Woloch, *Women and the American Experience*, 2nd ed. (New York: Alfred A. Knopf, 1994); and the collection by Linda K. Kerber and Jane DeHart, *Women's America: Refocusing the Past*, 4th ed. (New York: Oxford University Press, 1995); and Sara Evans, *Born for Liberty: A History of Women in America* (New York: Free Press, 1989).

The nineteenth-century movement has been well served by historians. Two landmark studies are by Eleanor Flexner, *A Century of Struggle: The Woman's Rights Movement in the United States* (Cambridge: Harvard University Press, 1959), and Aileen Kraditor, *Ideas of the Woman Suffrage Movement, 1890–1920* (New York: Columbia University Press, 1965). For useful information on the Woman's Party, see Loretta Ellen Zimmerman, "Alice Paul and the National Woman's Party, 1912–1920" (Ph.D. diss., Tulane University, 1964).

The women's movement interacted with other social movements. For incisive analysis, see Janet Zollinger Giele, *Two Paths to Women's Equality: Temperance, Suffrage, and the Origins of Modern Feminism* (New York: Twayne, 1995); David Pivar, *Purity Crusade: Sexual Morality and Social Control, 1868–1900* (Westport, Conn.: Greenwood Press, 1973); Ruth Bordin, *Women and Temperance: The Quest for Power and Liberty, 1873–1900* (Philadelphia: Temple University Press, 1981); Anne Firor Scott, *Natural Allies: Women's Associations in American History* (Champaign: University of Illinois Press, 1991); and Mari Jo Buhle, *Women and American Socialism, 1870–1920* (Champaign: University of Illinois Press, 1981).

Nancy Cott has written a significant monograph about feminist thought at the turn of the century, *The Grounding of Modern Feminism* (New Haven: Yale University Press, 1987). See also the nuanced discussion by Rosalind Rosenberg, *Beyond Separate Spheres: Intellectual Roots of Modern Feminism* (New Haven: Yale University Press, 1982).

Historians have begun revising our sense of women after World War II, discovering more than simply domesticity. A good place to start is with the collection of articles edited by Joanne Meyerowitz, *Not June Cleaver: Women and Gender in Postwar America, 1945–1960* (Philadelphia: Temple University Press, 1994).

As for the movement of the 1960s and 1970s, two early histories remain useful: Judith Hole and Ellen Levine, *Rebirth of Feminism* (New York: Quadrangle, 1971); and Jo Freeman, *The Politics of Women's Liberation: A Case Study of an Emerging Social Movement and Its Relation to the Policy Process* (New York: David McKay, 1975). But they have been supplemented by Winifred D. Wandersee, *On the Move: American Women in the 1970s* (Boston: Twayne, 1985). The now-classic interpretation is by Sara Evans, *Personal Politics: The Roots of Women's Liberation in the Civil Rights Movement and the New Left* (New York: Alfred A. Knopf, 1979). For a sophisticated theoretical as well as historical discussion, see William H. Chafe's *Women and Equality: Changing Patterns in American Culture* (New York: Oxford University Press, 1977).

Historians have recently begun to recognize the antifeminist side of the story. A particularly thoughtful analysis is by Donald Mathews and Jane DeHart, *Cultural Fundamentalism and the ERA* (New York: Oxford University Press, 1990). Also see Rebecca Klatch, *Women on the Right* (Philadelphia: Temple University Press, 1989). One of the most publicized and thoroughgoing attacks on contemporary feminism is by Christina Hoff Sommers, *Who Stole Feminism? How Women Have Betrayed Women* (New York: Simon and Schuster, 1994).

Education

For a fine overview, see Barbara Miller Solomon, *In the Company of Educated Women: A History of Women and Higher Education in America* (New Haven: Yale University Press, 1985). Patricia Ann Palmieri, *In Adamless Eden: The Community of Women Faculty at Wellesley* (New Haven: Yale University Press, 1995) provides a wonderfully textured portrait. Also see Helen Lefkowitz Horowitz's interesting analysis, *Alma Mater: Design and Experience in the Women's Colleges from Their Nineteenth-Century Beginnings to the 1930s* (New York: Alfred A. Knopf, 1985). Paula Fass, *The Damned and the Beautiful: American Youth in the 1920s* (New York: Oxford University Press, 1977), is very useful.

Employment

I have been well guided by two earlier surveys of middle-class women's work: Robert W. Smuts, *Women and Work in America* (New York: Columbia University Press, 1959), and Cynthia Fuchs Epstein, *Woman's Place: Options and Limits in Professional Careers* (Berkeley: University of California Press, 1970). A recent survey, filled with evidence and crisp analysis, is by Barbara F. Reskin and Irene Padavic, *Women and Men at Work* (Thousand Oaks, Calif.: Sage, 1994). More specialized studies include: Susan Porter-Benson, *Counter Cultures: Saleswomen, Managers, and Customers in American Department Stores, 1890–1940* (Champaign: University of Illinois Press, 1986); Regina Morantz-Sanchez, *Sympathy and Science: Women Physicians in American Medicine* (New York: Oxford University Press, 1985), and Mary Roth Walsh, *Doctors Wanted, No Women Need Apply: Sexual Barriers in the Medical Profession, 1835–1970* (New Haven: Yale University Press, 1970); Angel Kwolek-Folland, *Engendering Business: Men and Women in the Corporate Office, 1870–1930* (Baltimore: Johns Hopkins University Press, 1994); and Rosabeth Moss Kanter, *Men and Women of the Corporation* (New York: Basic Books, 1977).

If you want more complex economic analysis, see Joyce P. Jacobsen, *The Economics of Gender* (Cambridge, Mass.: Blackwell, 1994), and Barbara F. Reskin, ed., *Sex Segregation in the Workplace: Trends, Explanations, Remedies* (Washington, D.C.: National Academy Press, 1984).

Work has of course formed a major part of men's lives and identities. See, for example, Daniel T. Rodgers's lucid discussion in *The Work Ethic in Industrial America, 1850–1920* (Chicago: University of Chicago Press, 1978). On the basis of national poll data in 1957 and 1976, Joseph Veroff, Elizabeth Douvan, and Richard Kulka have produced a perceptive and readable pair of books: *Marriage and Work in America: A Study of Motives and Roles* (New York: Van Nostrand Reinhold, 1970) and *The Inner America: A Self-Portrait from 1957 to 1976* (New York: Basic Books, 1981). There is also the classic and exciting study by William H. Whyte, Jr., *The Organization Man* (New York: Simon and Schuster, 1956).

Work and Family

Since the trend of two-career couples began, sociologists have devoted increasing attention to the interplay (or conflict) between employment and domestic responsibilities. Two especially notable and readable studies are by Arlie Hochschild, *The Second Shift: Working Parents and the Revolution at Home* (New York: Viking, 1989) and *The Time Bind: When Work Becomes Home and Home Becomes Work* (New York: Metropolitan, 1997). For reviews of studies in the 1970s and 1980s, see two articles by Joseph H. Pleck: "Husbands' Paid Work and Family Roles: Current Research Issues," in *Research on the Interweave of Social Roles*, vol. 3, *Families and Jobs: A Research Annual*, ed. Helen Z. Lopata and Joseph H. Pleck (Greenwich, Conn.: JAI, 1983), 251–333; and "The 'Family Supportive' Employer Policies Relevant to Men," in *Men, Work, and Family*, ed. Jane Hood (Newbury Park, Calif.: Sage, 1993). For the 1950s and 1960s, Elaine Tyler May deals with family and work—and much more—in her influential book, *Homeward Bound: American Families in the Cold War* (New York: Basic Books, 1988).

Marriage and Family

Family historians have been doing creative work. For an excellent sampling, see Michael Gordon, ed., *The American Family in Social-Historical Perspective*, 3d ed. (New York: St. Martin's Press, 1983). Also see Carl Degler, *At Odds: Women and the Family in America from the Revolution to the Present* (New York: Oxford University Press, 1980); Theodore Caplow, *Middletown's Families: Fifty Years of Change and Continuity* (Minneapolis: University of Minnesota Press, 1982); and Stephanie Coontz, *The Way We Never Were: American Families and the Nostalgia Trap* (New York: Basic Books, 1992).

On courtship, Ellen Rothman has written a fine study, *Hands and Hearts: A History of Courtship in America* (New York: Basic Books, 1984).

After courtship usually come marriage and children. For the nineteenth century, see Bernard Wishy, *The Child and the Republic: The Dawn of Modern American Child Nurture* (Philadelphia: University of Pennsylvania Press, 1968), and the excellent compilation by Robert H. Bremner, ed., *Children and Youth in America: A Documentary History*, 3 vols. (Cambridge: Harvard University Press, 1971–74). On twentieth-century child-rearing there are many fascinating articles and books. For example, Martha Wolfenstein, "Fun Morality," in *Childhood in Contemporary Cultures*, ed. Margaret Mead and Martha Wolfenstein (Chicago: University of Chicago Press, 1955), 168–78; Nancy Pottishman Weiss, "Mother, the Invention of Necessity: Dr. Benjamin Spock's *Baby and Child Care*," *American Quarterly* 29 (Winter 1977): 519–46; Daniel R. Miller and Guy E. Swanson, *The Changing American Parent: A Study in the Detroit Area* (New York: John Wiley, 1958); and Melvin Kohn, *Class and Conformity: A Study in Values* (Homewood, Ill.: Dorsey Press, 1969).

Along with marriage and children comes housework, the subject of three thorough books: Glenna Matthews, *"Just a Housewife": The Rise and Fall of Domesticity in America* (New York: Oxford University Press, 1987); Susan Strasser, *Never Done: A History of American Housework* (New York: Pantheon, 1982); and Ruth Schwartz Cowan, *More Work for Mother: The Ironies of Household Technology from the Open Hearth to the Microwave* (New York: Basic Books, 1983).

And after marriage has come, increasingly, divorce. An excellent interpretation of the early twentieth century is Elaine Tyler May, *Great Expectations: Marriage and Divorce in Post-Victorian America* (Chicago: University of Chicago Press, 1980). For trends since 1945, see the lucid study by Andrew J. Cherlin, *Marriage, Divorce, Remarriage*, 2d ed. (Cambridge: Harvard University Press, 1992).

Sexuality

Two excellent general histories are by Peter Gay, *The Bourgeois Experience, Victoria to Freud: Education of the Senses* (New York: Oxford University Press, 1984), and

Estelle B. Friedman and John D'Emilio, *Intimate Matters: A History of Sexuality in America* (New York: Harper and Row, 1988). One will also profit from the collection of articles edited by Kathy Peiss and Christina Simmons, *Passion and Power: Sexuality in History* (Philadelphia: Temple University Press, 1989).

The ideology of sexuality has been treated with extraordinary insight by various historians: several of Carroll Smith-Rosenberg's essays in her collection, *Disorderly Conduct: Visions of Gender in Victorian America* (New York: Knopf, 1985); Nancy F. Cott, "Passionlessness: An Interpretation of Victorian Sexual Ideology, 1790–1850," *Signs* 4 (Winter 1978): 219–36; Peter T. Cominos, "Late-Victorian Sexual Respectability and the Social System," *International Review of Social History* 8 (1963): 18–48, 216–50; and Charles E. Rosenberg, "Sexuality, Class, and Role in Nineteenth-Century America," *American Quarterly* 25 (Summer 1973): 131–53. For a splendid reading of Ellis, Kinsey, and Masters and Johnson, see Paul Robinson, *The Modernization of Sex* (New York: Harper and Row, 1976).

From the era before Kinsey and polls, the most useful sources include: Katharine Bement Davis, *Factors in the Sex Life of Twenty-two Hundred Women* (New York: Harper, 1929); Dorothy Dunbar and Florence Haxton Britten, *Youth and Sex: A Study of 1,300 College Students* (New York: Harper, 1938); and Lewis M. Terman, *Psychological Factors in Marital Happiness* (New York: McGraw-Hill, 1938).

Gay and lesbian history has come into its own. The first notable monograph was by John D'Emilio, *Sexual Politics, Sexual Communities: The Making of a Homosexual Minority in the United States, 1940–1970* (Chicago: University of Chicago Press, 1983). Since then D'Emilio has written other thoughtful essays, which he has collected in *Making Trouble: Essays on Gay History, Politics, and the University* (New York: Routledge, 1992). The best survey of lesbian history is by Lillian Faderman, *Odd Girls and Twilight Lovers: A History of Lesbian Life in Twentieth-Century America* (New York: Columbia University Press, 1991). A book of enormous importance is by Allan Bérubé, *Coming Out under Fire: The History of Gay Men and Women in World War Two* (New York: Free Press, 1990). On the 1940s and 1950s, see Elizabeth Lapovsky Kennedy and Madeline D. Davis, *Boots of Leather, Slippers of Gold: The History of a Lesbian Community* (New York: Routledge, 1993). On the 1960s and since, I gained remarkable insights from Arlene Stein, *Sex and Sensibility: Stories of a Lesbian Generation* (Berkeley: University of California Press, 1997). Also useful is the overview by Barry D. Adam, *The Rise of a Gay and Lesbian Movement*, rev. ed. (New York: Twayne, 1995).

The history of birth control has been covered from different perspectives in three outstanding works: Linda Gordon, *Woman's Body, Woman's Right: A Social History of Birth Control in America* (New York: Grossman, 1977); James Reed, *From Private Vice to Public Virtue: The Birth Control Movement and American Society since 1830* (New York: Basic Books, 1978); and David Kennedy, *Birth Control in America: The Career of Margaret Sanger* (New Haven: Yale University Press, 1970).

On prostitution, a good place to start is with Ruth Rosen, *The Lost Sister-*

hood: Prostitution in America 1900–1918 (Baltimore: Johns Hopkins University Press, 1982).

Sport

The field of sport history is new but increasingly interesting for gender historians. An efficient survey is provided by Benjamin Rader, *American Sports: From the Age of Folk Games to the Age of Spectators* (Englewood Cliffs, N.J.: Prentice-Hall, 1983). More theoretical and exciting, though less informative, is Allan Guttmann's *From Ritual to Record* (New York: Columbia University Press, 1978). For a more psychological slant, see Michael A. Messner, *Power at Play: Sports and the Problem of Masculinity* (Boston: Beacon, 1992).

Steven Reiss has written two excellent studies of sports in historical and gender context: *Touching Base: Professional Baseball and American Culture in the Progressive Era* (Westport, Conn.: Greenwood, 1980); and *City Games: The Evolution of American Urban Society and the Rise of Sports* (Champaign: University of Illinois Press, 1989). For a stimulating examination of nineteenth-century sport, media, and manliness, see Michael Oriard, *Reading Football: How the Popular Press Created an American Spectacle* (Chapel Hill: University of North Carolina Press, 1993). A useful introduction is provided by Ronald A. Smith, *Sports and Freedom: The Rise of Big-Time College Athletics* (New York: Oxford University Press, 1983).

On women and sport in the twentieth century, consult these two pathbreaking books: Susan K. Cahn, *Coming On Strong: Gender and Sexuality in Twentieth-Century Women's Sport* (New York: Free Press, 1994); and Mary Jo Festle, *Playing Nice: Politics and Apologies in Women's Sports* (New York: Columbia University Press, 1996).

Social Psychology

As I tried to inform my historical interpretation with social-psychological understanding, I relied heavily on certain social psychologists. The most helpful guides were Kenneth Keniston, particularly his second appendix to *Young Radicals: Notes on Committed Youth* (New York: Harcourt, Brace, and World, 1968); Gordon W. Allport, *The Person in Psychology: Selected Essays* (Boston: Beacon Press, 1968); and Robert W. White, *Lives in Progress: A Study of the Natural Growth of Personality*, 2d ed. (New York: Holt, Rinehart, and Winston, 1966).

On the concept of "identity," I found especially useful John P. Hewitt, *Dilemmas of the American Self* (Philadelphia: Temple University Press, 1989).

On "role," I was benefited by a careful discussion by Shirley Angrist, "The Study of Sex Roles," *Journal of Social Issues* 25 (1969): 215–32. Also useful was *Family Roles and Interaction: An Anthology*, ed. Jerold Heiss (Chicago: Rand McNally, 1968). For critiques of "gender role" as a concept, see R. W. Connell, *Gender and*

Power: The Person and Sexual Politics (Cambridge: Polity Press, Blackwell, 1987), and Helena Z. Lopate and Barrie Thorne, "On the Term 'Sex Roles,'" *Signs* 3 (Spring 1978): 718–21.

On historical "generation," I acquired clarity and rigor from Norman B. Ryder, "The Cohort as a Concept in the Study of Social Change," *American Sociological Review* 30 (December 1965): 843–61; Bennett M. Berger, "How Long Is a Generation?" (1960), reprinted in his *Looking for America: Essays on Youth, Suburbia, and Other American Obsessions* (Englewood Cliffs, N.J.: Prentice Hall, 1971), 20–37; and the classic essay by Karl Mannheim, "The Sociological Problem of Generations," in *Essays on the Sociology of Knowledge*, ed. Paul Kecskemeti (New York: Oxford University Press, 1953), 276–322.

Index

Library of Congress Cataloging-in-Publication Data

Filene, Peter G.
    Him/her self : gender identities in modern America / Peter G. Filene : with a
foreword by Elaine Tyler May. — 3rd ed.
        p.   cm.
    Originally published: 1st ed. New York : Harcourt Brace Jovanovich, 1975.
    Includes bibliographical references and index.
    ISBN 0-8016-5920-4. — ISBN 0-8018-5921-2 (pbk.)
    1. Women—United States—History.   2. Sex role—United States—History.
3. United States—Social conditions.   I. Title.
HQ1426.F54   1998
305.3′0973—dc21   98-3328
                                                                                            CIP